# GERMAN
## COOKING

*Five Generations
of Family Recipes*

# GERMAN
# COOKING

## Eleanor A. Hinsch

Order this book online at www.trafford.com
or email orders@trafford.com

Most Trafford titles are also available at major online book retailers.

Printed in the United States of America.

ISBN: 978-1-4669-1327-1 (sc)
ISBN: 978-1-4669-1328-8 (e)

*Trafford rev. 03/13/2012*

 www.trafford.com

North America & international
toll-free: 1 888 232 4444 (USA & Canada)
phone: 250 383 6864 ♦ fax: 812 355 4082

In memory of my parents

Mathilde and Richard Bohlen

and

my brother, Walter

# PREFACE

I never met my great-grandmothers; they both died more than 100 years ago. I did have the great experience of going to Germany when I was 8 years old and meeting my Grandmothers. That was in 1956. I spent 3-½ months there, living on a working farm, collecting eggs, playing with geese and making friends with the pigs and cows. I also learned some really wonderful recipes.

My aunts shared their bread recipes with me. Watching them make the breads in a long trough was amazing. They would make white, rye, pumpernickel and a sweet bread, suck as raisin cinnamon. They would tell me about when they would take the breads to the town square where there was a huge brick oven. There the baker would bake all the loaves for the town.

My parents came from an area of Germany that borders Holland. I have recently discovered that some of the recipes handed down from my family are Dutch in origin. Where I could, I put both the German, Dutch and American names for the recipes. Since the area was also occupied by Sweden in the 1700s some recipes could also be Swedish in origin. I am still researching the idea.

I grew up in Brooklyn, New York where my parents had a Delicatessen. From my Dad I learned how to make those wonderful Deli salads and from my Mom I learned how to make pies, puddings and the meats that Delicatessens are famous for. Dad also had owned an ice cream shop before the Depression and shared some of his ice cream topping recipes with me. I hope you enjoy them as much as I do. I also included the recipes I used in my catering business and cake decorating and baking business. Some are German in origin, some are not.

I'm sure that by now you've figured out that, including me, my parents and grand and great grand-parents that's four generations. For this cookbook I've also included recipes from my daughters and even my son, hence the subtitle: *Five Generations of Family Recipes*. I hope you enjoy the recipes that I've collected from my family and ones that I've developed on my own. Also, with a direct request from my son, I've included basic, beginner recipes and cooking tips that he felt are never covered in recipe books.

My thanks to all who contributed to this book: my cousins; Margret Kayser, Margret Buck, Lorraine Keller, Ellen Kayser; my Aunts: Helen Buck, Mini Brommer, Meta Buck (great Aunt) Anna Roeloffs; my sister-in-law, Gwen; and my grandmothers, great-grandmothers, and to my children: Bethany, Sara and Jason.

# TABLE OF CONTENTS

# INFORMATION, HINTS AND TIPS

# CHART OF KITCHEN MATH

| MEASURE | EQUIVALENT | METRIC (ML) |
|---|---|---|
| 1 tablespoon | 3 teaspoons | 14.8 milliliters |
| 2 tablespoons | 1 ounce | 29.6 milliliters |
| 1 jigger | 1 ½ ounces | 44.4 milliliters |
| ¼ cup | 4 tablespoons | 59.2 milliliters |
| 1/3 cup | 5 tablespoons plus 1 teaspoon | 78.9 milliliters |
| ½ cup | 8 tablespoons | 118.4 milliliters |
| 1 cup | 16 tablespoons | 236.8 milliliters |
| 1 pint | 2 cups | 473.8 milliliters |
| 1 quart | 4 cups | 947.2 milliliters |
| 1 liter | 4 cups plus 3 ½ tablespoons | 1,000.0 milliliters |
| 1 ounce (dry) | 2 tablespoons | 28.35 grams |
| 1 pound | 16 ounces | 453.59 grams |
| 2.21 pounds | 35.3 ounces | 1.00 kilogram |

# STANDARD MEASURES FOR LIQUIDS

| | | | |
|---|---|---|---|
| 1 mixing glass equals | 12 ounces | 8 jiggers | 24 level tablespoons |
| 1 Jigger equals | 1 ½ ounces | | 4 level tablespoons |
| 1 pony glass | 1 ounce | | 2 level tablespoons |
| 1 sherry or port glass | 2 ounces | | 4 level tablespoons |
| 1 cocktail glass | 2 ounces | | 4 level tablespoons |
| 1 champagne glass | 5 ounces | | 10 level tablespoons |
| 1 tumbler | 9-12 ounces | | 16-24 level tablespoons. |

# WHAT EQUALS ONE POUND

| | | |
|---|---|---|
| 2 cups liquid | 4 cups white flour | 2 cups butter (packed) |
| 8-10 eggs in shells | 2 cups granulated sugar | 4 ½ cups ground coffee |
| 3 ½ cups confectioners' sugar | 3 bananas | 2 ¾ cups brown sugar |
| 2 cups salt | 2 ¾ cups oatmeal | 2 cups rice |

# WHAT EQUALS ONE OUNCE

2 tablespoons butter

4 tablespoons cocoa
4 tablespoons flour

1 square chocolate

1 cup evaporated milk equals 3 cups whipped

# DEEP-FAT FRYING TEMPERATURES
# WITHOUT A THERMOMETER

## 1 INCH CUBE OF WHITE BREAD WILL TURN GOLDEN BROWN:

| | |
|---|---|
| 345-355 degrees | 65 seconds |
| 355-365 degrees | 60 seconds |
| 365-375 degrees | 50 seconds |
| 375-385 degrees | 40 seconds |
| 385-395 degrees | 20 seconds |

# CANDY SYRUP TEMPERATURES
# WITHOUT A THERMOMETER

## A ½ TEASPOONFUL OF SYRUP DROPPED INTO FRESH COLD WATER:

| | |
|---|---|
| Thread: 230-234 degrees | spins a soft 3" thread |
| Soft ball 234-240 degrees | forms a ball, when pressed together but does not hold its shape |
| Firm ball 242-248 degrees | forms a ball that holds its shape |
| Hard ball 250-268 degrees | forms a hard, but plastic ball |
| Soft crack 270-290 degrees | forms hard, but not brittle, thread |
| Hard crack 300-310 degrees | forms hard, brittle thread that breaks when pressed |

# SUBSTITUTIONS AND AMOUNTS TO USE
# FOR SUBSTITUTIONS

| WHAT THE RECIPE CALLS FOR: | SUBSTITUTION |
| --- | --- |
| 1 tablespoon cornstarch | 2 tablespoons all-purpose flour (for thickening) |
| 1 whole egg | 2 egg yolks plus 1 tablespoon water |
| 1 cup homogenized milk | 1 cup skim milk plus 2 tablespoons butter or margarine OR ½ cup evaporated milk plus ½ cup water |
| 1 cup dairy sour cream | 1 cup plain yogurt, or 1 cup evaporated milk plus 1 tablespoon vinegar, or 1 cup cottage cheese mixed in blender with 2 tablespoons milk and 1 tablespoon lemon juice OR 1 tablespoon lemon juice plus evaporated milk to make 1 cup |
| 1 cup half and half | 7/8 cup milk plus 3 tablespoon margarine or butter or 1 cup evaporated milk |
| 1 ounce unsweetened chocolate | 3 tablespoons cocoa powder plus 1 tablespoon butter or margarine |
| 1 ounce (1 square) semi-sweet chocolate | 1 square unsweetened chocolate plus 1 tablespoon sugar |
| 1 teaspoon baking powder | ½ teaspoon cream of tartar plus ¼ teaspoon baking soda |
| 1 cup sifted cake flour | 7/8 cup sifted all-purpose flour (7/8 cup is 1 cup less 2 tablespoons) |
| ½ cup (1 stick) butter or margarine | 7 tablespoons vegetable shortening |
| 1 cup soured milk or buttermilk | 1 tablespoon white vinegar plus sweet milk to equal 1 cup Or combine 1 tablespoon lemon juice with enough Milk to equal 1 cup. Let stand 5 minutes. |
| 1 clove fresh garlic | 1 teaspoon garlic salt |
| 2 teaspoons minced onion | 1 teaspoon onion powder |
| 1 tbs. finely chopped fresh chives | 1 teaspoon freeze-dried chives |
| 1 teaspoon dry leaf herb | 1 tablespoon chopped fresh herbs |
| 1 package active dry yeast | 1 tbs. dry or 1 cake compressed yeast, crumbled |
| 1 cup honey | 1 ¼ cup sugar plus ¼ cup liquid |
| 1 cup oil | ½ pound butter or margarine |
| 1 cup brown sugar | 1 cup granulated sugar (+ 1 tablespoon molasses) |

| WHEN THE RECIPE CALLS FOR: | YOU START WITH |
|---|---|
| 5 ½ cups cooked fine noodles | 8 ounce package fine noodles |
| 4 cups slices raw potatoes | 4 medium-size potatoes |
| 2 ½ cups sliced carrots | 1 pound raw carrots |
| 4 cups shredded cabbage | 1 small cabbage (1 pound) |
| 1 teaspoon grated lemon rind | 1 medium-size lemon |
| 2 tablespoons lemon juice | 1 medium-size lemon |
| 4 teaspoons grated orange rind | 1 medium-size orange |
| 4 cups sliced apples | 4 medium-size apples |
| 2 cups shredded Swiss or Cheddar Cheese | 8 ounce piece Swiss or Cheddar Cheese |
| 1 cup soft bread crumbs | 2 slices fresh bread |
| 1 cup egg whites | 6-7 large eggs |
| 1 cup egg yolks | 11 or 12 large eggs |
| 4 cups chopped walnuts or pecans | 1 pound shelled walnuts or pecans |

| WHAT THE RECIPE CALLS FOR: | SUBSTITUTION |
|---|---|
| 1 cup canned tomatoes | 1 1/3 cup cut-up fresh tomatoes, simmered 10 minutes |
| 1 cup tomato sauce | 8 ounce can stewed tomatoes, blended in blender or 1 cup tomato puree seasoned or ¾ cup tomato paste plus ¼ cup water |
| ½ pound fresh mushrooms | 4 ounce can mushrooms |
| legumes | dried beans can be used interchangeably except for lentils |
| 1 tablespoon snipped fresh herbs | 1 teaspoon same herb dried OR ¼ teaspoon powdered or ground |
| 1 teaspoon dry mustard | 2 teaspoons prepared mustard |
| 1 teaspoon pumpkin pie spice | ½ teaspoon cinnamon, ½ teaspoon ginger, 1/8 teaspoon ground allspice, 1/8 teaspoon nutmeg |

# SALT SUBSTITUTES

| SPICE OR HERB | HOW TO USE IT (WITH SUGGESTED AMOUNTS) |
|---|---|
| BASIL | add ¼ to ½ teaspoon to 2 cups green vegetables; ¾ to 1 ½ teaspoons to 1 ½ pounds pork chops or roast; 1/8 to ¼ teaspoon to 2 tablespoons butter or margarine for basting 1 pound fish or 1 ½ pounds chicken |
| CHILLI POWDER | add 1 to 2 tablespoons to ground beef, noodle or rice skillet dishes (about 8 cups); 1 to 2 tablespoons to 4 pounds pot roast; ½ to ¾ teaspoon to 8 cups popped corn (1/3 cup corn, unpopped). |
| CURRY POWDER | add 1 to 2 tablespoons to 2 pounds lamb chops; 1 tablespoon to 2 pounds ground beef; 1 ½ teaspoons to 1 cup uncooked regular long-grain rice; ½ teaspoon to tuna salad using 6 ½ to 7 ounce can tuna. |
| DILL WEED | add ¼ to ¾ teaspoon to 2 cup green vegetables; ½ to 1 teaspoon to 4 cups cooked noodles. |
| DILL SEED | add ¼ to ½ teaspoon, crushed, to 2 tablespoons butter or margarine for seasoning fish, vegetables or bread |
| NUTMEG | add dash to ¼ teaspoon to 2 cups mixed vegetables, carrots, spinach; 1/8 teaspoon to 1 pound ground beef, dash to 1/8 teaspoon to 4 cups creamed chicken or tuna. |
| OREGANO | add ¼ to ¾ teaspoon to 4 cups eggs for egg salad; 1/8 to ¼ teaspoon to ¼ cup butter for basting fish; ¼ to ½ teaspoon to 2 cups spinach, green beans or 3 cups tomatoes. |
| PAPRIKA | add ½ teaspoon to ¼ cup flour for dredging chicken or meat; ½ teaspoon to ¼ cup butter for seasoning white vegetables. |
| PARSLEY (flaked) | add 2 to 4 teaspoons to 4 cups cooked noodles or 3 cups cooked rice; tablespoons to 2 pounds ground beef, ¼ to ½ teaspoon to ¼ cup butter for vegetables, fish, meats. |

| | |
|---|---|
| TARRAGON | add ¼ teaspoon to 1 pound fish; 1 teaspoon to 3 pounds chicken; ¼ to ½ teaspoon to ¼ cup butter for basting steak and chops. |
| THYME | add ¼ to ½ teaspoon to 1 cup flour for dredging 3 pounds chicken |

## THICKENERS
And substitutes

| Thickener | Substitute |
|---|---|
| 1 tablespoon cornstarch | 2 tablespoons flour or 1 1/3 tablespoons quick-cooking tapioca |
| 1 tablespoon flour | ½ tablespoon cornstarch, or 2 teaspoons quick-cooking tapioca, or two (2) egg yolks |
| 1 tablespoon tapioca | 1 ½ tablespoons all-purpose flour |

## PAN SUBSTITUTIONS

| RECIPE CALLS FOR: | SUBSTITUTIONS: |
|---|---|
| 4 cup baking dish | 9" pie plate<br>8x1 ¼" layer cake pan<br>7 3/8 x 3 ¾ x 2 ¼" loaf pan |
| 6 cup baking dish | 8 or 9x11" layer cake pan<br>10 inch pie plate<br>8 ½ x 3 5/8 x 2 5/8" loaf pan |
| 8 cup baking dish | 8x8x2" square pan<br>11x7x 11 ½" baking pan<br>9x5x3" loaf pan |
| 10 cup baking dish | 9x9x2 inch square pan<br>11 5/8 x 7 ½ x 3/8 inch baking pan<br>15x10x1" jellyroll pan |

| | |
|---|---|
| 12 cup baking dish | 13 ½ x 8 ½ x 2" glass baking pan |
| 15 cup baking dish | 13x9x2" metal baking pan |
| 19 cup baking dish | 14 x 10 ½ x 2 ½ inch roasting pan |

# LAST MINUTE COOKING CRISES

| PROBLEM | SOLUTION |
|---|---|
| scorched vegetables | disguise the burned taste by adding a tangy-flavored ingredient like barbecue sauce or curry powder. Or remove vegetables from scorched pan, put them in a clean one and place a small metal cap filled with salt on top of the food. Cover and let sit a few minutes, or, if not too badly burned, set the pan in a bigger pan of cold water till the steam stops. The burnt taste should disappear. |
| flavorless soup | add wine, tomato paste, mustard or lemon juice to taste depending on type of soup. |
| flavorless gravy | add pepper, salt, or wine to punch up the taste. |
| used too much salt | for an over-salted gravy, sauce or soup, sprinkle a little instant mashed potatoes and stir thoroughly. (or cold mashed potatoes beaten right in). For over salted vegetables add a bit of lemon juice, cream or sugar. |
| ruined the cake icing | coat with warm honey, sprinkle with chopped nuts, raisins, etc. or warmed preserves thinned with a few teaspoons orange or lemon juice (put preserves through a sieve first). Raspberry or strawberry jelly or jam or preserves used like icing make for a delicious cake. |

# TYPES OF CHEESES

ABERTAM

A hard cheese made from sheep's milk. It is native to Bohemia.

ALEMTEJO

A soft round cheese that is native to Alentejo, Portugal. It is made with sheep's milk and the flowers of a thistle. Some varieties have goat's milk also.

ALT KUHKASE

A German and domestic cheese also called Hand Cheese.

ALTENBURG

A small flat cheese made of goat's milk that is a from Germany.

ANCIEN IMPERIAL

A small, flat cheese about 2" square and ½" thick. It is French and is also known by the names Petite Carre and Carre Affine.

APPENZELL

A Swiss cheese which is similar to Emmentaler. It is made from cow's milk.

APPETITOST

A Danish cheese which is made from sour buttermilk. It is made also in the U.S.

ARMAVIR

A Russian cheese which is made from sour milk. It resembles Hand Cheese.

BACKSTEIN

A brick-shaped German cheese, similar to Limburger.

BARBEREY

A small, soft, rennet cheese resembling Camembert. It is also commonly known as known as Fromage de Troyes. Milk, while still fresh and warm is coagulated. with rennet. The uncut curd is put into a wooden mold having a perforated bottom. After Being drained for three hours, the cheese is turned into an earthenware mold. The cheese is salted, dried and ripened for about three weeks.

BATTLEMAT

Similar to Emmentaler cheese, if is softer and made in a large round approximately 16" in diameter and 4" thick. It is made in Switzerland and Northern Italy.

| | |
|---|---|
| BAUDEN | A sour-milk cheese, essentially the same as Harzkase. This cheese comes in two shapes. Either conical or cylindrical. It is made in Bohemia and Silesia. Also known as Koppen. |
| BEL PAESE | A creamy rich Italian cheese, milk flavored. |
| BELARNO | A hard, rich Italian cheese. |
| BERGQUARA | A Swedish cheese, resembling Gouda. It was known in Sweden in the 18th Century. |
| BERLINER KUHKASE | Another name for Hand Cheese. |
| BITTO | An Italian cheese of the Emmentaler type. It is usually ripened for two years. |
| BLUE: | Similar to French Roquefort, this is made in the US. The name comes from the veins of mold that give it a tangy flavor. |
| BLUE VINNY | A hard, flat, rich English cheese made from skimmed cow's milk. It is a white with a blue vein through it. |
| BRA | A small, mild, soft, creamy, Italian cheese. |
| BRAND | A German hand cheese made from sour-milk curd. During the manufacturing process. It is moistened with beer. It weighs about 1 pound. |
| BRANZA DEL BRAILA | A Rumanian cheese. Another name for Teleme cheese. |
| BRICK | This cheese has a mild to moderately sharp flavor, a soft to firm texture, and many tiny holes. It's sold both sliced and brick shaped. A rennet cheese, made from cow's milk. |
| BRIE | Originally from France, this cheese is now made in the US. It has a thin, edible crust and the flavor ranges from mild to pungent. It is a rennet cheese made from cow's milk. Depending on if it is made with skim or whole milk, there will be a variation in size and quality. Must be refrigerated. |

| | |
|---|---|
| BRINSEN | A rennet cheese made of sheep's milk, or a mixture of sheep's and goat's milk. Also known as Brinza cheese. It comes from the Carpathian Mountains of Hungary. |
| BROODKASSE | A hard, flat cheese, native to Holland. |
| CACCIO CAVALIO | A dry, hard, sharp cheese from Italy. |
| CACIO FIORE | An Italian, soft, rennet cheese, square in shape. Made from sheep's milk and has the consistency of butter and a sweetish taste. It may eaten fresh. |
| CAERPHILLY | A hard, rennet cheese made from cow's milk, It is native to Wales. |
| CAMBRIDGE | A soft, rennet English cheese made from cow's milk. |
| BURGUNDY | A soft, white, loaf-shaped cheese. Also known as Fromage de Bonrgagne. |
| CAMEMBERT | This is a creamy yellow cheese that has an almost liquid interior and a piquant flavor. The thin, grayish crust is also edible. Made from cow's milk. |
| CARRE AFFINE | Another name for Ancien Imperial cheese. |
| CASTELLO BRANCO | A cheese similar to Serra da Estrella. |
| CHAMPOLEON | A hard rennet cheese made from skimmed milk in the Dept. of Hautes Alpes, France. |
| CHAOURCE | A soft, whole-milk cheese resembling Camembert. It is 4" in diameter and 3" thick and is a product of Aube, France. |
| CHASCHOL DE CHASCHOSIS | a hard, rennet cheese, made from the skim cow's milk. |
| CHEDDAR | This popular cheese is mild, medium, or sharp in flavor, depending on age. Comes in wedges, sticks, sliced, shredded, and cubed. |

| | |
|---|---|
| CHESHIRE | The oldest English cheese, it is made of cow's milk and is supposed to owe its flavor to the saline content of the Cheshire soil. It is a hard cheese similar to Cheddar, and may come in red, white or blue types. |
| CHIAVARI | Hard, rennet, sour-milk cheese made from whole cow's milk. Also known as Caccio Romano. |
| CHRISTALINNA | A hard rennet cheese made from cow's milk, a product of Switzerland. |
| COMMISSION | A skimmed-milk cheese which is similar to Edam in its processing and shape, but darker in color. |
| COTHERSTONE | A rennet cheese made from cow's milk. It resembles Stilton and is also known as Yorkshire-Stilton. |
| COTTAGE | This is a simple, popular cheese that's also called pot cheese or schmierkase. Comes in in large or small curd, plain or creamed. |
| CREAM | Smooth and mild flavored, this cheese comes plain or flavored. Neufchatel, is similar to cream cheese but has more moisture and less fat. |
| CREUSE | A rennet, skim-milk, farm cheese. It is soft, yellow, and very flavorful. |
| CROISSANT | A small, soft, rich French cheese. |
| D'AMBERT | Another name for Forez Cheese. |
| DAMEN | A Hungarian cheese, also know as Glaire des Montagnes, It is a soft, uncured, rennet cheese made from cow's milk. |
| DANISH BLUE | A hard, rich, 4 pound cheese. This is a Danish imitation of Roquefort. |
| DAUPHIN | A French cheese made in Flanders. |
| DECIZE | A French cheese made in the Nivernais region. |

| | |
|---|---|
| DEMI-SEL | A French cream cheese necessarily consumed where it is made because of its fragility and perishable nature. It is made on the same principle as domestic cream cheese, but is softer, creamier, and lighter. |
| DERBYSHIRE | A hard, round, rennet cheese made from the whole milk of cows. From Derbyshire, England. Varies since it is made by local dairy farms. |
| DOTTER | A German cheese made of egg yolks and skimmed milk |
| DRY | A very hard German cheese. Also known as Sperrkase and Trockenkase. |
| EDAM OR GOUDA | Made in Holland and now in the US, these are mildly flavored cheeses. Flattened rounds are Gouda, ball shapes are Edam. |
| ENGADINE | A rennet cheese made in Switzerland, from whole cow's milk. |
| EPOISSE | A soft rennet cheese made from whole or partly skimmed milk. It is a produce of France. |
| ERIWANI | A Russian cheese made from sheep's cheese. Also called Karab, Tali, Kurini, Elisavetpolen and Kasach. |
| ETUVE | A Dutch cheese. It also comes half the full size, called Demi-Etuve. |
| FARM | Made in France and known as Fromage a la pie, mou, maigre, and Fresne. It is essentially the same as the cottage cheese of the U.S.A. |
| FEUILLE DE DREUX | A French cheese made in the Beauce region. |
| FILLED | A cheese like Cheddar, from which the butter fat is removed and other fats added during the processing. |
| FIN DE SIECLE | A French cheese made in Normandy. |
| FLOWER | A soft-cured, rennet cheese, made in England from whole cow's milk. It gets name because petals of various kinds of flowers are added during processing. |

| | |
|---|---|
| FONTAINEBLEAU | A French cream cheese made near Fontainebleau. |
| FONTINA | A round Italian cheese with a mellow flavor. Can also be from Finland and Denmark. |
| FOREZ | A round cheese, 10" in diameter and 6" high, with a flavor of Roquefort. Product of France. |
| FROMAGE DE CHEVRE | A hard goats' milk cheese made in France. |
| FROMAGE PERSILLE | Another name for Gex Cheese. It is a hard rennet cheese made in France. Resembles Roquefort, marbled and bluish. |
| FRUHSTUCK | An American cheese of the Limburger type. It is round in shape. Also known as Breakfast or Lunch cheese. |
| FTINOPORINO | A Macedonian cheese, similar to Brinsen, made from sheep's milk. |
| GAMMELOST | A Norwegian cheese made from sour skim milk. It varies in weight from 24 to 65 pounds. For shipment it is packed in a chest with wet straw. |
| GAUTRIAS | A round shaped cheese that is a product of France. |
| GERVAIS | A rennet cheese made from a mixture of whole milk and cream. It is of the Neufchatel group and can be eaten all the year round, but preferably during the summer. |
| GEX | A hard rennet cheese made from cow's milk. It is marbled and has a bluish appearance resembling Roquefort, and Septunoncel. |
| GISLEY | A Danish, hard, rennet cheese made from the skim of cow's milk. |
| GJETOST | A Scandinavian goat's milk cheese. |
| GLUMSE | A German cottage cheese, made from sour skim milk. |
| GOURNAY | A soft, rennet cheese of France. |

| | |
|---|---|
| GOYA | A rennet cheese made of whole or partly skimmed milk. From Argentina. |
| GORGONZOLA | An Italian blue veined cheese; sharp flavor. |
| GRAY | A sour skim-milk product of Tyrol. It is gray throughout and comes in a variety of shapes and sizes. |
| GREEN | A cheddar type of cheese that is flavored with sage. Also known as Sage Cheese. |
| GRUYERE | This is a nutty-flavored processed cheese that melts easily for a fondue. Originally Swiss made, it's now made in the US also. |
| GUSSING | A skim milk cheese, and Austrian cheese it resembles the U.S. Brick cheese. |
| HARZE | A hand cheese made in several sizes. It is a Belgian semi-cooked cheese similar to Port Salad and made at Harze. |
| HARZKASE | A sour milk cheese essentially the same as Bauden Cheese. |
| HERRGARDSOST | A Swedish cheese, it is a hard cheese and made with either cream or half cream. |
| HERVE | A Belgian soft cheese, turned out in cubes. |
| HOHENHEIM | A German cheese, it is soft, and round. |
| HOLSTEIN | A German cooked cheese made from sour skim milk. Aka Hostein Health. |
| HUSHALLSOST | A common cheese in Sweden, comes in three varieties. |
| INCANESTRATO | An Italian rennet cheese made of cow's, goat's, or sheep's milk, various spices and olive oil. Also known as Majocchino cheese. |
| ISIGNY | An American cheese, an attempt to make a Camembert, the proper ripening wasn't obtained. |
| JACK | A granular-cured Cheddar-type cheese made in America. |

| | |
|---|---|
| JOSEPHINE | A soft-curd rennet cheese made from cow's whole milk. A product of Silesia. |
| KAJMAR | A Serbian cheese similar to cream cheese. The flavor varies greatly with age. |
| KARAB | Another name for the Russian cheese, Erizvani, made from sheep's milk. |
| KARUT | A very, dry, hard, skim milk cheese of India. |
| KASACH | Another name for Eriwani, which is made from sheep's milk. It is made in the Caucasus. Different local names are given to this product, such as Karab, Tali, Kurini, and Elisavetpolem. |
| KATSCHAWALJ | A cream cheese made of sheep's milk in Serbia. It comes in various shapes and weighs about six pounds. |
| KJARGAARD | A Danish cheese that is hard, and made from skimmed cow's milk. |
| KLENCZ | A rennet cheese made from sheep's milk, sometimes combined with goat's milk. Also known as Brinsen cheese. |
| KLOSTER | A soft-ripened, rennet cheese made from cow's whole milk. It is made in France. |
| KNAOST | A sour milk, rennet cheese made in Norway and also called pultost cheese. |
| KOLOS-MONOSTOR | Made in Transylvania, it is a rennet cheese made from sheep's milk. |
| KOLOSVARER | A cheese made from buffalo milk. |
| KOMIJNE KASS | Another name for Leyden cheese. |
| KOPPEN | A goat's milk cheese with a sharp, pungent, slightly smoky flavor. |

| | |
|---|---|
| KUMBACH | A soft ripened, rennet cheese made from the whole or partly skimmed cow's milk. comes from upper Bavaria, Germany. |
| KURINI | A Russian cheese made from sheep's milk, also known as Eriwani cheese. |
| LAGUIOLE | A hard, rennet cheese, resembles Cantal and Roquefort. It derives its name from the village of Laguiole in France. |
| LANCASHIRE | A hard, round, rennet cheese seven inches in diameter and nine inches high. Comes from the Ribble, bordering on the Irish Sea coast. |
| LANGRES | A soft, square, rennet cheese. Full-flavored and strong scented, from France. |
| LAPLAND | A round, flat, hard cheese, it resembles a dumb-bell shape. |
| LAQUEUILLE-BLUE | A hard, rich cheese from France. |
| LEATHER | A round cheese made from skimmed cow's milk. It contains from 5-10% buttermilk. Comes from Germany. |
| LEICESTER | A hard, rennet cheese made from the whole cow's milk. It resembles Cheshire and Cheddar, and like them, it also comes from England. |
| LESCIN | A Russian rennet cheese, which is made from sheep's milk. |
| LEVEOUX | A French cheese made in Berry. |
| LEYDEN | A hard Dutch cheese, weighing about 25 pounds, which has cumin seed and cloves added. Also known as Komijna kaas, Liedsche Kaas or Kummel. |
| LIEDERKRANZ | This cheese is very similar to Limburger, but it's less pungent. It has a robust flavor and made exclusively in the US. |

| LIMBURGER | Cheese fans relish the pungent flavor and strong aroma of this appetizer cheese. It's available in pieces or as a spread. |
| LIVLANDER | A German sour milk cheese with a very sharp, pungent odor and taste. Also called Hand cheese. |
| LORRAINE | A small, hard cheese made with sour milk and seasoned with pepper, salt, and pistachio nuts. It is made in Lorraine, France. |
| LUNCH | A German cheese of the Limburger type, round in shape, and also called Frushstuck. |
| LUNEBERG | A German cheese which is a cross between Emmentaler and Limburger. |
| MACCONNAIS | A goat's milk cheese, made in France. |
| MACQUELINE | A soft rennet cheese of the Camembert type, made from whole or partly skimmed milk. Produced in the region of Senlis, France. |
| MAILE | A rennet cheese made of sheep's milk, produced in the Crimea. The ripened cheese keeps for a year, and has a crumbly texture inside. |
| MAJOCCHINO | An Italian rennet cheese made from the milk of cows, goats, sheep, plus various spices and olive oil. It contains about 15% alcohol. It is made in Spain, France, and the United States. |
| MALAKOFF | A form of Neufchatel cheese, made in Normandy, France. |
| MANURI | A Yugoslavian cheese made from sheep's or cow's milk. |
| MAQUEE | A soft, rennet, brick-shaped cheese made from cow's milk. Comes from Belgium. |
| MAROILLES | A French semi-hard, fermented, whole milk cheese. The rind is brownish red and the center is yellow. It has a sharp smell. |

| | |
|---|---|
| MASCONE | A white, soft, Italian cheese made from fresh cream. |
| MESITRA | A soft, unsalted cheese made of sheep's milk, which is produced in the Crimea. |
| MESOST | A sweet whey cheese made in Sweden. |
| METTON | A variety of French cheese made in the winter. |
| MIGNOT | A soft, rennet cheese, which may be either round or square in shape. A French cheese. |
| MIZITRA | A Yugoslavian soft cheese, made of sheep's milk. |
| MONTASIO | Italian cheese with a sharp taste and odor. When fresh it is white, when aged it turns yellow. It is soft and creamy. |
| MONT CENIS | A hard, rennet cheese made in France of cow's, sheep's and goat's milk. |
| MONTLHERY | A soft, rennet cheese from France. Made of cow's milk. |
| MAZARINELLI | A soft, rennet cheese, made in Italy, from cow's milk. |
| MOZZARELLA, SCAMORZE | These are favorite cheeses for use in pizzo and other Italian dishes. Scamorze comes in small rolls, Mozzarella sliced or shredded. |
| MUENSTER | This cheese has a mild to moderately sharp flavor, a soft to firm texture, and many tiny holes. It's sold sliced and brick-shaped. |
| MYSOST | A Scandinavian cheese made from whey. It is light brown and has a buttery consistency. It has a mild, sweetish taste. |
| NAGELKAZEN | This cheese is made from skimmed milk mixed with cloves and cumin seed. It is from Holland. |
| NESSEL | A round, very thin, soft-cured, rennet cheese made from whole cow's milk. English. |

| | |
|---|---|
| NEUFCHATEL | Soft, white and mild, similar to cream cheese. An unripened cheese that should be served chilled. |
| NIEHEIM | A sour milk cheese, made in Germany. |
| NIERDERUNGSKASE. | A hard, rennet cheese made from cow's milk. Also known as Elbing and Werderkase. |
| NOEKKELOST | A hard, flat pressed, Norwegian cheese similar in quality to rich Duren Gouda. |
| NOSTRALE | A hard, rennet, Italian cheese made from cow's milk. It is also known as Raschera. |
| OLIVET | A soft, rennet cheese made from cow's milk. Made in France. |
| OLMUTZER QUARGEL | A German hard cheese containing caraway seeds. Like hand cheese. |
| OSSETIN | A Russian cheese made from sheep's or cow's milk. |
| OSTIEPEK | A cheese made from sheep's milk from the Carpathian Mountains. |
| PAGLIA | A very soft cheese with an aromatic flavor, Made in Switzerland, similar to Gorgonzola. |
| PALPUSZTA | A strong-smelling Hungarian cheese similar to Limburger. |
| PARMESAN | These cheeses, also widely used in Italian cooking, are known as the grating cheeses. |
| ROMANO | They're sold grated, shredded and in wedges. |
| PECORINO | An Italian sheep's milk cheese which comes in several varieties. The interior is slightly greenish, somewhat granular, and devoid of eyes or holes. |
| PETITE GRUYERE | A soft, rich, yellowish cheese with a nutty flavor, made in Denmark. |

| | |
|---|---|
| PETIT SUISSE | A soft, rich, unsalted cream cheese, cylindrical in shape, made in France. |
| POMMEL | A soft, rich cheese, made in France. |
| PONT L'EVEQUE | A semi-hard fermented cheese made in Normandy. |
| PORT DU SALUT | A French, rennet cheese made from cow's milk. It has a soft, homogenous interior, a hard rind, and is similar in taste to Swiss cheese. |
| POTTED | This cheese is prepared from well-ripened Cheddar, butter, condiments, spirits, etc. Also known as club cheese. |
| PROVIDENCE | A French cheese resembling Port du Salut. |
| PROCESS CHESSE: | A pasteurized blend of fresh and aged natural cheese, these come packaged in many ways and may have flavors added. |
| PROVOLONE | Essential to Italian cooking, this cheese has a smoked, sharp flavor. Also called Provoloncini, Salami, and Provolette. |
| RABACAL | A round, firm cheese, made from sheep's milk or goat's milk. Comes from Portugal. |
| RADEN | A hand, rennet cheese, made from skim milk and resembling Emmenthaler. German. |
| RANGIPORT | Similar to Port du Salut cheese. Comes from France. |
| RAYON | A very dry, hard cheese used for grating. Made in Switzerland. |
| REBLOCHON | A soft, rennet cheese, made from fresh whole milk. |
| REGGIANO | An Italian cheese similar to Parmesan, used for grating. |
| RIESENGEBIRGE | A soft, rennet cheese, made from goat's milk in the mountains on the northern border of Bohemia. |
| RIOLA | Made from sheep or goat's milk. It has a soft texture and strong flavor. |

| | |
|---|---|
| ROQUEFORT | A French blue veined cheese with a sharp flavor. |
| RICOTTA | Another Italian favorite, this smooth, creamy cheese is similar to cottage cheese. It's a basic lasagna ingredient. |
| SALAMANA | A soft, sheep's milk cheese from Italy. A pronounced flavor and is eaten spread on bread or mixed with corn meal and cooked. |
| SANTE | A Kosher brand of cream cheese made in America. |
| SAP SAGO | A small, hard green cheese made from sour skimmed cow's milk and flavored with clover. Made in Switzerland. |
| SCHABZIEGER | A hard, skimmed milk cheese made in Switzerland. Used for grating. |
| SCHLOSS | This is a Limburg type cheese. It is a soft-cured rennet cheese. Made in Austria. |
| SERRA DA ESTRELLA | A Portuguese cheese make from sheep's milk |
| SLIPCOTE | A soft, un-ripened, rennet cheese, made from cow's milk. Made in England. |
| STILTON | An English blue veined cheese with a sharp flavor. |
| STRACCHINO | Several forms of Italian soft cheeses. It is very soft and highly colored. Usually eaten when fresh. |
| SVECIAOST | A Swedish cheese. It is made in three grades, full-cream, three-quarters cream and half cream. |
| SWISS | Originally made in Switzerland, this cheese with the sweet, nutty flavor, is now made in the US. It comes in chunks or slices. |
| SZEKELY | A soft Hungarian cheese made from ewe's milk. It is sold in sausage skins. |
| THENAY | A soft, rennet cheese, which resembles Camembert and Vendome, and is made in France. |

| | |
|---|---|
| TILSIT | A hard, rennet cheese resembling Brick cheese. Made in Germany, Yugoslavia, Hungary, Denmark and Switzerland. |
| TOPPEN | A sour milk cheese, made from skim milk in Germany. |
| TROUVILLE | A soft, rennet cheese, made from fresh, whole milk, in France. |
| ZIEGEL | A German cheese made from whole cow's milk. |
| *RENNET:* | *Calves gastric juice used to coagulate milk. Rennet rapidly loses its properties when heated above 60 degrees C.* |

# TYPES OF APPLES AND THEIR USES

| TYPE | GOOD FOR |
|---|---|
| BALDWIN | sauce, juice, cooking, baking |
| BEN DAVIS | salad, dessert, garnish, cooking |
| CORTLAND | eating, baking, cooking, sauces, salads, pie |
| CRAB APPLE | candied, juice, dessert, garnish, cooking |
| DELICIOUS | cocktail, candied, juice, dessert, eating |
| EARLY HARVEST | sauce, juice, salad, dessert, garnish, eating, cooking, baking |
| GRAVENSTEIN | eating, cooking, sauces, salads, pie, baking |
| GOLDEN DELICIOUS | cocktail, candied, juice, dessert, pie, eating |
| GREENING AND GRANNY SMITHS | sauce, juice, salad, dessert, pie, garnish, cooking, baking |
| JONATHAN | eating, cooking, baking, sauces, salads, pie |
| MACON | eating, this is an extra crisp eating apple |

| | |
|---|---|
| MCINTOSH | eating, cooking, sauces, salads, pie, juice, garnish |
| NORTHERN SPY | juice, dessert, garnish, eating, cooking, baking, salad |
| RIBATON PIPPIN | cocktail, candied, juice, salad, dessert, eating |
| ROME BEAUTY | juice, dessert, garnish, baking, cooking, sauce |
| SPITZENBERG | juice, garnish, cooking |
| STAYMAN | eating, baking, cooking, sauces, salads, pie |
| RED DELICIOUS | eating, salad |
| WEALTHY | juice, salad, dessert, cooking, baking |
| WINESAP | eating, baking, cooking, sauces, salads, pie |
| WOLF RIVER | dessert, garnish, cooking |
| WORCESTER PEARMAN | cocktail, candied, sauce, juice, salad, eating |
| YELLOW NEWTON | cocktail, candied, sauce, juice, salad, eating |
| YORK IMPERIAL | Baking, cooking, sauce, pie |

## QUICK GUIDE TO FREEZING

| TYPE | PREPARATION | BLANCH OR STEAM | PACKING |
|---|---|---|---|
| **VEGETABLES:** | | | |
| Asparagus | sort for size, break off woody base and remove scales. Leave whole or cut in 2" lengths | 2 to 4 minutes, depending on size | freeze on tray, dry pack in plastic bag |

| | | | |
|---|---|---|---|
| Beans-string | sort, wash, cut ends. Leave whole or cut beans | 3 minutes | freeze on tray, pack in plastic bag, glass jar or rigid container allow ¼" headspace in rigid container |
| Broccoli | soak in salted water To remove insects, wash, slice off stems | 3 minutes | freeze on tray. dry pack in plastic bag |
| Carrots | trim off greens. Cut large carrots in pieces leave small ones whole | 3 to 5 minutes, depending on size | pack in glass jars or rigid containers. allow ½" head-space |
| Chilies | Leave whole, wash | none | freeze on tray, dry pack in plastic bag |
| Corn on cob | husk, remove ends, trim, remove silk wash | 6 to 8 minutes, depending on size | wrap, individually. over-wrap in plastic bag |
| Mushrooms | sort by size. Soak 5 minutes in 1 tsp. lemon juice and 1 pint water, depending on size | 2 to 3 minutes | freeze on tray. Pack in plastic bag |
| peas | shell, soak in cold water to get rid of skin, etc. | 1 to 1 ½ minutes | dry pack in glass, jar or rigid container. allow ½" headspace |
| Peppers-bell | halve, seed, cut off ribs, halved or cut in forms wash | optional | freeze in trays. Pack in glass jar or freeze in containers. Allow ½' headspace |

**FRUITS:**

| | | | |
|---|---|---|---|
| Apples | peel, core, and slice drop in 1 qt. Water with 1 tsp. Salt to prevent darkening rinse and dry | dry pack or pack in syrup with ½ tsp ascorbic acid or lemon juice per qt. Or pack in pectin. | pack in glass jar or rigid plastic container. Allow ¼" headspace |

| | | | |
|---|---|---|---|
| Apricots | wash, pit, peel. Add pits to container to syrup formed from cooked fruit give flavor | | pack in glass jar or rigid container Allow 3/4" headspace |
| Berries | trim under cold water using care. Pick off stems. Leave whole or halve | a little honey if desired | freeze on tray, pack in rigid plastic container, allow ½" headspace |
| Cherries | sort, stem, wash, pit and chill. Leave whole | a little honey if desired | freeze on tray. Pack in container. Allow ½" headspace |
| Grapes | wash, stem, leave seedless grapes whole. seeded grapes, halve and seed | | freeze on tray. Pack in rigid container |
| Melons | halve, seed, cut into cubes or balls sprinkle with lemon juice or ascorbic acid | | freeze on tray. Pack in rigid containers. Allow ½" headspace. |
| Peaches | wash, peel, pit, halve or slice | a little honey or a syrup pack. Add ascorbic acid or lemon juice or pack in pectin | pack in glass jar or rigid container. Allow ¾" headspace |
| Plums | sort, wash, pit, halve or quarter | | freeze dry on tray. Pack in plastic bags |

## FREEZING FRUITS

*FRUITS CAN BE FROZEN FOR UP 12 MONTHS*

Pick fruits at the height of ripeness for maximum flavor and color. Do not use over-ripe fruit. Prepare fruit immediately and rush it to the freezer to halt ripening.

Wash, drain, sort by size, and trim fruits or berries Peel and seed fruits if necessary; and slice, halve or cut into chunks. Fruits can be frozen dry or in sweetening that helps preserve flavor, texture and color. For fruits and berries that don't discolor and can be prepared without rupturing the skins, freeze unsweetened or in a dry sugar pack. After washing, trimming and drying them on paper towels, lay the berries or fruit on a flat tray. Pre-freeze 1 hour, then pack.

Syrup packs are good when fruit must be sweetened to preserve quality. A natural sweetener for syrup that adds nutritive value is a mild-flavored honey. (In recipes calling for syrup). For thin syrup, dissolve 1 cup honey in 3 cups boiling hot water. Chill syrup before using to pack fruits. Use ½ cup syrup per pint, 1 cup per quart container.

To add vitamin C to fruit and preserve the quality add lemon juice or ascorbic acid. Use ½ teaspoon dissolved in a little cold water, per 1 quart syrup.

Fruits that darken very easily when frozen: peaches, pears; should be packed with pectin. Boil 1 box of commercial pectin in 1 cup water for 1 minute, stirring constantly. Add ¼ cup honey and stir until dissolved. Add cold water to make 2 cups.

## FREEZING FOODS

Most foods can be frozen, however some foods freeze better than others and some cannot be frozen at all.

Most meats can be frozen easily if well wrapped, organ meats cannot be stored as long as muscle cuts. Ground meats and sausage do not keep well over a long period of time. Raw steak can be frozen for up to 12 months. Raw bacon, 1 month. Raw pork chops can be frozen up to 6 months whereas ground beef should be used within 3 to 4 months. Raw chicken in pieces can be frozen for approximately 9 months, whole chickens and turkeys for up to 12 months.

Cooked casseroles with meat, soups and stews should be frozen no longer than 2 to 3 months.

Vegetables, which will be later cooked, can be frozen. Most can be blanched and fast frozen and placed into freezer bags, the exceptions are radishes, lettuce, green peppers, celery, cabbage and Chinese cabbage. They lose crispness after being defrosted. If they are going to be cooked you can freeze them as they freeze well for later cooking. Vegetables can be frozen up to 8 months.

Fruits don't freeze quite as well as vegetables but can be frozen, they only exception are bananas. They cannot be frozen. Orange, grapefruit and pineapple sections can be frozen in a prepared sugar syrup. Avocados, persimmons and watermelon are best frozen in a pureed form. Berries can be frozen up to 12 months. See previous section; freezing fruits for full information.

Tomatoes can be frozen directly into the freezer. They must be then treated as canned tomatoes and used for cooking. Treat as other vegetables. I store my plum tomatoes in a poly bag and just keep adding the tomatoes until I'm ready to make tomato sauce, I will use approximately 10 to 12 plum tomatoes instead of one can of tomatoes.

Cooked fish can be frozen up to 5 months and cooked shrimp can be frozen for approximately 3 months.

Baked goods and cooked dishes can be frozen successfully. Pies can be frozen, including fruit pies, but do not keep them in the freezer too long. Use within 1 to 2 months. Cake and breads freeze well but do not leave them in the freezer too long either as they will lose moisture. Quick breads last about 2 months, yeast breads and rolls can be kept 3 to 6 months. Cookies can be frozen for up to 12 months. Cheesecakes can be frozen up to 3 months. Otherwise, usually they should be frozen no longer than 1 to 3 months if unsure.

Most dairy products freeze well also. Even eggs can be frozen although I recommend freezing the yolks separately from the whites, but it isn't necessary. Butter, cheese and cream can all be frozen well. Butter can be frozen for up to 9 months, cheeses up to 6 months. Ice Cream should not be stored in the freezer longer than 2 months.

Please remember that over ripe fruits and vegetables will be mushy when defrosted, so make sure all fruits and vegetables are at peak of ripeness.

Nuts should be stored in the freezer and can be used straight out of the freezer. They remain fresh for up to 12 months.

## BROILING, STEAMING, SAUTEING, POACHING

*BROILING*; Broiling is food cooked by very hot direct heat on a rack. Most often thin, quick-cooking foods are broiled 3 to 4 inches from the heat while thicker foods or those that burn easily are placed 5-6 inches from the heat. To make sure the oven rack is in the right position, measure the distance between the heating element and the top of the broiler pan.

Arrange the food on a cold broiler pan to keep food from sticking. For dry foods, such as fish, lightly grease the broiler rack. For meat, slash the fat along the edges to keep the pieces from curling. Use tongs to turn the food, avoid piercing foods since that may allow the juices to escape. Very dry foods may need a marinade, glaze, etc or at least a bit of butter to keep it moist.

To test for doneness, fish should flake easily, meats, cut a slit in center, beef and lamb should be pink for medium, gray for pork, and white for poultry. Do not overcook, as meat will dry.

*STEAMING:* You suspend food over boiling water so that the steam from the water cooks the food. Used most often to cook vegetables, steaming also is ideal for meats, poultry, fish, fruits, and even breads.

Bring water in steamer to boil, hard enough to produce steam but not so hard that the pan becomes dry. Start by filling the steamer with 1 to 2 inches of water. Bring the water to a rolling boil over high heat, then reduce the heat to a gentle boil. Place the food in the steamer rack and lower the rack to about 1-½" above the water level. Cover the steamer and steam until food is done. Be sure to add more boiling water during cooking, if needed. In lieu of a steamer you can use a pot that fits over the first pot of boiling water OR a steamer insert that can be purchased separately (just make sure it fits properly in the pot you will be using).

*SAUTEING:* Sautéing is a way of cooking foods quickly in a small amount of fat. You can sauté in woks, sauté pans or simply use a skillet (10" to 12" best). Meat for sautéing should be cut thin, or thinly slice it across the grain. Use either butter, margarine, cooking oil, olive oil or shortening. Heat skillet over high heat and add fat, 1 to 2 tablespoons. Do not let the fat smoke or brown. Keep the meat in motion until done. If you plan to thicken your mixture, thoroughly dissolve flour or cornstarch in some type of cold liquid (such as milk or broth). Add the mixture to the center of the skillet where it's hottest. Continue cooking and stirring until the mixture bubbles.

*POACHING:* Poaching simply means simmering foods in a moderate amount of liquid. Water is the most used poaching liquid, but for soups and main dishes, milk, broth or dry wine are other options. For desserts fruit juice, milk or sweet wine can be used.

Start by putting 1 ½" liquid into a deep skillet or wide, shallow saucepan. Heat the liquid to simmering, bubbles should rise but not break the surface. Using a slotted spoon gently lower the food into the liquid. For eggs, break egg into custard cup and holding as close to liquid as possible, slid into the liquid. Do not boil the liquid as it makes the eggs tough. Remove cooked food with the slotted spoon or a pancake turner.

# LIQUEURS

Liqueurs range in alcohol content from 15% to 55% by volume. They are high-sugar beverages with added flavorings usually derived from herbs, fruits or nuts. Liqueurs can be broken down into the following categories:

**Chocolate liqueurs:** which includes Ashanti Gold, Crème de Cacao, Godiva Dark Chocolate, Godiva White Chocolate and Glodiva Cappuccino Liqueurs.

**Coffee liqueurs:** which includes Kahlua, Kona Gold, Kosaken Kaffee, and Toussaint Coffee Liqueurs.

**Cream liqueurs:** which includes Baileys Irish Cream, Dooley's, Starbucks Cream and Mozart Gold Chocolate Cream liqueurs.

**Crème liqueurs:** which includes Crème de Cacao, Crème de Menthe, and Parfait d'Amour liqueurs.

**Fruit liqueurs:** which includes Aurum, Cherry Heering, Cosa Gialla, Cointreau, Grand Marnier, Limoncello, Triple Sec, and Curacao liqueurs.

**Berry liqueurs:** which includes Chambord, Crème de Cassis, Lillehammer, Murtado, Razzmatazz and Sloe gin liqueurs.

**Flower liqueurs:** which includes Crème de Rose, Lavender Liqueur, Rosolio, St. Germain, and Shan Lotus liqueurs.

**Herbal liqueurs:** which can contain up to 50 or more different herbs includes:
    **Anise-flavored liqueurs:** such as Anisette, Ouzo and Pernod Ricard.
    **Other types of herbal liqueurs** such as Amaro, Benedictine, Chartreuse, Danzig Goldwasser, Goldschlager and Jagermeister.

**Nut-flavored liqueurs:** which includes Amaretto (almonds), Frangelico (hazelnuts), Kahana Royale (macadamia) and Ratafia (almonds).

**Whisky liqueurs:** which includes Drambuie, Irish Mist, Orangerie, Wild Turkey American Honey and Yukon Jack liqueurs.

**Other liqueurs:** which includes Advocaat (egg yolks and vanilla), Agnes (orange, apple, vanilla), Aurum (rum, tea, tangerines) and Barenjager (honey) liqueurs.

# WINES

| Types of Wine | Types of Food to serve with | Ideal serving temperature |
|---|---|---|
| Appetizer Wines:<br>Sherry (dry or sweet)<br>Vermouth (dry or sweet)<br>Flavored wines<br>Special natural wines | appetizers, canapés, bouillon | 45-50 degrees except for:<br>Sherry—60-70 degrees<br>Vermouth—serve over ice |
| Red Table Wines<br>Claret (dry)<br>Burgundy (dry)<br>Rose (pink, dry to sweet)<br>Red Chianti (dry)<br>Vino Rosso (semisweet) | steak, roast<br>game, roast, steak<br>ham, pork, veal<br>cheese, egg dishes, spaghetti | 60-70 degrees<br><br>45-50 degrees |
| White Table Wines<br>Chateau<br>Rhine Wine (dry to semisweet)<br>White Chianti (dry to semisweet)<br>Light Muscal (dry to sweet)<br>Chablis (dry)<br>Sauterne (dry to sweet)<br>Semillon | chicken, turkey<br>lamb, veal<br><br>seafood<br><br>shellfish | 45-50 degrees |
| Dessert Wines<br>Port (sweet)<br>Tawny Port (sweet)<br>White Tokay (sweet)<br>Cream or sweet Sherry<br>Muscatel (sweet) | sweet, nuts, fruit,<br>after coffee<br>all desserts | 60-70 degrees |
| Sparkling Wines<br>Sparkling Burgundy (red, Semisweet to sweet)<br>Sparkling Muscal (sweet) | all occasions and foods | 40-45 degrees |

| Sparkling Rose (dry to Semisweet) | all occasions | 40-45 degrees |

Sparkling Rose (dry to
Semisweet)                all occasions                40-45 degrees

Champagnes (gold or pink)  all occasions                40-45 degrees
Brut—very dry
Set-semidry
Demi-Sec

*When cooking with wines use the cheaper brands, rule of thumb would be: if you like it you use it, if you wouldn't drink it, don't!*

## COOKING WITH WINE

**USE BURGUNDY TO**
> Replace part of the liquid in beef stew
> Baste roast beef
> Replace part of the water when cooking beef tongue
> Pour over hamburger patties as they roast
> Flavor tomato sauces

**USE CLARET TO**
> Flavor clear soups just before removing them from heat
> Baste a baked ham
> Braise lamb shanks
> Make wine butter for steak—stir a little wine into melted butter, cook long enough
> To reduce liquid, and serve

**USE CHABLIS TO**
> Replace part of the liquid when poaching fish
> Replace part of the water when cooking carrots or artichoke or tiny whole onions

**USE RHINE WINE TO**
> Braise veal cutlets
> Replace part of the liquid in veal stew

**USE DRY SAUTERNE TO**
> Baste a lamb roast
> Braise lamb kidneys
> Flavor sauerkraut

## USE DRY SHERRY TO

Substitute for a little of the liquid when preparing cake, pudding, or salad dressing mixes

Glaze cooked sweet potatoes

Flavor seafood

Flavor cheese fondue

## CUTS OF STEAK: *and how to prepare them*

**Porterhouse:** choicest, most expensive, contains a large piece of tenderloin. Comes from large end of short loin. Should be at least 2" thick, broil or sauté.

**Strip or Boneless Loin (a/k/a New York Cut):** a porterhouse without the tenderloin. Broil or sauté.

**T-Bone:** includes small amount of tenderloin, but from opposite end of short loin than porter-house, smaller also. Sauté or broil.

**Shell:** a T-Bone or Porterhouse without the tenderloin. Sauté or broil.

**Delmonico or Boneless Club or Club:** no tenderloin, cut rather thin, makes great minute steak. Sauté quickly over high heat.

**Sirloin:** from high end of loin. More bones, cut thick, cook in broiler or over charcoal.

**Filet:** whole tenderloin, very tender, delicate flavor, most costly. Boneless, should be trimmed of fat before cooking. Must be barded or larded. **A/k/a Chateubriand.**

**Petit Filet, Tournedo and filet mignon:** chateubriand is largest cut from butt end and the filet mignon smallest cut from tip. All cut 1" thick except chateaubriand, which is cut 2" thick. All are either sautéed or broiled. Usually served with a sauce for more flavor.

# ROASTING TIME TABLES

| CUT | WEIGHT (POUNDS) | THERMOMETER READING (F) | COOKING TIME MINUTES PER POUND |
|---|---|---|---|

*BEEF ROAST-OVEN TEMPERATURE—325 DEGREES*

| CUT | WEIGHT (POUNDS) | THERMOMETER READING (F) | COOKING TIME MINUTES PER POUND |
|---|---|---|---|
| Rib (bone-in) | 6 to 8 | 140 degrees—rare | 23 to 25 |
|  |  | 160 degrees—medium | 27-30 |
|  |  | 170 degrees—well done | 32-35 |
| Rib (rolled or Boneless) | 4 to 6 | 140 degrees—rare | 26-32 |
|  |  | 160 degrees—medium | 34-38 |
|  |  | 170 degrees—well done | 40-42 |
| Ribeye Roast At 350 degrees | 4 to 6 | 140 degrees—rare | 18-20 |
|  |  | 160 degrees—medium | 20-22 |
|  |  | 170 degrees—well done | 22-24 |
| Rump (rolled Or boneless) | 4 to 6 | 150-170 degrees | 25-30 |
| Sirloin Tip | 3 ½ to 4 | 140-170 degrees | 35-40 |
|  | 6 to 8 | 140-170 degrees | 30-35 |
| Top Round | 4 to 6 | 140-170 degrees | 25-30 |

*VEAL ROAST-OVEN TEMPERATURE—325 DEGREES*

| CUT | WEIGHT (POUNDS) | THERMOMETER READING (F) | COOKING TIME MINUTES PER POUND |
|---|---|---|---|
| Loin | 4 to 6 | 170 degrees | 30-35 |

*LAMB ROAST-OVEN TEMPERATURE—325 DEGREES*

| CUT | WEIGHT (POUNDS) | THERMOMETER READING (F) | COOKING TIME MINUTES PER POUND |
|---|---|---|---|
| Leg (bone in) | 5 to 7 | 140 degrees—rare | 20-25 |
|  |  | 160 degrees—medium | 25-30 |
|  |  | 170 degrees—well done | 30-35 |
|  | 7 to 9 | 140 degrees—rare | 15-20 |
|  |  | 160 degrees—medium | 20-25 |

|  |  | 170 degrees—well done | 25-30 |
| Leg (boneless) | 4 to 7 | 140 degrees—rare | 25-30 |
|  |  | 160 degrees—medium | 30-35 |
|  |  | 170 degrees—well done | 35-40 |
| Shoulder (boneless) | 3 ½ to 5 | 140 degrees—rare | 30-35 |
|  |  | 160 degrees—medium | 35-40 |
|  |  | 170 degrees—well done | 40-45 |

## PORK ROAST-OVEN TEMPERATURE—325 DEGREES

| | | | |
|---|---|---|---|
| Loin | | | |
| Center | 3 to 5 | 165 degrees | 30-35 |
| Top | 2 to 4 | 165 degrees | 30-35 |
| Sirloin end | 3 to 4 | 165 degrees | 40-45 |
| Crown | 6 to 10 | 165 degrees | 25-30 |
| Arm Picnic | | | |
| Bone-in | 5 to 8 | 165 degrees | 30-35 |
| Boneless | 3 to 5 | 165 degrees | 35-40 |
| Tenderloin | ½ to 1 | 165 degrees | 45-60 |

| CUT | WEIGHT (POUNDS) | OVEN TEMPERATURE | TOTAL ROASTING TIME IN HOURS |
|---|---|---|---|
| *POULTRY* | | | |
| Chicken | 2 ½ to 4 ½ | 325 degrees | 2 to 3 ½ |
| Capon stuffed | 4 to 8 | 325 degrees | 2 ½ to 4 ½ |
| Cornish Hen | 1 to 1 ½ | 350 degrees | 1 to 2 |
| Duck stuffed | 4 to 8 | 350 degrees | 2 to 3 |
| Goose stuffed | 4 to 8 | 350 degrees | 2 ½ to 3 ½ |
|  | 8 to 14 | 350 degrees | 3 ½ to 5 |
| Turkey stuffed | 6 to 8 | 325 degrees | 3 to 3 ½ |
|  | 12 to 16 | 325 degrees | 4 ½ to 5 ½ |

# SPICES, HERBS AND BLENDS

## SPICES

ALLSPICE — sweet, good with fruits, desserts, breads, duckling, beef, pork, ham, yellow vegetables, tomato sauces, and relishes.

CINNAMON — sweet. Good with fruits, desserts, breads, tomato-meat sauces, yellow vegetables, beverages, pork, chicken, some beef and ground beef dishes.

CLOVES — sweet, pungent. Good with pickled fruits, desserts, baked goods, beverages, lamb, pork, corned beef, tongue, yellow vegetables, tomato sauces and beets.

GINGER — sweet. Good with fruits, squash, poultry, sauces for fish, port, some beef dishes, cheese and desserts.

NUTMEG — Sweet. Good with fruits, eggnog, cheese, desserts, ground beef, poultry, most vegetables and many sauces.

PAPRIKA — Mild. Good with beef, poultry, soups, salads, eggs and goulash.

SAFFRON — Pungent, aromatic. Good with meat, fish, poultry, vegetables, sauces and rice.

## HERBS

BASIL — Sweet, mild. Use with cheeses, pesto, vegetables, particularly green beans, tomatoes and tomato sauces, poultry, meat, rabbit, potato salad and sauces.

BAY — Sweet, mellow. Use with any foods requiring a bouquet garni, court bouillon, soups, stews, vegetables, pickling and other marinades and spaghetti sauce.

CHIVES — Mild, onion like. Use with sauces, salad dressings, cream, mild fish, poultry and veal.

| | |
|---|---|
| DILL | Mild. Use with fish, particularly salmon, pork, cottage cheese, potatoes, sauerkraut and other cabbage dishes, cauliflower, beans, pickles and sauces. |
| MARJORAM | Sweet, mild. Use with meat, particularly lamb, poultry, stuffing, cheese, vegetables, tomato-based sauces, soups and rabbit. |
| MINT | Strong, aromatic. Use with meats, vegetables, fruits, beverages and salads. |
| OREGANO | Spicy, pungent. Use with tomato dishes, fish, especially red snapper, vegetables used in Italian cuisine, stews, chili and beef and pork dishes. |
| PARSLEY | Mild. Use with court bouillon, soups, stews, meat poultry, fish, sauces, cheese, many vegetables and eggs. |
| ROSEMARY | Strong, acrid. Use with duckling, poultry, meat. Fish, stuffing and some vegetables like spinach, mushrooms, carrots, tomatoes and beans. |
| SAGE | Strong. Use with stuffing, pork, poultry, tomatoes, rice dishes, Brussels sprouts. |
| TARRAGON | Mild. Essential for Bearnaise sauce, good with fish, poultry, lamb, veal, salad dressings, vinegars, potato salad and some vegetables like beans, mushrooms and spinach. |
| THYME | Pungent, aromatic. Use with soups, stews, stuffing, rice dishes Mediterranean vegetables, dishes with red wine and/or tomatoes, rabbit, veal, lamb, fish and poultry. |

# BLENDS

BOUQUET
GARNI
Savory, aromatic, pungent. Good with meats, fish, poultry, vegetables, soups and stews.

CHILI
POWDER
Mild to hot. Good with chili con carne and other ground beef and pork dishes, cocktail and barbeque sauces, eggs, Creole and Mexican recipes, poultry.

CURRY
Mild to hot. Use with eggs, sauces, salad dressings, lamb, poultry, seafood, veal, cheese and fruit.

FINES
HERBES
Delicate. Use with eggs, mild fish, salad dressings, cream, white wine and butter sauces, poultry and veal.

## APPROXIMATE TEMPERATURE CONVERSIONS

|  | FAHRENHEIT | CELSIUS OR CENTIGRADE |
|---|---|---|
| Coldest spot in freezer | -10 degrees | -23 degrees |
| Freezer | 0 degrees | -17 degrees |
| Water freezes | 32 degrees | 0 degrees |
| Water simmers | 115 degrees | 46 degrees |
| Water boils (sea level) | 130 degrees | 100 degrees |
| Soft ball | 212 degrees | 112 degrees |
| Firm ball | 234 degrees | 117 degrees |
| Hard ball | 244 degrees | 121 degrees |
| Very low oven | 250-275 degrees | 121-133 degrees |
| Low oven | 300-325 degrees | 149-163 degrees |
| Moderate oven | 350-375 degrees | 177-190 degrees |
| Hot oven | 400-425 degrees | 204-218 degrees |
| Very hot oven | 450-475 degrees | 232-246 degrees |
| Extremely hot oven | 500-525 degrees | 260-274 degrees |

Note: to convert Fahrenheit into Centigrade, subtract 32, multiply by 5 and divide by 9. To convert Centigrade into Fahrenheit, reverse: multiply by 9, divide by 5, add 32.

Note: the freezer should be 0 degrees, it is a good idea to have a freezer thermometer to be sure, if the freezer is too warm the food will spoil.

## GRADES OF BEEF

**Prime:** the finest quality and most expensive usually not available at retail markets.

**Choice:** considered the best buy, retail, on the basis of palatability and cost.

**Good:** less desirable meat, also considerably less expensive.

## VEGETABLES IN SEASON

WINTER:     artichokes, avacados, broccoli, Brussel sprouts, cauliflower, mushrooms, parsnips, potatoes

SPRING:     asparagus, cabbage, carrots, green onions, spinach

SUMMER:     green beans, wax beans, beets, corn, okra, onions, peas, sweet green peppers, red peppers, summer squash, tomatoes, zucchini

FALL:     broccoli, cauliflower, eggplant, mushrooms, onions, parsnips, potatoes, sweet potatoes, acorn squash, hubbard squash

## STORING VEGETABLES

ROOT VEGETABLES: If already in netting bag or trays, store in their packaging in a dark, cool. dry place with plenty of air circulation. Since onions have a strong odor, keep them separate if possible. Hard rind squashes, acorn, Hubbard, butternut and turban, although not a root vegetable should also be stored in a dark, cool, dry place.

SALAD VEGETABLES: trim stems and droopy leaves from spinach and any kind of lettuce, wash leaves and dry well. Bundle them into transparent green bags and chill. Trim celery, Chinese Cabbage, radishes, and green onions and scrub them well; wash peppers and cucumbers, dry all of these foods thoroughly, wrap, and chill. Tomatoes that are firm and ripe can go into the refrigerator but any that are under-ripe are best kept at room temperature, away from sunlight, until they are ripe. Leave mushrooms in their original container and refrigerate, if in a transparent bag, punch a few holes in the bag for air.

YEAR ROUND VEGETABLES: fresh beans, peas, cabbage, cauliflower, corn, yellow squash, zucchini, artichokes, and asparagus. Store them in transparent bags to hold in natural moisture. Corn is the most delicate and should be stored no more than a day or two. Keep these vegetables cold and clean and wash them immediately before use.

## BASIC STAPLES FOR THE KITCHEN

| | | |
|---|---|---|
| Allspice | Garlic | Potatoes |
| American Cheese | Ketchup | Salt |
| Baking Powder | Maple Syrup | Stock-Chicken |
| Baking Soda | Mayonnaise | Stock-Beef |
| Basil | Measuring Cups & spoons | Sugar-granulated |
| Bay Leaves | Milk | Sugar-Powdered |
| Butter | Mixing Bowls | Sugar-Light Brown |
| Cinnamon | Nutmeg | Sugar-Dark Brown |
| Cloves, ground | Olive Oil | Tarragon |
| Cooking Wine | Oregano | Tomato Paste |
| Corn Starch | Parmesan Cheese | Tomato Sauce |
| Cream of Chicken Soup | Pasta Sauce | Vanilla Extract |
| Crushed Red Pepper | Pastas | Vegetable Oil |
| Flour-all purpose | Pepper, white & black | White Vinegar |

Knives: chef's knife (8-12"); serrated knife & paring knife

## OTHER USEFUL ITEMS FOR THE KITCHEN:

| | | |
|---|---|---|
| Electric Mixer | Wooden Spoons | Food Chopper/processor |
| Stand Mixer | Storage containers for food | Plastic Wrap |
| Pastry Blender | Foil Wrap | Parchment Paper |
| Pastry bag with tips | gravy ladle | Mustard |

# TIPS

**For Cooking:**

**Tip:** Cook vegetables that fruit (like string beans) above the ground in boiling water, cook vegetables that fruit below ground (potatoes, etc) in cold water and bring up to boil.

**Tip:** For hard or soft boiled eggs, put eggs in cold water and time from start of full boil; 4-5 minutes for soft boiled and 6-7 minutes for hard boiled depending on size of egg (small, medium, large or jumbo). Rinse eggs in cold water, by gradually adding cold water to the boiling water.

**Tip:** To peel tomatoes or apples pare boil in water for a few minutes. Skin removes easily.

**Tip:** Be sure to temper eggs into any hot mixture. (Add some hot mixture to egg mixture before adding egg mixture to hot mixture).

**Tip:** Take your bananas apart when you get them home from the store. If you leave them connected at the stem they ripen faster.

**Tip:** To see if egg are fresh put in cool water, if it sinks its good, if it floats, throw it out.

**Tip:** Add garlic immediately to a recipe if you want a light flavor of garlic. Add at the end of the recipe if you want a stronger taste of garlic.

**Tip:** Before you pour sticky substances into a measuring cup, fill it with hot water. Pour out the hot water but do not dry the cup. Add your ingredient (such as peanut butter) and watch how easily it pours right out.

**Tip:** When freezing food that has been prepared, first cover in plastic wrap, then tin foil. This prevents the foil from sticking to the food when defrosted.

**Tip:** Don't use skim milk when a recipe calls for milk. Whole milk should be used if the recipe doesn't specify.

**Tip:** Yes, bone-in-meat and poultry is juicier and more flavorful. However, if you are pressed for time; boneless meats cook faster.

**Tip:** Let meat rest for 10 minutes before slicing to allow juices to distribute and the proteins to relax.

**Tip:** When substituting dried in lieu of fresh herbs use 1/3 the amount of dried to replace the fresh. So, if recipe calls for 1 tablespoon fresh herbs, use 1 teaspoon dried herbs. However, if using Cilantro, basil or parsley, they lose their flavor when dried, so increase amount used. If you can only use dried you must add additional salt and pepper to add flavor.

**Tip:** If the recipe calls for reserved fluid from either potatoes or vegetables, use it, it contains starch that thickens what it is used in. It is also great to add to pan drippings to make a good tasting gravy. If necessary additional water or broth can be added if not enough reserved fluid is available.

**Tip:** If you can't find parmigiano-reggiano cheese you can use graapadano, asiago, or pecorino-romano instead.

**Tip:** Pure Vanilla extract has a better flavor that imitation, if you want the best, use the best! Its more expensive but its definitely a case of you get what you pay for.

**Tip:** If your meat is sticking to the pan when you are trying to sear it, your pan needs to be hotter.

**Tip:** Confused about what rack you should use when using the oven. Roast vegetables, casseroles and other dishes you need to be golden brown on top rack. Items to be browned go on bottom rack. Cookies, breads and other baked goods need the middle rack. Rotate the pans to keep browning even.

**Tip:** If a recipe calls for wine you can leave it out of the recipe if desired, just substitute an equal amount of fluid already used in the recipe for the wine.

**Tip:** Do not substitute table salt for coarse salt. It is a different consistency and will make the recipe taste more salty.

**Tip:** Nutmeg might sound and look like a nut but don't remove the shell. Just rub it on a grater to get the full fragrance of the spice.

**Tip:** Always remove bay leaf before serving, the same goes for whole garlic cloves and garni or fines herbes that are added. They are *not* edible.

**Tip:** Cooking Chicken: Over a half full can of beer place a whole chicken. (The can goes in the cavity. Season chicken well with salt, pepper and spices of choice. Place vertically in the oven, the beer evaporates creating a very moist chicken. Just follow regular roasting instructions.

**Tip:** When using eggs, milk and or butter in a recipe, bring them to room temperature unless the recipe says otherwise.

**For the Home:**
**Tip:** Wine and fruit stains can be removed from tablecloths, napkins and towels with salt. Cover the stain immediately with salt. Let it stand a short time and then wash in cool water.

**Tip:** To remove candle wax. If candle wax drips onto the carpeting, remove the wax by placing a brown paper bag over the area and gently run a warm iron over the bag.

**Tip:** To clean shower curtains. To remove soap and hard water film from plastic shower curtains and curtain liners, take down the curtain and place it on a flat surface. Wash it with a solution of ½ cup ammonia to 1 quart warm water. The film will vanish.

**Tip:** Clean out the lint filter in your dryer, but also clean it with soap and water and a brush every six months if you use dryer sheets. A dryer sheet builds up a waxy build up on the lint filter, which allows no water or air to go through after time. So wash the mesh and check it with water to see that the water flows through it to know its clean. It prevents the dryer from burning out.

**Tip:** Restore stainless steel. If your flatware has lost its luster, place your flatware in a pan and cover it with carbonated water, soda water, seltzer or club soda. Let set; after a few minutes, it will shine like new.

**Tip:** To sharpen scissors that are dull, cut through a sheet of sandpaper a couple of times. They will work like new.

**Tip:** To reattach loose knobs dip the screws in clear fingernail polish or shellac before resetting the knobs. This will help the knobs stay tight much longer.

**Tip:** To remove hard water buildup pour some white distilled vinegar in a plastic bag and place the bag around the shower head so the head is completely submerged. Tie the bag around the pipe and let the shower head soak overnight. Come morning the shower head will spray like new again.

**Tip** You can use parchment paper more than once, throw it out when it dries out or starts turning brown.

**Tip:** Use beer as a rinse for your hair, use flat beer and mix 1 cup with a egg yolk. Massage into hair, leave in 2 minutes and wash with shampoo. Beer also can be used as a simple final rinse for hair. Flat beer also works best as a rinse. (if you are a blonde use lemon juice instead, it doesn't dull the hair). Plain beer making a wonderful setting lotion. Just spray lightly with beer poured into a spray bottle.

**Tip:** To scrub a cast iron pan after use pour a little beer into still-warm pan. When cooled, clean. The liquid keeps the mess from sticking and can also season the pan.

Tip: Pour a cup of beer on the rusty bolts and screw that cannot turn. Wait a few seconds, then give a turn. Carbonation helps break down the rust.

**Tip:** Preventing garden pests is easy with beer. A small bowl will attract and kill slugs and other creepy crawlies. Also good at keeping wasps and bees away from the patio. Just place a bowl of beer 4-6 feet away from the main area.

**Tip:** Wash your pillowcase in beer spiked water (only a little) will help with insomnia. Leaves a light nutty scent on fabric.

**Tip:** Clean your jewelry with light ale, use soft clean cloth and use on gold jewelry to remove dirt. Brings back the shine. Also cleans tarnished copper pots.

**Tip:** Pour a ½ cup of beer on brown spots in lawn. It is an organic way to re-green the lawn.

## TYPES OF SAUSAGES

**FRANKFURTER:** The frankfurter or "hot dog" has been around for over 100 years. The original form of sausage has been around for over 3000 years. In Europe it is called a wienerwurst (which is dog sausage in German. The frankfurter is a combination of meats and spices. It can be all beef or beef and pork mixtures.

**BOLOGNA:** The most popular of the domestic sausages. Bologna originated in Bologna, Italy. Beef Bologna is made of beef, veal and pork trimmings, which are chopped finely, spiced, and put into casings. Ham bologna is made of pork shoulder or pork butt, and can be made with chunks of ham. Bologna can be used as a substitute for frankfurters in a recipe.

**BRATWURST:** made of finely chopped, lean fresh pork trimmings. Seasoned with spices, such as nutmeg, ginger, cloves and mace and herbs such as sage. Stuffed into hog casings it is delicious served with boiled cabbage, sauerkraut or mashed turnips. Bratwurst is a family favorite!

**BRAUNECHWEIGER:** Made like liverwurst, this has more liver in it and spreads easily on sandwiches, crackers or toast. More spices than liverwurst and less meat, it is good for frying. It comes in either smoked or regular types. Can also be used in stuffing for roast fowl, fresh pork, crown of lamb, veal, and baked stuffed potatoes, green peppers, etc.

**CAMBRIDGE:** A sausage that originated in England it is made of beef with a small amount of pork, very little seasonings and almost no spice. The casings must be pricked with a fork before frying or broiling.

**PINKELWURST:** This is made of onions, oats, beef fat, pork fat, salt, mustard, spices, flavoring and onion powder. Used in recipes it is also a grill favorite. German in origin.

**SALAMI:** A dry sausage that is made in many countries. Salami comes from Italy, Hungary and Germany. Italian salami is made of 2/3 pork and 1/3 beef which is chopped finely and moistened with red wine or grape juice. It was highly seasoned with garlic and other spices. It is air-dried. German and Hungarian salamis are smoked instead of air-dried and less highly spiced.

**CERVELAT:** A generic name of a number of sausages, which resemble salami in their preparation. The meat is usually more finely chopped and hog or beef casings are used in processing.

**HILDESHEIMER:** A pure pork sausage made of 65% belly fat and 35% pork liver. It is soft and spreadable. It is used for sandwiches, canapés, and snacks.

**LIVERWURST:** Made of pork liver and pork meat. It is highly seasoned with salt, pepper, cardamom, and other seasonings specially mixed for liverwurst. The liverwurst is hickory-wood smoke for three hours or more. Mixed with mayonnaise to make a smooth mixture similar to pate de foie gras.

**METTWURST:** Made with finely chopped pork and liver, cooked with spices and put into beef casings and then smoked. Used as a spread.

**MUENCHNER WEISSWURST (OR WEISSWURST):** A white sausage made of pork and veal, but mostly veal. It is slightly spiced and can be broiled, baked or steamed. Highly spiced.

# SYRUPS

**Simple syrup:** 4 cups of sugar to 1 cup of cold water. Dissolve the granulated sugar in cold water and bring to a boil. Boil only to sugar dissolves and the water turns clear. Cool and bottle. Keep under refrigeration.

**Lemon syrup:** 4 cups sugar, 2 cups hot water, 4 tablespoons corn syrup, and 6 tablespoons grated lemon rind. Combine the ingredients in a saucepan. Place over direct heat; stir only until the sugar is dissolved and simmer gently for 25 minutes. Strain through cheesecloth. Bottle and keep refrigerated.

**Mint syrup:** 4 cups sugar, 2 cups water, ¼ cup corn syrup and 40 stalks of crushed fresh mint. Combine the ingredients in a saucepan over direct heat. Stir until the sugar is dissolved, and then simmer for 20 minutes. Strain through cheesecloth and turn into hot sterilized jars. Keep tightly covered in the refrigerator. Makes 1 quart. Can be base for mint jelly or mint sauce, can also be used to sweeten iced tea.

**Raspberry syrup:** 2 quarts fresh raspberries, 4 cups sugar, 3 cups cold water. Wash and drain raspberries and mash. Add the sugar. Cover and let stand overnight. In the morning add the water and bring slowly to boiling over direct heat. Stirring occasionally, simmer for 20 minutes. Press through a fine sieve and then strain through cheesecloth. Return to heat and bring to boiling, skim and put into sterile jars. Makes 1 quart. A base for dessert sauces and ices. Can use frozen raspberries instead of fresh.
*Strawberry syrup: substitute strawberries instead of raspberries.*

# GLOSSARY OF FOOD TERMS

## A

*A La:* In the manner of; a la maison, in the style of the house or house specialty.

*A La carte:* Dining where the diner selects each course from the menu. The price for each course is separate.

*Al dente:* Italian phrase meaning "to the tooth" used to describe spaghetti or other pasta at the perfect stage of doneness—tender but with enough firmness to be felt between the teeth.

*Angelica:* The "herb of the angels," believed to ward off the plague in ancient times. Today, its pale, green celery-like, stalks are candied and used to decorate cakes, cookies and candies.

*Antipasto:* Italian meaning "before the meal." Food served before dinner, usually tart or biting in flavor.

*Aperitif:* A mild alcoholic drink sipped before meals to sharpen appetites.

*Aspic:* A clear gelatin made from vegetable or meat broth.

*Au gratin:* Topped with crumbs and or cheese and browned in the oven or broiler.

*Au Jus:* A roast dressed with its own pan juices.

## B

*Baba:* A small, round, fruit-studded, yeast-leavened cake soaked in syrup.

*Baguette:* The everyday bread of France, baked in long loaves.

*Bake:* To cook, uncovered, in the oven with dry heat.

*Bake blind:* To bake an unfilled pastry shell. Prick the bottom of the pie shell with a fork. This will prevent shrinkage. The pastry shell can be also weighed down with dried beans (which can be used over and over again).

*Barbeque:* To roast meat or other food, basting often with a richly seasoned sauce. Also the name for the food cooked this way.

*Baste:* To ladle drippings, marinade or other liquid over food as it roasts.

*Batter:* A flour-liquid mixture thin enough to pour.

*Beat:* To stir vigorously with a spoon or to beat with an egg-beater or electric mixer.

*Beurre manie:* French term meaning "kneaded butter." This is butter kneaded with flour into a soft paste that is used to thicken soups, sauces, and gravies. Its advantage is that it can be added pinch by pinch until the sauce is exactly the consistency the cook wants. It also can be added shortly before serving.

*Beurre noir:* French word for "browned butter."

*Bind:* To add egg, thick sauce, or other ingredient to a mixture to make it hold together.

*Bisque:* A smooth, creamy soup, often with a shellfish base.

*Blanch:* To scald quickly in boiling water.

*Blend:* To mix two or more ingredients until smooth.

*Boil:* To cook in boiling liquid.

*Bombe:* Frozen dessert of two or more flavors layered in a fancy mold; also the mold itself.

*Bone:* To remove bones.

*Bouillon:* A clear stock made of poultry, beef or veal, vegetables and seasonings.

*Bouquet garni:* a small herb bouquet, most often sprigs of fresh parsley and thyme plus a dried bay leaf, tied in cheese-cloth, then dropped into stocks, stews, sauces and soups as a seasoning.

*Braise:* To brown in fat, then to cook, covered in a small amount of liquid.

*Bread:* To coat with bread crumbs.

*Brochette:* French for skewer.

*Broil:* To cook under or on a grill by direct dry heat.

*Broth:* A clear meat, fish, fowl or vegetable stock, or a stock made of a combination of these.

## C

*Calorie:* A unit of heat used to measure potential energy value of food in the body.

*Canapé:* A small, decorative, open-face sandwich served with cocktails.

*Capon:* A male chicken castrated while young so that it grows plump, fat and tender.

*Caramelize:* To heat sugar or a sugar-water mixture until it turns a clear amber brown.

*Chantilly:* Sweetened, flavored cream that has been whipped just until it holds its shape softly.

*Chop:* To cut into small pieces.

*Clarify:* To make stock, aspic or other liquid crystal clear by adding egg shell or egg white; also to clear melted butter by spooning off the milk solids.

*Clove of garlic:* One segment of a bulb of garlic.

*Coat:* To cover with flour, crumbs or other dry mixture before frying.

*Coat the spoon:* Term used to describe egg-thickened sauces when cooked to perfect doneness, dip in spoon and should coat or stick to the spoon.

*Coddle:* To simmer gently in liquid, usually refers to poaching.

*Combine:* To mix together two or more ingredients.

*Compote:* A mixture of sweetened, cooked fruits.

*Consommé:* Clarified stock or bouillon.

*Coquilles:* The French word for shells. In this the country coquilles or scallop shells are available in sets of a dozen or half-dozen and used to make food more visually appealing.

*Court bouillon:* A delicate broth, usually fish and vegetable based, used for poaching fish.

*Couscous:* A fine semolina (wheat) grain that is a staple in North Africa. It is steamed in a couscousier (perforated container) over a bubbling piquant lamb or chicken stew.

*Cracklings:* The crisp brown bits left after lard has been rendered. In the South, cracklings are baked into a corn bread known as "crackling bread."

*Cream:* To beat butter or shortening alone or with sugar until fluffy.

*Crepe:* Very thin French pancake.

*Crimp:* To flute the edges of a piecrust.

*Crisp:* To warm in oven till crisp.

*Crostini:* Fried bread; squares usually served with soups.

*Croustade:* A toast, case used for serving creamed meats, fish, fowl or vegetables.

*Crumb:* To coat with bread, or cracker crumbs. For crumbs to stick, the food to be crumbed should first be dipped in milk or beaten egg.

*Cube:* To cut into cubes.

*Cut in:* To work shortening or other solid fat into a flour mixture with a pastry blender or two knives till texture of coarse meal.

*Cutlet:* A small, thin, boneless piece of meat—usually veal.

## D

*Dacquoise:* A dessert of almond meringue layers sandwiched with rich French butter cream.

*Dash:* A very small amount—less than 1/8th teaspoon.

*Deep fry:* To cook in hot deep fat.

*Deglaze:* To get up the "browned bits" left in a skillet or sauté pan after meat, poultry, vegetables or other foods have been browned. First remove excess fat and then add stock or wine or water and bring to a boil and stir. Thickeners can be added. The basis for gravies and sauces.

*Demitasse:* French for "half cup," usually a small cup used to serve after-dinner coffee.

*Devil:* To season with mustard, pepper and other spicy condiments.

*Dice:* To cut into small uniform pieces.

*Dilute:* To "water down" or weaken the strength of the soup, sauce, gravy or stew by adding liquid (usually milk, water or broth).

*Dot:* To scatter bits of butter or other seasoning over the surface of a food to be cooked.

*Double boiler:* Two saucepans in one—an upper pan fitted over a lower one. For cooking purposes, water goes into the lower pan. Cooking over simmering water keeps delicate mixtures just below the boiling point, and prevents over-cooking.

*Draw:* To remove the entrails or eviscerate. Also, to melt butter.

*Dredge:* To coat with flour prior to drying.

*Drippings:* Fats and juices released by meat as it cooks. They form the basis of many classic sauces and gravies.

*Duchesse:* Mashed potatoes, mixed with butter and cream, piped around meats, poultry or fish dishes as decorative borders, then browned in the oven or broiler just before serving.

*Dutch oven:* A large heavy metal cooking pot with a tight-fitting cover used for cooking pot roasts and stews.

## E

*En crocotte:* Cooked in a covered baking dish or pot.

*Enchiladas:* A spicy Mexican classic-tortillas rolled up around meat, vegetables and cheese.

*Entrée:* Main course of the meal.

*Entremets:* Side dishes served at a meal. May be savory or sweet.

*Espresso:* Robust, dark Italian coffee traditionally served in small cups.

## F

*File:* Also known as file powder and gumbo. A powder made of dried sassafras leaves used to thicken Creole soup
and stews. Creole cooks learned the secrets of file powder from the Choctaw Indians who invented it.

*Fillet:* A thin boneless piece of meat or fish.

*Fines herbes:* a mixture of minced fresh or dried parsley, chervil, tarragon and sometimes chives used to season salads, omelets and other dishes.

*Flambé or flambéed:* French word meaning flaming.

*Florentine:* In the style of Florence, Italy—which usually means served on a bed of spinach, topped with a delicate cheese sauce and browned in the oven, Fish and eggs, are two foods often served Florentine-style.

*Flute:* To crimp the edge of a piecrust in a fluted design.

*Fold in:* To mix a light, fluffy ingredient, such as beaten egg white, into a thicker mixture using a gentle over-and-over motion.

*Fondue:* Originated in Switzerland. A smooth mixture of melted cheese, white wine and kirsch made in an earthenware crock set over a burner. To eat, chunks of bread are speared with special long-handled fondue forks and twirled in the semi-liquid cheese mixture. Fondue Beurguignonne is a convivial Swiss version of a French dish: Cubes of steak speared with fondue forks, fried at the table in a pot of boiling oil then dipped into one of several assorted sauces. Very popular at parties in the 1970s and 1980s.

*Frappe:* A mushy frozen fruit dessert.

*Fritter:* A crisp, golden, deep-fried batter bread, often containing corn or minced fruits or vegetables. Also pieces of fruit or vegetables, batter dipped and deep fried.

*Fromage:* French meaning cheese.

*Frost:* To cover with frosting. Also, to chill until frosty.

*Fry:* To cook in a skillet in a small amount of fat.

**G**
*Giblets:* The heart, liver and gizzard of fowl.
*Goulash:* A stew.
*Grate:* To rub food across a grater to produce fine particles.
*Grease:* To rub butter or other fat over the surface of a food or container.
*Grissini:* Long, slim Italian bread sticks.
*Gumbo:* A Creole stew made with tomatoes and thickened either with file powder (ground dried sassafras leaves) or okra.

**H**
*Hors d'oeuvre:* Bite-sized appetizers served with cocktails.
*Hull:* To remove stems and hulls, from berries.
*Husk:* To remove leaves and silk strands from ears of corn.

**I**
*Ice:* To cover with icing. Also a frozen water-based fruit dessert.
*Italienne, a l':* Serve Italian-style with a garnish of spaghetti or other pasta.

**J**
*Jigger:* A bartender's measure holding 1 ½ fluid ounces.
*Julienne:* Food cut in uniformly long, thin slivers.

**K**
*Kasha:* Buckwheat groats braised or cooked in liquid and served in place of rice or potatoes.
*Kisses:* "Mini" meringues baked and served as candies or cookies.
*Knead:* To manipulate dough with the hands until it is light and springy.
*Kosher:* Food prepared or processed according to Jewish ritual and dietary law. Cannot contain pork or ham.

**L**
*Lard:* Creamy-white rendered pork fat; also the act of inserting small cubes (lardoons) of fat in a piece of meat prior to roasting.
*Line:* To cover the bottom, and sometimes sides, or a pan with paper or sometimes thin slices of food.
*Luau:* The traditional outdoor Hawaiian feast.
*Lyonnaise:* Seasoned in the style of Lyon, France—meaning with parsley and onions.

# M

*Macedoine:* A mixture of vegetables or fruits.

*Macerate:* To let steep in wine or spirits, or allow to steep after sprinkling with sugar.

*Maitre d'hotel:* Simply cooked dishes, seasoned with minced parsley, butter and lemon.

*Maitre d'hotel butter:* is a mixture of butter, parsley, lemon and salt.

*Marinade:* The medium in which food is marinated.

*Marinate:* To season or tenderize food by steeping in a piquant sauce prior to cooking.

*Marron:* The French word for chestnut.

*Marzipan:* A confection made from almond paste, sugar and egg white. It is usually molded into fruit and vegetable shapes.

*Mash:* To reduce to pulp.

*Mask:* To coat with sauce or aspic.

*Meringue:* A stiffly beaten mixture of sugar and egg white.

*Mince:* To cut into fine pieces.

*Mix:* To stir together.

*Mocha:* Coffee-chocolate flavoring.

*Monosodium glutamate:* A white crystalline compound used widely in Chinese and Japanese cookery.

*Mousse:* A rich, creamy frozen dessert; also a velvety hot or cold savory dish, rich, with cream, bound with eggs or cold, with gelatin.

*Mousseline:* A sauce to which whipped cream has been added.

*Mull:* To heat a liquid (often cider or wine) with spices.


# N

*Newburgh:* A rich cream-and-sherry sauce, usually for shellfish and chicken.

*Nicoise:* Prepared in the manner of Nice, France—with tomatoes, garlic, olive oil and ripe olives.


# O

*Oil:* To rub a pan or mold with vegetable oil.


# P

*Paclla:* A popular Spanish one-dish dinner containing rice, chicken, shellfish and vegetables served in their shallow metal cooking pan. Garlic and saffron are the dominant seasonings.

*Panbroil:* To cook in a skillet with a very small amount of fat, drippings are usually poured off as they accumulate.

*Parboil:* To boil food until about half done.

*Pare:* To remove the skin of a fruit or vegetable.

*Pasta:* The all inclusive Italian word for all kinds of macaroni and spaghetti.

*Pate:* A will-seasoned mixture of finely minced or ground meats and/or liver. *Pate de fois gras* is made of goose livers and truffles.

*Penne:* a form of pasta. Short hollow straight macaroni.

*Petits fours:* Tiny, fancily frosted cakes.

*Pilaf:* Rice cooked in a savory broth, often with small bits of meat or vegetables, herbs and spices.

*Pinch:* The amount of a dry ingredient that can be taken up between the thumb and index finger—less than 1/8th teaspoon.

*Pipe:* To press frosting, whipped cream, mashed potatoes or other soft mixture through a pastry bag with a decorative tip.

*Plank:* To broil steak, chops or fish on a well-seasoned (oiled) hardwood plank. Food will take in flavor of wood.

*Plump:* To soak raisins or other dried fruits in liquid until they plump up.

*Poach:* To cook in simmering liquid.

*Polenta:* A cornmeal porridge popular in Italy. It is often cooled, sliced or cubed, then breaded and fried.

*Pot pie:* A pastry-topped meat or poultry and vegetable stew baked in a casserole.

*Pot Roast:* A large, less-tender cut of beef often rump or chuck that is browned in oil, then cooked, covered, along with vegetables and some liquid. Other kinds of meat are said to be "pot roasted" when similarly cooked. But, technically, a pot roast is a cut of beef.

*Preheat:* To bring oven or broiler to recommended temperature before cooking.

*Prick:* To punch holes in the surface of pastry or other food with the tines of a fork. It prevents pastry from buckling and potatoes from bursting.

*Puree:* To reduce food to a smooth, velvety medium by whirling it an electric blender or pressing through a sieve or food mill.

## Q

*Quenelles:* Delicate fish, chicken or veal dumplings poached in hot liquid and smothered with a milky sauce.

*Quiche:* An open-faced savory tart. The best known is Quiche Lorraine, which is filled with bacon-studded cream and egg custard.

## R

*Ragout:* a stew.

*Ramekin:* A small individual size baking dish.

*Reduce:* To boil uncovered until quantity of liquid is less then when started.

*Render:* To melt solid fat.

*Rennet:* Material; from a pig's on calf's stomach, used to curdle milk, usually in cheese.

*Rice:* To press food through a ricer to mash or puree.

*Rijstafel:* Literally, "rice table," an opulent Indonesian curry dinner sometimes featuring as many as 40 different dishes.

*Risotto:* An Italian dish made with short-grained rice and tomatoes or mushrooms or onions or truffles. It is usually thick and topped with grated cheese.

*Rissole:* A small savory meat pie fried in deep fat.

*Roast:* To roast in the oven by dry heat.

*Roe:* The eggs of a fish.

*Roll:* To roll out with a rolling pin.

*Roux:* A fat-flour mixture used in making sauces.


S

*Sauté:* French for pan fry.

*Savory:* An adjective used to describe food that is piquant rather than sweet.

*Scald:* To heat a liquid almost to boiling—until bubbles form around edge of pan.

*Scallop:* To make small pieces of food in casserole, usually in a cream sauce.

*Scone:* A Scottish bread, shaped into flat round cakes and baked on a griddle or in the oven.

*Score:* To make crisscross cuts over food surface with a knife.

*Sear:* To brown under or over intense heat.

*Seed:* To remove seeds.

*Semolina:* The pale golden heart of duram (hard) wheat. It may be as finely milled as flour or as granular as couscous (see above).

*Shirr:* To cook whole eggs in ramekins with cream and crumbs.

*Short:* An adjective used to describe a bread, cake or pastry that has a high proportion of fat and is therefore is ultra tender or crisp.

*Shortening:* The fat used to make cakes, pastries, cookies, and breads, flaky and tender.

*Shred:* To cut in small thin slivers.

*Sieve:* To put through a sieve or strainer.

*Sift:* To put flour on other dry ingredient through a sifter.

*Simmer:* To cook in liquid to just below the boiling point.

*Skewer:* A long metal or wooden pin on which food is impaled before being grilled; also a name for the pin itself.

*Skim:* To remove fat or oil from the surface of a liquid or sauce.

*Silver:* To cut into thin strips.

*Spit:* To impale food on a long rod and roasted over glowing coals, also the name of the rod.

*Steam:* To cook, covered, over a small amount of boiling water so that the steam circulates freely around the food, making it tender.

*Steep:* To let food soak in liquid until liquid absorbs its flavor, as in steeping tea in hot water.

*Stir:* To mix with a spoon using a round-and-round motion.

*Stock:* Meat, fowl, fish or vegetable stock.

*Strain:* To put through a strainer or sieve.

*Stud:* To stick cloves, silvers of garlic or other seasoning into the surface of a food to be cooked.

## T

*Table d'hote:* Dining where the diner selects the entrée, the price of which determines the cost of the entire meal.

*Terrine:* A baked pate and/or the name of the rectangular earthenware or metal container the pate is baked in.

*Thicken:* To make a liquid thicker, usually by adding flour, cornstarch, or egg.

*Thin:* To make a liquid thinner by adding liquid.

*Timbale:* A savory meat, fish, fowl or vegetable custard.

*Top:* To lay or sprinkle on top of.

*Toss:* To mix as for a salad by gently turning ingredients over and over in a bowl.

*Truss:* To tie fowl into a compact shape before roasting.

*Turnover:* A folded pastry usually made by cutting a circle, adding a dollop of sweet or savory filling, folding into a semicircle and crimping the edges with the times of a fork. Most turnovers are baked but some are deep fat-fried.

*Tutti-frutti.* A mixture of minced fruits used as a dessert topping.

## V

*Vermicelli:* Very fine spaghetti.

*Veronique:* A dish garnished with white grapes.

*Vinaigrette:* Dressed with oil, vinegar, salt, pepper and herbs.

*Vol-ai-vent:* Puff pastry shells, large or small, filled with creamed chicken, seafood or mushrooms.

## W

*Whip:* To beat until frothy or stiff with an egg beater or in an electric mixer.

*Wok:* A round-bottomed, bowl-shaped Chinese skillet used for stir frying.

## Z

*Zest:* Oily, aromatic, colored part of the skin of citrus fruits, grated into various dishes.

# HOW TO BUY FRESH FISH

Start by looking at the eyes. They should be bright, clear and bulging. If they look dull or cloudy or sunken in, do not buy! Next look at the fish's gills to see that they're a fresh reddish pink color. Press the flesh of the fish. It should be firm and resilient. And remember that any fish with a pronounced "fishy" smell is the one to leave behind.

**Cleaning the fish:**

Dressed and cleaned means the fish monger will remove the tail and head, and the entrails. Fins and scales will also be removed.

Split and boned: all of the above plus it will be split down the middle and the center or large bone will be removed. Split and boned for stuffing: same as split and boned.

If you wish to serve with the head and tail you have to request it.

**Types of cuts:**

Steak: are cross-sectioned slices cut from a large fish. Tuna and swordfish are sold as steaks. Fillets: are boneless, skinless pieces of fish cut lengthwise from the fish. Any fish, regardless of size can be filleted. Flounder, mackerel, haddock are examples of fish that are sold as fillets.

## CLAMS (CLEANING AND SERVING)

Soft clams are steamed open before being brought to the table. The first step is the "bearding" of the clam—that is, removing the black hood from the neck together with its trailing "veil." The hard clam is opened with an oyster knife, like an oyster, It is beardless. The opened soft clams are served on a deep dish or large platter. An oyster or dinner fork may be used to remove the clam from its shell and the clam cap from the head. Most clam lovers prefer using their fingers. Along side of each plate a small warm dish containing melted butter seasoned with lemon juice, and each clam should be dipped into this sauce before eating. The broth should be strained and served in cups, the clams often being dipped first into broth, then into butter.

Clams may be boiled, steamed, broiled, sautéed, baked, etc. Clams, both fresh and canned, deserve to be used in more than just chowder. Tiny hard clams are prized raw or in a cocktail.

## PREPARATION OF CRABS

Crabs should always be alive when purchased. To prepare soft crabs, stick a sharp knifepoint into the body between the eyes. Lift up the pointed ends of the shell and remove the spongy white fibers. Turn the crab on its back and remove the "apron" (ventral plaque) or small loose shell running to a point at about the middle of the under-shell. Wash the crabs and fry them at once. To prepare hard crabs, drop them headfirst into boiling salted water to cover, and cook for 20 minutes. Drain, rinse, and cool. Crack the shell and claws to obtain the meat. Crabs are served with lemon and butter. They boil and broil well. Season the butter well. Pour seasoned butter over broiled crab as soon as they are removed from the broiler.

## OYSTERS

Oysters should never be really cooked, just heated through sufficiently to plump them up. Cooking until the 'edges curl' is a good test. Overcooking makes is tough and leathery. *Shucking:* Wash and rinse the oysters thoroughly in cold water. Place the oyster on a solid surface, flat shell up and holding it with left hand. With right hand force an oyster knife between the shells at or near the thin end. The knife is easier to insert if the thin end or 'bill' is broken off with a hammer. Cut the large muscle close to the flat upper shell in which it is attached, and remove the shell. Cut the lower end of the same muscle, which is attached to the deep half of the shell, and leave the oyster loose in the deep half if it is to be served on the half shell. Examine the oyster for bits of shell, which sometimes adhere to the muscle.

## LOBSTER

In choosing a live lobster, remember that there is a greater shrinkage than in any other fish. If the lobster is already cooked, pick it up, and if it is heavy in proportion to its size, the lobster is fresh. Straighten the tail, and if it springs back to its former place, the lobster was alive (as it should be) when it was put into the pot for boiling. In boiling a lobster, have salted water, or whatever other liquid the recipe calls for, boiling rapidly in a large fish kettle. Plunge the lobsters into the boiling liquid, head first, one at a time, bringing the liquid back to the boiling point between each lobster. The time usually required for cooking lobster is about 15 to 20 minutes, depending on the size. Do not stop the rapid boiling, as this will make the meat tough. In opening a cooked lobster first remove the large claws, then the small claws and tail. The tail meat may sometimes, after a little practice, be drawn out whole with a fork or a skewer, but more often it is necessary to cut the thin shell in the under part of the tail with a pair of kitchen scissors, before the tail meat can be removed. Divide the tail meat through the center and remove the small intestinal vein, which runs along the entire length. Hold the body of the shell firmly in the left hand, and with the right hand, draw out the body, leaving in the shell the stomach, which is not edible. The green liver is a particular delicacy. Discard the lungs. Break the body through the middle, and separate the body bones, picking out the meat that lies between them. which is the sweetest and tenderest part of the lobster. Separate the claws at the joints.

# FILLETING FISH

The fish needs to be large enough to lend itself to filleting. The flesh is divided down the middle of the back, separated from the fins, and raised clean from the bones with a very sharp knife. When cut, the filets may be cut into portions, dipped into a egg yolk, which has been beaten, rolled in fine bread crumbs and fried or broiled in the usual way. If the filet is smaller it can be rolled as one piece (divided if larger), and then fastened with thread or pierced with a skewer. Then proceed with the egg dip and bread crumb dip. The filets should then been seasoned with salt and pepper, and spices if the recipe calls for it.

# HOW TO PREPARE
# CHICKEN, TURKEY AND POULTRY

Remove poultry from wrapper. Discard wrapper and remove any giblets from interior of carcass. Wash inside and out. If desired, salt and pepper interior and exterior. Remove the tail and neck. If you wish to make gravy, add neck and tail, along with giblets to small pot with water and some onion, sliced into thin slices. Heat on low heat until needed for gravy, adding additional water if needed.

If you are stuffing the bird, do not do so until ready to roast. If you stuff the poultry make sure that the temperature of the poultry is 170 degrees F before removing from the oven. This will ensure that it is fully cooked.

To truss a turkey, when stuffed you can either use skewers and cord or leave open. This is a matter of personal preference. To use skewers and cord, pierce skin with the skewers on each side of the cavity and use cord to pull closed the opening by winding as you would shoe-laces, starting with cord folded in half and on bottom use one side from left to right and second side of cord from right to left with cord. Pull two sides together and tie in a bow.

If you wish, baste the poultry with some butter under the skin (pulling skin up gently and put pats between skin and meat). Butter can be flavored with some minced garlic or minced onion or your favorite herbs. Do this before trussing. If you wish you can rub the skin with butter or cooking oil instead of putting butter under the skin. This makes the skin tender and crispy.

# CRAVING

**FISH:** Fish should not be served on metal platters unless they are silver since the metal can change the flavor of the fish. The choicest cuts are in the middle of the fish, a planked fish should be cut through the center lengthwise. Small fish should be served individually without carving. A stuffed fish should have skewers and strings which should be removed before serving. The cut being made from head to tail, the backbone is left on the platter.

**HAM:** A bone runs through near the center; the broader side gives the best cuts. A small, thick slice is often taken almost at right angles to the bone, served with a little portion of fat. Or the carver may begin at the thick end of the ham and proceed to cut thin slices right on to the narrow end.

**LAMB:** Leg of Lamb is placed before the carver with the heavier side farthest from him. With a left leg the bone, which runs through it, should be at the carver's right; with the right leg this bone should be at his left. Beginning either at the center or at the heavy end, the carver should slice the meat heavy end, the carver should slice the meat, heavy end, the carver should slice the meat at right angles to the bone across the grain.

**PORK:** Roast Loin of port may be served with or without the tenderloin. The butcher should remove the back bone, and the rib bones should be carefully cut apart before cooking. The carver should cut between the ribs, each rib for thinner cuts or every other rib for a heavier cut.

**POULTRY:**
(Capon) A capon is carved somewhat like a turkey; that is, the legs should be separated from the body in a similar fashion, and the dark meat of the second joint put aside to be served with the filets, which will be cut out of each side of the breast. One should be able to carve four or five filets from the breast on each side.

For a chicken or turkey first remove the legs by slicing through the skin between the leg and body using a large carving knife. Pull leg outwards and cut through the hip joint, removing entire leg from the body.

Next remove the breast. Slice down one side of the breastbone until your knife meets the base of the turkey. Cut horizontally into the turkey near the base and remove the entire breast.

Slice the breast downward holding the breast firmly on a cutting board. Each of the sections of breast meat can then be lifted off and will have a layer or browned skin and rich fat on top. Slice the breast downward holding the breast firmly on a cutting board.

Next separate the drumstick from the thigh. Cut through the joint that connects the drumstick and thigh. Slice thigh meat thinly. You can also slice the leg if it is very large. Slice downwards through meat and then remove with vertical cuts.

The last step is to remove the wings by cutting through the joints connecting the wing bones to the back bones. Wings are served whole.

## MAKING GRAVY

Making gravy with pan drippings is quick and easy. After roasting meat, remove meat from pan and retain drippings in pan. Put pan on stove top, set to medium-high heat. Using a fine flour made commercially for gravy making, or regular all-purpose flour, slowly add flour to drippings making a roux. Slowly add either broth, water from boiled potatoes or vegetables, or plain tap water to the drippings. Bring mixture to a slow boil over medium-high heat. It thickens as it boils. A gravy browning sold in most markets can be added at this time for color, and salt and pepper, to taste. If desired, sautéed onions, or chopped giblets can be added. Skim off any fat that is floating on the gravy.

Use approximately 1 tablespoon of flour to 1-1 1/2 cups liquid. Make sure to get all the dripping from the bottom of the pan by using a fork to remove it from the bottom. Use beef broth for beef gravy, chicken broth for chicken gravy. Pork stock is also available at most super markets to make pork gravy. If too thick add more fluid, if too thin add a bit more flour. Can be put through a sieve or strainer if lumpy.

For turkey or chicken gravy the giblets can be simmered in water ahead of time and strained then added to the gravy. Do not add raw giblets to gravy, they must be cooked first. They can be cooked with celery and onions in water and simmered over low heat. The neck can be included and removed, along with the heart, etc. The liver can be chopped and added to the gravy. Meat can be removed from the neck and also chopped and added to the gravy.

**To make cream gravy:**

2 tablespoons drippings
½ cup chicken stock
cooked chopped giblets

3 tablespoons flour
1 ½ cups milk
salt and pepper to taste

Leave the fat in the pan in which the chicken has been cooked. Stir in the flour and, when well blended, but not browned, gradually add the stock and milk, stirring constantly over a low fire until smooth and thick. Add the giblets and season to taste with salt and pepper.

## SEASONED SALT

1 cup salt
1 teaspoon garlic salt
2 teaspoons dry mustard
2 ½ teaspoons paprika

1 teaspoon dried thyme
½ teaspoon dried oregano
½ teaspoon onion powder
1 teaspoon curry powder

*Mix all ingredients in a large bowl. Put into tightly covered containers. Makes about 1 ¼ cups.*

## SEASON A POT OR WOK

For a new pot or wok:
Wash the pot or wok thoroughly with soap and water. Dry completely. Preheat the pot over a high heat and add 3 tablespoons vegetable oil (for wok add also ½ cup sliced fresh ginger and 1 bunch scallions cut into 2 inch pieces). Fry the oil (or oil with scallions and ginger) over medium heat making sure that the entire surface is coated for 15 minutes.

Cool and then rinse the pan with hot water and wipe with a soft sponge. Dry with a terrycloth towel or put back on stovetop over low heat until thoroughly dried.

## VANILLA SUGAR

Sugar flavored with vanilla. It may be made easily at home by placing one or two vanilla beans in a jar containing granulated sugar and having a tightly fitting cover. It may be used in pastry, desserts, and for sweetening fresh berries.

# FINES HERBES

refers to a combination of edible herbs that is used to give more taste to bland dishes. The following ingredients are finely ground together. Keep in a tightly covered jar or a tightly-corked or covered bottle.

| | |
|---|---|
| 1 teaspoon burnet | 1 teaspoon chives |
| 1 tablespoon thyme | 2 tablespoon savory |
| 2 tablespoons marjoram | 2 tablespoons dried parsley |
| 1 tablespoon sage | 1 tablespoon grated lemon rind |
| 2 tablespoon celery seeds | 6 bay leaves |

*To use, place mixture in square of cheesecloth and tie tightly and put into the pot to simmer with meats, etc. Remove before serving.*

# MUSHROOMS
## some types of mushrooms

**Button:** Small white round "button" shaped mushrooms that are the most common mushroom sold. They are a cultivated variety that can be used in many recipes.

**Chanterelles:** Subtle in flavor, with a mild sweetness and slight peppery after-kick. Good for breakfast cooked with scrambled eggs. Sauté and put on sourdough toast seasoned with fresh herbs and nutmeg.

**Enoki:** small and pale, with skinny stems and barely there heads, these are Asian tree mushrooms taste as delicate as they look. They cook quickly in liquid without getting chewy—perfect for tossing in a broth type soup.

**Morels:** Great in spicy sauces and stews. May is peak time for morels. The look fragile but taste robust and meaty. Their powerful flavor can stand up to heat, strong spices and slow cooking. Their spongy caps soak up whatever you toss them in.

**Hen of the woods:** Great in tomato sauce. Also called maitake, this has a big beefy taste. Great as base for a mushroom tomato sauce, or to caramelize with onions to put on a steak.

**Oyster:** They have a look of oysters, they are broad capped mushrooms that taste briny and have a silky texture. Their creaminess works well in coconut or a milk based curry. They are a great addition to sauces also

**Portobello:** Mature cremini mushrooms, noted for rich flavor and meaty texture. Can grow up to 5 inches wide. Select firm, plump mushrooms that are not bruised or slimy. Store unwashed and wrapped in paper towels.

**Truffles:** These mushrooms are grown entirely underground and are considered to be integral to French cooking. It is a fleshy fungus, generally round in shape and black or brown in color. Has a delicate flavor, can be cooked slowly with butter, thyme, bay leaves, salt and pepper for approximately 1 hour. Can be stirred into sauces, or used for garnish, or left whole for dressing.

*NOTE: There are approximately 20 different types of cultivated mushrooms currently sold on the market, add to that there are more than 30 varieties of wild mushrooms sold internationally. There are also types of mushrooms that are called conditionally edible mushrooms. They must be prepared correctly or they can be toxic. The ones mentioned above are only a small sampling of mushrooms available.*

# MEAT AND DESSERT SAUCES AND SALAD DRESSINGS

# BARBEQUE SAUCE
For chicken, ribs, hamburgers and franks

3 tablespoons butter
1 medium onion, diced
1 clove garlic, diced
½ cup chopped celery, with leaves
1 lb. can crushed tomatoes
¼ cup chopped green peppers
8 ounce can tomato sauce
2 slices of lemon

3 tablespoons molasses
2 teaspoons dried mustard
1/3 cup vinegar
½ teaspoon ground cloves
½ teaspoon allspice
1 ½ teaspoons salt
2 teaspoons Tabasco sauce
1 bay leaf

In a saucepan, melt butter and add onion and garlic; cook until onion is tender but not browned. Add remaining ingredients and simmer 30 minutes. Strain.

Brush over chicken, ribs, hamburgers, or franks during grilling, baking or broiling.

Makes approximately 2 cups.


# SAVORY BARBEQUE SAUCE
For grilled meats such as steaks and hamburgers

1 cup catsup
¼ cup Worcestershire Sauce
¼ cup steak sauce
2 tablespoons brown sugar
2 tablespoons finely chopped onion
½ teaspoon garlic powder

¼ teaspoon ground nutmeg
¼ teaspoon ground cinnamon
¼ teaspoon ground cloves
1/8 teaspoon ground ginger
1/8 teaspoon pepper

In a saucepan, combine all ingredients. Heat to boiling. When barbequing, baste the steak or burgers with the sauce during grilling. Serve additional sauce on top of the grilled meat or on side, as preferred.

Makes approximately 2 cups.

# SPICY BARBEQUE SAUCE
## For grilled meats

1 tablespoon butter
½ cup chopped onion
½ cup maple syrup
3/4 cup vinegar
1/8 teaspoon pepper

1 can beef broth
1 tablespoon Worcestershire Sauce
1 ½ teaspoons salt
2 drops Tabasco Sauce
1 cup catsup

In a saucepan, melt butter. Add onions and sauté until lightly browned. Add additional ingredients. Boil on medium low heat, for about 15 minutes, or until sauce is glossy and thick.

Makes approximately 2 cups.

# SARA'S BARBEQUE SAUCE
## For ribs
Sara H.

2 bottles store brand steak sauce
2 bay leaves
SAUCE:
½ bottle Saucy Susan (or can apricot preserves)
2 tablespoons lemon juice
2 dabs Dijon Mustard

3 tablespoons vinegar
water to cover ribs

½ bottle honey BBQ sauce
2 tablespoons cinnamon

Boil ribs in large pot with steak sauce, vinegar, bay leaves and water for 1 hour or till meat is very tender. Warm sauce ingredients in pot. Put ribs in roasting pan and cover with sauce. Cook at 350 degrees for 1 or so hours. When meat starts to fall off bone it is ready to serve.

# BASIC BROWN SAUCE
## basis for other meat sauces

2 cans of beef broth (13 oz)
3 sprigs parsley or 1 teaspoon dried
1 stalk celery, cut into 1" pieces
6 medium mushrooms, diced
1 tomato, peeled, seeded & chopped
½ bay leaf

1 pinch dried thyme
½ clove garlic, minced
2 tablespoons onion, finely chopped
3 tablespoons butter
3 tablespoons flour

In a heavy saucepan heat bouillon, parsley, celery, mushrooms, tomato, bay leaf, thyme and garlic and bring to a boil. Lower heat and simmer, covered for one hour. Cool and strain. In a skillet sauté onion until translucent. On a low flame whisk in flour until blended. Add butter, blend. When butter flour mixture is smooth, gradually add broth, stirring constantly until blended and smooth. Bring sauce to a boil, lower heat and simmer for ½ hour, stirring occasionally to keep sauce smooth. Cool. Sauce may be stored in the refrigerator for later use or frozen.

Makes approximately 3 cups.


# BASIC BUTTER SAUCE

3 tablespoons butter
3 drops of lemon juice
2 or 3 egg yolks

1 tablespoon flour
1 cup water
salt and white pepper

Blend together over a low flame (without browning) 1 tablespoon of the butter and 1 tablespoon of flour. Then increase heat to high and add gradually 1 cup of water, stirring constantly. Bring mixture to a boil, then remove the pan from the heat and add egg yolks, one at a time, beating the sauce vigorously with a whisk. Season the sauce to taste with salt and white pepper and beat in 2 tablespoons of butter piece by piece and add a few drops of lemon juice. To prevent curdling do not allow sauce to boil after eggs have been added.

## CHEESE SAUCE
### For Vegetables and Fish

½ cup mayonnaise
1/2 cup milk

1/3 cup shredded cheddar cheese
or American, grated Parmesan or
crumbled blue cheese

Stir together all ingredients in a small saucepan. Heat over medium low heat for about 5 minutes or until heated. Serve over hot vegetables or fish.

*Use cheddar or American cheese on Asparagus*
*Use Blue Cheese on fried flounder*
*Use Parmesan on zucchini*

Makes approximately 1 cup.


## COCKTAIL SAUCE
### For Seafood

¼ teaspoon Tabasco
1 cup ketchup or chili sauce
2 tablespoons lemon juice

½ teaspoon salt
1 tablespoon horseradish
1 teaspoon grated onion (optional)

Add Tabasco to ketchup or chili sauce, mix well. Stir in remaining ingredients. Chill before serving. Serve with seafood cocktail.

Makes about 1 cup.

# CRAN ORANGE SAUCE
### For Ham or Turkey (Great for the Holidays)
*Margaret B*

Simply add ½ jar of Orange Marmalade to 1 can of whole cranberries. Simmer and stir over low heat and serve warm. Stores and reheats well. Also, the aroma while simmering will add to the holiday mood.

*NOTE: you can use jellied cranberry sauce if you choose. I think the whole berries look and taste better.*

# CUMBERLAND SAUCE
### For Pate, baked ham or roast pork

1 tablespoon finely chopped shallots
    or 1 small onion
zest of one orange
3 tablespoons fresh lemon juice, strained
1 teaspoon Dijon Mustard
¼ tsp. fresh ginger root (or 1/8 tsp. powdered)

1 cup red currant jelly
few grains of salt
zest of one lemon
3 tbs. strained, fresh orange juice
1 cup port wine
dash cayenne pepper

Blanch and drain shallots (or onion) and set aside. In heavy saucepan melt jelly add onion, orange and lemon zest, lemon and orange juice, mustard and simmer until smooth (about 10 minutes) add wine, ginger root, cayenne pepper and salt. Pour sauce in to sauceboat and serve with sliced meat.

Makes about 2 cups.

## DRAWN BUTTER SAUCE
### For Seafood

8 tablespoons butter
½ teaspoon salt
1 ½ cups hot water

3 tablespoons flour
¼ teaspoon pepper
1 teaspoon lemon juice

Melt 3 tablespoons of butter and blend with flour. Add salt and pepper to taste and stir in hot water gradually. Let sauce boil for 5 minutes; then stir in 3 tablespoons of butter, bit by bit, alternately with 1 teaspoon lemon juice.


## GARGONZOLA/BLUE CHEESE TOPPING
### For hamburgers
Margaret B

Add 4 ounces of crumbled Gorgonzola or Blue Cheese to just enough ranch style salad dressing or sour cream that will allow the cheese to bind with the sauce and hold together. Generously spoon on top of your cooked hamburger patty. You can add a thick slice of tomato if desired. For added crunch add either cole slaw or lettuce.

# HARD SAUCE
## For meats

3 tablespoons butter
¾ cup sifted confectioners' sugar

3 tablespoons heated brandy or rum

Melt butter in a small saucepan. Remove from heat and stir in confectioners' sugar and brandy or rum. Beat until smooth.

Makes about 2/3 cup.


# HOLLANDAISE SAUCE
## For meats

10 tablespoons unsalted butter
2 tablespoon flour
1 cup heavy cream heated to just boiling
1 tablespoon fresh lemon juice, strained

1/8 teaspoon Salt
3-4 grindings of white pepper
3 egg yolks

In a heavy saucepan melt 2 tablespoons butter over low heat. Blend in flour and stir constantly with a whisk until blended. Gradually add heavy cream and stir until sauce is creamy and smooth. Remove from heat and add salt and pepper.

In a bowl beat egg yolks until lemon colored. Add white sauce, a little at a time, beating until yolks and white sauce are thoroughly blended. Pour sauce back into saucepan and place over simmering hot water. Cut the remaining butter into 8 pieces and add to sauce, one at a time, stirring. Stir in lemon juice.

Makes about 1 cup.

# HORSE RADISH SAUCE
## For fish

4 tablespoons freshly grated horseradish
½ cup drawn butter sauce
1 cup freshly made soft bread crumbs

1 cup fish stock
1 tablespoon heavy cream
2 egg yolks

Combine horseradish with fish stock and bring to boil; reduce heat and let simmer for 20 minutes. Add drawn butter sauce, cream, and bread crumbs. Bring to a boil again and season with salt and pepper. Remove the pan from the heat and add the egg yolks stirring gently and constantly.

Serve with fish.

# HUNTER SAUCE
## For beef, lamb or pasta

2 tablespoons butter
1 tablespoon shallots, chopped
¼ pound fresh mushrooms. sliced
1 cup dry white wine
½ cup tomato sauce
½ cup basic Brown Sauce

2 tablespoons unsalted butter
1/8 teaspoon salt
fresh black pepper to taste
½ teaspoon dried chervil
¼ teaspoon dried tarragon

In a skillet sauté butter and shallots until limp but not brown. Add mushrooms and wine and stir over medium heat for 10 minutes. Add tomato sauce and brown sauce and simmer, stirring for 5 minutes. Just before serving, add sweet butter, salt, pepper, chervil and tarragon.

Makes about 2 cups.

*A flavorful sauce for lamb, beef and pasta dishes.*

# MUSHROOM SAUCE FOR STEAK

1 can whole mushrooms, 6 oz.
1 tablespoon chopped parsley
4 tablespoons butter

¼ teaspoon Tabasco Sauce
½ teaspoon salt

Combine mushrooms with liquid and remaining ingredients in saucepan; heat. Serve with steak.

Makes ½ cup.


# NEWBURG SAUCE
## For Seafood

1 can condensed cream of shrimp soup
½ cup mayonnaise

¾ cup dry Sherry

In a small saucepan with a wire whisk, beat all ingredients until smooth. Stirring constantly, cook over medium heat until hot, *Do Not Boil.* Serve over seafood. Garnish with chopped parsley.

Makes about 2 cups.

Microwave: In 1 quart microwave proof bowl stir together all ingredients. Microwave with full power 3 minutes or until hot. Stir after each minute.

# ROYAL MUSHROOM SAUCE
## For beef

½ cup mushroom stems, chopped fresh
¼ cup finely chopped green onion
4 teaspoons cornstarch
1 cup Burgundy

½ cup water
2 tablespoons parsley, snipped
1 teaspoon salt
dash pepper

Add mushrooms and onion to fat remaining in skillet after meat has been browned. Cook vegetables till tender, but not brown. Blend in cornstarch. Add remaining ingredients; cook, stirring till mixture thickens. Spoon about 2 Tablespoons sauce over each serving of beef. At serving time, reheat remaining sauce and serve during meal.

Makes about 1 ½ cups.

# SAUCE BORDELAISE
## For Grilled Meats

1 cup red wine, Bordeaux type
1 tablespoon minced shallots
1 sprig fresh thyme (1/8 teaspoons. dried)
1 small bay leaf

pinch salt
1 cup Basic Brown Sauce
2 tablespoons sweet butter
2 tablespoons chopped parsley

In a heavy saucepan heat wine, shallots, thyme, bay leaf, and salt. Bring to a boil. Reduce heat to a simmer and continue to cook for 10 minutes. Add basic brown sauce and simmer, uncovered, about 15 minutes, stirring from time to time. Add butter and fold in sauce. Just before serving add parsley and serve over meats.

*Great with steak or other grilled meat.*

# SAUCE DIANE
## For all types steak

Steak
2 tablespoons butter
1 tablespoon olive oil
2 shallots, finely chopped
½ clove garlic, minced
2 tablespoons Cognac
tarragon

dash of Worcestershire Sauce
1 tablespoon chili sauce
2 tablespoons Brown Sauce
2 tablespoons sweet butter
¼ cup chopped parsley
small amount of fresh or dried
salt and pepper to taste

Broil steak to desired doneness. Remove from pan and keep warm. Degrease skillet by wiping it out with a paper towel. Add to pan: butter, olive oil, shallots, garlic and cook, stirring over low heat until limp. Add cognac to the pan, step back, and flame using a long match. When the flames subside, add salt, pepper, Worcestershire sauce, chili sauce, and brown sauce.

Stirring constantly, bring sauce to a boil. Lower heat and simmer and stir in sweet butter, parsley and tarragon. Pour sauce over steak and serve immediately.
Serves 2.

*The most widely loved of steak sauces, will work well with filet mignon.*

# BASIC WHITE SAUCE

There are 3 varieties of basic white sauce. The first is a thin sauce, the second is a medium consistency and the third is a thick sauce. They all have the same basic ingredients in different amounts. The following are the ingredients.

| SAUCE | THIN SAUCE | MEDIUM SAUCE | THICK |
|---|---|---|---|
| butter | 1 tablespoon | 2 tablespoons | 3 tablespoons |
| flour | 1 tablespoon | 2 tablespoons | 3 tablespoons |
| cream | | | |
| or scalded milk | 1 cup | 1 cup | 1 cup |
| salt | ½ teaspoon | ½ teaspoon | ½ teaspoon |
| white pepper | 1/8 teaspoon | 1/8 teaspoon | 1/8 teaspoon |

Melt the butter in a saucepan, and the flour and blend thoroughly. When completely smooth and free from lumps but not browned, add the seasonings and then gradually add the cream or milk. Stir constantly over a low heat until the sauce boils gently. Continue cooking for approximately 5 minutes. This sauce can be made in a larger quantity and will keep several days refrigerated.

Cream sauce is an enriched version of white sauce and you can add several beaten egg yolks after totally cooking the sauce.

*Variations:*

*Bechamel Sauce: use chicken or beef stock instead of milk or cream.*

*Cheese Sauce: add ¼ cup of grated American or Swiss cheese, stirring constantly while adding. Serve over fish, eggs or vegetables.*

*Mushroom Sauce: add ¼ cup of cooked mushroom stock and 1 teaspoon minced onion, cooked in butter until tender Serve over fowl, fish or eggs.*

## WHITE SAUCE
### Quick and Easy
### For meats, pasta, vegetables

¼ cup mayonnaise  
2 tablespoons flour  
¼ teaspoon salt

dash pepper  
1 cup milk

In a small saucepan stir together first 4 ingredients. Stirring constantly, cook over medium heat for 1 minute. Gradually stir in milk until smooth. Constantly stirring, cook until thick. *Do Not Boil.*

Makes about 1 ¼ cup.

To make into cheese sauce add 1 cup of shredded cheese after milk. Makes 2 cups.


## BASIC TOMATO SAUCE
### For Spaghetti or in other pasta dishes

2 cups chopped onion  
3 cloves garlic, chopped  
3 tablespoons olive oil  
3 ½ cups canned Italian-style plum tomatoes, include fluid  
2 small cans tomato paste

1 bay leaf  
½ teaspoon salt  
¼ tsp. freshly ground black pepper  
½ teaspoon oregano  
or: ¼ tsp. oregano & ¼ tsp. basil  
2 cups water

Sauté the onion and garlic in the olive oil until brown, stirring often. In a stock pot add tomatoes, tomato paste, water, bay leaf, salt and pepper. Add onion and garlic. Simmer uncovered, stirring occasionally, about 2 hours. Add more water as necessary. Add oregano and continue cooling about 15 minutes. Remove the bay leaf. The sauce should be thick. Serve over cooked spaghetti or use as an ingredient in other dishes.

*Variations: add ½ pound browned chopped beef*  
  *Add ½ pound browned chopped sweet (or spicy) Italian Sausage*

# HOMEMADE ITALIAN MEAT SAUCE
## For use in pasta dishes
*Eleanor H*

1 cup chopped onion
2 cloves minced garlic
¼ cup vegetable oil
1 pound ground beef
1 pound ground Italian sausage
2 cans Italian tomatoes (2 lb 3oz), peeled
2 cans tomato paste (6 oz)

2 tablespoons sugar
1 tablespoon oregano, crumbled
1 tablespoon leaf basil, crumbled
1 tablespoon salt
½ teaspoon pepper
¼ cup grated Parmesan cheese
1-8 ounce can tomato sauce

Sauté onions and garlic in oil until soft in a large skillet (large enough for all ingredients), brown beef and sausage. Pour off all but 2 Tbs. Fat in skillet. Stir in tomatoes, tomato paste, tomato sauce, sugar, oregano, basil, salt and pepper. Simmer, uncovered, stirring frequently, for 45 minutes or until sauce thickens. Stir in Parmesan cheese, cool. Can be frozen for future use.

Make 10 cups. **Can be doubled.**

*Variations: add sautéed sliced mushrooms.*
*Leave out meats.*

# QUICK APPLESAUCE
*Eleanor H*

6 medium apples, Granny Smith
or other cooking apples
1/3 cup sugar

1 teaspoon lemon juice
dash cinnamon

About ½ hour ahead:
Quarter apples, do not peel or core. In a 3 quart saucepan, add ½ cup water and heat over high heat to boiling. Reduce heat to low and cover, simmering approximately 12 minutes or until apples are fork tender. Stir in sugar, lemon juice and cinnamon. Press mixture through a sieve or food mill to remove skin and seeds. Add more sugar if necessary. Applesauce will be pink if red skinned apples are used. If you use Granny Smiths you will probably need additional sugar.

Makes 4 servings.

*Variation: use mixed cooking apples for more flavor.*
*The applesauce can be frozen, keep well sealed.*


# CLASSIC MAYONNAISE

4 egg yolks
2 teaspoons salt
2 teaspoons dry mustard
dash cayenne

½ lemon, juiced
2 tablespoons water
2 cups vegetable oil

Begin with all ingredients at room temperature, they will emulsify more readily. In a food processor combine yolks, salt, mustard, cayenne, lemon juice and water together to form base. With the motor running add a few drops of the oil; the mixture will begin to thicken. Begin adding the remainder of the oil slowly. Scrape down sides of processor. Taste. Adjust seasonings if needed. Keep covered and refrigerated for up to 3 days.

Makes approximately 2 cups.

Serve with seafood, poultry, salads and cold cuts.

# TARTAR SAUCE
## For Seafood

1 cup mayonnaise
3 tablespoons finely chopped dill pickle
1 tablespoon finely chopped onion

1 teaspoon finely chopped parsley
½ teaspoon sugar

*You can use pickle relish instead of pickle, onion, parsley and sugar (4 Tablespoons)*
In a small bowl stir together all ingredients. Cover and chill. Serve with seafood. Store in refrigerator.

Makes about 1 cup.


# OLD FASHIONED CRANBERRY SAUCE

5 cups water
grated rind 1 orange

2 cups sugar
4 cups cranberries

Cook together the water, sugar and orange rind for 3 minutes. Pick over, wash and add the cranberries. Then cook just until the berries cease popping, about 5 minutes. Do not stir. Serve cold.


# BLUE CHEESE SALAD DRESSING

1 cup mayonnaise
4 ounces Blue Cheese, crumbled
3 tablespoons milk
2 tablespoons lemon juice
1 tablespoon finely chopped onion

2 teaspoons sugar
¼ teaspoon Worcestershire Sauce
¼ teaspoon dry mustard
¼ teaspoon salt

Mix all ingredients together, cover and chill.
Makes approximately 1 cup.

# CAESAR DRESSING

1 cup mayonnaise
3 tablespoons milk
2 tablespoons cider vinegar

2 tablespoons grated Parmesan cheese
½ teaspoon sugar
1/8 teaspoon garlic powder

Stir together all ingredients, cover, chill.
Makes approximately 1 ¼ cups.

# CHEESE AND HERB DRESSING

1 cup mayonnaise
½ cup chopped parsley
¼ cup grated Parmesan cheese

2 tablespoons lemon juice
1 clove garlic, minced
1 teaspoon dried basil

Mix all ingredients, cover and chill.
Makes approximately 1 ¼ cups.

# CREAMY FRENCH DRESSING

1 cup mayonnaise
2 tablespoons lemon juice
4 teaspoons sugar
1 tablespoon milk

1 teaspoon paprika
½ teaspoon dry mustard
¼ teaspoon salt
1/8 teaspoon pepper

Mix all ingredients together, cover and chill.
Makes approximately 1 ¼ cups.

# CREAMY GARLIC DRESSING

1 cup mayonnaise
3 tablespoons milk
2 tablespoons cider vinegar
1 medium clove of garlic, crushed

½ teaspoon sugar
¼ teaspoon salt
1/8 teaspoon pepper

Stir together all ingredients, cover and chill.
Makes about 1 cup.

## CREAMY ITALIAN DRESSING

1 cup mayonnaise
3 tablespoons milk
2 tablespoons cider vinegar
1 clove minced garlic

½ teaspoon dried oregano
½ teaspoon sugar
¼ teaspoon salt
1/8 teaspoon pepper

Mix together all ingredients, cover and chill.
Makes approximately 1 cup.

## CUCUMBER DILL DRESSING

1 ½ cups cucumber, peeled, seeded, chopped
2 tablespoons finely chopped onion
1 tablespoon milk

1 tablespoon lemon juice
½ teaspoon dill weed
¼ teaspoon salt

Mix all ingredients together, cover and chill.
Makes approximately 1 cup.

# RUSSIAN DRESSING

1 cup mayonnaise
1/3 cup catsup
1/3 cup chopped pickles

2 teaspoons lemon juice
2 teaspoons sugar

Mix together all ingredients, cover and chill.
Makes approximately 1 ½ cups.

# THOUSAND ISLAND DRESSING

1 cup mayonnaise
1/3 cup ketchup

3 tablespoons sweet pickle relish
1 hard cooked egg, finely chopped

Stir together all ingredients, cover and chill.
Makes approximately 1 ½ cups.

# YOGURT DRESSING
### For fruit salad

1 tablespoon mayonnaise

1 8oz container vanilla yogurt.

Fold mayonnaise into yogurt, cover, and chill. Serve over fruit salad.
Makes over 1 cup.

# BUTTERSCOTCH SAUCE
## For puddings

1 ½ cups firmly packed brown sugar
½ cup dark corn syrup
½ cup water

½ teaspoon salt
2 tablespoons butter
1 teaspoon vanilla

Combine sugar, corn syrup, water and salt in a medium sized heavy saucepan. Cook over low heat, stirring constantly until sugar dissolves; stir in butter. Heat to boiling, cook, without stirring, until candy thermometer reads 230 degrees (a fine thread spins from the end of a fork when dipped into hot syrup). Pour into a bowl and stir in vanilla, cool. Serve warm over pudding.

Makes about 1 ¾ cups.


# BUTTERSCOTCH SAUCE
## For Ice Cream

1 cup firmly packed brown sugar
1 tablespoon vinegar
1/8 teaspoon salt

4 tablespoons butter
½ cup cold water
½ teaspoon vanilla

Cook sugar, butter, vinegar, water and salt, stirring frequently until a portion will form a soft ball in cold water. Add the vanilla and serve over ice cream.

This sauce can be reheated just before serving.

# CHERRIES JUBILEE SAUCE
### For Ice Cream or Slices of Pound Cake

2 cups canned cherries                          ¼ cup brandy
2 tablespoons sweet wine, such as port

Heat cherries with wine in the top of a chafing dish, add brandy, ignite and stir until the flames die.

Serve over ice cream or slices of pound cake.

Makes approximately 4 servings.


# CHOCOLATE SAUCE
### For ice cream and puddings

1 cup water                                     1 tablespoon cornstarch
½ cup sugar                                     1 teaspoon vanilla
1 square dark chocolate                         few grains of salt
¼ cup cold water

Boil sugar and one cup water to a syrup, about 5 minutes. Stir cornstarch and cold water together. Add melted chocolate to the hot syrup and pour this into cornstarch mixture. Stir well, return to fire and cook several minutes. Flavor and serve hot on ice cream or pudding.

## DELICATE SAUCE
### For plain cakes, pudding, ice cream

¼ cup butter
½ cup powdered sugar
1 cup whipped cream

1 teaspoon vanilla
1 tablespoon orange juice

Beat butter and sugar to a cream. Add whipped cream. Put over hot water and beat until thick. When smooth and thick, add vanilla and orange juice. Serve warm.


## HOT BLUEBERRY SAUCE
### For ice cream, waffles, pancakes

2 cups fresh blueberries
1/3 cup sugar
3/4 teaspoon cinnamon

¼ teaspoon freshly grated nutmeg
grated lemon rind

Combine all ingredients in a heavy saucepan. Mix well. Bring to a boil, then simmer for 5 minutes, stirring occasionally. Good over vanilla ice cream, waffles and pancakes.

# MANDARIN ORANGE SAUCE
## For pudding

1/3 cup sugar

2 tablespoons cornstarch

1 can mandarin oranges (11 oz)

1/2 cup orange juice

Combine sugar and cornstarch in a medium sized saucepan. Drain juice from mandarin oranges into a 1 cup measure, add orange juice to make 1 cup. Stir juice mixture gradually into saucepan until smooth. Heat to boiling, stirring constantly until thickened, add oranges, serve warm over pudding.

Makes 2 cups.


# ORANGE LIQUEUR SAUCE
## For puddings and ice cream

½ cup sugar

2 eggs

2 tablespoons orange liqueur

½ cup heavy cream

1 teaspoon grated orange rind

Combine sugar and eggs in the top of a double boiler or in a medium size heatproof ceramic bowl. Beat just to blend. Place over hot—not boiling—water and stir until sugar dissolves. Beat with a rotary hand or an electric beater until mixture thickens and triples in volume. Remove from water, stir in orange liqueur. Beat until mixture has cooled to room temperature. Beat cream until stiff in a small bowl; fold into egg mixture with orange rind, chill until serving time.

Makes approximately 1 ½ cups.

## RASPBERRY SAUCE
### For ice cream

2 cups raspberries
½ cup sugar (approx).
1 tablespoon cornstarch

1 tablespoon lemon juice
1 tablespoon cognac

Mix the raspberries with the sugar and heat, stirring frequently, to a boil. Strain and add more sugar if desired. Mix the cornstarch with 2 tablespoons of cooled raspberry juice. Heat the remaining juice to a boil, stir in the cornstarch and cook, stirring, until thickened. Cool and add the lemon juice and cognac. Serve over vanilla ice cream.

Makes approximately 2 cups.


## VANILLA OR LEMON SAUCE
### For cakes, pudding or ice cream

½ cup sugar
1 tablespoon cornstarch
1 teaspoon vanilla

2 tablespoons butter
1 cup water
few grains of salt

Mix sugar, salt and cornstarch, add boiling water. Cook until thick and clear, stirring constantly. Continue to cook over hot water for approximately 20 minutes. Remove from heat and add butter and vanilla.

*For lemon sauce: use grated lemon rind and juice of ½ lemon instead of vanilla.*
*For orange sauce: use grated orange rind and juice of ½ orange instead of vanilla.*

## TABASCO FLAVORED MARINADE
### For meat

¼ cup lime juice
½ cup salad oil
½ teaspoon sugar
1 teaspoon dry mustard
1 teaspoon salt

¼ teaspoon thyme
¼ teaspoon rosemary
¼ teaspoon basil
1 bay leaf
¼ teaspoon Tabasco Sauce

Beat together lime juice and salad oil. Stir in remaining ingredients. Add beef or lamb and stir to cover. Refrigerate 5 hours or overnight, turning occasionally. Drain.

Enough for about 2 pounds of meat.


## TERIYAKI SAUCE FOR MARINADE
### For Yakitori (chicken)

1 cup soy sauce
1 cup dry sherry
¼ cup canned beef broth
1 cup dry sherry

1 teaspoon sugar
1 clove garlic, crushed
1 tablespoon finely minced ginger

Combine all ingredients in a bowl. Marinate meat at least 1 hour in mixture.
See Yakitori (chicken).

# SOUPS

# STOCK
## *Basic Information*

1. 6 to 8 quart covered soup pot
2. use onions, leeks, carrots, celery and parsley for flavor
3. use only small amounts of salt
4. always use cold water
5. skim off material on top after it boils
6. after coming to a boil, cover and simmer
7. broths may be made stronger and more delicious if a combination of beef, veal and chicken is used.
8. collect and freeze chicken necks, wings, gizzards and backs for pot soups and chicken broths for use in stock
9. veal knuckles, marrow bones, chicken bones, and chicken feet give soups extra flavor. They also provide the gelatinous substance necessary for aspics. These broths, when clarified, will jell without the use of gelatin.
10. to prepare a light a white stock, use only veal and chicken with their bones.
11. to prepare a brown stock it is best to use some beef. On a baking pan, brown the bones, some beef also, if you wish, slice carrots and onions (400 degrees) for 45 minutes. Proceed with the basic directions for beef broth but be sure to deglaze (extract brownness from) the browned pan with 1 cup (reserved from the recipe) of boiling water.

# BEEF BROTH

2 pounds shin of beef (if eating beef
use flank or chuck
1 carrot
1 stalk celery, with leaves
2 leeks, cut lengthwise for easy cleaning
1 teaspoon salt
2 veal bones

2 beef bones
1 quart cold water
2 sprigs curly parsley or Italian parsley
1 onion, studded with 2 cloves
1 bay leaf
¼ teaspoon white pepper

Place everything in a heavy soup pot that has a tight cover. With pot uncovered, bring ingredients to a boil. As scum comes to the top, skim it off with a large spoon. Cover pot, reduce heat to a simmer and cook for 3 hours if meat is to be eaten, remove it when tender. Strain soup. If soup is too concentrated add water, if not concentrated enough, cook it down slightly. Adjust seasoning right before serving.
Makes 6 servings.

# CONSOMME

4 cups strained beef broth (fat removed)
½ cup wine (white or red)
1 cup cold water

½ cup ground beef
1 fresh tomato, cut up

Place all ingredients except water into a soup pot. Bring to a boil and skim. Cover pot. Simmer for 1 hour and add cold water. Bring to a boil uncovered. Skim again. Cover and cook 30 minutes. Strain through a fine strainer covered with triple thickness cheese cloth. To clarify consommé: first adjust seasoning. Beat one egg white till frothy. Add egg white and broken shell to soup. Beating constantly, bring soup to a boil. Cook for a few minutes. Strain again as above. The soup should now be clear.

Makes 6-8 servings.

# OMA'S GERMAN DUMPLINGS FOR SOUP
*Mathilde Bohlen*

1 cup milk
3 eggs

3/4 cup flour
pinch salt

Heat milk to just boiling, take from heat and add flour and salt, all at once, stir (if thin put back on heat) until ball forms. Then add one egg at a time, stirring each egg in. Drop by spoonfuls into finished soup and let steam (cover soup, on medium heat) for about 5 to 10 minutes. They will be white and floating on surface when done. Fork tender. Enough for one large pot of soup.

*This is great for chicken soup. They steam in the soup and float to the top when done. About 5 to 10 minutes. Can be left cooking longer, however. Can be frozen in leftover soup.*

# CHICKEN SOUP
*Eleanor Hinsch*

12 cups water
4 pouches Noodle Soup mix*
1 chicken, cleaned & washed, neck removed
2 stalks celery diced
½ small onion, diced

2 cans chicken broth
1 recipe of Oma's dumplings
2 cups water
2 peeled, diced carrots

In large stock pot put in 12 cups of water, bouillon cubes, broth or soup mix, (enough for 12 cups water) diced celery, carrots, onions, and chicken. Bring to a boil and turn down heat to simmer. Allow to simmer until chicken is fully cooked. Remove chicken, debone and cut chicken into 1" cubes. If chicken is done it should come off bones very easily. Re-add chicken to pot, discard bones. About ¾-1 hour.

In separate small pot, put 2 cups water, and gizzard, neck, etc from chicken. Simmer for 1 hour, put aside. Into large stockpot add Noodle soup mixes and juice from the gizzard mixture that was set aside. Discard the rest except the liver, which can be used for chopped chicken livers, if kept in refrigerator (about 1 week, well wrapped) or in freezer for a few months (well wrapped). Allow to simmer for about ½ hour covered. Add dumplings, recover pot and allow dumplings to come to top of soup. Serve hot.

*Additional veggies can be added, such as corn, peas, cut green beans, etc. The cooked liver can also be chopped into the soup.*

*This is a hearty soup great if you're feeling sick, or just have a cold. Good for those cold winter nights.*

*Can add a grating of nutmeg just before serving.*

*Can be frozen, if desired, for up to 3 months.*

*\*You can use noodles and chicken broth or stock instead of Noodle soup mix if you have time. Use 1/3 bag of noodles, either broad or soup noodles. Use broth mixed in water, to taste.*

# CHICKEN STOCK

1 whole chicken carcass
2 quarts water
1 carrot coarsely chopped
1 celery stalk
1 small onion quartered

1 bay leaf
¼ teaspoon dried basil
6 whole peppercorns
¼ cup fresh parsley, chopped

Break up carcass. Add giblets, if available. Combine all ingredients in a large soup kettle. Bring to a boil and simmer over low heat for 1 ½ to 2 hours. Strain. Store leftover in refrigerator for 1 week, in freezer for up to 3 months.

Can be frozen.

# NOODLES FOR SOUP

1 cup flour
½ teaspoon salt

2 eggs, beaten

Sift flour and salt together into a bowl. Make a well in center of flour mixture and add eggs; blend thoroughly. Knead dough on a floured surface, cover, and let stand 30 minutes. Roll to about 1/8" thickness. Turn dough over and continue rolling until paper thin. Allow dough to partially dry about 1 hour. Cut dough into lengthwise strips, 2 ½" wide, and stack on top of each other. Slice into short strips, 1/8" wide. Separate noodles and allow to dry thoroughly (noodles can be stored in refrigerator in a tightly covered container) if not cooked immediately.

Makes 2 cups of noodles.

# CHICKEN NOODLE SOUP

4 ½ pound stewing chicken
3 quarts cold water
1 medium sized onion, sliced
1 carrot, sliced

1 bay leaf
1 teaspoon chopped parsley
1 tablespoon salt
2 cups noodles for soup

Rinse and disjoint chicken; put into a sauce pot and add remaining ingredients except noodles. Cover and bring to boiling. Cook over low heat about 3 hours, or until thickest pieces of chicken are tender. Skim off fat as necessary. Remove chicken. Add noodles to broth and cook 15 minutes until noodles are tender. Remove bay leaf. Serve hot.

Makes 8 to 10 servings.

# GERMAN SOUP BALLS IN BROTH

2 quarts water
3 pounds lean beef
salt
pepper
1 cup flour

½ teaspoon salt
2 tablespoons butter
4 eggs, beaten
1 to 2 tablespoons milk

Add the water to the meat, season to taste, and cook slowly for several hours until meat is just tender ½ hour before serving time make soup balls as follows: sift flour and salt together. Cut in the butter with a pastry blender or 2 knives. Blend the eggs into the flour; stir in only enough milk to make a batter thin enough to drop from end of spoon. Drop by spoonfuls into the boiling broth (meat removed) and cook for 10 minutes. Serve soup hot with the meat.

Makes approximately 10 servings.

# COLD MUSHROOM SOUP

1 pound fresh, white mushroom buttons with stems, coarsely chopped
½ cup heavy cream
freshly ground nutmeg

2 cans (10 ½ oz) condensed chicken broth
salt
minced parsley

Puree the mushrooms, a small amount at the time, in an electric blender with some of the chicken broth. Pour into a heavy saucepan; add any remaining broth and the heavy cream. Season to taste with salt and freshly ground nutmeg. Bring to a boil over low heat. Do not cook further. Chill. To serve, sprinkle with parsley, serve over ice.

Makes 3-4 servings.

# CREAM OF ASPARAGUS SOUP

1 pound asparagus
3 scallions (white and light green only) chopped
2 tablespoons brown rice
2 cups water

½ teaspoon salt
fresh-ground pepper to taste
3 tablespoons sour cream
few drops lemon juice

Wash the asparagus well, then slice each spear on the diagonal into several pieces, reserving a few of the asparagus tips for a garnish. In a saucepan, combine the asparagus, scallions, brown rice, water, salt and pepper. Bring to a simmer. Cover and simmer until asparagus and rice are very tender, 20-25 minutes.
In bender or food processor, puree the asparagus mixture (with a blender, this will have to be done in several batches). Pour puree into clean saucepan and heat through. Stir in sour cream and lemon juice. Chill thoroughly. Taste and correct seasonings. Garnish with raw asparagus tips.

Makes 4 servings.

# CREAM OF BROCCOLI SOUP

2 tablespoons butter
½ cup heavy cream
1 onion, chopped
half and half
1 russet potato, peeled & chopped
pepper to taste

nutmeg to taste
6 cups chicken stock, warmed
salt to taste
3 cups chopped broccoli, florets &
stems

In a large pot, melt butter and cook onion until tender over medium high heat. Add potato and toss to coat with butter. Add hot stock and bring to a simmer. Stir in broccoli and return to a simmer. When potato and broccoli are tender, puree in batches in a blender or food processor. Return to pot and add cream. Season to taste and serve warm.

Makes approximately 4 servings.

# CREAM OF MUSHROOM SOUP

1 pound fresh mushrooms
2 slices onion
¼ cup butter
2 tablespoons flour

2 cups Evaporated Milk diluted with
2 cups water
salt and paprika to taste
chopped Parsley

Clean mushrooms. Slice onions fine. Heat butter in a saucepan and cook the mushrooms and onions in this for 10 minutes. Add the flour and blend well. Add the milk, stirring constantly until thickened. Bring to a boil and boil 2 minutes. Season. Serve hot, with chopped parsley sprinkled over the top.

Makes approximately 4 servings.

# CREAM OF POTATO SOUP

6 cups sliced raw potatoes
3 teaspoons salt
3 cups milk

1 large onion
4 tablespoons butter
1 tablespoon parsley

Slice the onion and put the potatoes and onion into a saucepan. Barely cover with cold water. Add the salt, cover, and bring to a boil. Let simmer for 10 minutes, or until the potatoes are very tender. Mash the potatoes and onions in the liquid. Add the butter and the milk. Taste for seasoning. Reheat, but do not let boil. Just before serving, add the chopped parsley. Serve hot.

8 servings.

# CREAM OF ROASTED TOMATO SOUP

1 ½ pounds ripe plum tomatoes
5 tablespoons olive oil
2 garlic cloves, minced
½ teaspoon dried oregano. crumbled
¼ teaspoon dried basil, crumbled
½ teaspoon freshly ground black pepper
½ cup finely chopped onion

1 cup chicken broth
¾ cup heavy cream
½ cup tomato puree
sugar to taste, if needed
2 tablespoons freshly grated Parmesan cheese, optional

Preheat oven to 475 degrees. Halve tomatoes lengthwise and lay them cut sides down in a jelly-roll pan. Brush generously with 3 tablespoons oil and sprinkle with garlic, oregano, basil and pepper. Roast tomatoes until their edges are charred, about 15-20 minutes. Scrape tomatoes, oil and herbs from pan into food processor. Process until not quite smooth (leaving small chunks and charred black specks).

In a saucepan cook onion in remaining 2 tablespoons of oil until translucent. Whisk in roasted tomato puree, broth and wine. Then whisk tomato paste. Heat the cream and whisk in to the tomato mixture. Taste and add sugar if necessary. Stir in Parmesan. Add salt and pepper to taste and bring soup to a simmer.

Makes approximately 6 servings.

# CREAMY BUTTERNUT SQUASH SOUP

¼ cup chopped onion
1 tablespoon butter
3 cups cubed peeled butternut squash
1 medium potato, peeled and cubed
1 ½ cups water

1 ½ tsp. Chicken broth granules
¼ tsp. salt
dash pepper
¼ cup evaporated milk

In a small saucepan, sauté onion in butter until tender. Add squash and potato, cook and stir for 2 minutes. Add the water, bouillon, salt and pepper, bring to a boil. Reduce heat, cover and simmer for 15-20 minutes or until vegetables are tender.

Cool slightly in a blender, cover and process soup until smooth. Return to the pan, stir in milk and heat through.

Makes approximately 2 servings.

# FRENCH ONION SOUP GRATINEE

| | |
|---|---|
| 5 large yellow onions | 2 tablespoons flour |
| 3 tablespoons butter | ½ cup dry white wine (or vermouth) |
| 1 tablespoon oil | salt and pepper to taste |
| ¼ teaspoon sugar | 6-1/2 inch thick slices French bread |
| 2-13 ¾ ounce cans beef broth | butter |
| ½ cup shredded Swiss or Gruyere cheese | ½ cup shredded Parmesan cheese |

Day before:
Peel and thinly slice onions. In a large heavy casserole or Dutch Oven, heat butter, and oil, cook onions and sugar very slowly over low to medium heat, stirring often till golden brown. (This may take up to 30 minutes).

Meanwhile bring broth to a simmer. When onions are done, sprinkle with flour and stir over low heat for 2 minutes. Off heat, stir in broth and wine, season to taste with salt and pepper. Simmer partially covered, for 15 minutes.

Lightly toast French bread slices on a baking sheet in 325 degree oven for about 20 minutes. Store in a plastic bag until ready to serve. Do ahead to here, let soup cool and keep in refrigerator.

**To serve:**
Preheat broiler. Heat soup in pot on stove top until hot. Taste the soup, add salt and pepper if needed, and ladle into individual ovenproof bowls or into oven-proof casserole. Lightly butter toasted French bread slices and top each bowl with a slice or cover soup in casserole with an even layer of the bread. Sprinkle with the shredded cheeses, place under broiler and keep a close watch until cheese melts and browns lightly. Serve at once.

Serves 6.

# LEEK AND POTATO SOUP

4 medium sized potatoes
2 cups water
1 tablespoon flour
1 tablespoon butter

4 small leeks
4 cups milk
2 teaspoons salt

Peel the potatoes and dice into small pieces. Trim the leeks and cut into thin slices. Put the potatoes, leeks, and water into a saucepan. Cover and bring to a boil. Simmer 10 minutes, or until very tender. With ½ cup milk make a smooth paste with the flour and salt. Mash the potatoes and leeks. Add the 3 ½ cups of milk, and then stir in the flour paste. Stir well and add the butter. Reheat, stirring constantly, until the mixture bubbles, and let simmer for a few minutes to cook the flour and soup thickens. Serve hot or cold.

Makes approximately 5 servings.

# LENTIL SOUP

½ pound (2 cups) dried lentils
1 ham bone, left from cooked shank
1 cup diced celery with leaves
1 carrot, pared and sliced
2 medium onions, sliced
2 bay leaves

6 cups water
2 teaspoons salt
½ teaspoon Tabasco Sauce
½ teaspoon dried mustard
2 tablespoons lemon juice

Put lentils in a large, deep kettle. Add water to cover, soak over night. Drain. Return lentils to kettle with remaining ingredients except lemon juice. Bring to a boil. Cover; reduce heat and simmer 2 to 2 ½ hours, or until lentils are tender. Remove bay leaves and ham bone. Force through a sieve if desired, and return to kettle. Remove meat from bone and add to soup. Stir in lemon juice; heat 10 minutes longer.

Makes 6 to 8 servings.

# ONION SOUP

4 tablespoons butter
4 cups beef broth, hot
½ cup freshly grated Parmesan cheese
4 ½" slices toasted French bread

4 large onions, sliced thin
2 slices Swiss or Gruyere cheese, in
strips

Melt butter in skillet and brown onions. Add hot broth to onions. Hot broth extracts the flavor and color from the onions to make the soup very tasty. Add Swiss cheese and 1 tablespoon Parmesan cheese. Divide into 4 oven soup bowls. Bake in a 350 degree oven for 30 minutes. Soup may also be baked in one casserole and divided later. Serve topped with toasted croutons. Serve with Parmesan cheese.

Makes 4 servings.

# PUMPKIN SOUP

2 tablespoons chopped onion
2 tablespoons butter
1 cup cooked pumpkin
pepper
chopped parsley

2 teaspoons chopped green pepper
2 cups milk
¾ teaspoon salt
1/8 teaspoon Worcestershire Sauce

Sauté onion and green pepper slowly in the butter for 5 minutes. Add next five ingredients and cook over hot water until very hot. Add parsley just before serving.

Makes approximately 4 servings.

# SPLIT PEA CREAM SOUP

1 cup dried split peas
2 quarts cold water
small piece fat salt pork
4 tablespoons fat
½ small onion

3 tablespoons flour
1 ¼ teaspoons salt
1/8 teaspoon pepper
1 cup evaporated milk,
diluted with 1 cup water

Pick over peas, cover with cold water and soak overnight. Add the cold water, pork and onion. Simmer 4 hours, or until soft. Press through sieve or potato ricer. Meanwhile, melt the fat and add flour, stir to smooth paste. Add pea pulp, salt, pepper and milk. If too thick add more milk. Garnish with croutons and toasted almond slices if desired.

Makes approximately 4 servings.

# SPLIT PEA SOUP

16 ounces package of green split peas
3 quarts water
1 small ham shank
1 large onion finely chopped
2 chicken bouillon cubes or 2 teaspoons.
powdered

½ teaspoon oregano leaves
¼ teaspoon pepper or to taste
1 bay leaf
1 ½ cups carrot thinly sliced
1 cup celery chopped
½ teaspoon garlic powder

In a large deep pot, combine peas, water, ham shank, onion, chicken bouillon and seasonings. Simmer, uncovered for 1 ½ hours. Remove ham shank; trim meat off bone and return meat to pot. Stir in carrots and celery. Simmer uncovered an additional 2 to 2 ½ hours or until soup reaches desired thickness

Makes approximately 6 servings.

*For hard water areas add 1/8 teaspoon baking soda per pound of beans or use bottled water for cooking, otherwise cooking time must be lengthened.*

# SQUASH SOUP

1 ½ pounds yellow summer squash
1 cup medium white sauce
2 eggs, slightly beaten
2 tablespoons grated Parmesan cheese

1 medium onion, chopped
½ cup grated American cheese
1 cup buttered crumbs

Wash and cube the squash. Cook with the onion until tender in a very little boiling salted water. Drain thoroughly and combine with the white sauce, American cheese, and eggs. Turn into a greased baking dish, sprinkle with the buttered crumbs and the Parmesan cheese. Bake in 350 degree F. oven for about 30 minutes, or until browned.

Makes approximately 4 servings.

# VEGETABLE SOUP
## Germuseuppe

*For Stock*:
1 soup bone, cracked
3 quarts water
1 tablespoon salt
*Other Ingredients*:
1 pound potatoes
1 pound green beans
3 small carrots

2 medium onions
2 stalks celery
2 tablespoons chopped parsley
2 tablespoons sugar
2 28 oz. cans tomatoes
2 tablespoons shortening
¼ cup flour

Place the bone in a large soup pot or kettle. Cover with cold water and add salt. Bring to a boil, cover and simmer 1 ½ hours. Occasionally skim off any foam that rises to the surface during cooking. Meanwhile, prepare vegetables and cut them into even-sized pieces. After stock has simmered add vegetables, sugar, salt and simmer for a further 30 minutes or until vegetables are tender. Remove bone and add tomatoes. In a separate pan melt the shortening, then blend in flour. Remove 1 cup of liquid from the soup and gradually stir into flour mixture. When blended, add to soup, stirring well. Bring soup to the boiling point, then simmer 5 minutes.

Makes 8 servings.

# WILD RICE AND CHICKEN SOUP

3 cans chicken broth (10.5 oz)
2 cups water
½ cup wild rice
½ cup chopped green onions
½ cup butter
¾ cup all-purpose flour

¾ teaspoon salt
½ teaspoon poultry seasoning
¼ teaspoon ground black pepper
2 cups heavy cream
2 cups cubed, cooked chicken meat
1 4 0z jar sliced pimento peppers, drained

Combine the broth, water, and rice in a large soup pot, and bring to a boil. Reduce heat, and cover. Simmer for 35 to 40 minutes, until rice is tender. Sauté onions in butter in a medium saucepan, over low heat, stir in flour, salt, poultry seasoning, and pepper. Cook, stirring constantly, until mixture is bubbly and thick. Stir in cream. Cook for 6 minutes, or until mixture thickens slightly, stirring constantly. Stir into broth. Add cubed chicken and pimientos. Heat through. Serve warm.

Makes 6 servings.

# SALADS

## OPA'S DELI COLE SLAW
*Richard B*

1/2 cup white vinegar, store brand
1/2 cup sugar
1/2 cup water
mayonnaise
1 carrot, shredded (optional)

salt & white pepper to taste
1/2 onion grated
1 medium head of cabbage or bag
of shredded cabbage

Cut out hard center of cabbage and shred by cutting on a diagonal, thinly. Boil together vinegar, sugar, water, cool to room temperature. In large bowl mix cabbage and half of the vinegar mixture. Add salt and pepper, and grated onion. Add mayonnaise to taste. Refrigerate until cool. Serve. Keep leftovers refrigerated.

Makes about 8 servings

Reserve additional vinegar mixture for another time. Can be refrigerated for 3 weeks.

## OPA'S DELI CUCUMBER SALAD
*Richard B*

2 cucumbers, peeled and sliced thinly
1 teaspoon salt
1 teaspoon parsley, fresh or dried
2 tablespoons white vinegar, store brand

1 small onion, finely chopped
2 teaspoons sugar
dash pepper to taste
1 tablespoon salad oil

Put sliced cucumbers in medium bowl, salt. Press for 1 hour at room temperature, with a heavy plate directly on cucumbers. Drain. Let stand for at least 30 minutes more (pressed) and then add rest of ingredients a little at a time (to taste) add more if needed. Keep refrigerated.

## OPA'S DELI MACARONI SALAD
*Richard B*

1 pound macaroni, uncooked
1 green peppers, finely chopped
1 ½ teaspoons salt
¼ cup white vinegar (store brand)
2 tablespoons prepared mustard
½ teaspoon ground black pepper.

1 tomato, finely chopped
1/2 small onion, finely chopped
mayonnaise to taste (approx. 1 cup)
2/3 cups granulated sugar
¼ cup grated carrot (optional)
1 stalk celery, chopped (optional)

Cook macaroni and drain well. In a bowl, add tomato, peppers and onion. Add salt and pepper add additional ingredients and add mayonnaise to coat lightly. Let sand over night in refrigerator. Toss before serving.

Garnish with parsley, if desired. Keep refrigerated.

## MACARONI SALAD
*Lorraine K.*

½ green or red pepper, minced
1 medium onion, grated
2 carrots, grated
4 tablespoons vinegar
½ teaspoon salt
mayonnaise, approximately ½ cup

1 stalk celery, minced
1 small apple, grated
2 tablespoons sweet pickle relish
4 tablespoons sugar
½ teaspoon white pepper
1 pound elbow macaronis (5 lbs. cooked)

Boil elbows in salted water for 20 minutes. Turn off heat and allow the elbows to remain in hot cooking water for another 20 minutes. Drain in colander and let elbows cool and dry for at least one hour. Add other ingredients and stir together. Keep refrigerated. After a day or so the flavor can go sort of flat—just add a teaspoon of vinegar, a teaspoon of sugar and a pinch of salt.

# OPA'S DELI POTATO SALAD
*Richard Bohlen*

Dressing for 6-8 lbs. Potatoes
1 ¾ cups water
1 cup sugar
2 tablespoons salt
mayonnaise to taste

1 1/3 cups white vinegar, store brand
3 pounds red bliss potatoes
½ medium onion, grated
½ teaspoon white pepper

For Dressing:
Boil water, sugar and salt together, when salt and sugar are dissolved add vinegar—this mixture can be stored in the refrigerator indefinitely for use.

Boil potatoes in their skins until tender but still firm, peel while hot, then cool for 1 or more hours. Slice potatoes thinly, and mix in onion and pepper. Pour dressing over potatoes a little at a time then shake bowl (a small dishpan is better if using more potatoes) back and forth until the dressing is absorbed. You can turn it over by hand but don't stir with a spoon (it breaks the potatoes). Keep adding dressing until it is saturated, but not soupy. Allow resting one hour or more, and then adding more dressing if dry. (Some potatoes absorb more dressing than others). Add a bit of mayonnaise or salad oil. Keep refrigerated.

*To make German Style Potato Salad: do not add mayonnaise or salad oil. Fry diced bacon (about ½ pound for 3 pounds potatoes) in large skillet. Lower heat to medium and add a couple tablespoons of cooking oil (do not drain bacon) and slowly add the potato salad to skillet. Heat until warmed thoroughly; add more oil if needed or butter pats can be used to keep salad moist while heating (I prefer butter). Add extra pepper and salt to taste, if needed.*

*Serving size is approximately ¼ to 1/3 pound per person. Mayonnaise can be thinned by mixing with a couple tablespoons of milk to make it easier to mix.*

*This is exactly like the salad served in the deli (but for less than 50 pounds of potatoes) thanks to my cousin, Lorraine K, for the recipe in an amount that is useable.*

# HAM AND MACARONI SALAD

2 cups cubed, cooked ham
1 ½ cups uncooked macaroni
½ cup celery
¼ cup green pepper
1 tablespoon minced onion

1 tablespoon vinegar
1 ½ teaspoons salt
1 ½ teaspoons dry mustard
¾ cup mayonnaise

Cook macaroni. Combine with remaining ingredients. Serves eight as a main dish served on lettuce leaves with choice of garnishes, more if used as a side dish. Keep refrigerated.

Approximately 9 servings.

# NEW JERSEY STYLE POTATO SALAD

2 pounds Yukon Gold potatoes
2 hard boiled eggs, finely chopped
½ cup mayonnaise
½ medium yellow onion finely chopped

2 stalks celery finely chopped
kosher salt
black pepper, finely ground
sugar to taste

Boil potatoes in skin and let cool. Slice into quarters, add eggs, mayonnaise, onion and celery, and fold together. Season to taste with salt, pepper and sugar. Keep refrigerated.

# OLD FASHIONED GERMAN POTATO SALAD
*Mathilde Bohlen*

1 pound bacon
1 cup chopped onion
4 tablespoons flour
4 teaspoons salt
pepper to taste

2 teaspoons celery seed
½ cup chopped celery
1 cup vinegar
10-12 cups potatoes, peeled &
thinly sliced

Cook bacon till crisp, drain (reserving ½ cup fat), and crumble bacon. Combine vinegar, onion salt, pepper, celery seed and chopped celery. Add potatoes and allow to stand for 1/2 to 1 hour. Using retained fat, put potato mixture into skillet and heat thoroughly, do not turn potatoes or stir. Check to see if potatoes are lightly browned on bottom, turn with spatula, add crumbled bacon, and pat of butter. Cook until potatoes are tender and potatoes are lightly browned.

Serve warm or chilled. Store in refrigerator.


# VEGETABLE SALAD
*Aunt Helen B.*

2 sliced cucumbers
2 tomatoes cut into small pieces
1/2 onion, sliced
1 shredded carrots
1 tablespoon salt
3/4 cups of vinegar 1/2 cup of vegetable oil

1 bunch of celery, cut into small pieces
1 bell pepper, cut into small pieces
1 dill pickle, sliced
2 gherkin pickles, sliced
1/2 cup of sugar

Combine all ingredients and mix well without crushing vegetables. Chill before using, keep refrigerated.

# BEET SALAD
*Aunt Helen B.*

1 small pan full of sliced & peeled beets
1 jar of sweet pickles
½ small onion, sliced

Cover beets with sweet pickle juice and top with sliced onion. Chill before using, keep refrigerated.


# HERRING SALAD
*Aunt Helen B.*

6 Salt Herrings
6 Milk Herrings
2-3 hard boiled eggs, finely diced
1 apple, finely diced
1 tablespoon capers
3-4 sweet gherkins, finely diced
mayonnaise

1 stalk celery, finely diced
2-3 beets, peeled and finely diced
1 small onion, grated
1-2 russet potatoes, finely grated
1 dill pickle, finely diced
salt & pepper to taste

Mix all ingredients except mayonnaise together; add mayonnaise to taste, after ingredients are mixed well. Cover and keep refrigerated until use. Herring salad is traditionally served as a New Years dish in Northern Germany for good luck. Chill before using, keep refrigerated.


# SHRIMP OR CRABMEAT SALAD
*Aunt Helen B.*

1 recipe of macaroni salad

1 pound of shrimp or crabmeat

Make macaroni salad according to recipe and add seafood. (Can also use broiled fish). Mix gently and season to taste. Keep refrigerated.

# HAM SALAD
*Aunt Helen B.*

2-3 hard boiled eggs, diced
2 pounds potato salad, prepared
mayonnaise, to taste

6-8 ounces ham, diced
2-3 sweet gherkins and juice from jar

Gently mix together eggs, ham, and potato salad. Add gherkins, diced, and add some juice from pickle jar. Add mayonnaise to taste. Keep refrigerated.


# PICKLED BEETS

½ cup cider vinegar
2 teaspoons dried mustard
1/3 cup sugar
2 cups sliced peeled, cooked beets

¼ cup water
½ teaspoon salt
½ teaspoon celery seed
1 medium onion, sliced

Heat the vinegar and water to boiling. Add the mustard, salt and sugar. Blend until mixed, and let boil again; then pour over the combined celery seed, beets, and onion. Cover and place in the refrigerator, marinate overnight or longer. Serve cold.

# BREAKFAST AND BRUNCH

# BAKED EGGS

eggs (one for each serving needed)
2 tablespoons light cream or milk (per egg)
butter

2 drops Tabasco sauce for each egg
paprika and salt to taste

Lightly butter individual baking dishes. Add 2 tablespoons light cream or milk with 2 drops of Tabasco to each dish. Carefully break in eggs. Sprinkle lightly with salt and paprika. Bake in 325 degree F. oven for 12 to 18 minutes, or until eggs are set.


# EGGS: FRIED WITH FRIED TOAST

2 eggs
butter

2 slices white or wheat bread
salt and pepper to taste

Heat a fry pan over medium-high heat. Butter one side of each slice of bread. Put bread, butter side down, into pan. Allow to lightly brown in pan and flip over. Brown second side and remove to plate. Lower heat to medium and add an additional pat of butter to pan. Break eggs and carefully add to pan, one at a time. Season tops of eggs with a pinch of salt and pinch of pepper, to taste. Add few drops of water to pan and cover. Lower heat to low and allow egg tops to set. Do not brown eggs or flip eggs for sunny side up. Flip eggs carefully to not break the yolks for over-easy, remove from pan and place over the toast.

Makes 1 serving.

*This was and is my favorite breakfast. I love the flavor of the pan fried bread.*
*To make scrambled eggs, lightly stir eggs and put into hot pan. While cooking, move egg mixture from outside of pan to the inside. Work your way around the pan, and repeat. Slide onto the toast when set but not browned.*

# OMA'S BASIC BATTER—FOR PANCAKES
*Oma Anna Margaretha Bohlen.*

2 serving spoons of flour (heaping)
2-3 tablespoons milk
butter

1 egg
pinch salt
fruit for topping (blueberries, apples, strawberries or other berries)

Mix floor, milk, egg and salt together until well blended.
The trick to Oma's pancakes is to have the pan hot on a medium heat, put vegetable oil in the pan and make sure the egg/flour mixture is well beaten. Pour evenly into pan and make it spread to sides by turning pan. Put a pat of butter in the middle and fruit desired on top. If using apples make sure they are sliced thinly. Put either applies, blueberries or other sliced berries on top of pancake. Cook till lightly browned on both sides and serve with sugar and syrup.

Makes 1 pan sized pancake.

*If you like your pancakes fluffy add 1 teaspoon baking powder. Otherwise these pancakes resemble crepes. This pancake is a family favorite. My brother and I love them with blueberries or apples, my son loves them plain, my daughters eat them with berries. This was one of the first recipes my Mom taught me. I use it as an alternative for crepes when I'm in a hurry.*

# OMA'S BASIC BATTER—FOR FRENCH TOAST
*Oma Anna Margaretha B.*

1 Egg
dash salt
2 slices white bread

2-3 tablespoons milk
butter

Same recipe as pancake batter without the flour, which is why it's so easy to remember. Mix well together; dip the bread in the mixture and transfer to hot pan where you have melted a pat of butter. Brown both sides.
Yield: 2 slices which is one serving.

*Serve with maple syrup.*

# BELGIAN WAFFLES

1 package dry yeast
2 cups lukewarm milk
4 eggs, separated
1 teaspoon vanilla

2 ½ cups sifted all-purpose flour
1 tablespoon sugar
½ teaspoon salt
½ cup melted butter

Sprinkle yeast over warm milk; stir to dissolve. Beat egg yolks and add yeast mixture with the vanilla. Sift together flour, sugar, and salt. Add to the yeast mixture. Stir in the melted butter and combine thoroughly. Beat the egg whites until stiff and stir ¼ of the egg whites into the batter. Carefully fold in remaining whites. Let mixture stand in a warm place for 45 minutes or until double in bulk. Heat waffler; pour in approximately 1 to 1 ¼ cups batter and cook until brown or steaming stops. Sprinkle with powdered sugar.

Makes 4 servings.

# (FEATHER LIGHT) BISCUITS

2 cups flour
1 teaspoon salt
2 teaspoons baking powder
1 tablespoon sugar

½ cup heavy cream to ¾ cup
½ cup sour cream
4 tbs. unsalted butter, melted (1/2 stick)

Preheat oven to 425 degrees F. Line a 10" cake pan with parchment paper. Combine the flour, salt, baking powder, and sugar in a mixing bowl. Stir in the ingredients with a fork. In a small bowl, whisk together ½ cup of heavy cream and the sour cream. Slowly add the cream mixture to the dry ingredients, mixing lightly with a fork. Gather the dough together by hand, and if the doesn't completely come together; add a little more heavy cream until it does. Put the dough into a ball, and then roll it out on a lightly floured board to form a 9" square. Cut the dough into 12 squares, dip both sides of each square in the melted butter, and place them in the prepared pan so the sides are touching. Bake in the center of the oven until the biscuits are lightly browned and puffed, 13-15 minutes. Remove from the oven, and serve immediately.

Makes 12.

# BUTTERMILK BISCUITS

3 cups all-purpose flour
1 ½ tablespoons double-acting baking powder
¾ teaspoon baking soda
¾ teaspoon salt

2 tablespoons sugar
¾ cup butter, cold
1 egg, slightly beaten
¾ cup buttermilk

Sift dry ingredients together. Cut butter into tablespoons and, with a pastry blender, blend into dry ingredients until texture of cornmeal. Stir ½ cup buttermilk into beaten egg and add mixture to flour mixture. Stir quickly, adding remainder of buttermilk as necessary until dough forms a ball. Turn onto floured surface and knead once. Let dough rest for a minute, then roll out to ¾" thickness. Cut into 2" rounds. Place biscuits on buttered baking sheet, 1" apart. Bake at 400 degrees for 15 minutes or until golden brown.

Makes 8 servings.

*For cheese biscuits: when kneading dough, knead in ½ cup grated cheese.*


# CINNAMON ROLLS

1 egg
3 cups Bisquick baking mix
¾ cup milk

3 tablespoons softened butter
¼ cup sugar
2 teaspoons cinnamon

Heat oven to 400 degrees F. Beat egg; add Bisquick and milk. Stir to make soft dough. Turn onto lightly floured cloth-covered board. Knead lightly, just until smooth. Pat or roll out into a rectangle 11"x8". Spread with butter, sprinkle with mixture of sugar and cinnamon. Roll up tightly beginning at wide side; seal well by pinching edge of dough into roll. Place sealed side down on ungreased baking sheet. Make cuts with scissors almost through roll at intervals of 1". Bake about 20 minutes. While warm, glaze top with mixture of ¼ cup confectioners' sugar and 2 tablespoons warm water.

Makes 10 to 12 slices.

# CREPE—BLINTZES

For Crepes:
1 1/3 cups flour
1 cup milk
3 large eggs
1 cup soda water
¼ teaspoon salt
¼ cup sugar
1 teaspoon vanilla
1 teaspoon grated lemon rind
¼ cup butter melted

For Cheese Filling:
2 lbs. dry cottage cheese or farmers cheese
½ cup sugar
1 teaspoon vanilla
1 lemon rind, grated
½ cup golden raisins, soaked in water drained
powdered sugar for dusting

Place flour, milk, eggs, soda, water, salt, sugar, vanilla and grated lemon rind in a blender and blend for 30 seconds. Add the melted butter and blend for 30 seconds more. Let batter stand for 1 hour. Meanwhile, make the cheese filling by mixing the cottage cheese, sugar, vanilla, grated lemon rind and golden raisins in a medium bow. Set aside.

To make the crepes, heat in a small frying pan until hot and then brush with melted butter. Using a ladle or large spoon, pour about 2 tablespoons of the batter into the pan, tilting the pan so that it covers the bottom. As soon as the crepe looks set, about 1 minute, flip with a spatula and fry the other side for 1 minute. Remove from heat and place on a plate. Repeat until all the batter is used. Brushing the pan with melted butter between each crepe and stacking finished crepes.

Lay a crepe on a plate and top with 1 tablespoon or more of the cheese mixture. Turn 2 sides of the crepe in over the filling then roll them up. After all the crepes are filled, gently reheat in a frying pan with 2 tablespoons of butter until lightly golden brown. Sprinkle with powdered sugar and serve.

Makes 2 dozen.

# CREPES

3 eggs
1 tablespoon heavy cream
pinch salt

2 tablespoons flour
2 tablespoons milk
4 teaspoon butter

Beat together eggs, flour, cream, milk, and salt until mixture is the consistency of cream. Melt a teaspoon of butter in a six-inch skillet. When butter foams, pour a tablespoon of batter into skillet. Cook over moderately high meat, swirling skillet so that batter coats the bottom of the pan. Cook one minute, check to be sure bottom is browned, then flip crepe and brown other side (about ½ minute). Continue making crepes this way until all of batter is used. Fold crepes into quarters and stack on a plate covered with a tea towel.

Enough for 4 servings

# CREPES SUZETTE

*Use crepe recipe above*
For filling:
1 orange
1 cup powdered sugar, sifted
2 ponies kirsch
2 ponies maraschino

1 lemon
2 tablespoons butter
2 ponies white Curacao

Prepare crepes. Then grate rind of orange and lemon. Squeeze the orange and lemon juice into a saucepan. Combine with rind and powdered sugar and heat, stirring, until mixture is smooth. Pour into a pitcher.

Have ready a chafing dish, crepes, pitcher of orange/lemon sauce and liquors. Melt butter in chafing dish.

When it bubbles, add half of the liquors and ignite with long match, do not stir. When flame dies down, add sauce to chafing dish and stir. Add crepes to dish, dipping and turning them to coat with sauce, then arranging in an overlapping layer. Add remaining liquor and ignite. Serve as soon as flame dies down.

Approximately 4 servings.

# GERMAN PANCAKES
## *Pfnannkuchen*

1-1/2 cups milk
½ cup flour
3 eggs, beaten

1/3 cup butter
powdered sugar
syrup

Combine milk and flour. Add eggs and mix well. Butter an 8" round cake pan and place in a 400 degree F oven till the butter melts. Pour in batter and bake 20 minutes and serve warm with powdered sugar and syrup.
Serves 2.

*Very similar to my Grandmother's recipe, but the baked version. Can use regular granular sugar instead of powdered sugar.*


# MUSHROOM FILLING FOR OMELETS OR CREPES

1 pound mushrooms, fresh, sliced
1/3 cup sliced scallions
2 tablespoons butter
1 tablespoon flour

1 cup sour cream
1 teaspoon Worcestershire Sauce
salt and pepper to taste

In skillet, sauté mushrooms and scallions in butter till tender. Blend in flour, lower heat and stir in sour cream, Worcestershire Sauce and seasonings. *Don't let it boil.*

Spoon about 3 tablespoons mushroom mixture onto lower center of each warm crepe or omelet. Roll up and garnish with a few more mushrooms.

3 servings.

# NORWEGIAN APPLE PANCAKES

For Filling:
4 tablespoons butter
4 cups very thinly sliced peeled, cored apples
¼ teaspoon ground cinnamon
1 teaspoon grated lemon zest
5 tablespoons red currant jelly
For Batter:
2 eggs, plus 1 egg yolk

¼ teaspoon vanilla
1/8 teaspoon ground cardamom
1/8 teaspoon salt
¼ cup unsalted butter, melted
1 cup flour
For Topping:
sugar
slivered almonds

To make the filling, melt the butter in a large skillet over a low heat. When foam subsides, add the apples, cinnamon and lemon zest. Cook, stirring frequently, until the apples are soft, about 4 minutes. When the apples begin to get soft, add the red currant jelly and stir until it melts. Keep the mixture warm. In medium-sized bowl beat the eggs and egg yolk until they are light in color and thickened. Add the milk, vanilla, cardamom, salt and butter and beat well. Sift in the flour and beat well to mix. The batter will be thin. Preheat the oven to 150 degrees.

Lightly grease an 8-9 inch skillet, preferably one with sloping sides, which make turning easier, and place it over medium high heat. Once the skillet is hot, pour in about ¼ cut of the batter. When the pancake is brown on the bottom, slide an egg turner under a corner of the pancake, and flip it over. Let the pancake cook until brown on the bottom.

Remove the pancake, put 2-3 tablespoons of filling in center and gently fold on edge over and then the other to cover the filling and then gently turn the rolled pancake over so it lies seam down. Sprinkle with sugar and slivered almonds. Keep warm on platter in oven until all are done. Only if needed, brush oil on skillet and repeat process until batter is used up.

*Can be served for brunch or dessert, serves 6 for dessert or 12 for brunch served with other dishes.*

# OMELET—BASIC RECIPE

8 eggs
½ teaspoon salt
¼ teaspoon hot pepper sauce (optional)

2 tablespoons butter
½ cup water (or milk for creamy omelet)
choice of filling (see note)

Put first 3 ingredients in a bowl and add the ½ cup water. Beat mixture briskly with a fork for 30 seconds, or until blended. Heat 6-8" omelet pan, then add 1 ½ teaspoons butter to pan. When pan is hot and butter melted add ½ cup egg mixture (egg mixture should bubble and begin to cook at once on other edge). Push egg in from sides of pan with a spatula so that the uncooked portion flows to the bottom of the pan. Lower heat and cover. When set the omelet is still moist and creamy on top. Cook 1 minute longer, uncovered, to brown bottom slightly. With handle of pan directly in front, put filling (if used) on left side of the omelet (if you are right handed, right side if you are left handed). Hold spatula as you would a mixing spoon and turn uncovered side of omelet over filled side. Slide on to serving platter. Bring up heat on pan and repeat 3 times.

Makes 4 servings (each omelet is 2 eggs).

*Fillings: see Spanish Omelet Filling, Mushroom Omelet Filling; or simply put strips of American or other cheese on for filling. Omelet can also be eaten plain.*

# GERMAN POTATO PANCAKES

2 pounds Idaho potatoes
(3 large)
1 medium onion
2 eggs
2 tablespoons flour

¾ teaspoon salt
dash nutmeg
dash pepper
oil for frying

Grate potatoes, put in ice water and let stand for 15 minutes. Grate onion and add to potatoes. Add flour, salt, nutmeg and pepper. Drain and pat dry with paper towels. Measure out 4 cups. Beat eggs with a whisk. Add onion and potato mixture to eggs. Heat oil in heavy skillet (1/8" deep). Drop mixture in hot oil by tablespoon, making 2 to 3 pancakes at a time. Fry 2-3 minutes on each side, until crisp and golden brown. Drain well on paper towels. Serve hot with apple sauce or sour cream.

Makes 12 pancakes, serves approximately 3-4.

# POTATO PANCAKES

6 large baking potatoes
1 large onion, grated
1 teaspoon salt
½ teaspoon pepper

½ teaspoon baking powder
4 eggs, separated
1 cup vegetable oil

Pare and grate potatoes. Drain well in sieve, pressing out excess liquid with a spoon. Combine potatoes, onion, salt, pepper, baking powder and egg yolks in a large bowl. Beat egg whites until stiff but not dry in a medium-size bowl; fold into potato mixture. Heat oil in a large skillet until a small amount of batter sizzles when dropped into it. Drop batter by large spoonfuls into hot oil. Sauté pancakes until golden brown, turning once, drain on paper toweling. Keep pancakes warm in oven on lowest setting until all are done. Serve with applesauce.

Makes about 30 pancakes, serves approximately 4-6.

# OMA'S POTATO PANCAKES
*Mathilde Bohlen*

6 medium potatoes, peeled
2 eggs, beaten
¼ teaspoon freshly ground black pepper

1 medium onion
1 teaspoon salt
¼ cup vegetable oil

Shred or grate potatoes and onion. Combine onion, eggs, salt and pepper in a large mixing bowl. Pat dry potatoes with paper towels. Add to onion mixture and mix thoroughly. Heat oil in heavy skillet over medium heat. Drop potato mixture by rounded teaspoonfuls into oil. Cook until golden brown, turn and repeat. Serve with applesauce or sour cream.

Makes 4 servings.

*Each of the potato pancake recipes are very good.*

# CHEESE OMELET
*Eleanor Hinsch*

2 eggs
pinch salt
pinch pepper

2 Tablespoons milk
1-2 slices American Cheese
large pat of butter

Mix eggs, salt and pepper, with milk. Beat till smooth. Heat 10" covered pan on medium heat, melt butter in pan. pour in egg mixture, and shred cheese over the top of egg mixture. Put a few drops of water in pan and cover. Eggs are done when top is set but bottom in not brown. Fold in half and remove to plate for serving.

Makes 1 serving.

*One of my favorite quick breakfast or brunch omelets. The few drops of water allow the top to set better without browning the bottom of the omelet. Covered, it steams and fries at the same time. Reduce heat or turn off heat completely when close to set. This method can be used to set the tops of sunny side up eggs, also.*

*Bacon bits can be added to this omelet for a bacon, cheese, and egg omelet. Serve on an English Muffin or a nice roll for on the go.*

# PANCAKES—BASIC RECIPE

1 ½ cups flour
1 tablespoon baking powder
1 tablespoon sugar
1 egg

1 tablespoon vegetable oil
1 cup milk
1 teaspoon vanilla
vegetable oil for pan

Mix all ingredients together except for oil for pan, use a fork or spoon and don't over-beat.

Heat a griddle or heavy-bottomed pan to 300-350 degrees or medium heat. Coat pan with vegetable oil, then wipe out excess with a paper towel.

Pour ¼ cup batter into pan to test for proper temperature. Watch for bubbles to form and break on the surface of the pancake before turning. Then cook until golden brown on the second side. When satisfied that the pancakes will cook evenly, remove the test pancake from the pan. Pancakes should cook for about

2-4 minutes on first side, depending on size, and about 2 minutes on the second side. Lift edge of pancakes to check for brown color on the second side, if necessary.

*Variations: add any combination of apples and cinnamon; peaches; blueberries; strawberries; raspberries; bananas or nuts. Dense fruits should be partially cooked, then cooled before gently stirring into the batter. Avoid over-mixing. Smaller ingredients, such as blueberries, can be sprinkled directly onto the pancake that's been poured onto the griddle.*

*Makes about 12—3" pancakes.*

# PUFFED APPLE PANCAKES

¼ cup butter or margarine
6 cups peeled, cored apple slices
¼ cup sugar
½ teaspoon cinnamon
2 eggs, slightly beaten

½ cup flour
½ cup milk
¼ teaspoon salt
1 tablespoon butter
strawberry preserves

Melt butter or margarine in large skillet over low heat. Add apples, sugar and cinnamon to skillet and cook until apples are tender. In a separate bowl combine eggs, flour, milk and salt. Beat until smooth.

Heat an oven proof 8" skillet in a 450 degree F. oven until very hot. Coat skillet with margarine, immediately pour in batter. Bake pancake on lowest rack in oven at 450 degree oven for 10 minutes. Reduce heat to 350 degrees and continue baking for an additional 10 minutes or until golden brown. Fill with apple mixture and top with preserves. Serve immediately.

Makes approximately 4 to 6 servings.

# OVEN PUFFED PANCAKES
## With fruit topping

PANCAKE:
½ cup all-purpose flour
2 tablespoons sugar
¼ teaspoon sugar
½ cup milk
2 eggs
2 tablespoons butter

FRUIT TOPPING:
½ cup sugar
1 tablespoon cornstarch
½ cup orange juice
2 tablespoons orange-flavored liqueur
or orange juice
3 cups sliced fruits and/or berries

Heat oven to 425 degrees F. Lightly spoon flour into measuring cup; level off. In a medium bowl, combine all pancake ingredients except butter, beat with wire whisk or rotary beater until smooth. Place butter in 9" pie pan; melt in 425-degree oven just until butter sizzles (2-4 minutes). Remove pan from oven, tilt to coat bottom with melted butter. Immediately pour batter into hot pan. Bake at 425 degrees for 14-18 minutes until puffed and golden brown.

Meanwhile in small saucepan, combine ½ cup sugar and cornstarch, mix well, Stir in orange juice and orange-flavored liqueur. Cook and stir over medium heat 5-7 minutes or until sugar dissolves and mixture thickens. Remove pancake from oven; immediately arrange peaches and strawberries over pancake and drizzle with orange sauce. Cut into wedges. SERVE IMMEDIATELY.

2-3 servings. Can be doubled using 2 pans.


# POACHED EGGS

Butter                                           eggs
2 drops Tabasco Sauce

Fill poaching pan half full with water; boil, lower to simmering temperature. Grease poaching unit with a little butter combined with 2 drops Tabasco; heat until butter is melted. Carefully break eggs into unit and cook over simmering water 4 to 6 minutes until whites are solid and yolks are of desired firmness.

You can use a small pot in a fry pan or a small ovenproof baking cup in a pot for same effect.

# SHIRRED EGGS

4 eggs                                       black pepper
salt                                         ¼ cup light cream

Butter four custard cups. Break an egg carefully into each cup. Season with salt and pepper, to taste. Pour 1 tablespoon of cream over each egg. Bake at 350 degrees F. for 10 minutes.

*Can be served with toast fingers.*


# SPANISH OMELET FILLING

1 tablespoon minced onions                   1 teaspoon sugar
2 tablespoons minced green pepper            1 teaspoon Worcestershire Sauce
1 tablespoon butter                          dash hot pepper sauce
1 can tomato sauce (8 ounce)

Sauté minced onion and green pepper with 1 tablespoon butter. When soft add remaining ingredients and simmer, stirring frequently about 5-10 minutes, or until fairly thick.

Makes enough for 2 omelets.


# WAFFLES

2 cups cake flour                            4 tablespoons melted butter
3 teaspoons baking powder                    ½ teaspoon salt
½ cup evaporated milk diluted with           3 eggs, separated
½ cup cold water

Sift dry ingredients together. Add beaten egg yolks, milk, and butter. Fold in stiffly beaten egg whites. Pour into waffle iron. Bake until golden brown.

# BREADS AND MUFFINS

# APPLE BREAD

2 cups flour
1 teaspoon baking powder
½ teaspoon baking soda
1 teaspoon salt
½ cup shortening
1 teaspoon vanilla

2/3 cup sugar
2 eggs
1 cup peeled, ground apples plus juice
½ cup grated sharp cheese
¼ cup chopped nutmeats

Preheat oven to 350 degrees F. Sift flour, baking powder, baking soda, and salt together. Cream the shortening, add the sugar gradually and continue working until light and fluffy. Add the eggs, one at a time, beating about one minute after each addition. Add the apples, vanilla, cheese and nuts and mix well. Add the dry ingredients in two portions, mixing only until all the flour is dampened. Turn into a greased 9x5x3 inch loaf pan. Push the batter well up into the corners of the pan, leaving the center slightly hollow. Bake one hour.
Yield: 1 loaf.

# APPLE-CINNAMON SWIRL LOAF

1 package active dry yeast
1 ¼ cups warm water (115-120 degrees)
1 egg
1 package single layer white cake mix
1 teaspoon salt
4 tablespoons butter

3 ½-3 ¾ cups chopped, cored, and pared apples
1/3 cup sugar
1/3 cup chopped pecans
2 teaspoons ground cinnamon

In a large mixing bowl, dissolve 1 package of dry yeast in warm water. Add the egg, cake mix and salt, beat till smooth. By hand, stir in flour, knead on lightly floured surface till smooth and elastic. Place in greased bowl. Cover and let rise until doubled in size, about 1 ¼ hours. Pinch down, divide in half. Cover; let rest for 10 minutes. Combine apples, sugar, pecans and cinnamon. Melt butter, set aside. Roll half the dough to 12x8" loaf pan. Brush surface with some of the butter. Sprinkle with half the apple mixture. Beginning at the short side, roll up; seal side and ends. Place in greased 8x4x2" loaf pan. Brush top with additional butter. Repeat with remaining dough, filling, and butter. Cover, let rise in warm place till nearly double. About 1 hour. Bake at 375 degrees for 30-35 minutes. Remove from pans, cool on a rack.
Makes 2 loaves.

# APPLE SPICE BREAD

2 cups flour
2 teaspoons baking powder
1 teaspoon salt
1 teaspoon cinnamon
½ teaspoon nutmeg
¼ teaspoon ground cheese

½ cup butter, softened
1 cup brown sugar, packed
2 eggs
1 ½ cups apples, peeled, grated coarsely (approximately 2 apples)
½ cup chopped walnuts

Sift first six ingredients together and set aside. Cream butter and sugar together until light and fluffy. Add eggs and beat well. Stir in sifted dry ingredients and mix well. Fold in apples and nuts. Grease and flour 9x5x3" loaf pan. Pour batter in pan and bake at 350 degrees for 1 hour. Cool in pan 10 minutes before turning out onto wire rack. Cool completely before slicing.
Yield: 1 loaf.

# BANANA BREAD

1 ½ cups flour
1 teaspoon baking soda
1 teaspoon salt
½ cup shortening
¾ cup firmly packed light brown sugar

2 eggs
1 cup mashed ripe bananas (2-3)
½ cup milk
½ cup walnuts, chopped

Sift flour, soda, and salt together. Cream shortening and sugar thoroughly. Add eggs and bananas, beating until light. Alternately add flour mixture and milk. Beat after each addition until smooth. Add nuts. Pour batter into greased 9x5x3" loaf pan. Bake at 350 degrees F. 1 hour and 5 minutes or until done. Remove pan, cool on rack. Wrap in foil or plastic wrap and store overnight before slicing.

# BANANA TEA BREAD

1 ¾ cups flour
2 teaspoons baking powder
¼ teaspoon baking soda
½ teaspoon salt

1/3 cup shortening
2/3 cup sugar
2 eggs, well beaten
1 cup mashed ripe bananas (2-3)

Preheat oven to 350 degrees F. Sift together the flour, baking powder, baking soda, and salt. Cream the shortening, add the sugar gradually and continue working until light and fluffy. Add the eggs and beat well. Add the flour mixture alternately with the banana, a small amount at a time. Beating after each addition until smooth. Turn into a greased bread pan 81/2x4 1/2x3", and bake about 1 hour 10 minutes.

*Variations: for raisin loaf: add one cup seedless raisins.*
   *For Date loaf: add 1 cup finely chopped dates to the batter.*
   *For nuts loaf: add ½ cup coarsely broken nutmeats.*


# BRAN BREAD

3 ½ cups un-sifted all-purpose flour
½ cup instant non-fat dry milk
1 ½ teaspoon salt
2 packages active dry yeast
1 egg (at room temperature)

¼ cup sugar
1 ½ cups warm water (105-115 degrees)
1/3 cup softened margarine or butter
2 cups all bran cereal

In large bowl, stir together 3 cups of flour, non-fat dry milk and salt. Set aside. Combine yeast, sugar and warm water in another large bowl. Stir in cereal. Let stand for about 2 minutes or until cereal is softened. Add batter, egg and about half of the flour mixture. Beat at medium speed for 2 minutes, scraping bowl occasionally. Stir in remaining flour mixture by hand. Add ½ cup flour, if necessary, to form a stiff, sticky dough. Cover; let rise in warm place, free from drafts, until double in bulk, about 1 hour. Stir down dough. Place into 9x5x3" loaf pan generously greased. Bake at 375 degrees about 40 minutes. Remove from pan and cool on wire rack.

Makes 1 loaf

# CINNAMON LOAF

1 cup sugar
½ cup shortening
2 eggs
1 teaspoon vanilla
1 cup dairy sour cream
¼ cup milk
2 cups all purpose flour

1 ½ teaspoons baking powder
1 teaspoon baking soda
½ teaspoon salt
¼ cup sugar
2 teaspoons ground cinnamon
1 ½ teaspoons orange peel, finely shredded

Grease a 9x5x3" loaf pan. Cream together the 1 cup sugar and the shortening till light and fluffy. Add eggs and vanilla, beat well. Blend in sour cream and milk. Stir together flour, baking powder, baking soda, and salt, add to creamed mixture. Mix well. Spread ½ batter in pan. Combine the remaining sugar, the cinnamon and orange peel. Sprinkle all but 1 tablespoon over the batter in the pan. Top with the remaining batter. Cut through batter gently with knife to make swirling effect with cinnamon. Top with remaining sugar mixture.

Bake in 350 degree F. oven about 35 to 40 minutes.

# CORN BREAD

1 cup cornmeal
1 cup flour
2 teaspoons baking powder
½ teaspoon baking soda

1 teaspoon salt
1 large egg, lightly beaten
1 cup buttermilk
1/ cup vegetable shortening, melted

Preheat the oven to 400 degrees F. Lightly grease an 8-9" square pan. In a large bowl, stir in cornmeal. flour, baking powder, baking soda, and salt. In a small bowl, beat the egg and the buttermilk until well blended. Stir into the dry ingredients just until mixed. Blend in melted shortening. Pour batter into pan and bake for 20-25 minutes or until lightly browned on top and toothpick inserted into center comes out clean. Turn onto wire rack and cool. Cut into squares and serve.

Approximately 8 servings.

# COTTAGE CHEESE NUT LOAF

2 cups cottage cheese, sieved
1 cup crushed corn flakes
1 tablespoon grated onion
2 tablespoons finely minced parsley
½ teaspoon salt

1 cup nut meats, coarsely cut (any kind)
1/8 tsp. each sage, thyme, cloves
1 tablespoon bacon fat
1/8 teaspoon peppers

Combine all ingredients, and blend thoroughly. Form into a loaf and bake in a generously greased bread pan at 400 degrees F for about 45 minutes or until the top and sides are well browned. Turn onto warmed platter, serve with tomato sauce.

Serves 6.

# CRANBERRY FRUIT BREAD

1 cup fresh or frozen cranberries, coarsely chopped
½ cup chopped pecans
1 tablespoon grated orange peel
2 cups flour
1 cup sugar

1 ½ teaspoon baking powder
1 teaspoon salt
½ teaspoon baking soda
2 tablespoons shortening
¾ cup orange juice
1 egg, well beaten

Preheat oven to 350 degrees F.
Grease and lightly flour a 9x5x3" loaf pan. Prepare cranberries, nuts and orange peel. Set aside. In a bowl mix together flour, sugar, baking powder, salt, and baking soda. Cut in shortening. Stir in orange juice, egg, and orange peel mixing just to moisten. Fold in cranberries and nuts. Spoon into prepared pan. Bake 60 minutes or until wooden pick inserted in center comes out clean. Cool on a rack 15 minutes. Remove from pan, cool completely. Wrap and store overnight.

Makes 1 loaf.

*This is really good, I used to sell them at craft shows—it also can be made ahead and frozen.*

# FRENCH HERB BREAD

5-6 cups all-purpose flour
2 packages active dry yeast
1 package (at least ¾ ounce or 4 teaspoons)
dry ranch-style buttermilk salad dressing mix
(reserve 1 teaspoon)

1 ½ cup buttermilk
½ cup water
¼ cup shortening
1 egg
1 tablespoon melted butter

Bake at 375 degrees.
In large mixing bowl, combine 2 cups flour, yeast, 3 teaspoons salad dressing mix; mix well. Heat buttermilk, water, shortening until warm (120-130 degrees), add to flour mixture. Add egg. Blend until moistened, beat 3 minutes at medium speed. Gradually stir in enough remaining flour to make a firm dough. Knead on well-floured surface until smooth and elastic (5 to 10 minutes). Place in greased bowl, turning to grease top. Cover, let rise in warm oven (turn to lowest setting for 1 minute turn off) for 20 minutes.

Punch down dough, divide into 2 parts. On lightly-floured surface, roll or pat each half to a 12x7" rectangle. Starting with longer side, roll up tightly sealing edges and ends. Place seam side down on greased cookie sheet. Make diagonal slashes about 2" apart in tops of loaves. Cover, let rise in warm oven until light and doubled in size, about 30 minutes. Bake in preheated oven at 375 degrees for 25 to 30 minutes, while warm, brush with melted butter and sprinkle with 1 teaspoon salad dressing mix. Cool on wire racks.

Makes 2 loaves.

# LEMON TEA LOAF

3 cups sifted flour
¾ cup granulated sugar
3 teaspoons baking powder
1 teaspoon salt
¼ teaspoon baking soda
¼ teaspoon nutmeg
½ cup finely chopped walnuts

1 tablespoon grated lemon rind
1 egg
1 ¼ cups milk
4 tablespoons butter, melted-1/2 stick
1 tablespoon granulated sugar
1 tablespoon lemon juice
¼ cup firmly packed brown sugar

Bake at 350 degrees F for 1 hour 15 minutes.

Sift flour, ¾ cup granulated sugar, baking powder, salt, baking soda, and nutmeg into a large bowl; stir in walnuts, brown sugar and lemon rind.

Beat egg slightly with milk in a small bowl, stir in melted butter, and pour all at once into flour mixture. Stir about 30 strokes, or just until evenly moist. Spoon into a well-greased loaf pan, 9x5x3"; let stand 20 minutes.

Bake in moderate oven (350 degrees F.), 1 hour and 15 minutes.

Cook in pan on a wire rack 5 minutes and turn onto rack.
Mix the 1 tablespoon granulated sugar and lemon juice in a cup; brush over top of loaf several times to glaze. Cool loaf.

Yield: 1 loaf.

# NORWEGIAN SWEET BREAD

2 packages active dry yeast
1 ¼ cups lukewarm water (115 to 120 degrees)
5 ¼-6 cups unbleached flour
½ cup sugar
1 tablespoon salt
½ teaspoon ground cloves

½ teaspoon pepper
1-12 ounce can of beer
½ cup light corn syrup
2 cups rye flour
1 cup raisins

In large bowl, soften yeast in warm milk; let stand 5 minutes. Beat in 1 cup of unbleached flour, sugar, salt, cloves and pepper. Cover; let stand in a warm place about 40 minutes or till dough becomes light and bubbly. Add beer and corn syrup. Stir in rye flour, raisins and enough of the remaining unbleached flour to make a moderately stiff dough. Turn out onto floured surface; knead till smooth and elastic about 8 to 10 minutes. Place in greased bowl, turning once to grease surface. Cover; let rise till double, about 1 hour. Punch dough down; let rest 10 minutes. Divide dough in thirds; shape in round loaves. Place on greased baking sheets. Cover; let rise till double, 30 to 40 minutes. Bake at 375 degrees for 40 minutes or till done. Cover each loaf with foil cap last 20 minutes of baking time to prevent over browning.

Makes 3 loaves.

# NUT BREAD

3 teaspoons baking powder
1 teaspoon cinnamon
3 cups whole wheat flour
½ cup dark molasses
½ cup water
2 tablespoons melted butter

1 teaspoon baking soda
1 ½ teaspoon salt
1/3 cup brown sugar
1 cup milk
1 cup broken walnut meats

Mix the dry ingredients and combine with the molasses, milk and water. Blend thoroughly. Add the nuts and melted butter to the ingredients and beat well. Pour the mixture into one large or two small bread pans that have been well greased. Let stand at room temperature for 20 minutes, then bake in a 325 degree F. oven until the bread is brown and shrinks slightly from the sides of the pan. If baked in one pan the baking time will take 1 hour; if baked in two pans the baking time will be 40 to 50 minutes. Turn onto a rack and allow to cool. Serve with cream cheese or butter.

# OATMEAL-RAISIN BREAD

2 cups sifted all-purpose flour
2 teaspoons baking powder
¾ teaspoon baking soda
1 ½ teaspoons salt
1 cup uncooked rolled oats

1/3 cup shortening
1/3 cup brown sugar, packed
1 cup seedless raisins
1 egg, beaten
1 ¼ cups buttermilk

Preheat oven to 350 degrees F. (moderate oven). Sift together flour and next 3 ingredients. Add oats and raisins. Cream together shortening and brown sugar till light and fluffy. Add egg and buttermilk. Add milk mixture in thirds to flour mixture stirring till blended after each addition. Bake in greased 9x5x3" loaf pan in 350 degree oven for 1 hour or until done.

Yield: 1 loaf.

# ORANGE PECAN BREAD

½ cup butter
1 ¼ cups sugar
2 eggs
2 teaspoons baking powder
2 cups flour

1 teaspoon salt
½ cup orange juice
1 tablespoon grated orange peel
1/2 cup chopped pecans

Cream butter and sugar until light and fluffy. Add eggs and beat well. Sift together flour, baking powder and salt and add to creamed mixture, mixing well. Add orange juice and stir to blend. Fold in orange peel and pecans. Grease and flour a 9x5x3" loaf pan or 6 miniature pans. Put batter in pans and bake at 350 degrees F. for 1 hour to full-size pan for 25-30 minutes in miniature pans. Cool in pan 10 minutes before turning out onto wire rack. Cool completely before slicing.

# PECAN CARAMEL ROLLS

¼ cup firmly packed brown sugar
¼ cup butter softened
2 tablespoons light corn syrup
1 can refrigerated crescent dinner rolls (8 oz).

2 tablespoons sugar
½ teaspoon cinnamon
¼ cup finely chopped pecans

Heat oven to 375 degrees F. In a small bowl, combine brown sugar, butter and corn syrup; blend well. Spread in bottom of ungreased 8 or 9" round cake pan.

Separate dough into 4 rectangles; firmly press perforations to seal. In a small bowl, combine sugar and cinnamon; sprinkle mixture evenly over rectangles. Sprinkle 1 tablespoon of the pecans on each rectangle. Starting at shorter side, roll up each rectangle; pinch edges to seal. Cut each roll into 4 slices. Place, cut side down, over brown sugar mixture in pan.

Bake at 375 degrees for 20 to 27 minutes or until golden brown. Cool in pan 1 minute; invert onto serving platter or foil, serve warm or cool. *This is another favorite with the craft shows that I did for years.*

Makes 16 rolls.

# PUMPKIN BREAD

2 packages yeast
¼ cup sugar
1 tablespoon salt
2 cups pureed cooked pumpkin (or canned)

¼ cup lukewarm water
1 ¾ cups milk, scalded
8 to 8 ½ cups sifted flour
¼ melted shortening

Soften the yeast in the water with 1 spoonful of sugar. Let stand for 10 minutes. Combine hot milk, salt, and the remaining sugar. Stir and cool until lukewarm. Combine yeast and cooled-milk mixtures and stir to blend. Add 2 ½ cups of the flour and beat until batter is very smooth. Add the pumpkin and the cooled shortening and mix well. Add enough of the remaining flour to make a stiff dough; use any remaining flour on the board for kneading and shaping the dough.

Turn dough out on a lightly floured board. Cover dough with a bowl, let rest for 10 minutes. Place in a greased bowl, turn once to bring greased side up. Cover and let stand in warm place and let rise until double in bulk. Approximately 1 hour. Punch down dough, turn over in bowl and let rise again until double in size, about 45 minutes. Turn out on board and divide into 3 equal portions.

Cover with bowls or towels and let rest for 10 minutes. Shape into loaves and place in greased loaf pans. Cover and let stand until doubled. Bake in 400 degree F. oven for 15 minutes and then reduce heat to 375 degrees F and continue baking 20 to 30 minutes until well browned. Turn out onto racks to cool, uncovered.

Makes 3 loaves.

# OMA'S RAISIN BREAD
*Mathilde Bohlen*

3 ½ cups sifted flour
1/8 pound butter (1/2 stick)
1 egg
1 cup milk

1 tablespoon sugar
pinch salt
2 packages active yeast
6 ounces raisins (mixed golden & dark-seedless)

Dissolve yeast in ¼ cup lukewarm water with ½ teaspoon sugar, set aside. Sift flour, sugar and salt, add the raisins. Beat egg and add to flour mixture (make a hole in the center and add the other ingredients). Add yeast, melt butter in the milk to lukewarm and add slowly to flour.

Set aside to double in bulk near heat. Knead mixture thoroughly. Put in greased pan; set aside for 5 to 10 minutes, cover with towel. Bake at 425 degrees, approximately 25 minutes.

Makes 2 loaves.


# RYE BREAD

2 cups milk
2 tablespoons brown sugar (or ¼ cup molasses)
3 cups white flour
1 tablespoon caraway seeds

1 teaspoon salt
2 yeast cakes
3 cups rye flour

Scald 2 cups milk; add salt and brown sugar or molasses. Cool and add 2 cakes crumbled yeast. Stir in 3 cups white flour. Beat well and then stir in 3 cups rye flour. When smooth, turn dough onto lightly floured board and knead until elastic. Place in greased bowl, cover, and let rise until double in bulk. Add caraway seeds to dough, knead and shape into two loaves. Place in greased pans, brush with butter and let rise until double in bulk. Bake in a moderately hot oven (375 degrees F.) for 45 to 60 minutes. The white flour may be reduced to 1 cup and increase rye flour to 5 cups, if desired. Unlike wheat breads, it will not be stiff enough to knead. Makes 2 loaves.

# GERMAN RYE BREAD
## *Deutsches Roggenbrot*

2 tablespoons butter
2 tablespoons sugar
1 teaspoon salt
1 yeast cake

½ cup lukewarm water
6 cups rye flour, divided
1-1/2 cups bread flour
2 tablespoons caraway seeds

Put butter, sugar, salt in top of a double boiler, add scalded milk. Dissolve yeast in ½ cup lukewarm water. When milk mixture is lukewarm add dissolved yeast plus 3 cups of rye flour. Mix with a spoon. Add rest of the rye flour and mix thoroughly. Turn onto floured board and knead dough until smooth and elastic to the touch. Bubbles may be seen under the surface. Return dough to bowl, cover, let rise till double in size. Punch down and knead again adding caraway seeds and bread dough. Knead again and then shape into 2 loaves and place into greased loaf pans. Fill halfway, cover and let double in size.

Bake at 425 degrees F. for 15 minutes and reduce temperature to 375 degrees F for an additional 30 to 35 minutes, till firm to touch.


# ORANGE PECAN BREAD 2

½ cup butter, softened
1 ¼ cup sugar
2 eggs
2 cups flour
2 teaspoons baking powder

1 teaspoon salt
½ cup orange juice
1 tablespoon grated orange peel
½ cup chopped pecans

Cream butter and sugar until light and fluffy. Add eggs and beat well.
Sift together flour, baking powder and salt and add to creamed mixture, mixing well. Add orange juice and stir to blend. Fold in orange peel and pecans.

Grease and flour a 9x5x3" loaf pan (or 6 4 1/2x2 1/2x1 ½" miniature pans). Pour batter in pans and bake at 350 degrees for 1 hour in full-size pan (or 25 to 30 minutes in miniature pans). Cool in pan 10 minutes before turning out onto wire rack. Cool completely before slicing.

Makes 1 loaf or 6 miniature loaves.

# STRAWBERRY BREAD

3 cups flour
1 teaspoon baking soda
1 teaspoon salt
1 ½ teaspoon cinnamon
1 ¼ cups chopped walnuts

2 cups sugar
4 eggs
1 ¼ cups vegetable oil
2 cups fresh or 16 ounces frozen
(thawed) strawberries

In a large bowl, combine flour, soda, salt, cinnamon and sugar. Add eggs and oil and mix well. Stir in strawberries and nuts until evenly distributed.

Grease and flour 2 9x5x3" loaf pans or 4-1 pound coffee cans. Divide batter among pans and bake at 350 degrees for 1 hour in loaf pan or 35-40 minutes in coffee cans. Cool in pans for 10 minutes before turning out on wire racks. Cool completely before slicing.

Makes 2 loaves or 4 coffee can sized loaves.


# SWEDISH RYE

1 package active dry yeast
½ cup warm water
2 cups sifted rye flour
¾ cup dark molasses

1/3 cup shortening
2 teaspoons salt
2 cups boiling water
6 ½ cups sifted enriched flour

Soften active dry yeast in the warm water. Combine rye flour, molasses, shortening, and salt; add boiling water and blend well. Cool to lukewarm. Add softened yeast. Gradually stir in enriched flour to make soft dough; mix well. Turn out on well-floured surface. Cover and let rest 10 minutes. Knead till dough is smooth and satiny, about 10 minutes. Place in lightly greased bowl, turning once to grease surface. Cover; let rise in warm place till double, about 1 ½ to 2 hours. Punch down. Cover, and let rise till almost double, about 30 minutes. Turn out on lightly floured surface and divide in 3 equal parts; form in balls. Cover; let rest 15 minutes.

Shape in 3 round loaves and place on greased baking sheets. Cover; let rise till almost double, about 1 hour. Brush loaves with slightly beaten egg. Bake in moderate oven (350 degrees F), for 35-40 minutes.

Makes 3 loaves.

# WHITE BREAD

1 yeast cake

2 tablespoons melted butter or shortening

6 ½ cups flour

1 tablespoon sugar

2 teaspoons salt

2 cups lukewarm water

Add the sugar to the water, and stir in the broken yeast. When dissolved thoroughly, set it aside for about 10 minutes. Add the melted butter and salt; then gradually stir in 3 cups of flour and beat until smooth. Add balance of the flour, reserving some to place on the board. Knead dough on floured board until smooth and elastic and until all the flour is worked in. Place it in greased bowl, cover, and set it aside in warm place for about 2 hours, or until well risen. Mold it in two loaves; place them in well-greased bread pans, filling half full. Make a slight incision down center or each loaf. Cover, and let rise 1 hour or more. Bake in moderately hot oven from 45 to 60 minutes. (For milk bread substitute 2 cups of milk for the water plus ¼ cup water).
Makes 2 loaves.

# BREAD MAKING PROBLEMS:

## BREAD DIDN'T RISE WELL OR NOT AT ALL
Yeast was not fresh.
Liquid was too hot and killed the yeast.
Dough was kneaded too much or not enough. Knead only until the dough does not tear easily when stretched.
Oven temperature was too low. To check your oven's temperature, place an oven thermometer at the center of the oven and set the oven to 350 degrees. Check the temperature indicated on the thermometer after 20 minutes. If it's not within 5 degrees of 350 degrees, you'll need to adjust the oven's temperature control.

## BREAD IS HEAVY AND COARSE
There's too much liquid or not enough flour in dough. When mixing dough, start with a minimum amount of flour until the dough reaches desired consistency (soft, sticky, stiff or firm). Dough was allowed to rise for too long. Proper rising helps the development of the bread texture. Let dough rise in a warm (80 to 85 degrees), draft-free area.
Oven temperature was too low.

## BREAD IS DRY AND CRUMBLY
Too much flour was used.
Dough was allowed to rise too long.

## BREAD IS DOUGHY ON THE BOTTOM OR HAS A SLIGHTLY GUMMY TEXTURE
Bread was under baked. Test for doneness at the minimum recommended baking time. Bread is done when it's golden brown and sounds hollow when tapped on the bottom. Or insert an instant-read thermometer in the thickest part of the loaf. The bread is done when the thermometer read 200 degrees. Bread stayed in the pan too long after baking. Remove breads from pans and cool on wire racks. Let breads cool for at least 20 minutes before slicing. Use a serrated knife and a sawing motion when cutting.

## LOAF SINKS IN THE CENTER.
Dough rose too long during the second rise time in the pain.

## BREAD HAS LARGE HOLES
Dough was not kneaded enough.
Air was not compressed out of the dough during shaping.

## BREAD CRUMBLES WHEN CUT
Too much flour was used.

**Baking Tips:**
- Use stick butter or margarine (with at least 80% oil) or shortening. Don't use light or whipped butter, diet spread or tub margarine.
- Use aluminum pans with a dull rather than shin or dark finish. Glass dishes and dark finishes will produce darker crusts.
- To allow for good air circulation while baking, leave at least 1 inch of space between pans and the sides of the oven.

**Note for breads and muffin making: Avoid over-beating the batter for either muffins or breads. It makes the breads/muffins tough and chewy.**

# APPLE-CRANBERRY MUFFINS

1 ¾ cups plus 2 tablespoons flour
½ cup sugar
1 ½ teaspoon baking powder
½ teaspoon baking soda
½ teaspoon salt
½ teaspoon cinnamon

1 egg
¾ cup milk
¾ cup sweetened applesauce
¼ cup butter, melted
1 cup cranberries coarsely, chopped

In medium bowl, combine 1 ¾ cups of the flour, ¼ cup of the sugar, the baking powder, baking soda, and salt. In a small bowl, combine egg, milk, applesauce and butter, mix well. Add egg mixture to flour mixture, stirring just until moistened. Batter will be lumpy. In small bowl, toss cranberries with remaining 2 tablespoons flour, fold into batter. Spoon batter into 12 greased 2 ½" muffin cups. In another small bowl, combine remaining ¼ cup sugar and the cinnamon. Sprinkle over muffins. Bake in preheated 400 degree oven 20 to 25 minutes or until wooden pick inserted in center comes out clean. Remove from pan, cool on wire rack.

Makes 12 muffins.

# APPLE-WALNUT MUFFINS

2 cups all-purpose flour
1 teaspoon baking soda
¼ teaspoon ground cinnamon
¼ teaspoon ground ginger
¼ teaspoon ground allspice
¼ teaspoon ground nutmeg
¼ teaspoon salt, rounded
2 large eggs
1 cup frozen, thawed apple juice concentrate plus

2 tablespoons frozen, thawed apple juice concentrate
½ cup buttermilk
2 tablespoons oat bran
2 small Granny Smith apples, peeled, cored, and chopped
1/3 cup chopped walnuts
GARNISH:
1 small Granny Smith apple, peeled, cored, cut into 12 thin slices

Preheat oven to 375 degrees F.
Grease 12 standard size muffin pan cups or line with paper liners. Mix together flour, baking soda, cinnamon, ginger, allspice, nutmeg and salt. Mix together eggs, apple juice and buttermilk. Stir flour mixture and oat bran into egg mixture until dry ingredients are just moistened. Do not over mix. Gently stir in chopped apples and nuts.

Spoon batter into prepared pan, filling cups 2/3 full. Garnish each muffin with an apple slice. Bake muffins until lightly golden and tops spring back when pressed, 25 minutes. Transfer pan to a wire rack to cool slightly. Turn muffins out onto rack to cool completely.

Makes 12 muffins.

# BANANA-NUT MUFFINS

½ cups butter, softened
1 cup granulated sugar
2 large eggs
2 large ripe bananas, mashed
2 cups all-purpose flour
1 teaspoon salt

1 teaspoon baking powder
½ teaspoon baking soda
1 cup buttermilk
½ cup chopped pecans
1 teaspoon vanilla extract

Preheat oven to 400 degrees F. Grease 12 standard size muffin pan cups or use paper liners. Beat together butter and sugar at medium speed until light and fluffy. Add eggs, 1 at a time, beating well after each addition. Beat in bananas until smooth.

Mix together flour, salt, baking powder and baking soda.

Alternately stir flour mixture and buttermilk into egg mixture until dry ingredients are just moistened.

Stir in nuts and vanilla. Do not over mix batter; it should not be completely smooth. Spoon batter into prepared pan, filling 2/3 fill. Bake until lightly golden, about 18 minutes. Transfer muffin pan cups to a wire rack to cool slightly. Turn out onto rack. Serve warm.

# BLUEBERRY MUFFINS

½ cup unsalted butter (1 stick), room temperature
1 cup sugar
2 tablespoons sugar
2 teaspoons baking powder
1 teaspoon vanilla extract
½ teaspoon finely grated lemon zest

1 ¾ cups all-purpose flour
¼ cup finely ground yellow cornmeal
¼ teaspoon salt
1/8 teaspoon ground cinnamon
½ cup milk
2 ½ cups blueberries, rinsed & dried

Preheat oven to 375 degrees F. Grease 12 regular muffin cups or line with paper liners. Using an electric mixer, cream the butter and 1 cup of the sugar together in a large bowl. Add the eggs one at a time, beating well after each addition. Add the baking powder and mix well. Add the vanilla extract and lemon zest to the batter, mix well.

In another bowl, combine the flour, cornmeal, salt, and cinnamon. Add half of this dry mixture to the batter and mix lightly; then add the milk and stir well. Add remaining dry mixture and stir just to combine, do not over-mix.

Fold in the blueberries. Spoon the batter into the muffin cups, then sprinkle them evenly with the remaining 2 tablespoons of sugar. Bake in the center of the oven until the muffins are golden brown and a toothpick comes out clean when inserted in the center of the muffins, about 25 to 30 minutes.

Cool the muffins in the pan on a wire rack for 15 minutes. Then un-mold them onto a rack to cool completely.

*Follow the instructions carefully when adding the ingredients, taking care not to over-mix the batter, or you will end up with tough muffins.*

# BRAN MUFFINS

1 ¼ cups flour
3 teaspoons baking powder
½ teaspoon salt
½ cup sugar

1 ½ cups bran flakes
1 cup milk
1 egg
¼ cup vegetable oil

Stir together flour, baking powder, salt and sugar. Set aside.

Measure bran flakes and milk into mixing bowl. Stir to combine. Let stand 1 to 2 minutes or until cereal is softened. Add egg and oil. Beat well. Add dry ingredients to cereal mixture, stirring only until combined. Portion batter evenly into 12 greased 2 ½" muffin pan cups. Bake at 400 degrees F. for 25 minutes or until golden brown. Serve hot or cold.

Makes 12 muffins.

# ORANGE SPICE MUFFINS

1/3 cup brown sugar, packed
¼ cup butter, softened
1 egg, beaten
¾ cup milk
½ cup orange juice
1 tablespoon grated orange peel

3 cups biscuit baking mix
1 pkg. mincemeat, crumbled, 9 ounces
Cinnamon Topping:
2 tablespoons sugar
2 teaspoons cinnamon

Preheat oven to 375 degrees F. In a large bowl, beat sugar and butter until fluffy. Add egg, milk, orange juice and peel; mix well. Stir in biscuit mix and mincemeat only until moistened (do not over-mix). Fill greased or paper-lined 2 ½" muffin cups ¾ full. Sprinkle Cinnamon and Sugar Topping evenly over muffins. Bake 18 to 22 minutes or until golden brown. Remove from pan. Serve warm.

Makes about 18 muffins.

Topping: in a small bowl, combine sugar and cinnamon.

# TAFFY APPLE MUFFINS

2 cups flour
½ cup sugar
1 tablespoon baking powder
½ teaspoon salt
¼ teaspoon nutmeg
½ cup milk
¼ cup butter, melted

2 eggs
1 teaspoon vanilla
1 cup apple chopped
½ cup honey
½ cup dark brown sugar, packed
¾ cup walnuts finely chopped

Preheat oven to 400 degrees F. Grease 36 miniature muffin cups. In a large bowl, combine flour, sugar, baking powder, salt and nutmeg. In a small bowl, combine milk, butter, eggs and vanilla until blended. Stir into flour mixture just until moistened. Fold in apple. Spoon into muffin cups. Bake 10-12 minutes or until lightly browned and wooden pick inserted in center comes out clean. Remove from pan.

Meanwhile in a small saucepan, heat honey and brown sugar over medium-high heat to a boil, stir to dissolve sugar. Dip warm muffins into hot glaze, then into chopped nuts. Spear with Popsicle sticks or wooden skewers, if desired.

Makes 36 miniature muffins.

# POPOVERS

1 cup flour, sifted
¼ teaspoon salt
¼ cup milk, at room temperature
½ teaspoon melted butter or margarine

2 eggs, at room temperature,
slightly beaten
½ cup milk, room temperature
additional butter, melted

Sift 1 cup sifted flour with ¼ teaspoon salt into a deep bowl and make a well in the center. Add 2 eggs (at room temperature), slightly beaten, to well with ½ cup milk (at room temperature) and ½ teaspoon melted butter or margarine. Slowly stir flour into liquids until mixture is fairly smooth and like sour cream. Stir in an additional ½ cup milk (at room temperature). Mixture should be smooth but not over-beaten and should be the thickness of heavy cream. While making batter, heat muffin pan (preferably iron), adding between ¼ and ½ teaspoon melted butter or other fat, to each muffin cup. Fill each cup about 2/3 of the way with batter.

Bake at 350 degrees F. and bake 20 minutes—do not open door to the oven. Test one popover to see if it is crisp and dry inside. When done, remove from the pan and prick a small hole in one side of each popover so steam can escape. If this step is not done the popover will collapse and turn soggy inside.

Makes 10 to 12 popovers.

*When I was little my parents and my Aunt and Uncle used to take me to this wonderful restaurant in upstate New York, I don't remember what I ate except for the wonderful popovers they served. It took me quite a while to find a recipe for popovers that I really liked enough. Still not like that restaurant but close!*

# HORS D'OEUVRES AND PARTY FARE

## APPETIZER MEAT BALLS

1 ½ pounds ground beef, veal and pork, mixed
1 cup seasoned bread crumbs
½ cup chili sauce
1 egg
¼ cup minced onions

2 tablespoons chopped parsley
1 ½ teaspoons salt
½ teaspoon Tabasco sauce
½ teaspoon garlic powder
3 tablespoons butter

Combine meat, breadcrumbs, chili sauce, egg, onion, parsley, salt, Tabasco sauce and garlic powder in a large bowl. Shape meat into balls 1" in diameter. Pan fry a few at a time in the butter, put into chaffing dish. Serve with food picks.

Makes 8 dozen.


## ASPARAGUS QUICHE

9" pie shell (do not prick pastry)
¾ lb. fresh asparagus or 1 8 ounce frozen pkg.
3 eggs, beaten
1 ½ cups light cream

¾ teaspoon salt
dash nutmeg
1 ½ cups shredded Swiss cheese

Line baking sheet with foil and fill pie shell with dry beans; put shell on foil-lined sheet. Bake 5 minutes at 450 degrees. Remove from the oven, remove foil and beans. Reduce oven to 325 degrees. If using fresh asparagus, wash and scrape off scales. Break off the woody stems. Cut asparagus into 1 ½" pieces. In saucepan cook asparagus pieces, uncovered in a small amount of boiling salted water for 8 to 10 minutes or till just tender. (or cook frozen asparagus according to package directions). Drain well.
In medium bowl combine eggs, cream, salt and nutmeg. Stir in cooked asparagus pieces. Sprinkle cheese in pre-cooked pastry shell, pour egg mixture over cheese. Bake until set when knife inserted in middle comes out clean, approximately 25-30 minutes, remove from oven and allow to sit on wire rack till cool.

Makes 8 servings.

# BAKED CLAMS
## *Aunt Helen B*

4 large cans minced clams, retain juice
1 clove garlic, minced
4 ounces white vermouth
butter, melted
additional seasoned bread crumbs

3-4 strips of bacon
4-5 tbs. seasoned bread crumbs
2 tablespoons all-purpose flour
paprika to taste
clam shells

Dice the bacon and fry in 12" skillet. Add minced clove of garlic and continue frying until lightly browned. Add minced clams and stir into garlic and bacon. Add clam broth from the 4 cans of clams and stir over low heat. Add 4 to 5 tablespoons of seasoned bread crumbs and the vermouth. Add flour to thicken, approximately 2 tablespoons. Let simmer and continue to stir. Spread shells on tray and sprinkle with additional bread crumbs. Spoon in clam mixture and top with light sprinkle of additional bread crumbs, baste with melted butter to cover lightly. Sprinkle with paprika and put in top rack of oven and broil until lightly golden brown. This step takes just a few minutes, so watch closely.

# BACON AND DOUBLE CHEESE QUICHE

CRUST:
1 1/3 cups all-purpose flour
1/8 teaspoon salt
½ cup chilled butter
3 tablespoon cold water
FILLING:
10 strips lean bacon

4 large eggs
1 1/3 cups light cream
¼ teaspoon dried thyme
1/8 teaspoon white pepper
½ cup shredded Gruyere cheese (2oz.)
½ cup shredded white cheddar cheese
(2 ounces)

To prepare the crust; in a large bowl, mix together the flour and salt. Using a pastry blender cut in the butter until coarse crumbs form. Add water, 1 tablespoon at a time, tossing with a fork, until a dough forms. Use only enough water to form dough. Shape into a disk, wrap in plastic wrap, and chill in refrigerator for 30 minutes. Preheat oven to 375 degrees F. On a lightly floured surface, using a lightly floured rolling pin, roll the dough into 11" circle. Fit into 9" pie pan. Trim edge, leaving ¼" overhang. Fold under to form standup edge. Prick dough with a fork. Line with foil and fill with pie weights or dried beans. Bake piecrust for 10 minutes. Remove foil and weights. Bake until lightly golden, about 5 minutes, transfer to a wire rack to cool.

Meanwhile, prepare the filling. In a medium skillet, cook the bacon over medium heat until crisp, 8-10 minutes. Transfer to a paper towel to drain. In a small bowl, whisk together the eggs cream thyme and pepper. Pour mixture into crust. Crumble bacon. Sprinkle the egg mixture with the bacon Gruyere cheese and cheddar cheese. Bake until golden and custard to set about 30 minutes. Serve warm.

Makes 8 servings.

# BEER SHRIMP

1 quart beer
2 teaspoons salt
1 teaspoon tarragon
3-4 sprigs of fresh dill

¼ cup lemon juice
1 teaspoon whole peppercorns
2 pounds raw shrimp in shells
1 small jar of stuffed green olives

Pour beer into 2 quarts saucepan, add lemon juice, salt, peppercorns, tarragon, bring to a boil. Reduce heat and simmer 10 minutes. Add shrimp, bring to a boil again, then simmer 3-5 minutes (depending on size of shrimp) or until shrimp are deep pink. Drain, cool, shell, devein shrimp. Arrange in a bowl on cracked ice, garnish with the dill and olives. Chill until serving.

# BLUE CHEESE DIP

4 ounces cream cheese
4 ounces bleu cheese
1 tablespoon heavy cream sweet

1 teaspoon Worcestershire sauce
1 tablespoon chopped chives

Allow cheese to come to room temperature. Blend all ingredients together by hand or with electric mixer. Serve with chips raw vegetables.

Make 1 ½ cups.

# CHEESE STRAWS

1 cup grated American cheese
1 cup flour
1 teaspoon baking powder
½ teaspoon salt

1/8 teaspoon cayenne pepper
¼ teaspoon paprika
1 egg
2 tablespoons milk

Mix together cheese flour baking powder salt cayenne pepper and paprika; add beaten egg; mix well, add milk enough to make stiff dough. Roll out 1/8 inch thick, on floured board; cut into strips five inches long and ¼" wide. Bake in hot oven at 450 degrees F. for 10 minutes.

Makes 30 cheese straws.

# CHICKEN LIVER PATE

½ pound chicken livers
1/3 cups butter, softened
½ small onion, finely chopped
2 tablespoons sherry or brandy

½ teaspoon salt
½ teaspoon prepared mustard
pinch nutmeg
pinch allspice

In a small saucepan cover chicken livers with water, bring to a bowl and simmer 17-19 minutes. Drain. Cut livers into pieces and put in food processor or blend until smooth. Chill. You can omit the sherry, use chicken broth instead—add slowly 1 tablespoon first and see if more is necessary.

Serve with crackers or toast.

Makes 1 ½ cups.

# CHEESE QUICHE

½ pound sharp cheddar cheese
1 tablespoon flour
3 eggs
1 cup heavy cream

½ teaspoon salt
¼ teaspoon pepper
1 unbaked 9" pie pastry or 10" flat
scalloped Quiche pan, pastry lined

Preheat oven to 400 degrees. Grate cheese and stir in flour. Beat eggs. Stir cream and seasonings into eggs. Line the bottom of the pastry with the cheese. Pour on eggs and cream. Bake at 400 degrees for 35 minutes.

Serves 8.

# INDIVIDUAL CHEESE QUICHES
*Eleanor Hinsch*

½ pound Fontina cheese
3 eggs
1 cup heavy cream
½ teaspoon salt

¼ teaspoon pepper
2 teaspoons flour
Fillo dough cups—2 pkgs.

Preheat oven to 400 degrees. Cut cheese into small cubes. Beat eggs. Stir cream and seasonings into eggs, stir in flour. Line the bottom of pastry cups with the cheese cubes, spread evenly between cups. Pour on eggs and cream mixture. Bake at 400 degrees for 35 minutes or until knife inserted into middle comes out clean.

Makes 8-16 servings.

# CHEESE WEDGES

12 slices white bread
½ cup processed cheddar cheese spread
¼ teaspoon Tabasco sauce

¼ teaspoon mustard
rolled anchovies, optional

Remove crusts from the bread slice diagonally to make 4 wedges from each slice. Combine cheese spread Tabasco and mustard until well blended. Spread on bread wedges. Bake in 400 degree oven for 5 minutes or until cheese is bubbly. Top with anchovies if desired. Serve hot.

Makes 48 wedges.


# CHICKEN LIVER SPREAD

¼ cup margarine or butter
½ cup minced onions
2 hard cooked eggs, chopped
½ cup mayonnaise
1 tablespoon dry sherry

1/2 teaspoon salt
1 tablespoon chopped parsley
½ teaspoon dry mustard
1 pound chicken livers

In medium skillet melt 2 tablespoons butter over medium heat. Add onion, cook until tender. Melt 2 additional tablespoons butter in pan, cook livers, a few at a time, 3-5 minutes or until lightly browned and tender. Remove from heat, cool. Finely chop livers. In separate bowl mix chopped eggs with salt, parsley, and dried mustard. Mix together. Reserve 1 tablespoon of the egg mixture for garnish In same bowl stir together onion, livers, remaining eggs, mayonnaise and sherry until well blended. Cover and chill at least 4 hours. Garnish with reserved egg and parsley.

Makes about 2 cups, serve on crackers.

# CHINESE BARBECUED SPARERIBS

4 pounds spareribs
1 cup soy sauce
1/3 cup water
3 tablespoons red wine

1 tablespoon sugar
1 teaspoon salt
1 clove garlic

Score the meat between the ribs but do not cut all the way through.
Place the meat in a large bowl. Combine the remaining ingredients and pour over the ribs. Let stand for 1 hour turning once. Remove the meat from the marinade. Reserve the liquid. Place the ribs on a grill over medium coals and cook about 1 and ½ hours. Turn the meat frequently and brush with the marinade. Cut with scissors into individual ribs if desired. Spareribs may be baked and basted in a roasting pan in a moderate (350 degree) oven for 1 ½ hours.

Makes about 20-30 ribs.

# CORNED BEEF RIBBONS

4 cans corned beef spread, 4 ½ ounces each
¼ cup finely chopped dill pickle
6 teaspoons bottled horseradish

8 tablespoons sour cream
1 ½ loaves thinly sliced bread (1 lb. each)

Mix corned beef spread, pickle, horseradish, and sour cream in a medium sized bowl. Spread evenly on 24 slices of bread, leaving remaining 12 slices plain. Make 12 stacks of 2 spread slices (spread side up), and 1 un-spread slice each. Wrap in plastic wrap and refrigerate overnight or until serving time. To serve, trim off crusts, cut each sandwich into four strips, cut strips crosswise to make 8 little sandwiches.

Makes 50 servings.

# CRABMEAT REMOULADE

1.7 ounce can crabmeat
1 cup mayonnaise
¼ cup olive oil
2 tablespoon lemon juice
2 cloves crushed garlic

1 teaspoon celery seed
2 stalks celery, finely chopped
¼ teaspoon salt
1/8 teaspoon pepper

pick over and shred crab meat. Blend all ingredients by hand. Refrigerate. Serve with crackers,. chips, and raw vegetables.

Makes 3 cups.

# CRABMEAT SPREAD

2 cups fresh white crabmeat
½ cup mayonnaise
1 tablespoon horseradish
1 teaspoon Tabasco
1 teaspoon lemon juice

1 3 ounce package cream cheese
6 ripe black olives, chopped fine
1 clove garlic, minced
2 tablespoons chili sauce

Chop crabmeat. Combine with ingredients. Spread on crackers.
Makes four servings.

# CURRIED EGG SANDWICHES

12 hard cooked eggs finely chopped
½ cup mayonnaise
4 teaspoons curry powder
2 teaspoons Dijon mustard
1 ¼ loaves thin sliced whole wheat or rye 24 slices

3 tbs. finely chopped green onion
1 teaspoon salt
1 ¼ loaves thin sliced white bread—24 slices.

Combine eggs; mayonnaise; curry powder; mustard; onion and salt in a large bowl. Spread egg mixture on all the white slices top with the whole-wheat slices. Stack sandwiches in plastic bags refrigerate overnight or until serving time.

To serve; trim off crusts, cut each sandwich into fourths.

Makes 50 servings.

# DEVILED EGGS

1 dozen hard cooked eggs
3 ounces cream cheese
¼ cup mayonnaise
¾ teaspoon salt
¼ teaspoon pepper

¼ teaspoon powdered mustard
¼ teaspoon curry
½ teaspoon monosodium glutamate
½ teaspoon Worcestershire sauce

Cut each egg in half (lengthwise). Remove egg yolks and sieve or mash thoroughly. Reserve egg whites. Combine yolks with other ingredients to make a smooth mixture. Store separately if mixture is to be used at later date. Allow yolk mixture to soften to room temperature before use. Fill egg whites 1 to 2 hours before using with either a decorating bag or with a spoon or spatula.

Makes 24.

# FETTUCINI FLORENTINE

pound package of fettucini noodles
1-10 ounce package frozen chopped spinach
boiling water
2-tablespoons olive oil
1 small onion, thinly sliced
1 16 ounce container ricotta cheese (2 cups)

1 ½ cups milk
1 ½ teaspoons salt
2 tablespoons slivered cooked ham
grated Parmesan cheese
freshly ground black pepper

In a 6 quart saucepot prepare the fettucini as label directs, drain and return fettucini to saucepot, cover and keep warm. Meanwhile, place frozen chopped spinach in medium bowl; cover with boiling water and let stand 5 minutes to thaw. Drain spinach well, squeeze dry. In 10" skillet over medium heat, in hot olive oil, cook onion until tender, stirring occasionally. Add spinach and cook, stirring frequently, until mixture is heated through. To the fettucini in saucepot, add spinach mixture, ricotta cheese, milk and salt, over low heat. Heat through, gently tossing to mix well.

To serve, spoon fettucini mixture onto warm large platter, top with slivered ham. Pass grated Parmesan cheese and freshly ground black pepper, if you like, to sprinkle over each serving.

Makes 8 main-dish sized servings.

# GARLIC AND HERB CHEESE BALL

8 ounces cream cheese softened
3 ounces herb and garlic cheese at room temperature
Tabasco sauce

chopped onion
chopped nuts

Mix together cream cheese and herb/garlic cheese add a few dashes of Tabasco sauce and about 2-3 tablespoons of finely chopped onions. Refrigerate. When hard enough to handle roll into a ball or log shape (wrap in plastic wrap to make handling easier) depending on what you prefer. Roll in chopped nuts.

*This can be frozen ahead without the nuts. Freeze the nuts separately.* If you have frozen it defrost in the refrigerator and then roll in nuts. Use as soon as possible if you have frozen it. Otherwise it can be refrigerated for 2-3 weeks. *Nice for small parties.*

Makes 10 servings.

# HAE KUNG
# SHRIMP ROLLS

PASTRY:
1 cup sifted flour
½ teaspoon salt
¼ pound butter
3 tablespoons heavy cream
FILLING;
½ pound raw shrimp shelled & deveined

1 teaspoon salt
dash cayenne pepper
1 egg beaten
1 clove garlic minced
4 tablespoons melted butter
2 tablespoons cornstarch

PASTRY:

Sift the flour and salt into a bowl cut in the butter with a pastry blender or two knives. Stir in the cream with a fork until a ball of dough is formed. Wrap in waxed paper or foil and chill for 2 hours. Can substitute pastry with packaged prepared wrappers in frozen food section of market.

FILLING:

Mix all ingredients together. Roll out the dough very thin and cut into 3" circles. Place a heaping teaspoon of the filling on each turn in opposite ends then roll up like a sausage. Seal the edges well. Arrange on baking sheet and bake in a preheated 400 degree oven 15 minutes or until golden. Serve hot with Chinese duck sauce and hot mustard. Makes 12 rolls.

*This recipe can be doubled. It a good party finger food. Can use ground beef or chopped chicken, sautéed, instead of shrimp if you wish.*

# HAM STUFFED CHERRY TOMATOES

½ cup finely chopped cooked ham
¼ cup (1 ounce) Roquefort cheese crumbled
¼ cup dairy sour cream

¼ teaspoon lemon juice
dash of pepper
36 cherry tomatoes

Combine ham cheese sour cream lemon juice and pepper in a small bowl blend. Refrigerate.

With a sharp small knife. cut the tops of the tomatoes and scoop out the insides. Spoon about ½ teaspoon of ham and cheese mixture into each tomato. Try to find large cherry tomatoes, it makes them easier to stuff.

Makes 36 servings.


# ITALIAN SPINACH RICOTTA QUICHE

1 pre-baked pie shell
1 tablespoon butter
1 cup minced onion
1 package frozen chopped spinach thawed 10 oz.
1-15 ounce container Ricotta cheese

2 eggs
¾ teaspoon salt
¼ teaspoon pepper
¼ teaspoon ground nutmeg
3/8 cup grated Parmesan cheese

Preheat oven to 350 degrees.

Thoroughly drain spinach, using hands to squeeze out as much moisture as possible or wrap in cheesecloth and squeeze. Melt butter and fry onion until soft and translucent. Add spinach and stir until most of the moisture is gone. Remove from the heat. In a large bowl, add all the other ingredients in the spinach and stir until mixture looks like green and white marble. Pour into baked pie shell. Bake at 350 degrees for about 40 minutes or until top is golden and filling is set.

Makes 8 servings.

# QUICHE LORRAINE

PIE CRUST:
2 cups sifted flour
1 teaspoon salt
1 stick chilled butter, cut into ½" pieces
3 tablespoons vegetable shortening
QUICHE LORRAINE:
9-10" unbaked pastry shell
3 ounces Gruyere cheese, grated about ¾ cup

7 slices bacon
1 small onion, thinly sliced
4 eggs
1 ½ cups half and half
½ teaspoon salt
1/8 teaspoon pepper
pinch nutmeg
1 tablespoon butter

In large mixing bowl, blend flour, salt, butter, shortening with pastry blender. Blend until mixture looks mealy. The fat should be broken down into pieces the size of small peas. Sprinkle ice water, a tablespoon at a time, over the flour and toss with a fork. Go sparingly on the water as too much water makes the dough sticky and tough. Work mixture together with your hands until the ball of dough holds together. Briefly knead the ball with the heel of your hand, pressing hard down and away from you. Form it into a ball, wrap it in waxed paper and chill at least 1 hour. This can be done up to 2 days ahead.

Place the dough on a lightly floured board. If the dough is hard, knead it a little to soften. Roll with a rolling pin a few strokes to flatten. Roll lightly from center to edge away from you, lift dough, turn it and roll again until it is about ¼" thick and 2" larger all around that the pie pan.

To transfer dough to pie plate, gently and loosely roll about half the pastry circle onto a rolling pin. Carefully lift over the pie plate, center, then unroll. Fit the pastry into the pan, pressing gently. Do not stretch the dough—it can cause shrinkage in baking. Flute edges.

This can be partially baked ahead of time.

QUICHE:
Heat oven to 400 degrees F. Prick bottom of pie shell with a fork at ½" intervals. Line the shell with buttered foil, buttered side down, press well against sides, fill it with dried beans or raw rice to keep the empty shell from puffing as it bakes. Bake for 10 minutes, remove foil and beans and bake for 5 more minutes until it just begins to brown. Let shell cool.

Lower oven to 375 degrees. Coarsely grate the cheese on a flat grater over waxed paper. Fry the bacon until crisp and drain. Pour out all but 1 tablespoon of fat from skillet and in it cook onion rings until transparent. Crumble bacon and sprinkle it in a pie shell. Add onion and grated cheese.

In a bowl beat eggs, half and half and seasonings until well blended. Slowly pour custard into pastry shell. Leave ¼" at top to allow for puffing. Dot top of custard with bits of butter. Bake for about 30 minutes on upper rack of preheated oven until the top is puffed and brown and knife inserted in center comes out clean.

Makes approximately 8 servings.

## ONION QUICHE

1 tablespoon butter
3 large onions sliced
3 tablespoons flour
½ cup light cream

¾ teaspoon salt
¼ teaspoon pepper
2 eggs
1 unbaked 8" pie pastry

Preheat oven to 400 degrees. Melt butter in a skillet. Sauté onions until they are translucent sprinkle flour on onions and stir. Blend in light cream and seasonings and remove from flame. Beat eggs. Add eggs to the onions and pour mixture into pie pastry. Bake for 45 minutes at 400 degrees F.

Makes 8-10 servings.

## SENF GHERKINS
### Sweet Pickles
*Aunt Helen B.*

8 large cucumbers
2 cups sugar
1 tablespoon pickling spices

2 cups vinegar
2 tablespoons mustard seeds
pickling salt, per box directions

Combine the spices and put into cheesecloth and tie off. Combine sugar and vinegar in saucepan and bring to a boil. Drop in spices packet. Clean and cut cucumbers in stripes. Soak in pickling salt for one hour. Cook juice and spices together and when boiling add cucumber spears and bring up to a boil again. Put into clean, hot jars and close. Let cool and store in refrigerator until you use them.


## SHRIMP CATALINA

4 hard cooked eggs, sieved
3 tablespoons mayonnaise
1 tablespoon lemon juice
pinch of cayenne
¼ teaspoon pepper

1 pound cooked shrimp, diced fine
2 tablespoons chili sauce
1 teaspoon Worcestershire Sauce
½ teaspoon salt
cucumber and onion

Mash eggs with a fork or put through a sieve. Combine all ingredients until well mixed. Place in a 2 to 3 cup bowl. Refrigerate at least 2 hours. Unmold on a chilled platter. Garnish with paper thin slices of cucumber and sieved onion. Serve with thinly sliced rye bread.

Makes about 2 cups.

# STUFFED EGGS

6 hard-boiled eggs
1 tablespoon mayonnaise
dash French mustard

1 teaspoon fresh chives chopped
2 teaspoons minced parsley
salt and pepper to taste

Peel eggs and cut in half lengthwise. Lift out yolks and mash in small bowl; reserve whites. Mix yolks with mayonnaise, mustard, chives and parsley. Season with salt and pepper to taste. Fill each egg white with mixture.

*Variation: omit chives, parsley and mustard; add ¼ teaspoon paprika and sprinkle on top as garnish.*

Makes 12 servings.


# STUFFED MUSHROOMS
*Sara H.*

24 large fresh mushrooms 1 ½-2" in diameter
2 green onions sliced into 1 ½" strips
1 clove garlic minced
¼ cup butter
2/3 cup fine dry breadcrumbs

½ cup shredded cheddar (or diced proseiutto)
¼ cup shredded Provolone cheese
if Proseiutto is used
½ teaspoon Italian seasoning

*Note: for the Proseiutto Stuffed Mushrooms: omit shredded cheddar. Stir 1/3 cup chopped proseiutto ¼ cup shredded provolone and ½ teaspoon Italian seasoning into crumb mixture.*

Clean mushrooms remove stems reserve caps. Chop enough stems to make 1 cup. In medium saucepan cook the chopped stems green onions and garlic in butter until tender. Stir in breadcrumbs and cheese. Spoon crumb mixture into mushroom caps. Arrange stuffed mushrooms in a 15x10x1" baking pan. Bake in 425 degree F. oven 8 to 10 minutes or until heated through.

Makes 24 servings.

*Great for parties, usually the first to go. Can be prepared before and heated when you want to serve them.*

# STUFFED MUSHROOMS PARMIGIANA

12 large fresh mushrooms (appro. 24 ounces)
2 tablespoons butter
1 medium onion finely chopped
2 ounces pepperoni diced (1/2 cup)
¼ cup finely chopped green pepper
1 small clove of garlic minced
½ cup finely ground bread crumbs

3 tablespoons grated Parmesan cheese
1 tablespoon snipped parsley
½ teaspoon seasoned salt
¼ teaspoon dried oregano crushed
dash pepper
1/3 cup chicken broth

Wipe mushrooms clean remove stems set aside caps, finely chop stems and reserve. Melt butter in skillet, add onion, pepperoni, green pepper, garlic and chopped mushroom stems. Cook till vegetables are tender but not brown. Add bread crumbs, cheese, parsley, seasoned salt, oregano and pepper. Mix well. Stir in chicken broth. Spoon stuffing into mushroom caps rounding tops. Place caps in a shallow baking pan with about ¼ inch water covering bottom of pan. Bake uncovered at 350 degrees for about 25 minutes or until heated through.

Makes 12 stuffed mushrooms. (can be frozen for a few weeks).

# STUFFED HOT POTATOES

7 small yellow fleshed potatoes, like Yukon gold
1 cup broccoli florets
2 ounces Monterey jack cheese, shredded
3 tablespoons reduced fat plain yogurt
Chili powder, for sprinkling

2 tablespoons finely chopped pickled
jalapeno chili
salt and pepper
olive oil cooking spray

Place the potatoes in a large saucepan with enough water to cover. Bring to a boil, lower the heat and simmer until fork tender, about 25 minutes. Drain and let cool slightly.

Meanwhile, in a small saucepan of boiling water, cook the broccoli until crisp-tender, about 5 minutes, drain. Finely chop the broccoli and place in a medium bowl.

Slice 6 potatoes in half. Scoop out half of the flesh from each piece and add to the broccoli. Peel and finely chop the remaining potato and add to the mixture. Add the cheese, 2 tablespoons yogurt and the jalapeno, mash coarsely and season with salt and pepper.

Preheat the oven to 425 degrees. Arrange the potato halves cut side down on a baking sheet and lightly coat them with cooking spray, invert and season tops with salt and pepper. Divide the stuffing among the potato halves. Lightly coat with cooking spray and sprinkle with chili powder. Bake until golden about 20 minutes. Garnish with the remaining 1 tablespoon yogurt and more chili powder.
Makes 6 servings.

# SWEET AND SOUR PORK BALLS

3 pounds pork ground, lean

3 cans 5 3/4 oz. each—water chestnuts drained and finely chopped

1 ½ cups green onions finely chopped (2 to 3)

1 tbs. ginger, fresh or crystallized finely chopped

3 teaspoons salt

3 tablespoons soy sauce

4 eggs lightly beaten

cornstarch

SWEET & SOUR SAUCE

2 cups unsweetened pineapple juice

1 cup cider vinegar

¼ cup soy sauce

2/3 cup sugar

1 ½ cups beef broth

1/3 cup cornstarch

2/3 cup cold water

½ cup vegetable oil

Combine pork; water; chestnuts; green onions; ginger, salt, soy sauce and eggs in a large bowl. Mix well with hands; add breadcrumbs and mix just until combined. Chill mixture for 1 hour. Shape into ¾" to 1" in diameter balls. Roll the balls in cornstarch to coat lightly. Brown meatballs about ¼ at a time, on all sides in hot oil, in large skillet. Remove balls to a roasting pan as they brown. Cover loosely with foil. Bake in moderate oven (350 degrees) for 15-20 minutes or until cooked through. To serve place in chafing dish and stir in enough sauce to coat balls.

*Serve with sweet and sour sauce. Makes 50 servings.*

*To freeze ahead: freeze meatballs in a single layer on a jellyroll pan or cookie sheet, when frozen solid place in plastic bags and seal.*

**To reheat:** *place in large roasting pan; heat covered in hot oven (350-375 degrees) for 30 minutes or piping hot.*

*NOTE: for 12 servings: use 1 pound pork 1 can water chestnuts ½ cup onion 1 teaspoon ginger ½ teaspoon salt 2 teaspoons soy sauce, 1 egg and 1/3 cup bread crumbs. Follow directions.*

*SWEET AND SOUR SAUCE* (MAKES 6 CUPS): Combine pineapple juice, vinegar, soy sauce sugar, beef broth and ginger in a large saucepan bring to a boil.

Mix cornstarch with water, add to boiling mixture, stirring constantly. Continue cooking and stirring until sauce is thickened and clear, 1 minute.

**For 12 servings:** use 1 6 ounce can pineapple juice, ¼ cup vinegar, 1 tablespoon soy sauce, 2 ½ tablespoons sugar 1/3 cup beef broth 2 teaspoons ginger, 1 ½ tablespoons cornstarch and 3 tablespoons water.

*MAKE AHEAD NOTE:*

Sauce keeps covered in refrigerator up to 1 week. Reheat in heavy saucepan over low heat until bubbly hot.

# SWEET AND TANGY BARBECUED SPARERIBS

4 lbs. pork spareribs cut into serving size pieces
1 ½ teaspoons salt
¼ cup honey
2 tablespoons Worcestershire sauce

2 tablespoons soy sauce
2 tablespoons catsup
2 tablespoons water

Sprinkle both sides of the ribs with salt. Place on a rack in a baking pan. Bake in a preheated very hot oven (450 degrees F) for 20 minutes, turning once. Reduce oven heat to 350 degrees. Cook until almost tender, about 20 minutes longer. To prepare barbecue sauce combine remaining ingredients; blend well. Brush over ribs, cook 30 minutes longer, brushing and turning frequently.

Makes 10 servings.


# TWO MINUTE SHRIMP
## In a chafing dish

1 tablespoon butter
1 shallot, diced fine, or 2 tbs. minced onion
1 lb. medium shrimp, cooked & cleaned (22-26 shrimp)
½ cup heavy sweet cream
½ teaspoon tomato paste
¼ cup sherry

¼ teaspoon salt
1/8 teaspoon pepper

1 tablespoon chopped parsley
1 tablespoon chopped chives

Place butter in blazer pan, directly on flame. Sauté shallots in butter for 30 seconds. Add shrimp, cream, tomato paste, salt and pepper. Allow cream to cook down for 1 minute, then add sherry. Sprinkle parsley and chives over all. Stir for 30 seconds and serve on toast points or pastry shells.

Serves 6.

# VEGETABLES AND VEGETARIAN DISHES

# ACORN SQUASH

1 medium acorn squash, halved and seeded          2 tablespoons brown sugar
1 tablespoon butter

Preheat oven to 350 degrees F.
Turn acorn squash upside down onto a cookie sheet. Bake in a 350 degrees F. oven until it begins to soften, approximately 30 to 45 minutes. Remove squash from the oven and turn onto a plate so that the flesh is facing upwards. Place butter and brown sugar into the squash, and place remaining squash over the other piece. Place squash in a baking dish (so the squash won't slide around too much) while baking. Place squash in the 350 degrees F. oven and bake another 30 minutes.

# STUFFED ARTICHOKE HEARTS

12 artichoke hearts                          ¼ cup butter
2 cups boiled chicken, shredded              ¼ cup flour
grated Parmesan cheese                       2 cups light cream
½ pound melted butter                        1 tablespoon salt
SAUCE:                                       ¼ teaspoon pepper

Cook artichoke hearts for about 15 minutes and drain. Blot them dry and continue cooking till tender by steaming in butter. Prepare cream sauce by melting ¼ cup butter in saucepan or double boiler. Remove from heat and stir in ¼ cup flour. Return to flame and add cream gradually, stirring constantly as the mixture thickens. Cook about 3 minutes more and add seasoning. Use half the cream sauce and mix with boiled chicken. When the artichokes are tender, stuff them with chicken mixture. Arrange the hearts on a buttered pan and cover with balance of cream sauce. Sprinkle with grated Parmesan cheese and melted butter and broil in oven for a few minutes.
Serve immediately.

Makes 6 servings.

# PAN FRIED ASPARAGUS

1 ¼ cups butter
2 tablespoons olive oil
1 teaspoon coarse salt

¼ teaspoon ground black pepper
3 cloves garlic, minced
½ pound fresh asparagus spears, trimmed

Melt butter in a skillet over medium-high heat. Stir in the olive oil, salt, and pepper. Cook garlic in butter for a minute, but do not brown. Add asparagus, and cook for 10 minutes, turning asparagus to ensure even cooking.

Makes 4 servings.

# BAKED BEANS

1 pound dried beans, cooked according to package directions
¼ cup chopped onion
¼ pound finely diced salt pork
¾ cup molasses

½ cup ketchup
1 teaspoon dry mustard
1 teaspoon salt
1 teaspoon Worcestershire Sauce

Mix all ingredients together. Bake 4 to 5 hours at about 350 degrees F. Serve hot. Makes 6 servings.

# BALSAMIC GLAZED PEARL ONIONS

2 ½-3 pounds pearl onion                    1 cup balsamic vinegar
2 tablespoons extra virgin olive oil        ½ cup water

Blanch onions in boiling water for 3 minutes and then drain, cool and peel them. Heat oil over moderately high heat in a large heavy skillet until hot but not smoking. Add onions and sauté until lightly browned (about 5 minutes). Reduce heat and pour balsamic vinegar and water over the onions. Simmer, stirring occasionally, until onions are tender (about 15 minutes). Using a slotted spoon, transfer onions to a platter.

Increase heat slightly and simmer until liquid is reduced to about ½ cup and is thick and syrupy. Spoon over onions. Best served at room temperature.

*Glazed onions can be made up to 2 days in advance. After removing onions from mixture, place onions and liquid in separate, covered containers and refrigerate. To serve, warm the onions in the liquid and simmer until liquid is reduced to ½ cup and is thick and syrupy. Spoon over onions and serve.*

# BOHNEN MIT KARTOFFEIN
## Green Beans with Potatoes

Boiling water
4 medium potatoes, pared, sliced
2 teaspoons salt
1 package frozen regular cut green beans
4 slices bacon, diced

¼ teaspoon dried thyme
1 ¾ teaspoons salt
¼ teaspoon pepper
1 ½ tablespoons vinegar

About 45 minutes before serving:
Cook potatoes with 2 teaspoons salt in boiling water to cover, cover saucepan. Cook until almost tender. Then lay block of beans on top of potatoes; cover and cook all till tender, drain. Meanwhile in a small skillet, sauté bacon until crisp; remove bacon, crumb into bits, retain bacon fat. For sauce; combine flour, thyme, salt and pepper.

Then stir this into hot bacon drippings; cook till thickened, slightly browned. Add vinegar; stir smooth.

Pour sauce over vegetables. Then sprinkle with bacon, and toss all with two forks. Serve hot, with pot roast or Rouladen.

Makes 4 to 5 servings.

*Variation: Instead of potatoes make this green beans recipe with Spatzle. Cook Spatzle according to the directions for the Spatzle and then follow the directions for this recipe. When using Spatzle it is an accent to the beans not to be in equal amounts as the potatoes would be.*

# SHREDDED BRUSSEL SPROUTS

½ pound sliced bacon
¼ cup butter
2/3 cup pine nuts
2 pounds Brussel Sprouts cored and shredded

3 green onions, minced
½ teaspoon seasoned salt
pepper to taste

Place bacon in a large, deep skillet. Cook over medium-high heat until crisp. Drain, reserving 2 tablespoons grease, crumble bacon and set aside.

In the same skillet, melt butter in with reserved bacon grease over medium heat. Add pine nuts and cook, stirring until browned. Add Brussel sprouts and green onions to the pan and season with seasoned salt and pepper. Cook over medium heat until sprouts are wilted and tender, 10 to 15 minutes.

Stir in crumbled bacon just before serving.

Makes approximately 8 servings.

# SPICED CREAMED BRUSSEL SPROUTS

2 packages frozen Brussel sprouts, cooked
¼ teaspoon marjoram
1/8 teaspoon black pepper

2 cups medium white sauce (see sauces)
¼ teaspoon thyme

Cook and drain Brussel sprouts. Heat 2 cups of medium white sauce and stir in marjoram, thyme and pepper. Gently stir in Brussel sprouts.

Serves 6 to 8 servings.

*Substitution: use 2 pounds of fresh Brussel sprouts, cored and washed. Then follow recipe directions.*

# CABBAGE AND POTATOES

4-5 large all-purpose potatoes
Salt, to taste
¼ cup olive oil, divided
1 medium head green cabbage (2 pounds), halved and cored, sliced thinly

freshly ground black pepper to taste
1 large egg, lightly beaten
1 tablespoon finely snipped chives or 2 scallions trimmed and sliced

Cook potatoes until tender, about 20-25 minutes, salt to taste. Drain well and puree in food processor. Transfer into large bowl. In large skillet, heat ½ of the oil. Add cabbage and season with salt and pepper.

Cook over medium-high heat, stirring often. Add cabbage, egg, chives or scallions, and salt and pepper to the potatoes. Mix well to blend and divide into 16 equal portions. Use your dampened hands to form thick patties.

In a large skillet over medium-high heat, heat remaining oil. Add patties and cook, turning once or twice, until golden brown on both sides, 7-10 minutes. Drain on paper towels and season with salt and pepper before serving. Serve hot.

Can be served as a side dish

# GLAZED CARROTS

2 pounds carrots
¼ cup molasses

¼ cup water

Pare carrots. Cut in half or quarters lengthwise (depending on size). In a large skillet combine carrots, molasses and water. Heat to boiling. Reduce heat, cover tightly and simmer 20-25 minutes.

Shake pan frequently during cooking and check once or twice that water has not boiled away. Carrots should be fork tender.

Makes 6 servings.

# TANGY CARROTS

2-16 ounce cans, small sliced carrots
1 tablespoon cornstarch
1 tablespoon orange flavored instant breakfast
drink (powder)

¼ teaspoon salt
several dashes nutmeg
2 tablespoons butter
chopped parsley

Drain carrots, reserving liquid. If necessary add water to liquid to make ¾ cup. In saucepan, blend cornstarch with instant breakfast drink powder, salt and nutmeg. Stir in the reserved liquid. Bring to boiling, stirring constantly. Reduce heat; cook and stir till mixture thickens. Add butter and carrots; heat through. Before serving, sprinkle with parsley.

Makes 6-8 servings.

# CELERY IN BUTTER

1 large bunch of celery
1 teaspoon salt
dash of pepper

6 tablespoons butter
½ cup minced onion (1 medium)
1 tablespoon chopped parsley

Wash and trim celery. Cut into 2"x1/2" pieces. Place in saucepan with enough water to just cover. Add salt and pepper. Cover, bring to boiling. Simmer about 20 minutes or until celery is just tender. Drain well. Melt butter in saucepan. Add onions and celery. Cover, cook over low heat for 3 to 4 minutes, stirring occasionally. Arrange in serving dish, sprinkle with parsley.

Makes 4 servings.

*The cooked celery can be added to other vegetables besides being served separately. I like it with cherry tomatoes.*

# EGGPLANT AND CHEESE
## Greek Style

4 tablespoons oil
1 large eggplant, sliced ½" slices. lengthwise
1 cup chopped onion
1 clove garlic, crushed
1 can (1 pound) tomatoes, cut up
3 tablespoons parsley

¾ teaspoon salt
1/8 teaspoon pepper
1/8 teaspoon cinnamon
1 ½ cups cottage cheese
½ cup grated Parmesan cheese
1 egg

In large skillet, using about 1 teaspoon of oil at a time, lightly brown eggplant, adding more oil as necessary (total 3 tablespoons). Remove and drain on paper towels. Add remaining 1 tablespoon oil and sauté onion and garlic until onion is tender. Add tomatoes, parsley, salt, pepper and cinnamon. Simmer, uncovered, 5 minutes.

Spread half the tomato mixture in 12x8x2" baking dish. Mix cottage cheese, ¼ cup Parmesan and the egg Spread over tomato mixture, arrange eggplant, slightly overlapping, on cheese mixture. Sprinkle with 2 tablespoons Parmesan. Top with remaining 2 tablespoons Parmesan.

Bake uncovered in 375 degree oven 35-40 minutes or until eggplant is tender. Good with warm pita bread and tossed salad.

Makes 4 servings.

# EGGPLANT PARMESAN WITH MARINARA SAUCE

1 eggplant, peeled and sliced thinly, lengthwise
1 egg, beaten
salt and pepper, to taste
garlic powder, to taste
finely grated flavored breadcrumbs
SAUCE:
1 can tomato sauce, 8 ounce

1 can tomatoes puree (1 ½ pounds)
oil
2 onions
1 large clove garlic
salt & pepper to taste
mozzarella cheese, grated
grated Parmesan cheese

Dip slices of eggplant in a mixture of egg, salt, pepper, and garlic powder and then into breadcrumbs mixed with the grated Parmesan cheese. Fry in hot pan with oil until browned.

SAUCE: Sauté cut up onion in oil till clear, then brown minced garlic in oil, add tomato sauce, the tomatoes (pureed in blender if crushed is only available). Put in salt and pepper to taste and mix in a good tablespoon oregano, cook for ½ hour. Take a baking dish, put some sauce in the bottom and then layer eggplant, sauce, mozzarella cheese, Parmesan cheese, then repeat until finished, ending with sauce.
Bake at 300 degrees F. for ½ hour or until bubbly.

*Even my Dad, who hated eggplant loved this dish. Of course, I never did tell him it was eggplant!*

Makes 4 servings.

# ROASTED GARLIC BULBS

garlic bulbs
salt and pepper to taste

extra virgin olive oil

Heat oven to 350 degrees F. Cut ¼ to ½" off top of garlic bulb to expose cloves. Remove most of outer skin from bulb, leaving bulb intact and cloves unpeeled. Place bulb, cut side up, on 8" piece of aluminum foil. Drizzle with 1 teaspoon olive oil; sprinkle lightly with salt and pepper. Wrap in foil. Bake for 45 to 55 minutes or until softened. Cool slightly. Separate cloves; press cloves slightly to squeeze out soften garlic. Use roasted garlic in recipes or spread on French bread. (parchment paper can be used instead of foil, reduce baking time).

# GREEN BEANS WITH HERBS

½ teaspoon chevil leaves
2 tablespoons butter
1 pound fresh green beans

1 teaspoon tarragon leaves
mayonnaise

Cook green beans, drain and add chrvil and tarragon and butter. Mix well and add mayonnaise to taste.


# FETTUCINI FLORENTINE

1 package fettuccini noodles (12 ounces)
1 package frozen chopped spinach (10 oz)
boiling water
3 tablespoons olive oil
1 small onion, thinly sliced
1 container ricotta cheese, 16 ounces

1 ½ cups milk
1 ½ teaspoons salt
2 tablespoons slivered cooked ham
grated Parmesan cheese
freshly ground black pepper

In 6 quart saucepot, prepare noodles per label directions, drain.

Return noodles to saucepot, cover to keep warm. Meanwhile place frozen chopped spinach in medium bowl; cover with boiling water and let stand 5 minutes to thaw. Drain spinach well, squeeze dry. In a 10" skillet over medium heat, in hot olive oil, cook onion until tender, stirring occasionally. Add spinach and cook, stirring frequently, until mixture is heated through.

To fettucini in saucepot, add spinach mixture, ricotta cheese, milk and salt; over low heat, heat through, gently tossing to mix well. To serve, spoon fettuccini mixture onto warm platter; top with slivered ham. Serve with grated Parmesan cheese and freshly ground black pepper on side.
Makes 8 servings.

# BROILED MUSHROOMS

¾ teaspoon oregano leaves
1/8 teaspoon black pepper
1 pound mushrooms

1/8 teaspoon garlic powder
¼ cup vegetable oil (or olive oil)

Remove any dirt from mushrooms and wipe with paper toweling. Arrange on broiler tray. Combine ingredients and brush on mushrooms, broil and brush again half way through broiling Broil till tender.


# HERBED MUSHROOMS WITH WHITE WINE

1 tablespoon olive oil
1 ½ pounds fresh mushrooms
1 teaspoon Italian seasoning
¼ cup dry white wine

2 cloves garlic, minced
salt and pepper to taste
2 tablespoons chopped fresh chives

Heat the oil in a skillet over medium heat. Place mushrooms in the skillet, season with Italian seasonings, and cook 10 minutes, stirring frequently. Mix the wine and garlic into the skillet, and continue cooking until most of the wine has evaporated. Season with salt and pepper and sprinkle with chives. Continue cooking 1 minute.

Makes approximately 6 servings.

# MARINATED MUSHROOMS

2 ½ pounds small mushrooms-very fresh, not soft
2 teaspoons salt
FOR MARINATE:
3 crushed cloves of garlic
1 teaspoon oregano

½ cup olive oil
½ teaspoon salt
juice of one lemon
bay leaf

Wash and trim mushrooms, toss with salt. Bring enough water to a boil to cover mushrooms. Place mushrooms in boiling water and cook for 15 minutes. Combine marinate ingredients in earthenware, enamel or stainless steel bowl (don't use plastic). Place mushrooms in marinate and refrigerate for 48 hours. Serve chilled. Makes 1 quart.


# MUSHROOMS IN CREAM SAUCE

1 pound fresh mushrooms, trimmed
½ stick unsalted butter
1 cup heavy cream

1 tbs. fresh parsley, finely chopped
salt & white pepper to taste

Cut mushrooms into quarters. In a large skillet over medium-high heat, melt the butter. Add mushrooms and cook, stirring often, until lightly browned and softened, about 5 minutes. Pour in cream, increase the heat to high and boil rapidly until slightly thickened, 3-5 minutes. Stir in parsley, season with salt and pepper and serve hot.

Makes approximately 4 servings.

# SAUTEED MUSHROOMS AND ONIONS
*Eleanor Hinsch*

1 package of fresh mushrooms, 8 ounces
½ stick butter (4 tablespoons)
salt and pepper to taste

1 medium onion
flour for thickening

Slice onion in thin slices, wipe off mushrooms with a paper towel and slice them thinly. Put butter into sauté pan and heat on medium-high heat. When hot, add the onion slices and mushroom slices. Sauté until mushrooms are golden brown and onions are opaque. Salt and Pepper to taste, then slowly add flour, stirring constantly, until thickened. Serve while hot.

Makes approximately 4-6 servings.

*My son loves this so I had to include it in this book. I know its a simple recipe but it tastes great on burgers, steaks, etc. I love it over meatloaf also.*

# STUFFED MUSHROOMS PARMESAN

1 pound fresh mushrooms (approx. 12 large)
2 tablespoons butter
1 clove garlic, chopped finely
2 tablespoons finely chopped onion
3 tablespoons grated Parmesan cheese
½ cup dry breadcrumbs

1 tablespoon olive oil
1 tablespoon finely chopped parsley
pinch marjoram or oregano
salt and pepper to taste
1 tablespoon olive oil

Remove stems from mushrooms, cut off dried end of stems and reserve caps for stuffing. Chop the stems. In a skillet, heat the butter and sauté the garlic and onion until onion is just tender. Add the chopped mushroom stems and cook over low heat until the mushroom juices are exuded. Raise the heat and cook until liquid is evaporated. In mixing bowl, combine the cooked, chopped mushroom stems with the breadcrumbs, cheese, 1 tablespoon olive oil, parsley and oregano.

Season to taste with salt and pepper. Stuff the mushrooms with the mixture and arrange stuffed caps on a baking sheet or in baking pan. Brush tops with remaining 1 tablespoon olive oil. Bake in preheated 350 degree F. oven about 20 to 35 minutes. To prepare ahead, bake for half the time, cool to room temperature then freeze or store in refrigerator (for up to 1 day) then return to room temperature and cook about 25 minutes or until heated through.

Makes 6 servings.

# BEER FRIED ONION RINGS

1 1/3 cups all-purpose flour
1 ½ cups beer, active or flat, warm or cold

1 quart vegetable oil
3 very large yellow or Bermuda onions

Combine flour and beer in a large bowl and blend thoroughly, using a rotary beater. Cover, allow batter to stand at room temperature for at least 3 hours.

20 minutes before the batter is ready, preheat over to 200 degrees. Place layers of paper toweling on a jelly roll pan. Carefully peal the papery skin from the onions so that you do not cut into the outside onion layer. Cut onions into ¼" thick slices. Separate the slices into rings. Pour enough oil into a 10" skillet to come 2" up the sides of the pan. Heat to 375 degrees on a deep fat frying thermometer.

Drop a few onion rings into the batter with metal tongs, then carefully place them in the hot fat. Fry the rings, turning them once until all the onion rings have been fried golden color. Transfer to the paper lined jellyroll pan. To keep warm, place them on the middle rack of the preheated oven until all the onion rings have been fried.

# CREAMED ONIONS

2 pounds small white onions (about 18)
3 tablespoons butter
3 tablespoons flour
salt and white pepper, to taste

1 ½ cups milk
1/3 cup chopped parsley
¼ teaspoon paprika

To prevent weeping, cook the onions in their skins until tender, 20 minutes or longer. Drain and peel. In a saucepan melt the butter, add the flour and stir with a wire whisk, until blended. Meanwhile, bring the milk to a boil and add all at once to the butter-flour mixture, stirring vigorously with the whisk until the sauce is smooth and thickened. Add the sauce to the onions and reheat. Sprinkle with the parsley and paprika.

*Variations: add ½ cup grated sharp cheddar cheese in the sauce before adding the onions.*
*Add mushrooms: sauté ½ pounds sliced mushrooms in butter and add to the*
*sauce with the onions. Use 1 teaspoon of thyme instead of paprika.*

# CREAMED PEARL ONIONS AND PEAS

2 packages pearl onions, (10 ounces each)
3 tablespoons butter
3 tablespoons all-purpose flour
½ teaspoon caraway seeds, crushed

½ teaspoon salt
¼ teaspoon ground black pepper
2 ¼ cups milk
2 packages frozen peas, thawed
(10 ounces each)

In a 10" skillet, heat 1 inch water to boiling over high heat. Add onions, heat to boiling, reduce heat to low, cover and simmer 10 to 15 minutes until onions are tender; drain onions. When cool enough to handle; peel onions, leaving a little of the root ends to help onions to hold their shape during cooking.

Meanwhile, in a 2 quart saucepan, melt butter over medium heat. Stir in flour, caraway seeds, salt and pepper until blended and cook 2 minutes, stirring constantly. Gradually stir in milk and cook, stirring constantly, until sauce thickens and boils. Return onions to skillet. Add peas and sauce and cook, stirring, until heated through.

Makes 10 servings.


# FRENCH FRIES—QUICK AND EASY

2-3 Yukon Gold potatoes, sliced ¼" wide,
unpeeled to resemble French fries

6 cups peanut oil, room temperature

Square sides on potatoes and cut in ¼" slices. In a 10 cup Dutch oven, add peanut oil and potatoes and bring to a boil. (about 5 minutes). At full boil set time for 15 minutes, DO NOT STIR, after 15 minutes gently stir nudging stuck fries off of bottom of pot. Boil additional 6 to 8 minutes. Remove from oil immediately, salt and serve.

# FRENCH FRIED ONION RINGS

1 ½ cups all-purpose flour
3 very large yellow or Bermuda onions
1 quart vegetable oil

1 ½ cups beer, active or flat at
room temperature

Combine flour and beer in a large bowl and blend thoroughly using a rotary beater. Cover, allow batter to stand at room temperature for at least 3 hours.
20 minutes before the batter is ready, preheat oven to 200 degrees. Place layers of paper toweling on a jelly-roll pan. Carefully peel the papery skins from the onions so that you do not cut into the outside onion layer. Cut onions into ¼" thick slices. Separate the slices into rings.

Pour enough oil into a 10" skillet to come to 2" up the sides of the pan. Heat to 375 degrees on a deep-fat frying thermometer.

Dip a few onion rings into the batter with metal tongs, carefully place them in the hot fat. Fry rings, turning them once or twice until they are an even, delicate golden color. Transfer to the paper-lined jelly roll pan. To keep warm, place them on the middle shelf of the preheated oven until all the onion rings have been fried.

# FRENCH FRIED ONIONS

1 1/3 cups all-purpose flour or breadcrumbs
1 can evaporated milk
salt to taste

1 quart vegetable oil
3 very large yellow or Bermuda onions

Peel and cut onions in ¼" slices. Separate into circles. Salt; dip into evaporated milk, undiluted, then into flour or breadcrumbs. Fry in hot fat (190 degrees F.), 4 to 5 minutes. Shake onto a sheet or paper to absorb any fat.

Any vegetable may be fried in this way.

# HERBED CREAMED ONIONS

2/5 teaspoon sage leaves
2 cups medium white sauce (see sauces)

1/8 teaspoon black pepper
1 pound small white onions
or 2-1 pound cans

Add sage and pepper to white sauce. Peel and cook onions in water, drain well. Add heated white sauce and stir together. Serve while warm.


# HERBED PEAS

½ teaspoon basil leaves
6 portions of peas or 2 boxes frozen

1/8 teaspoon black pepper

Cook peas and drain well. Add basil and pepper, mix gently.


# PEAS AND CARROTS IN THYME SAUCE

1 tablespoon butter
1 small onion, chopped
¼ teaspoon dried thyme leaves, crushed
1 can cream of celery soup (10.75 ounces)

1/3 cup milk
large dash of pepper
1 cup carrots, cut into 2" julienne strips
1 cup peas or 1 package frozen peas

In a 2 quart saucepan over medium heat, in hot butter, cook onion and thyme, until onion is tender, stirring occasionally. Stir in soup, milk and pepper. Add peas and carrots. Heat to boiling. Reduce to low heat. Cover, simmer 8 minutes or until vegetables are tender, stirring occasionally.

Makes 3-4 servings.

# BAKED POTATOES

Idaho Potatoes, one per person                          butter
sour cream, optional

Preheat oven to 425 degrees.
Wash potatoes, scrub lightly with brush, pat dry. Lightly piece skins with sharp fork or a paring knife. 2-3 pricks per potato. If you wish you can loosely wrap them in aluminum foil. When the oven is heated, put potatoes onto baking rack and bake for approximately one hour or until you can lightly squeeze the potato and the potato has a give, or if the potato is fork tender. Serve with butter or sour cream.

Each potato is one serving.


# TWICE BAKED POTATOES

**Follow recipe for baked potatoes above**
When potatoes are fully cooked. Remove from oven and cut horizontally. Remove all the potato from the skin, leaving approximately ¼" of potato in the skin. Whip the potatoes with milk and butter until fluffy. Fill the potato skins until peaked. Put on tray and put into oven preheated at 425 degrees for about 15 minutes, or until golden. Serve with gravy, butter, or favorite topping.


# BAKED POTATO WEDGES

2 teaspoons olive oil                                    ½ cup melted butter
5 large russet potatoes, peeled & cut into wedges        1 cup seasoned bread crumbs

Preheat oven to 350 degrees F. Grease a baking sheet with olive oil. Brush potato wedges with butter, and roll in breadcrumbs. Place wedges on prepared baking sheet. Bake in preheated oven for 20 minutes. Remove from oven and turn wedges; cook for 10 to 15 minutes, or until tender.

# BOILED POTATOES

cold water                                                          potatoes: see notes below
salt

**Note:** Certain types of potatoes are more starchy than others. Idaho potatoes have a high starch content, red potatoes have a low starch content. What it means is that a starchy potato takes longer to boil or bake or even fry, whereas a low starch content takes less time to cook.

For each person you want to give a boiled potato to you have 1 potato. So if you have 5 people that would be 5 potatoes (plus one for the pot!) to 6 potatoes.

Start by peeling and cutting potatoes in half or quarters, depending on size of potatoes. Unless you wish to serve each potato whole, the cut potatoes cook faster. Put potatoes into cold, salted water in pot. Make sure the water covers the potatoes.

Bring up to a boil on high heat and continue boiling until potatoes are fork tender. Remove from heat and drain off water. Serve as is or use for mashed potatoes or stuffed baked potatoes.


# ITALIAN POTATO WEDGES

1 teaspoon vegetable oil                         1 medium unpeeled potato, cut
¼ teaspoon Italian seasoning                   into 8 wedges lengthwise
¼ teaspoon paprika                                 1 tablespoon Parmesan cheese
1/8 teaspoon salt

On dinner plate, combine oil, Italian seasoning, paprika and salt. Add potato wedges, turning to coat with mixture, arrange in spokes like tire spokes, cut side down. Cook, covered with waxed paper, on high in microwave for 4-5 minutes, until potatoes are tender, rotate each wedge halfway through cooking. Sprinkle with Parmesan cheese. Let stand for 3 minutes. If you like serve with ketchup or tomato sauce.

Makes 1 serving.

# POTATO DUMPLINGS
## Kartoffelknodel or Klosse

1 ½ pounds medium potatoes baked or boiled, in skins, a day ahead
2 eggs
1 cup flour

3 ½ pounds medium potatoes
½ teaspoon salt
1/8 teaspoon pepper
¼ teaspoon nutmeg

Peel and mash cooked potatoes. Peel raw (3 ½ pounds) potatoes and grate, put in cheesecloth and ring out as much fluid as possible. Mix potatoes together and add eggs, flour and seasonings, and mix well. Form into balls about 3" in diameter and drop carefully into a pot of boiling, salted water. Allow dumplings to rise to the surface, turn heat down, cover pot and simmer for 20 minutes. Remove with slotted spoon onto a warm serving dish.

Makes approximately 5 servings.

*The water used to boil dumplings makes a good start for gravy.*


# GARLIC MASHED POTATOES

6 medium potatoes peeled, cut into 1/8 slices
1 teaspoon salt
½ cup warm milk

6 tablespoons butter
1 teaspoon roasted garlic
salt and pepper to taste

Place potatoes in 4 quart saucepan or Dutch oven. Add enough water to cover, add 1 teaspoon salt, bring to a boil over high heat (7 to 9 minutes). Reduce heat to medium. Cook until potatoes are fork tender (15 to 18 minutes) drain. Place potatoes in large mixing bowl. Add milk, butter and garlic, beat at medium speed until smooth, (2-3 minutes). Season with salt and pepper. Can be made without garlic if desired.

Makes 6 servings.

# GARLIC MASHED POTATOES WITH CHEESE
*Sara H.*

3 pounds unpeeled red potatoes, quartered
½ pound butter, room temperature
3 ounces Romano cheese, grated

3 tablespoons chopped garlic
1 ½ teaspoon salt
1 ½ teaspoons dried oregano

Bring a large pot of salted water to a boil. Add potatoes and cook until tender but still firm, about 45 minutes; drain. Stir in butter, cheese, garlic, salt and oregano. Mash with a potato masher or with an electric mixer.

Approximately 6 servings.

*My younger daughter loves making these for every occasion. Amazingly I actually like them too.*


# QUICK AND EASY MASHED POTATOES

6 russet potatoes, peeled and quartered
salted water for boiling potatoes

3-4 tablespoons butter
¼-½ cups milk or cream

Bring water and potatoes in a large pot to a boil. Boil until fork tender, about 30-45 minutes. Drain water from pot and stir in butter and ¼ cup milk or cream. Using either an electric mixer or potato masher, beat potatoes until smooth. If creamier potatoes are desired add more milk or cream.

Serves 6.

# SCALLOPED POTATOES

2 pounds boiling potatoes (5-6 cups) sliced
1 lg clove of garlic, peeled; crushed, chopped finely
2 cups milk
1 ½ cups heavy cream

¾ teaspoon salt (approximately)
½ tsp. freshly ground white pepper
1 tablespoon butter
½ cup grated Swiss cheese @ 2 oz.

Peel the potatoes, wash and dry thoroughly. Slice fairly thin with a slicer or sharp knife. At this point, do not soak the potatoes in water or you will lose the starch needed for the dish to be smooth. Combine the potato slices with the garlic, milk, cream, salt and pepper in a large heavy saucepan.

Bring to a boil over medium heat, stirring with a wooden spoon to prevent scorching (and the mixture can scorch very easily). As the liquid reaches a higher temperature, the mixture should begin to thicken slightly. When the mixture has thickened a bit, butter a shallow baking dish (about 1 ½" deep) and pour in the potato mixture. Sprinkle with cheese all over the top of the dish and then place on a cookie sheet (both to catch spills and to allow a more even transfer of heat) and bake in a preheated 400 degree F. oven for about 1 hour, until the potatoes are nicely browned and tender when pierced with the point of a paring knife.

Allow the dish to rest for 15 to 20 minutes before you serve it.
Makes about 8 servings.


# SWEDISH POTATOES

9 oval potatoes, about 3" long, each
2 tablespoons melted butter

salt and pepper to taste

Pare the potatoes and trim them with a knife so they are evenly shaped ovals. Cut potatoes crosswise at 1/8" intervals, slicing only ¾ of the way through. Drop into cold water to prevent discoloration. Before roasting, dry potatoes, roll in melted butter, sprinkle with salt and pepper. Roast in same pan with meat. Bake at 450 degrees for 20 minutes and then at 325 degrees for 1 hour.

Brush potatoes with meat dripping every 15 minutes. Roast potatoes until knife penetrates to the center easily and the outsides are nicely browned (approximately 1 ½ hours). Makes 9 servings.

# WARM POTATO AND GREEN BEAN TOSS

3 ½ cups quartered small red potatoes in skins
1 package frozen cut green beans thawed & drained
16 ounce size
1/3 cup oil
¼ cup cider vinegar

1 teaspoon sugar
1 teaspoon dried tarragon leaves
¼ teaspoon salt
1/8 teaspoon pepper

Place potatoes in large saucepan; add water to cover. Bring to a boil over high heat. Reduce heat to low; cover and cook 12 to 16 minutes or until potatoes are tender. Add green beans, cook 3-5 minutes or until green beans are warm. Drain well. Place in serving bowl.

Meanwhile, in small jar with tight fitting lid combine remaining ingredients; shake well, pour over potatoes and green beans; toss gently, serve immediately.

Makes 12 ½ cup servings.

# BAKED SWEET POTATOES

4 medium sweet potatoes (about 2 ½ pounds) boiled or baked until tender, skinned & sliced
4 cups melted butter
¼ cup brown sugar, packed

1 tablespoon grated orange rind
¼ cup orange juice
¼ cup bourbon (optional)
¼ cup finely chopped, preserved ginger

Preheat oven to 375 degrees F. Place the potato slices in a buttered baking dish. Combine the remaining ingredients and pour over the potatoes. Bake 15 minutes or until bubbly-hot.

# CANDIED SWEET POTATOES

4 large sweet potatoes, scrubbed
4 tablespoons butter, melted
ground cinnamon

1 cup firmly packed dark brown sugar
1 teaspoon grated orange zest
½ cup orange juice

Preheat oven to 250 degrees F.
In a large pot, place the potatoes in boiling water to cover and cook them until they are tender when pierced with the tip or a sharp knife, 25 to 30 minutes.

Drain potatoes. When they are cool enough to handle, peel and thinly slice them.

In a 1 to 2 quart buttered casserole, layer about 1/3 of the potatoes, drizzle them with about 1/3 of the butter and sprinkle them with some cinnamon and 1/3 of the sugar. Repeat this procedure twice. Sprinkle the top with the orange zest, and pour the orange juice over all.

Bake the casserole until the potatoes are well candied and the juices are bubbling, about 30 minutes.
Makes approximately 8 servings.

# PENNSYLVANIA DUTCH EGG CASSEROLE

1 8 ounce package of fine egg noodles
1 can condensed cream of onion soup
½ cup milk
¼ cup mayonnaise

2 teaspoons Worcestershire sauce
8 eggs, hard-boiled, shelled and sliced
1/3 cup Parmesan cheese, grated

Cook noodles, following label directions, drain. Place in a greased 8 cup, shallow casserole dish. Combine soup, milk, mayonnaise, and Worcestershire sauce in a small saucepan; heat slowly, stirring constantly, until smooth and hot; stir half into noodles. Place egg slices over noodle mixture; spoon remaining sauce over eggs. Sprinkle cheese over top.

Bake in moderate oven (350 degrees F.) for 20 minutes or until bubbly.

Makes about 6 servings.

# RED CABBAGE
## PORT BRAISED

1 small red cabbage (1 ½ pounds)          salt and pepper to taste
¼ cup unsalted butter (1/2 stick)          ½ cup red wine vinegar
1 cup port

Preheat oven to 350 degrees F.
Remove tough outer leaves from the head of cabbage, cut in half and remove core. Thinly slice the cabbage and rinse under cold running water. Drain well.

In a large covered casserole on top of the stove, melt the butter. Add the port and the cabbage. Stir well and season with the salt and pepper. Cover tightly and place in the oven. Cook, stirring often, until the cabbage is slightly tender, about 20 minutes. Pour in the vinegar, cover and cook until the cabbage is very soft, about 15 minutes watch carefully and add a small amount of water if the cabbage starts to scorch. Season with salt and pepper just before serving.

# RED CABBAGE
### (Aunt) Anna R.

3 cups shredded red cabbage                1 teaspoon salt
2 medium unpeeled apples, cubed (1 ¾ cups)  1/8 teaspoon pepper
¼ cup cider vinegar                        2 tbs. bacon drippings or salad oil
¼ cup brown sugar, packed                  dash caraway seeds
¼ cup water

Combine all ingredients; cover tightly and steam until cabbage is tender, about 30 minutes. Stir occasionally (more vinegar may be added for a tart flavor).

Serves 4.

Note: *add some unsweetened applesauce instead of apples if you don't have fresh apples.*

# RED CABBAGE WITH APPLES
## ROTKOHL MIT APFEL

2 ½ pounds red cabbage, shredded
¾ cup boiling water
3 large cooking apples, pared, cored, sliced
3 tablespoons melted butter
¼ cup vinegar

1 ½ teaspoons flour
¼ cup packed brown sugar
2 teaspoons salt
dash pepper

Put shredded cabbage in kettle. Add water; cook, covered, 10 minutes. Add apples; cook, covered, 10 minutes or until tender. Combine butter, vinegar, flour, sugar, salt, pepper; add to cabbage-apple mixture.

Makes 4-6 servings.


# SWEET SOUR RED CABBAGE
## Suss Saur Rotkohl

1 head red cabbage, cleaned & shredded (4 cups)
1 cup water
4 tablespoons sugar
½ teaspoon salt
4 tablespoons vinegar

2 apples, chopped, peeled and cored, sliced
1 tablespoon butter
¼ teaspoon pepper

Cook cabbage and apples in water till tender approximately 15 to 20 minutes. Add remaining ingredients and cook a few more minutes. Serve with chicken or pork.

Makes 6 to 8 servings.

# RICE PILAF

1 tablespoon finely chopped onion
2 tablespoons butter
1 cup uncooked rice

2 cups chicken stock
1 teaspoon salt (omit if stock is salty)

Preheat oven to 350 degrees F. In an oven proof casserole dish cook onion in 1 tablespoon butter until soft but not brown. Add rice to mixture and mix well. In a separate saucepan add chicken stock and salt and bring to a boil. Add the liquid to the rice mixture, cover and cook in the oven until the liquid has cooked away, (approximately 20 minutes). Turn rice onto hot serving dish, separate grains and sprinkle with 1 tablespoon melted butter.

This dish will keep warm in a casserole for 1-2 hours without drying.

Serves 8 as an accompaniment to meat.

# HOMEMADE SAUERKRAUT

1 cabbage

2 tbs. salt (for each canning jar)

Clean, core and shred cabbage. Place a small amount of cut cabbage in quart jar. Press down in jar, using handle of heavy knife. Keep adding cabbage and pressing in like manner. To each jar use 2 tablespoons of salt, sprinkling it in as you add cabbage to the jar. When jar is packed tightly, add enough hot water to each jar to fill completely. Place lid on jars, but do not tighten. Stand on tray. It will ferment for several days. When it stops fermenting, remove lid, add enough cold water to fill jar, and screw lids tightly. Makes 10 servings.

# BAKED SQUASH AND APPLES

½ cup pomegranate juice, optional
2 ½ lbs. butternut squash, peeled and cut into 2" cubes
4 apples, cored and thickly sliced

½ cup light brown sugar
2 tablespoons butter, melted
salt to taste

Preheat oven to 350 degrees F.
Arrange squash and apples in buttered 13x9x2" baking dish. Mix light brown sugar and pomegranate juice (optional) and pour over squash and apples. Drizzle with melted butter and bake until squash is tender and easily pierced with a fork (about 20-30 minutes).

Makes 8 servings.

# SPATZLE
## German Noodles

1 ½ cups flour
2 eggs

½ cup water
salt and pepper to taste

Mix eggs, flour, salt, and pepper together. Add water until moist enough for the batter to go through a sieve without to much effort. Drop the batter through the strainer into boiling water or chicken stock. Bring up to boil again and cook for approximately three minutes—when spaetzle rises to top of the pot. Remove and drain. Can be served as a side dish or mixed with vegetables, such as green beans.

Can also be rolled out and cut into narrow stripes with a pizza cutter if strainer unavailable. Squish the stripes and drop into boiling water and follow instructions above. Tastes great mixed in green beans mixed with browned butter.

Makes enough for either soup or for a side dish, about 4 servings.

# SPATZLE
## Swabian Noodles

4 cups flour
4 eggs, beaten

2 teaspoons salt, divided
9 cups water, divided

In a bowl, combine flour, eggs and 1 teaspoon salt. Add just enough water to make a firm dough. (When pulled up on a spoon, dough should tear at 6 to 8"). Fill large pot with remaining water and remaining salt, bring to a boil. Press dough through a ricer or colander directly into boiling water. Rinse cooking utensils in cold water and keep pot boiling. Spatzle needs only 2 to 3 minutes to cook. Remove with a slotted spoon and repeat until all the dough is used.

Serve as a side dish to roast with gravy or alone tossed with Swiss or other cheese.


# FRIED GREEN TOMATOES

1 cup all-purpose flour
1 teaspoon salt
1 teaspoon pepper
5 green tomatoes, sliced ½" thick

1 cup breadcrumbs
2 eggs, beaten
½ cup butter

In a small bowl, stir together the flour, salt and pepper. Place the crushed crackers (or breadcrumbs) in another small bowl, and the beaten eggs in a third bowl. Melt the butter in a large skillet over medium heat. Dip each tomato slice in the egg to coat, then in the flour mixture. Dip the floured tomato slice back into the egg, and then into the crumbs. Place the coated tomato slices in the hot skillet, and fry until golden brown on each side, about 3 to 5 minutes per side. Add more butter to the pan if necessary. Serve hot.

Makes approximately 6 servings.

# PROVINCIAL TOMATOES

2 large tomatoes, cut into ¼" squares
salt and pepper to taste
1 tablespoon olive oil, as needed
½ cup grated Parmesan cheese

¼ cup dry bread crumbs
2 tablespoons dried parsley
¼ cup grated Asleago cheese

Preheat broiler.
Place tomato slices in a single layer on a baking sheet or in a baking dish, season with salt and pepper, and drizzle with olive oil. Mix together the Parmesan cheese, Asleago cheese, breadcrumbs and parsley; sprinkle over the tomato slices. Drizzle a little bit more olive oil over the top. Broil tomatoes for 5 minutes, or until the top is golden and toasty.

Makes 4 servings.

# GLAZED TURNIPS
## Teltower Rubchen

3 pounds small turnips
3 tablespoons butter
1 tablespoon sugar

2 tablespoons flour
salt and pepper, to taste
¼ teaspoon paprika

Peel and cut the turnips into cubes approximately 1"x1"x1" square. Boil for 10 to 15 minutes in salted water. Drain and reserve the cooking water. In the same pan melt the butter and add the sugar stirring until brown. Add the turnips, stirring until they are covered with the butter mixture. Sprinkle the flour over the turnips. Add the reserved cooking liquid with more water, if necessary. Cover and simmer for about 30 minutes, or until tender. Season with salt, pepper, and paprika. Good served with lamb or pork roasts.

Serves 6.

# TURNIPS

3 pounds either turnips or rutabagas        butter
salt and pepper to taste        brown sugar
1 carrot, pared and chopped        water for boiling

Peel turnips, slice top and bottom to make it easier to remove rest of rind. Dice into cubes and bring to a boil in water along with the chopped carrot.
When turnips and carrots are fork tender remove from heat and drain off water. Add 2-3 tablespoons of butter to pot and mash with a potato masher or use an electric mixer. Add salt and pepper to taste and add 1 tablespoon of brown sugar. Stir. Taste and if you wish to, add more brown sugar. If you like the turnips more buttery you can also add more and stir in.

Serves 6.

*Turnips are great with Thanksgiving turkey or Baked Ham.*

# BEEF DISHES

# BEEF FILETS

6 large mushroom caps
6 beef filets

3 tablespoons butter
Royal Mushroom Sauce (see sauces)

Trim and carve mushroom crowns with v shapes around edges, not too deep.

Heat butter in heavy skillet till golden brown and bubbling. Quickly brown steaks on both sides over moderately high heat. Place filets on squares of heavy foil on baking sheet.

Spoon 2 tablespoons royal mushroom sauce over each filet, top each with a fluted mushroom crown. Bring corners of each foil square up over steak, and twist gently, leaving top slightly open. Complete cooking in extremely hot oven, 500 degrees F for 12 minutes for rare, 15 minutes for medium and 18 minutes for well done.

*Note: meat can be refrigerated after foil wrapping, to finish off in oven, just add an extra 10 minutes of cooking time.*

Makes 6 servings.


# BEEF-CHEDDAR BAKE

3 ½ cups onion chopped
4 tablespoons butter
2 pounds ground round steak
3 cups grated sharp Cheddar cheese
3 cups milk

6 eggs, beaten
2 teaspoons dried thyme
pinch cayenne pepper
½ cup Bisquick mix

In large skillet, sauté onion in butter until soft but not browned, about 5 minutes. Stir in ground round, sauté 10 minutes longer; drain, place in large mixing bowl. Stir in remaining ingredients. Spoon into buttered 10" baking dish. Bake in a pre-heated 350 degrees F. oven for 35-45 minutes or until mixture is set and lightly browned on top.

# BELGIAN BEEF OVEN STEW (FOR 2)

½ pound beef stew meat
1 tablespoon cooking oil
salt and pepper to taste
½ cup chopped onion
2 small carrots, sliced
1 tablespoon flour

¾ cup beer
½ small garlic clove, minced
1 beef bouillon cube
1/8 teaspoon dried thyme crushed
2 servings of instant mashed potatoes

In a skillet, brown meat on all sides in hot cooking oil, sprinkle with salt and pepper. Place stew meat, onion and carrots in 1 quart casserole dish. In the same skillet blend flour into skillet drippings. Add beer and remaining ingredients except potatoes. Cook and stir until mixture thickens and bubbles. Pour over meat in casserole. Cover and bake in 350 degree F. oven until meat is tender, about 1 ¾ hours. Prepare potatoes for 2 servings as directed on package. Spoon potatoes on top of stew, forming a ring around the casserole dish, return to oven and bake, uncovered, 15 more minutes.

Makes 2 servings.

# BROWNED BEEF STEW

2 ½ pounds beef for stew, cut in 1 ½" cubes
1/3 cup all-purpose flour
1/3 cup salad oil
1 cup chopped onion
1 clove garlic minced
24 ounces (3 cups) beef broth

½ teaspoon Worcestershire sauce
¼ teaspoon pepper
5 medium potatoes, cut into chunks
1 pound carrots, cut into chunks
1 package frozen peas 10 ounces
1 teaspoon salt

About 3 ½ hours before serving.

On waxed paper, coat stew meat with flour, reserve remaining flour. In 6 quart Dutch oven, over medium-high heat; in hot salad oil, cook meat, a few pieces at a time until well browned on all sides, removing pieces as they brown.

Reduce heat to medium, to drippings in pot add onions and garlic, cook until onion is almost tender, about 3 minutes, stirring occasionally. Stir in reserved flour until blended. Gradually stir in broth, salt, Worcestershire, pepper and cook, stirring constantly, until mixture is slightly thickened.

Return meat to Dutch oven, heat to boiling, stirring occasionally. Reduce heat to low, cover and simmer about 2 ½ hours or until meat is almost tender, stirring occasionally.

Add potatoes and carrots and over medium heat to boiling. Reduce heat to low, cover and simmer 20 minutes. Stir in frozen peas, cover and simmer 5-10 minutes until all vegetables are tender.

Makes 8 servings.

# CLASSIC STANDING RIB ROAST

1 standing rib roast (the bigger the better)     salt & pepper to taste.

Buy at least three ribs, remembering that leftover beef makes good cold meat for sandwiches or cut in strips for a stir fry. Have the butcher cut off the short ribs and remove the chine (backbone), attaching a piece of suet where the chine was removed (optional), tying the roast properly. Meat should be at room temperature, at least 3 hours. Salt and pepper meat well.

Place, fat side up, standing on a rack in a shallow pan in a preheated 325 degree oven. Roast 13-15 minutes per pound (112-115 degrees on meat thermometer) for rare about 18 minutes for medium rare (115-120 degrees). Once cooked, the roast should rest 20 to 30 minutes to let the juices settle and to make carving easier. As is true of all foods, the meat continues to cook after it comes from the oven.

*This is a favorite, so easy to make, of course, it is expensive. But definitely worth the price for a special occasion!*

*Serve with baked or stuffed baked potatoes and your favorite vegetables. Serve au jus or a thin gravy.*

# OVEN-GLAZED CORNED BEEF

5 pounds corned beef brisket
2 onions
6 whole cloves
6 peppercorns

2 large bay leaves
2 cloves garlic, peeled
1/3 cup firmly packed light brown sugar
1 tablespoon Dijon mustard

Place corned beef in kettle, cover with cold water. Bring to boiling, drain water. Cover meat with fresh cold water. Stud onions with the whole cloves; add to corned beef with peppercorns, bay leaves and garlic cloves. Cover kettle, bring to boiling, lower heat. Simmer 4 hours, or until meat is very tender. Allow meat to cool slightly in the cooking liquid, remove to shallow pan. Cover meat with another shallow pan, weigh the top with several large books or something equally heavy. This will ensure neat slices. Refrigerate meat with weights, if possible, otherwise leave under weights 1 hour, wrap and refrigerate overnight.

About 1 hour before serving, remove corned beef from refrigerator. Combine brown sugar with mustard to make a smooth paste, spread over the top (fat) surface of meat. Bake at 350 degrees for 30 minutes or until meat is hot and glaze is bubbly and brown. Remove the bay leaves and garlic before serving. Cut into thin slices across the grain. This can be served with vegetables and potatoes, can be served with cooked cabbage, if desired. Make 10 servings.

# LASAGNA
*Eleanor Hinsch*

2-1 lb. 13 oz. cans Italian style peeled tomatoes
4 8-ounce cans tomato sauce
2 teaspoons salt
3 teaspoons dried oregano
¼ teaspoon pepper
2 teaspoons onion salt
2 cups minced onions
2 cloves garlic minced

1/3 cup oil
2 pounds ground beef
1 pound sweet Italian sausage
2 teaspoons salt
1 pound lasagna noodles
1 ½ pounds ricotta cheese
1 lb. mozzarella cheese, thinly sliced
1 cup grated Parmesan cheese

In large saucepan or kettle, combine tomatoes and next 5 ingredients; start simmering, uncovered. In skillet, sauté onion and garlic in oil until lightly browned; add beef, remove sausage from casing and cut into small pieces, add to beef, also add 2 teaspoons salt. Cook until meat and sausage loses the red color; add to tomato sauce; simmer 2 ½ hours or until thickened. (1 can of tomato paste can be added for thicker sauce).

Meanwhile cook lasagna according to package directions, stirring occasionally, drain, separating noodles. Heat oven to 350 degrees F. In bottoms of 2 12x8x2" baking dishes, place several spoonfuls of sauce, top with crisscross layers of lasagna, then with ricotta (split ricotta, mozzarella and parmesan between the 2 casseroles), 1/3 mozzarella and parmesan, ending with sauce. Repeat, ending with sauce. Top with remaining mozzarella. Repeat with second casserole dish. Bake for 50 minutes. Remove from oven, let stand for 15 minutes.

*This dish can be frozen. After assembling the casserole, cover well with plastic wrap and foil and freeze. Thaw completely, bake about 20 minutes longer than recipe directs, must be fully thawed first.*

*This is my all time favorite lasagna recipe and the most requested by my family and friends. I usually double the sauce recipe and freeze ½ of the sauce for another time, or other dishes.*

Makes 16 servings.

# GOULASH

3 tablespoons butter
2 tablespoons vegetable oil
4 medium onions, thinly sliced
3 cloves garlic, finely chopped
1 tablespoon marjoram
2 pounds lean beef, cut into 1" cubes
salt and pepper, to taste
1 tablespoon Hungarian paprika, mild or hot
1 teaspoon thyme

2 Italian or green bell peppers, sliced
6 plum tomatoes, chopped
3 tablespoons tomato paste
½ cup finely chopped Italian parsley, flat leaf
3 leaves from celery ribs, chopped
2 bay leaves
1 cup beef stock or bouillon
sour cream

In Dutch oven, heat butter and oil and brown meat on all sides over medium-high heat. Remove meat, lower heat, add onions and cook until wilted. Add garlic and marjoram, and cook for several minutes, stirring to mix. Add beef, salt, pepper, paprika and thyme. Mix well. Cover with lid and cook. Simmer slowly on low heat for 30 minutes, stirring occasionally. Add green peppers, tomatoes, tomato paste, ¼ cup parsley, celery leaves, bay leaves and beef stock. Bring to boil, reduce heat, cover and cook slowly for 1 ½ hours, or until beef is tender. Top with sour cream and rest of parsley. Serve with spaetzle or broad egg noodles.

Makes 4-6 servings.

*This recipe came to me from a neighbor over 50 years ago. Her name was Lillian and although she is long gone, thanks again!*

# HUNGARIAN GOULASH

2 ½ pounds lean round of beef
3 medium red onions, sliced thinly
1 tablespoon paprika
1 clove garlic, crushed
1 tablespoon butter
1 cup sour cream

3 tbs. beef drippings (or beef broth)
salt and pepper
1 blade of marjoram
2 ½ pounds sauerkraut
1 tablespoon flour
1 teaspoon caraway seeds

Cut the meat into 1" cubes. Melt the drippings in a skillet and brown the red onions. Skim out the onions and place in a stew pan. Brown the meat in the drippings and then turn the contents of the skillet into the stew pan. Season with salt and pepper, the paprika, marjoram, and garlic. Stir in the seasonings until blended and then add boiling water just to cover the meat. Simmer gently for 30 minutes. Add sauerkraut and continue simmering for another hour, or until the meat is tender. Cream together the flour and butter and stir into the sauce, cooking until it is smooth and thickened. Add the sour cream and caraway seeds and cook for a few minutes longer. Serve very hot.

Serves 6 to 8.
Serve over noodles.

*Years ago I went to Hungary and tried their goulash. What a great feast! I asked for the recipe, its close, although they spoke a very broken English and I didn't speak Hungarian. But its still good.*

# MEATBALL OVEN STEW (for 2)

1 egg
2 tablespoons cornmeal
2 teaspoons minced onions
½ teaspoon dry mustard
¼ teaspoon chili powder
½ teaspoon salt
½ pound ground beef
1 tablespoon salad oil

2 small potatoes, pared & quartered
2 small carrots, sliced
1 small onion, quartered
1 tablespoon flour
1 can tomatoes, 8 ounces
1 beef bouillon cube
salt and pepper to taste
2 tablespoons water

Combine egg, cornmeal, onion, mustard, salt and chili powder. Add beef, mix well, and form into 6 balls. Brown on all sides in hot oil. Place in 1 ½ quart casserole dish. Add potatoes, carrots and onion. Sprinkle with salt and pepper. Blend flour into drippings in skillet. Add tomatoes, 2 tablespoons water, and 1 beef bouillon cube. Cook and stir till mixture is bubbly. Pour over meat and vegetables. Cover and bake in 350 degrees F. oven till vegetables are tender, about 1 hour.

Serves 2.

# MEATLOAF
*Eleanor Hinsch*

2 pounds ground round beef
2 eggs
salt & pepper to taste
½ small onion, grated

2 slices white bread, shredded
½ cup milk or half & half
3 tablespoons tomato ketchup
1 teaspoon parsley

Mix all ingredients thoroughly; mixture should be soft but not soupy. If needed, an additional slice of bread can be added, put into loaf pan. Bake at 350 degrees F. for 1 hour. If the meatloaf is done it will start pulling away from the sides of the pan. It will also be firm to the touch when lightly touched with finger. Drain fat, halfway through baking and once more 10 minutes before finished. *For additional flavor a package of meatloaf seasoning or powdered onion soup mix can be added to raw ingredients.*

Makes 6 servings.


# MINUTE STEAKS (FOR 2)

2 minute or cubed steaks, ½ to ¾ pounds
½ teaspoon salt
2 tablespoons water

2 tablespoons ketchup
2 teaspoons Worcestershire sauce
1/8 teaspoon Tabasco sauce

Heat skillet; brown steaks on both sides in skillet. Reduce heat and cook about 2 minutes on each side or until meat is desired doneness. Sprinkle with salt and remove steaks. To pan juices, add water, ketchup, Worcestershire sauce and Tabasco sauce. Return steaks to skillet and heat in sauce, for a few minutes.

Serves 2.

# PATE EN CROUTE

**PASTRY:**
2 ¼ cups flour
½ teaspoon salt
1 ½ sticks butter
1 egg
2-3 tablespoons sour cream

**FILLING:**
4 tablespoons butter
¾ lbs. each of ground veal, beef, pork
1 cup finely chopped mushrooms
salt and pepper to taste
½ cup finely chopped onion
¼ cup chopped parsley
1 cup shredded Gruyere Cheese
4 egg yolks

*Serve with sour cream and a sprinkling of dill.*

**PASTRY:** Sift flour and salt onto a board. Make a well in the center. Add the butter, cut up into small pieces and the egg. Add sour cream. Quickly work ingredients into a soft ball. Chill in the refrigerator in wax paper for 30 minutes. *Frozen, prepared pastry can be substituted. Thaw and use per instructions Puff pastry can also be used instead. Roll out 1 sheet following pastry directions below. Remember not to trim too small since the puff pastry will shrink back somewhat.*

**FILLING:** Heat butter in a large skillet and add meats. Brown meats, breaking up with a fork. Do not overcook. Season with salt and pepper. Remove from heat. Combine with mushrooms, onion, parsley and cheese. Add egg yolks. Blend well, cook slightly. Drain off excess liquid.

Butter a cookie sheet lightly. Roll out the pastry to 12"x15". Center one half of the pastry in the middle of the sheet. Form the meat in a loaf in the center allowing at least an inch margin of pastry. Fold over the second half of the pastry to cover first half and seal edges with a fork. Roll out trimmings and make long ½" wide pieces to crisscross (3) top of loaf. Brush crust with 1 egg and 2 tablespoons heavy cream beaten together. Cross pastry strips diagonally across crust. Brush with egg mixture and bake in 375 degree oven until golden brown, about 40 minutes.

Makes 6-8 servings.

# PEPPER STEAK

1 ½ lbs. sirloin steak, cut into strips 1/8" thick
1 tablespoon paprika
2 cloves garlic, crushed
3 tablespoons butter
1 cup sliced green onions with tops
2 green peppers cut in strips

2 large fresh tomatoes, diced
1 cup beef broth
¼ cup water
2 tablespoons cornstarch
2 tablespoons soy sauce
3 cups hot cooked rice

Sprinkle steak with paprika and allow to stand while preparing other ingredients. Cook steak and garlic in butter until meat is browned. Add onions and green peppers; continue cooking until vegetables are wilted. Add tomatoes and broth; cover and simmer about 15 minutes. Blend water with cornstarch and soy sauce. Stir into steak mixture and cook until thickened, serve over beds of fluffy rice.

Makes 6 servings.

# POOR BOY FILLETS

5 slices bacon
1 pound lean ground beef
lemon pepper
¼ cup grated Parmesan cheese

1 can mushroom pieces, drained (2oz)
2 tablespoons finely chopped onion
2 tablespoons finely chopped green pepper

In a skillet partially cook bacon, drain on paper toweling. Pat ground beef on waxed paper to a 12x7 1/2x ¼" rectangle. Sprinkle lightly with salt and lemon pepper. Top with cheese. Combine mushrooms, onion and green pepper; sprinkle evenly over meat. Roll up jellyroll fashion, starting with short end. Cut into 1 ½" slices. Wrap edge of each slice with a strip of partially cooked bacon, securing with wooden picks. Grill over medium coals 8 minutes turn and grill 8 minutes more.

Serve on a platter with cherry tomatoes and parsley sprigs, if desired.

Makes 5 servings.

# POT ROAST
*Eleanor Hinsch*

| | |
|---|---|
| 2 tablespoons vegetable oil | ½ teaspoon salt |
| 4 ½ pounds bottom or beef eye of round | 1 cup diced onion |
| 6 cups beef broth | 2 bay leaves |
| 1 tablespoon minced garlic | 3 tablespoon flour |
| salt and pepper to taste | gravy master (1 teaspoon), optional |

Heat the oil in a large, heavy bottomed pot. The pot should be large enough that all the meat and stock should fit with 1 to 2 inches of space remaining below the rim. Sear the meat on all sides. Add the onion and bay leaves, and sauté for 4 to 5 minutes. Add the garlic and seasonings, and sauté for 3 to 4 minutes.

Remove beef and add the flour to the pot and whisk together with drippings, add beef broth slowly whisking with the roux and bring to a boil, add the meat back into pot. Decrease the heat and simmer, covered, stirring occasionally, for approximately 2 hours, or until the meat offers little or no resistance when pierced with a fork. Reduce heat, remove meat and bay leaves. Discard bay leaves. Taste and adjust seasoning, if needed. Add gravy master if needed (optional). If sauce needs thickening, add additional flour and whisk well.

*This pot roast recipe works well in a slow cooker or a pressure cooker. If using a pressure cooker make sure it is large enough to allow steam room. It takes approximately 45 minutes to 1 hour cook time once cooker is hot enough. You must still sear all sides of the meat before cooking. This can be done in the pressure cooker and then take off burner to allow pot to cool down after making gravy. Put meat back into pressure cooker and bring up to proper temperature and then cook for the above cooking time. See settings on instruction manual for settings. See manual for settings for slow cooker also.*

Makes 8 servings.

# GARLIC PRIME RIB

1-10 pound prime rib roast
10 cloves garlic minced
2 tablespoons olive oil

2 teaspoons salt
2 teaspoons ground black pepper
2 teaspoons dried thyme

Place the roast in a roasting pan with the fatty side up. In a small bowl, mix together the garlic, olive oil, salt, pepper and thyme. Spread the mixture over the fatty layer of the roast, and let the roast sit out until it is at room temperature, no longer than 1 hour. Preheat the oven to 500 degrees.

Bake the roast for 20 minutes in the preheated oven, then reduce the temperature to 325 degrees and continue roasting for an additional 60 to 75 minutes. The internal temperature of the roast should be at 145 degrees for medium rare.

Allow the roast to rest for 10 to 15 minutes before carving so the meat. You can retain its juices for gravy.

# OMA'S BEEF ROULADEN
*Mathilde Bohlen (my mom)*

5 slices round or sirloin, cut into thin slices
¾ to 1 pound bacon cut in half
5 carrots, peeled, cleaned, cut lengthwise OR
2 dill pickles cut lengthwise into 1/8s
2 tablespoons oil
3 whole onions, peeled and sliced

2 cups beef broth
2 bay leaves
2 teaspoons gravy master
4 tablespoons flour, or more
toothpicks or string for cooking
salt and pepper to taste

Lay out each slice of beef, if over 1/8" thick, use meat mallet to pound thinner (cover beef with waxed paper), cut meat slices into 2-3 slices so they are approximately 3" wide and 6" long. On short end of each piece lay ½ slice bacon (more if desired) carrot or pickle (can substitute dill pickle with gherkin pickles if you prefer a sweeter pickle) and onion (at least ¼ onion each slice of beef. Salt and pepper to taste. Roll up beef and either secure with 2 toothpicks or tie with kitchen string. Brown the rolls in a large, deep skillet with oil. When meat loses all redness and is browned, remove from pan. When all are removed, dissolve bouillon cubes in ½ cup water and add to pan.

Into a small shaker or covered cup add 1 to 2 tablespoons flour to cold water, ½ to ¾ cup at a time. Shake together until blended and add to skillet. Do this with the water and flour until used up. Stir and simmer until lightly boiling and reduce heat, add gravy master, stir and add back the beef rolls. On a low heat simmer for an additional hour or until beef is tender. Remove the bay leaves and serve, with potatoes, noodles, potato dumplings or Spatzle.

Tastes great served with red cabbage.

*One slice cut into 3 should be enough for 1 adult, but I have had 1 person eat as many as 12 (4 slices of beef) so err on the side of more for less people. This recipe is what we use for our Christmas Eve celebration, my children's favorite, and mine. My parents loved them. Can be frozen and reheated after thawing.*

Makes 3-6 servings.

# OMA'S POT ROAST
*Mathilde Bohlen*

4 pounds rump roast trimmed
pepper to taste
3 cloves
2 carrots peeled and sliced
2 tablespoons cooling oil
2-3 tablespoons flour

seasoned salt to taste
1 bay leaf
1 small onion chopped
4 firm potatoes peeled & quartered
3 cups water
dash gravy master, to taste

In a heavy cooking pot 6-8 quart size heat oil sprinkle seasoned salt and pepper on meat and brown meat on all sides to a nice dark brown color. Lower heat to medium-low and add water carrots bay leaf cloves and onion. Cover and allow to cook on medium-low for at least 2 to 3 hours add more water if needed (enough for gravy). You can also add a beef bouillon cube for more flavor if you want. Stir occasionally. Put the potatoes on to boil and continue cooking the meat until potatoes and any vegetable you want are finished. Remove meat pot from heat and transfer meat to serving platter, put in warm oven or wrap with foil to keep warm.

Remove the bay leaf and cloves from the meat juices. In a small lidded jar put the flour and some cold water and shake vigorously. Add to meat juices stirring constantly. Return to heat increasing heat to medium. Add gravy master if you want to at this point. Bring to a slow boil if gravy isn't thick enough add a little more flour using the water and flour method. If the gravy gets lumpy strain it before serving. If gravy gets to thick add some water from either the potatoes or the vegetables.
Makes approximately 6-8 servings.

# SAUERBRATEN
## PICKLED BEEF ROAST

3 pounds beef roast (sirloin tip or rump)
MARINADE:
2 onions quartered
6 cups cold water

3 cups white vinegar
10 peppercorns
1 teaspoon salt
1 bay leaf

Prepare marinade by combining all ingredients except meat. Place the roast in a large bowl and cover with the marinade. Refrigerate 5-7 days.

Preheat oven to 325 degrees F. Place beef in roasting pan. Add 1 cup of marinade, cover and roast in the oven for 1 ½ hours or until tender.

For a real German meal, serve beef thinly sliced with potato dumplings and red cabbage.

Makes 5 servings.


## SHORT RIBS WITH VEGETABLES

3-4 pounds beef short ribs
salt and pepper to taste
1 sliced onion
1 cup water
8 small white onions, peeled
flour

4 medium potatoes, peeled, quartered
6-8 carrots, halved lengthwise
¾ pounds whole green beans
minced parsley

Brown ribs fat side down slowly in heavy saucepan or Dutch oven. Pour off fat, season with salt and pepper. Add sliced onion and water, cover and bake in 325 degree oven for 2 hours or until meat is fork tender, basting occasionally with pan juices. During last 45 minutes add onions and potatoes; 15 minutes before meat is done add carrots and beans. Remove to warm platter, sprinkle with parsley. Skim fat from pan juices and thicken with a few tablespoons flour; whisk and add gravy master (about 1 teaspoon), serve hot with the gravy.

Makes 4 servings.

# STEAK AND PEPPERS
# ITALIAN STYLE

2 medium green peppers, cut into strips    2 tablespoons vegetable oil
1 jar Italian sauce                        3 pounds London broil

Preheat broiler. In skillet, sauté pepper strips in oil until tender. Add sauce and simmer 10 minutes. Cut steak diagonally in 3/8" thick slices. Broil 3 minutes on each side. Arrange steak slices on a platter, spoon sauce over steak.

Makes 8 servings.


# STUFFED STEAK

4 shell steaks—1" thick                          ¼ cup chopped parsley
2 tablespoons butter                             1 cup green onion minced
24 oysters, fresh, frozen, canned, coarsely chopped    salt and pepper to taste
2 tablespoons butter, melted

Make a pocket in each steak by cutting through meat with a small, sharp knife. Cut from 1 side of meat almost to the fat on the opposite side. Keep opening as small as possible. Melt 2 tablespoons butter in a skillet over medium heat. Add onions, cook until pale yellow and soft. Add oysters; cook 1 minute, stirring constantly. Remove from heat. Stir in parsley. Divide stuffing into 4 parts Spoon 1 part into pocket in each steak. Close opening by inserting wooded picks at a slant. Brush steak with melted butter. Broil to doneness desired. Seasoning each side after it has browned with salt and pepper.

Makes 4 servings.

# STUFFED PEPPERS

10-12 medium green peppers, washed with tops and seeds removed
1 32 ounce jar of spaghetti sauce
4 cups cooked elbow macaroni (1/2 lb. uncooked)

1 ½ pounds ground beef
1 cup chopped onions
2 cups herb seasoned stuffing cubes
1 can (10 ¾ ounces) beef broth

Boil peppers for 5 minutes, drain. Brown beef with onions in large skillet. Drain off fat. Mix in spaghetti sauce and stuffing cubes. Stuff peppers. Place half of peppers in a 2 quart freezer-oven proof casserole dish with half can of beef broth and half of remaining spaghetti sauce and ½ cup of water. Repeat with remaining peppers in another 2 quart dish. Stand peppers upright in the sauce and baste tops with mixture. Bring to a boil. Cover, simmer, for 20 minutes. Mix ½ of the macaroni in the first dish around peppers and half the macaroni in second dish. Cook 1 for 15 minutes uncovered. Wrap and freeze the other casserole for another time. To reheat, place covered casserole in preheated oven at 400 degrees F for 1 ¼ hours.
Each casserole serves 5-6 people.


# SWEDISH CABBAGE ROLLS

12 large cabbage leaves
1 beaten egg
¼ cup milk
¼ cup finely chopped onion
1 teaspoon salt
¼ teaspoon pepper

1 pound lean ground beef
1 cup cooked rice
1 can 8 ounce tomato sauce
1 tablespoon brown sugar, packed
1 tablespoon lemon juice
1 teaspoon Worcestershire sauce

Immerse cabbage leaves in large kettle of boiling water for about 3 minutes or until limp; drain. Combine egg, milk, onion, salt, pepper, beef and cooked rice. Place about ¼ cup meat mixture in center of each leaf; fold in sides and roll ends over meat. Place in slow cooking pot. Combine tomato sauce with brown sugar, lemon juice and Worcestershire sauce. Pour over cabbage rolls. Cover and cook on low for 7 to 9 hours.
Makes 6 servings.

*This is an easy recipe and can be made in a slow cooker if you have one. Otherwise, make it in a heavy pot and on low heat. Its easy to make and can be frozen. I usually freeze one of the casseroles. Make sure you cover first with plastic wrap and then tightly with aluminum foil.*

# SWEDISH MEATBALLS
## Margret K.

1 pound beef
¼ pound pork
¼ pound veal
1 teaspoon salt
2 eggs
¼ cup minced onion
3 tablespoons parsley
¼ teaspoon paprika

½ teaspoon grated lemon rind
1 teaspoon lemon juice
1 teaspoon Worcestershire sauce
2 slices white bread
¼ cup flour
¾ cup cream or evaporated milk
2 tablespoons butter
3 cups chicken broth

Sauté onions in butter Soak bread in cream in large bowl. Add onions to the bread mixture, also add meat and other ingredients except broth, butter and flour into bread mixture. Mix everything together and shape into loosely packed balls. Add butter into pan and brown meatballs. Remove meatballs. Add broth and flour and make gravy, add meatballs into pan and simmer in closely covered pan until done (approximately 15 minutes). Makes 6 servings.

*For larger amounts simply double or triple accordingly. This recipe can be frozen. Great for parties, and can be made ahead. Serve on a bed of fine egg noodles.*
*This recipe was used both in the Deli for catering and also in my catering business.*


# ZITI CASSEROLE
## Jason H.

1 pound ziti pasta
1 pound ricotta cheese
¼ pound diced mozzarella cheese
½ cup grated Parmesan cheese

1 egg
¾ teaspoon salt
¼ teaspoon pepper
6 cups meat sauce (see sauces)
or large jar sauce

Cook ziti and drain, following package directions.
While noodles are cooking, make filling; combine ricotta, mozzarella, Parmesan, egg, salt and pepper in a large bowl. Layer ziti, filling and meat sauce in a 13x9x2" baking dish, starting and ending with meat sauce.
Bake in 350 degree F. oven for 40 minutes or until bubbly hot.
Makes 8 servings.

# CHICKEN POULTRY AND STUFFINGS

# CHICKEN A LA SUISSE

6 medium chicken breasts skinned & boned
8 ounces Swiss cheese slices
8 ounces sliced cooked ham
3 tablespoons flour
1 teaspoon paprika
6 tablespoons butter

½ cup white wine
1 chicken bouillon cube
1 tablespoon cornstarch
1 cup heavy cream
minced cooked ham for garnish
parsley sprigs for garnish

About 1 ¼ hours before serving, spread chicken breasts flat; cut cheese and ham slices to fit on top; fold breasts over filling; fasten edges with toothpicks, enclosing filling well. On waxed paper, mix flour and paprika; use to coat chicken.

In 12" skillet, over medium heat, in hot butter, cook chicken breasts until browned on all sides. Add white wine and chicken bouillon. Reduce heat to low, cover and simmer for 30 minutes or until tender; remove chicken to warm platter, remove toothpicks, keep chicken warm.

In cup, with a fork, blend cornstarch and cream until smooth. Gradually stir cornstarch mixture into liquid in skillet. Cook, stirring constantly, until thickened. Spoon sauce over chicken. Sprinkle with minced ham, garnish with parsley sprigs.
Makes 6 servings.

# BROILED STUFFED CHICKEN
## For 2

2 pounds broiler-fryer, split
2 tablespoons butter
salt and pepper to taste
1 cup chopped apples
¼ cup chopped onion

¼ cup chopped celery
4 tablespoons butter
2 cups herb-seasoned stuffing cubes
¼ teaspoon salt
dash pepper

Preheat broiler. Tuck wings of chicken back. Place chicken, skin side up, on broiler pan. Brush chicken with half of the 2 tablespoons melted butter; sprinkle with salt and pepper. Broil at least 4" from heat about 20 minutes. Turn and brush cavity side with the remaining 1 tablespoon butter, sprinkle with salt and pepper. Continue broiling 20 minutes or till tender. Meanwhile, cook apple, onion and celery in the 4 tablespoons of butter until soft, combine with stuffing croutons, salt, pepper and ¼ cup water. Heap the cavity of each chicken half with stuffing. Return to broiler for 10 minutes.

Makes 2 servings.


# STUFFED SAVORY CABBAGE WITH MUSHROOM SAUCE

1 head Savoy cabbage, or regular green @ 4 lbs.
1 pound ground sausage
3 small onions, finely chopped ¾ cup
1/3 cup butter
2 cups ground raw (or cooked) chicken breast
2/3 cup water
1 package herb-seasoned stuffing cubes (8 oz) ground in blender
½ cup chopped parsley
2 eggs, lightly beaten
1 teaspoon leaf sage, crumbled

1 teaspoon salt
¼ tsp. freshly ground black pepper
2 cans chicken broth—13 ¾ ounce size
MUSHROOM SAUCE
¼ cup butter
¼ pound sliced mushrooms
¼ cup flour
1 teaspoon salt
¼ tsp. freshly ground black pepper
2 cups reserved cooking liquid from cabbage

Line a large mixing bowl (about 12 cups) with 3 layers of cheesecloth that hangs over the edge of the bowl, set aside. Using a sharp pointed paring knife, remove the core of the cabbage. Carefully pull the leaves off the cabbage one by one. Green cabbage might need blanching first. Reserve 8 large leaves, plunge remaining leaves into large kettle of boiling water; heat 3-5 minutes or until pliable. Remove with tongs to tray lined with paper towel; drain, reserve.

Cook sausage meat in a large skillet, breaking up with a wooden spoon as it cooks, until meat is lightly browned and no pink remains. Add onion, cook, stirring occasionally, until tender but not brown, about 5 minutes. If using cooked chicken (or turkey), stir in. Stir in water; bringing to a boil. Remove from heat; add stuffing mix, blend thoroughly. Mix in parsley, eggs, sage, salt and pepper. Taste and add additional seasonings, if you wish. Mixture should be spicy, since the cabbage will absorb much of the flavor.

Line the cheesecloth-lined bowl with a double layer of large cabbage leaves, overlapping slightly, with top edges hanging over the side of the bowl.

Divide meat mixture in thirds. Place 1/3 in bowl; layer with cabbage leaves. Repeat 2 more times, ending with cabbage. You may have to press down slightly to compress the filling. Fold the overhanging cabbage leaves neatly over the top of the layered mixture. Gather the cheesecloth tightly around the stuffed cabbage and squeeze into a ball shape. Tie securely with twine or string.

Place cabbage ball in a deep saucepan so there is a minimum of space between the cabbage ball and the pan. Pour in chicken broth; bring to boiling, cover tightly. Lower heat; simmer gently for 1 ¼ hours. Check occasionally, adding additional chicken broth if necessary. Carefully remove stuffed cabbage from sauce pan onto tray or plate and let stand 15 minutes. Measure out and reserve 2 cups cooking broth for mushroom sauce.

To serve: untie and loosen cheesecloth. Place platter over cabbage. Quickly turn upside down and remove cheesecloth. Overlap 3-4 of the reserved cabbage leaves over the stuffed cabbage to make it resembles the top of a cabbage. Line the platter with the remaining cabbage leaves.

MUSHROOM SAUCE: melt ¼ cup butter in a medium size saucepan. Add ¼ pound sliced mushrooms, sauté 5 minutes or until just golden. Add ¼ cup flour, 1 teaspoon freshly ground black pepper, stirring to coat; remove from heat. Slowly stir in the reserved 2 cups cooking liquid until mixture is smooth. Cook, stirring constantly until mixture thickens and bubbles.
Makes 10 servings.

# CHEESE AND CHICKEN ON ASPARAGUS

¼ cup butter
1/3 cup flour
2 cups milk
1 cup grated American cheese
2 cups diced cooked chicken
2 tomatoes

1-10 oz. package frozen kernel corn
1 ½ teaspoon salt
2-10 ounce packages frozen asparagus
spears
2 hard cooked eggs

In a saucepan melt butter. Stir in flour gradually blend in milk. Cook over low heat, stirring constantly, until sauce bubbles and thickens. Add grated cheese, stir until melted. Stir in chicken, frozen corn and salt. Simmer, covered, over low heat. Keep warm.

Cook asparagus spears according to package directions. Drain and arrange with layer of tomatoes; then layer of asparagus. Shell hard cooked eggs. Chop whites finely. Add to chicken mixture. Spoon chicken down center and over asparagus. Garnish with finely sieved egg yolks and tomato slices.

Makes 6 servings.


# CHICKEN BROCCOLI CASSEROLE

1 package frozen broccoli clusters
2 tablespoons melted butter
grated cheese
1 chicken or 2 chicken breasts, cooked, cut into
bite sized pieces

1 can cream of chicken soup
1 egg yolk
½ cup half and half

Cook broccoli in salted, boiling water for 2-3 minutes. Drain well. Place in buttered casserole. Sprinkle butter and 2 tablespoons cheese over broccoli. Spread chicken over broccoli mixture. Mix soup, egg yolk and cream together. Spoon over chicken. Sprinkle with cheese. Bake at 350 degrees for 45-50 minutes.

Makes 4 servings.

# HERB ROASTED CHICKEN

4 skinless boneless chicken breasts          1/8 teaspoon pepper
1 can condensed cream of chicken soup, 10 ¾ oz.          ½ cup water

Spray skillet with vegetable cooking spray. Heat over medium-high heat for 1 minute. Cook chicken 10 minutes or until browned; set aside. Add soup, pepper and water. Return chicken to pan. Cover and cook over low heat for 5 minutes or until chicken is done. *Serve over rice or bed of egg noodles.*

Makes 4 servings.


# CHICKEN AND PASTA PRIMAVERA

1 can condensed cream          1/8 teaspoon pepper
of mushroom soup, 10.75 oz          2 cups broccoli flowerets
¾ cup milk          2 ½ cups cooked corkscrew or elbow
¼ cup grated Parmesan cheese          macaroni
1/8 teaspoon garlic powder          2 cans chunk white chicken, drained (5oz)
2 carrots, pared, peeled and cut in small pieces

In a saucepan, mix soup, milk, cheese, garlic powder, pepper, broccoli and carrots. Over medium heat, heat to a boil. Cover and cook over low heat for 10 minutes or until vegetables are tender-crisp, stirring occasionally. Stir in macaroni and chicken and heat through.

Makes 4 servings.
*Instead of 2 cans of chicken, use leftover chicken, approximately 2 cups, chopped into bite sized pieces.*

# CHICKEN AND VEGETABLE STIR-FRY

3 whole chicken breasts, approx. 2 ½ lbs. each
1 tablespoon cornstarch
3 tablespoons soy sauce
2 tablespoons dry sherry
1 teaspoon sugar
1 teaspoon ground ginger

½ teaspoon crushed red pepper
1 ½ teaspoon salt
3 medium zucchini
1 pkg. frozen Chinese pea pods (6oz)
1 pound small mushrooms
½ cup salad oil

Remove bones from chicken breasts, cut chicken into 1 ½" chunks. In medium bowl, mix chicken, cornstarch, soy sauce, sherry, sugar, ginger, red pepper and 1 ½ teaspoon salt. Cut zucchini into bite-size pieces. Thaw frozen pea pods with running hot water; pat dry with paper towels. Quickly rinse mushrooms with running cold water, pat dry with paper towels.

In 8 quart Dutch oven or wok over medium-high heat, in hot salad oil, cook zucchini and mushrooms with ½ teaspoon salt until zucchini is tender-crisp, stirring constantly with slotted spoon, about 5 minutes. Spoon zucchini mixture onto platter, leaving oil in Dutch oven. In remaining oil, cook chicken mixture until chicken is tender, stirring frequently, about 10 minutes. Add snow peas and zucchini mixture, toss gently to mix well; heat through. Serve immediately. If desired, serve with white rice.

Makes 6 servings.

# CHICKEN 'N DUMPLINGS

6 cups chicken broth (about 4-13.75 oz. cans)
2 cups cut-up cooked chicken
1 cup leftover cooked vegetables (optional)
¼ cup butter
¼ teaspoon garlic powder

½ teaspoon salt
¼ teaspoon pepper
¼ cup vegetable shortening
1 ½ cups self-rising flour
½ cup ice water (to 2/3 cup)

Combine chicken broth, chicken, vegetables, butter, garlic powder, salt and pepper in a large saucepan. Bring to a boil, lower heat and simmer for 1 minute. Taste, add additional salt and pepper if needed. Cut shortening into flour in a medium sized bowl, until crumbly; stir in enough water to make soft dough. Bring chicken mixture to a boil again, lower heat and simmer an additional minute. Drop dumpling dough by rounded teaspoonfuls onto the gently bubbling broth, spacing as evenly as possible. Cover and simmer 15 minutes without lifting cover. Ladle soup into soup plates to serve, to round out meal, add a green salad and fresh fruit for dessert.

*Instead of self-raising flour: 1 ½ cups all-purpose flour mixed with 3 teaspoon double-acting baking powder and 1/3 teaspoon, salt.*

*If starting front scratch, cook one 2 ½ to 3 pounds broiler-fryer cut up, with 1 carrot, 1 onion, 6 pepper corns, 1 teaspoon salt and water to cover, about 7 cups. In a large kettle or Dutch oven, 50 minutes or until tender. Strain broth, and add water, if needed, to make 6 cups.*

*Can add chopped celery ribs (1) if desired.*

Makes 6 servings.

# MOM'S CHICKEN AND DUMPLINGS

*CHICKEN:*
1 stewing chicken (4-5 pounds)
1 small onion, sliced
1 carrot, sliced
2 celery ribs, finely chopped
1 teaspoon salt
*SAUCE:*
¼ cup unsalted butter6 tablespoons flour
white pepper to taste
6 tablespoons flour

1/8 teaspoon paprika
½ cup half and half
*DUMPLINGS:*
2 cups flour
1 teaspoon salt
1 tablespoon baking powder
1 tablespoon vegetable shortening
¾ cup milk

In a large kettle, place chicken. Add onion, carrot, celery and salt and pour in enough water to cover chicken. Bring to a boil over high heat. Reduce heat to medium-low and simmer, partially covered, until the chicken is tender, about 2 hours.

Remove chicken from pot and cool. When cool enough remove skin and remove meat from bones. Dice the chicken into 1"-1 ½" cubes. Strain the broth, discard the solids and de-fat the stock. Measure 4 cups of the stock (remainder can be refrigerated or frozen for use in another recipe; if less than 4 cups add water to chicken stock to make the 4 cups).

In a large saucepan using medium-high heat, melt the butter; stir in the flour and paprika. Stir until well blended and lemon colored, about 3-4 minutes. Pour in the 4 cups of stock, increase the heat to high, and bring to a boil, stirring often. Reduce the heat to medium-low and cook, stirring occasionally, until the sauce is thickened and smooth, about 10 minutes. Add the cubed chicken, half and half, and pepper. Season with additional salt and pepper if needed. Reduce heat to medium-low and cook slowly while preparing the dumplings.

In a large bowl, sift the flour, salt and baking powder together. Blend in the shortening with a pastry blender or a fork. Add the milk and mix well. Using a teaspoon; spoon dumpling mixture onto the gently bubbling chicken mixture. Cover and cook for an additional 15 minutes without lifting the lid. Serve at once.

Makes 6 servings.

# OVEN CHICKEN
## Low Calorie

3 broiler-fryer chickens, halved
2 teaspoons salt
½ teaspoon Tabasco sauce
4 tablespoons lime juice

1 teaspoon paprika
2 tablespoons salad oil
2 teaspoons dried tarragon
pepper to taste

Place chicken halves, skin side down, in shallow, foil-lined pan. Combine remaining ingredients to make marinade, brush over chicken. Bake in a 375 degree oven for 45-50 minutes; turning over after 25 minutes and brushing occasionally with the marinade.

Makes 6 servings.

# CHICKEN AND CHEESE

½ chicken broiler, cut in pieces
salt and pepper to taste
butter

garlic salt
2 tablespoons melted butter
2 tbs. Fontina cheese, shredded
OR 2 tablespoons Roquefort cheese

Rub chicken with salt and pepper. Place on broiling pan, skin side down. Dot with butter. Sprinkle with garlic salt, broil. When brown, turn, brush with 2 tablespoons melted butter, sprinkle with 2 tablespoons cheese. Broil until cheese has melted and chicken is tender.

Makes 2-3 servings.

# CHICKEN CACCIATORE
## For 2

1 ½ pounds of chicken (parts)
2 tablespoons butter
1 small onion, peeled and sliced
½ clove of garlic, minced
1 green pepper, sliced in strips
1 can tomatoes, 8 ounces

½ can tomato sauce, (4 ounces)
½ teaspoon salt
1/8 teaspoon pepper
¼ cup dry white wine
1/2 teaspoon dried oregano leaves
1 bay leaf

Wash and dry chicken. Heat butter in a large skillet over medium heat, add chicken pieces and brown evenly. Remove chicken; add onion, garlic and green peppers to skillet and cook until tender. Drain fat from skillet, return chicken pieces. Add remaining ingredients. Cover and cook over medium-low heat for 30 minutes, stirring occasionally. Uncover skillet and cook an additional 15 minutes or until the chicken is fork tender. Remove bay leaf.

Makes 2 servings.

# CHICKEN CONFETTI
*Ellen K.*

4-5 pounds cut up chicken
1 teaspoon salt
1/8 teaspoon pepper
¼ cup salad oil
½ cup chopped onion
¼ cup chopped green pepper
1 clove minced garlic
2 cans (16 ounce) tomatoes

1 can (8 ounce) tomato sauce
1 can (6 ounce) tomato paste
2 tablespoons parsley
2 teaspoons salt
1 teaspoon basil
¼ teaspoon pepper
2 tablespoons sugar
8 ounces spaghetti (cooked, cooled)
Grated Parmesan Cheese

Wash chicken and pat dry. Season with 1 teaspoon salt plus 1/8 teaspoon pepper. In large skillet or Dutch oven, brown chicken in oil. Remove chicken. Pour off all but 3 tablespoons of fat. Add onion, green pepper and garlic, cook and stir until onion is tender. Stir in chicken and remaining ingredients except spaghetti and cheese.

Cover tightly, cook chicken slowly 1 to 1 ½ hours or until tender, stirring occasionally and adding water if necessary. Skim off excess fat. Serve on spaghetti, sprinkle with Parmesan Cheese.

Makes 4-6 servings.

# CHICKEN CASSEROLE
## *Julie V.*

4 skinless boneless chicken breasts
2 cans cream of mushroom soup, condensed
or cream of broccoli soup
1 can water chestnuts, canned, sliced
1 cup mayonnaise
½ cup celery ribs chopped

1 scoop horseradish
1 teaspoon cayenne pepper
1 teaspoon white pepper
1 bag corn bread cubes
1 teaspoon Worcestershire sauce
½ small onion, chopped

Cook 4 chicken cutlets in a little salted water with chopped onion and celery for flavor. Dice cooked chicken and add to other ingredients, except bread cubs. Turn into buttered 9x13" oblong baking pan. Top with the bread cubes just as they come from the bag. Bake at 350 degrees for 30 minutes.

Makes 8 servings.


# CHICKEN CORDEN BLEU

PER PERSON;
2 slices boiled or baked ham
1 ½ ounces Gruyere cheese
salt and pepper to taste

1 boneless breast of chicken
¼ cup seasoned bread crumbs
1 tablespoon melted butter

Cut each breast cutlet lengthwise, making 2 pieces. Pound with a mallet to make each piece 1/8" thick. Place a slice of ham and ½ of the cheese on each half of cutlet and roll up jellyroll fashion. Dip each rolled cutlet in butter then in breadcrumbs. (a dash of dry mustard can be added to the butter for more flavor). Tuck in ends firmly. Bake on a greased pan in a 400 degree oven for 40 minutes.

*Note: ends must be firmly tucked in or melted cheese will run out!*

Makes 1 serving.

# CHICKEN A LA FRANCAISE

3-cups hot cooked rice
2 whole chicken breasts, skinned, boned, cut into
thin strips (about 1 ½ pounds before deboning)
1 ½ teaspoon salt
¼ teaspoon pepper
3-tablespoons butter
3-1 cup sliced green onions with tops

1 can (8 ounce) sliced mushrooms
(drain, reserve liquid)
½ cup dry sherry
1 cup fresh or frozen green peas
3 tomatoes, peeled, cut into eighths
2 tablespoons cornstarch

While rice is cooking, season chicken with salt and pepper, sauté in butter until browned. Add onions and mushrooms, continue cooking 2 minutes longer. Stir in sherry, peas, and broth. Cover and simmer about 20 minutes, add tomatoes. Dissolve cornstarch in mushroom liquid and stir into chicken mixture. Cook, stirring frequently, about 5 minutes longer. Serve over beds of fluffy rice. Garnish with chopped fresh parsley, if desired.

Makes 6 servings.

# CHICKEN FRICASSEE
# WITH DUMPLINGS

1 stewing chicken (4-5 pounds), cut up
¼ cup fat
2 sprigs parsley
4 celery tops
1 carrot, sliced
1 slice of onion
2 teaspoons salt

1/8 teaspoon pepper
Dumplings:
2 cups Bisquick baking mix
¾ cup milk
Gravy:
½ cup Bisquick mix
1 cup milk or cold water

Brown chicken slowly in fat, place in a kettle with just enough boiling water to cover. Add rest of ingredients except dumplings and gravy ingredients. Boil for 5 minutes; then turn down heat and simmer for 2-3 hours, until chicken is fork tender. Make dumplings and drop on simmering stew. Remove dumplings and chicken to a platter; keep hot while making gravy. Pour gravy over chicken and dumplings and serve.

*Dumplings:*
Mix ingredients together with a fork. Spoon into boiling stew. Cook over low heat for 10 minutes uncovered or covered.

*Gravy:*
Leave approximate 4 cups of chicken broth in the kettle over low heat, skimming off excess fat; mix ½ cup Bisquick and 1 cup milk or cold water to a smooth paste. Stir into broth; cook until thickened—about 15 minutes stirring occasionally. Season to taste.

Makes 8 servings.

# CHICKEN FRICASSEE
# WITH HERBS

3 cups chicken broth
1 onion, studded with 4 cloves
1 small carrot, diced
3 peppercorns
1 tablespoon chopped chives
½ bay leaf
2-3 ½ pound frying chickens, cutup
6 tablespoons flour
2 tablespoons chopped parsley

5 tablespoons butter
12 small white onions, peeled, whole
½ teaspoon rosemary
½ teaspoon marjoram
¼ teaspoon powdered saffron
3 tablespoons light cream
2 egg yolks
1 teaspoon lemon juice

In a heavy kettle combine the broth, onion, carrot, peppercorns, chives, parsley, salt and bay leaf. Bring to a boil. Dredge the chicken pieces in 3 tablespoons of the flour. In a skillet, heat 3 tablespoons of the butter; add the chicken and brown on all sides. Add to the simmering broth and cook, covered, over low heat until the chicken is tender, about 45 minutes.

Remove the chicken pieces to a warm platter and keep hot. Strain the stock, return it to the heat and add the onions. Cover and cook 45 minutes. Remove the onions to the platter and keep hot. In a heavy saucepan melt the remaining butter, add the remaining flour and stir with a wire whisk until blended. Add the simmering chicken broth all at once to the butter-flour mixture, stirring vigorously with the whisk until the sauce is thickened and smooth. Add the herbs and additional salt to taste. In a small mixing bowl combine the cream and egg yolks. Add a little of the hot sauce to the yolk mixture and stir it into the remaining sauce. Do not let it boil. Stir in the lemon juice. Pour the sauce over the chicken and onions.

Makes 6 servings.

# CHICKEN KIEV

½ cup butter, softened
2 tablespoons finely chopped parsley
1 clove garlic, crushed
1/8 teaspoon cayenne pepper
2 tablespoons lemon juice

4 whole boned, chicken breasts
½ cup flour
2 eggs, slightly beaten
½ cup dry bread crumbs, very fine
vegetable oil for frying

Mix the butter, parsley, garlic and cayenne. Gradually add the lemon juice, beating well to blend. Chill until firm enough to shape. Measure out 1 tablespoon of the mixture and shape into a cube. Divide the remainder into quarters and shape into an elongated roll about 2 ½ inches long. Refrigerate overnight, or place in freezer for about 1 hour. Flatten chicken breasts with meat mallet to 1/8" thick.

Place a roll of butter mixture on each breast and roll up. Tucking in edges to thoroughly seal in the butter. Secure loose edge with a toothpick. Roll breasts in flour to coat thoroughly, then coat with beaten eggs. Finally, roll in breadcrumbs to cover all sides. Heat 3-4" of vegetable oil in a deep saucepan over medium high heat or to a temperature of 350 degrees on frying thermometer. Fry breasts until dark brown, about 8-10 minutes. Remove toothpicks and arrange on a warm platter. Cut the chilled cube into 4 slices and place a slice on each roll. Garnish with parsley and lemon wedges if desired.

Makes 4 servings.

*Rich and buttery, rolled cutlets fried in oil. Can be baked instead, at 350 degrees for approximately 40 to 45 minutes.*

# CHICKEN IN MUSHROOM SAUCE

4 chicken breasts split in half lengthwise  
2 lemons  
pepper to taste  
¼ cup butter  

2 cups sliced fresh mushrooms  
2 tsp. fresh or frozen snipped chives  
½ cup whipping cream  

Zest and juice lemons, mix juice and zest together and add pepper for marinade; add chicken to marinade, put in plastic bag and refrigerate for at least an hour. In a large skillet, cook the chicken breasts in hot butter over medium heat for 8-10 minutes or until chicken is fork tender and no pink remains, turning occasionally so chicken browns evenly. Transfer chicken to a serving platter, reserving the drippings in the skillet. Cover the chicken and keep warm.

Add the mushrooms and chives to the reserved drippings in the skillet. Cook and stir for 1 to 2 minutes or till the mushrooms are tender. Stir in the whipping cream, boil gently for 3 minutes or till the sauce is slightly thickened, scraping up the browned hits on the bottom of the skillet. To serve, spoon the sauce over the chicken.

Makes 4 servings.

# CHICKEN PARMESAN
*Eleanor Hinsch*

6 boneless, skinless chicken breasts, split in half  
¼ cup Parmesan cheese  
1 jar spaghetti sauce or homemade sauce  
¼ stick butter  

1 cup plain, or Italian bread crumbs  
½ pound spaghetti, uncooked  
1 pound Mozzarella cheese  

Mix Parmesan cheese and bread crumbs together. Wash cutlets and dreg each cutlet in the bread crumb mixture. Prepare spaghetti as per box directions. Drain. In a casserole pan pour thin layer of sauce and arrange spaghetti over sauce evenly. In a skillet, add butter and on medium high heat sauté chicken until done, add more butter if needed. Arrange chicken on top of spaghetti. Bake in oven at 350 degrees F. for about 30 minutes, or until heated through. Slice Mozzarella cheese and cover top of dish with the cheese slices. Bake until the Mozzarella is melted. Can be frozen.

Makes approximately 6 servings.

# CLASSIC CHICKEN POT PIE

PASTRY:
1 ½ cups all-purpose flour
1 teaspoon salt
1/3 cup chilled butter, cut into pieces
1 large egg
3 tablespoons ice water
FILLING:
4 cups cubed cooked chicken
1 tablespoon butter
1 pound fresh mushrooms, sliced

¼ cup whipping cream
¼ cup dry white wine or water
2 tablespoons all-purpose flour
1 ½ teaspoon paprika
½ teaspoon salt
½ teaspoon black pepper
¾ cup chicken broth
GLAZE:
1 large egg, lightly beaten

To Prepare Pastry:
In a medium bowl, mix together flour and salt. Using pastry blender, cut butter into flour until coarse crumbs form. In a small bowl, beat together egg and water. Add to the flour mixture; mix lightly until a soft dough forms. Shape into a disk, wrap in plastic wrap and chill in the refrigerator for 1 hour.

To Prepare Filling:
Place chicken in a 2 quart casserole. In a large skillet, melt butter over low heat. Add mushrooms; increase the heat to medium-high; and sauté until browned and the liquid evaporates, about 5 minutes. Add the wine; cook until almost evaporated, about 2 minutes. Add mushroom mixture to chicken; stir to combine.

In a medium saucepan, whisk together cream, flour, paprika, salt, and pepper, over low heat; cook until thickened, about 5 minutes. Whisk in broth. Pour sauce over chicken mixture.

Preheat oven to 400 degrees F.

On a lightly floured surface; using a lightly floured rolling pin; roll the pastry to fit the top of the casserole Place on top of pie; trim and seal the edges. Roll out trimmings. Cut out leaves and flowers, brush pastry with glaze; add the decorations; brush again with glaze. Bake until filling is bubbly and crust is browned, 25-30 minutes. Transfer to a wire rack to cool slightly. Serve warm.

Makes 6 servings.

# QUICK CHICKEN POT PIE

1 can cream of mushroom soup
1 cup milk
¼ teaspoon pepper
1 can cream of chicken soup
¼ teaspoon dried thyme

4 cups cooked, cut-up vegetables frozen or fresh: broccoli, potatoes, mushrooms, etc)
2 cups cubes chicken or turkey
1 can refrigerator flaky biscuits (10 oz) or puff pastry cut slightly larger than baking dish

In a 3 quart oblong baking dish, combine soup, milk, thyme, pepper, stir in vegetables and chicken. Bake at 400 degrees F., for 15 minutes or until mixture begins to bubble. Meanwhile, cut biscuits into quarters. Remove dish from oven, stir. Arrange biscuits over mixture. Bake an additional 15 minutes or until biscuits are golden brown.

Makes 5 servings.


# CHICKEN AND RICE BAKE

1 can cream of mushroom soup (10.75 oz)
1 cup water (for creamier rice use 1 1/3 cup)
¾ cup uncooked regular white rice

¼ teaspoon paprika
¼ teaspoon pepper
4 skinless boneless chicken breasts

In 2 quart shallow baking dish mix soup, water, rice, paprika and pepper. Place chicken on rice mixture. Sprinkle with additional paprika and pepper, Cover. Bake at 375 degrees F. for 45 minutes or until chicken and rice are done.

Makes 4 servings.

# CHICKEN AND HAM ROULADE

3 large chicken breasts, skinned,
boned & halved, lengthwise
6 thin slices boiled ham
3 slices mozzarella cheese, halved
1 medium tomato, seeded and chopped

½ teaspoon dried sage, crushed
1/3 cup fine dried bread crumbs
2 tablespoons grated Parmesan cheese
2 tablespoons snipped parsley
4 tablespoons butter, melted

Place chicken, boned side up, on cutting board. Place a piece of clear plastic wrap over. Working from center out, pound lightly with meat mallet to 5x3". Remove wrap. Place a ham slice and half slice cheese on each cutlet, cutting to fit. Top with some tomato and a dash of sage. Tuck in sides; roll up jellyroll style, pressing well to seal. Combine breadcrumbs, Parmesan and parsley. Dip chicken into melted butter, then roll in crumbs. Place in shallow baking dish.

Bake at 350 degrees for 40 to 45 minutes.

Makes 6 servings.

*Tastes great and is a nice alternate to Chicken Corden Bleu.*


# CHICKEN SALAD

3 cups cooked chicken, cut into 1" cubes
¼ cup capers
½ cup vinegar
salt
Dash of Tabasco sauce

2 cups diced celery
½ cup chicken fat
1 teaspoon onion juice
mayonnaise

Make a marinade of the chicken fat, vinegar, onion juice, Tabasco and salt. Pour the marinade over the chicken and let stand for several hours, turning once or twice. Drain off the marinade, combine the chicken with the celery and capers and mix with mayonnaise to taste. Pile the salad in lettuce cups or fill scooped out tomatoes. Chill before serving. Can be garnished with hard cooked eggs and additional mayonnaise.

Makes approximately 5 cups.

# CHICKEN SCALOPINI WITH FONTINA CHEESE
# AND MUSHROOMS

4 boneless and skinless chicken breasts
1 stick unsalted butter
½ cup olive oil
½ cup all-purpose flour
3 tbs. freshly & finely grated Parmesan cheese
½ teaspoon salt

1/8 teaspoon freshly ground pepper
2 large eggs
½ pound button or cremini
mushrooms, sliced thinly
½ lb. diced cooked ham (1 cup)
¼ pound shredded Fontina cheese

Preheat oven to 350 degrees F.

Place each chicken breast half between two sheets of wax paper and pound them with mallet until they are thin scaloppini and about 9x6 inches. In a large 12" skillet, melt the butter with the olive oil over medium heat. On a sheet of wax paper, mix together the flour, grated Parmesan cheese, salt and pepper. In a bowl, beat the eggs. Dredge the chicken in the flour mixture, tapping off the excess flour and then dip them in the egg. Working in batches, place the chicken breasts in the skillet and cook until golden, turning once, about 5 minutes a side.

Remove the chicken breasts from the skillet and arrange in a 12x9x2" baking casserole. In the same skillet, cook the mushrooms, stirring until softened, about 5 minutes. One minute before the mushrooms are tender, add the ham. Spoon the mushroom and ham mixture over the scaloppini. Sprinkle the Fontina cheese over the mushrooms and bake until bubbly, for 20 to 25 minutes. Serve immediately.

Makes 4 servings.

*This is a real favorite. I love Fontina cheese and I have used Deli country ham diced, which has a nice flavor that makes it more family style.*

# CHICKEN STICKS

3 pounds chicken wings
1 cup butter (2 sticks)
1 ½ cups flour

1/3 cup sesame seeds
1 tablespoon salt
½ teaspoon ground ginger

Singe chicken wings; if necessary; cut off and discard tips. Divide each wing in half by cutting through joint with a sharp knife. Wash, drain on paper toweling. Melt butter in large pan. Mix flour, sesame seeds, salt and ginger in pie plate. Roll chicken pieces, one at a time, in butter in pan, letting any excess drip back. Roll in flour mixture, then set aside until all are coated. Put in single layer in same pan.

Bake at 350 degrees for 1 hour, or until tender. Slide pan in heated broiler for 5 minutes.

Makes 25 servings

# CHICKEN-BROCCOLI CORDEN BLEU

2 whole chicken breast halves without skin
4 slices cooked ham, thinly sliced
4 slices Swiss cheese, thinly sliced
2 tablespoons vegetable oil
chopped fresh parsley for garnish

1 can cream of broccoli soup—10.75ox
1/3 cup milk
¼ cup sliced green onions
1/8 tsp. dried thyme leaves, crushed

Place chicken between 2 pieces of plastic wrap. With a meat mallet or rolling pin, pound chicken to ¼ inch thickness. Place a ham slice and cheese slice on each breast half. Roll up chicken from narrow end, jelly-roll fashion. Tuck in ham and cheese if necessary; secure with wooden toothpicks.

In a 10" skillet over medium heat, in hot oil, cook chicken 10 minutes or until browned on all sides. Spoon off fat. Stir in soup, milk, green onions and thyme. Heat to boiling. Reduce heat to low. Cover; simmer 10 minutes or until chicken is tender and juices run clear. Garnish with parsley.

Makes 4 servings.

# CHICKEN DRUMSTICKS

3 pounds small chicken wings (about 15)
½ cup sugar
3 tablespoons cornstarch
½ teaspoon ground ginger

¼ teaspoon pepper
¾ cup water
1/3 cup lemon juice
¼ cup soy sauce

Cut off tips and discard. Divide each wing in half by cutting through joint with a sharp knife. Wash and place on paper towels and pat dry. Place in a single layer on rack in broiler pan.

Mix sugar, cornstarch, salt, ginger and pepper in a small saucepan; stir in water, lemon juice and soy sauce. Cook, stirring constantly, until mixture thickens and boils, 3 minutes. Brush part over chicken wings. Bake in 400 degree oven, turning once, for 30 minutes. Continue baking, turning and brushing several times with remaining lemon mixture, for an additional 30 to 40 minutes, or until richly glazed. When ready to serve, place in a chafing dish or keep-hot server.

Frame with a ring of thin lemon slices, if you wish. Serve hot.

Makes 12 servings.

# CHICKEN BREASTS STUFFED WITH RICE

1 package wild rice pilaf (10 ounce size)
1 tablespoon slivered almonds
2 lg. whole boneless chicken breasts,
skinned, halved
1/8 teaspoon salt
2 tsp. Dijon mustard
2 ounces Swiss cheese, shredded (1/2 cup)
(do not use pre-shredded)

SAUCE:
1 cup chicken broth
½ cup half and half
2 tablespoons flour
dash paprika
2 pkgs. frozen chopped spinach (9 oz)

Heat oven to 350 degrees F. Prepare rice pilaf according to package directions. Stir in almonds. Using a sharp knife, cut 3" slit in meaty side of each chicken breast half to form pocket. Spoon ½ cup of cooked rice mixture into each pocket. Arrange filled chicken breasts in un-greased 13x9" (3 quart) baking dish. Lightly sprinkle with salt and paprika.

Bake at 350 degrees for 45 to 50 minutes or until chicken is tender. In medium saucepan, combine all sauce ingredients except cheese. Using wire whisk, stir mixture until smooth. Stir in cheese. Cook over medium heat until sauce is thickened and begins to bubble, stirring constantly. Keep warm. Just before serving prepare spinach according to package directions; drain. Spread cooked spinach in thin layer on serving platter, arrange chicken breasts over spinach. Spoon some of the sauce over each stuffed chicken breast, serve with remaining sauce.
Makes 4 servings.

# CREAMED CHICKEN OVER RICE
*Eleanor Hinsch*

2 cups water
2 cups instant white rice
¼ teaspoon pepper
1 tablespoon butter

1/1-2 cups leftover chicken, cut up
3 cans cream of chicken soup
1-1 1/2 cups peas
1 cup whole milk

Bring 2 cups of water to a boil, add tablespoon butter and instant rice and following box directions cook rice. In separate saucepan, add 3 cans of soup with whole milk and bring to slow simmer, add chicken and pepper and continue to simmer until warmed through.

Prepare peas to taste.
To serve, put rice on plate and ladle creamed chicken over the rice. Add the peas on top or side as desired.

Makes approximately 4 servings.

*My children always loved this, and still do. It's a quick and easy meal to make instead of take out. Canned chicken can be used instead of leftovers if they aren't available.*

# MARINATED CHICKEN KABOBS
## for grilling

1 cup vegetable oil
½ cup soy sauce
½ cup light corn syrup
¼ cup lemon juice
2 tablespoons sesame seeds
1 green bell pepper cut into chunks

½ teaspoon garlic powder
salt to taste
4 skinless boneless chicken breast
halved, cut into 1 ½ inch cubes
8 ounces fresh mushrooms

In a medium bowl, blend vegetable oil, soy sauce, light corn syrup, lemon juice, sesame seeds, garlic powder and salt. Place chicken in the mixture. Cover and marinate in the refrigerator at least 2 hours. Preheat an outdoor grill to medium heat, and lightly oil grate. Thread chicken onto skewers alternately with mushrooms, onions and green bell peppers. Pour marinade into a saucepan, and bring to a boil. Cook for 5 to 10 minutes. Place skewers on the prepared grill. Cook 15 to 20 minutes, turning frequently, until chicken is no longer pink and juices run clear. Baste with the boiled marinade frequently during the last 10 minutes.

Makes 8 servings.

*I love this, its quick and easy and my son does the grilling. I usually leave out the sesame seeds, though, they get in my teeth!*

# CRUSTY CHICKEN

3 pounds frying chicken, cut up
½ stick butter, melted
1 teaspoon salt

½ teaspoon pepper
1 cup corn flake crumbs

Wash and dry chicken pieces. Combine melted butter with salt and pepper. Dip chicken pieces in seasoned butter, then roll in corn flake crumbs until well-coated. Place skin side up in single layer in shallow baking pan lined with aluminum foil, do not crowd pieces. Bake at 350 degrees about 1 hour or until tender. Do not cover pan or turn pieces.

Makes 4-5 servings.

*Variations: add salt and pepper to cornflake crumbs and substitute evaporated milk for butter.*

# BRANDIED DUCK

6 lbs. duck, cleaned, cut into serving portions
salt and pepper to taste
2 large onions, chopped
2 tablespoons parsley, chopped
1 bay leaf
1 teaspoon thyme

1 clove garlic, pureed
4-1/2 ounces cognac
1 pint claret wine
¼ cup olive oil
½ pound mushrooms, sliced

Have butcher cut duck into serving pieces. Sprinkle with salt and pepper. Put into a deep bowl; add onions, parsley, bay leaf, garlic, thyme, cognac and claret. Let duck marinate in mixture for 4 hours, turning occasionally.

Put the oil in a heavy heat-proof casserole, when oil is hot, add duck and brown well on all sides on top of stove. Add cognac and claret in which duck had marinated and sliced mushrooms. Cover and simmer over low heat until duck is cooked. (fork tender and cooked through). Serve hot.

Makes 4 servings.

# ROCK CORNISH GAME HENS
*With Mushroom Stuffing and Sauce*

4 Rock Cornish game hens
½ pound fresh mushrooms, sliced
¼ cup butter, melted
½ cup butter, melted

½ cup water
salt and pepper to taste
1 can cream of mushroom soup
10.75 oz.

Thaw hens and remove giblets. Preheat oven to 400 degrees. Rinse and dry birds. Season inside with salt and pepper. Sauté mushrooms quickly in ¼ cup butter. Stuff all but 8 large slices of mushrooms into hens. Place hens, breast side up into shallow roasting pan. Brush with butter. Add ½ cup water to bottom of roasting pan to keep the drippings from burning. Cover pan with foil. Roast for 25-30 minutes depending on size of birds. Uncover, brush with butter. Roast uncovered for 20-30 minutes, until the drumsticks are soft and juices are not tinged with pink when thickest part of thigh is pierced with fork. The skin should be brown. Brush with butter every 10-15 minutes.

Combine and heat soup and drippings. Serve as a sauce. Garnish birds with reserved mushroom slices.

Makes 4 servings.

*This is an easy and delicious recipe. Kids like it as much as adults.*

# ROCK CORNISH GAME HENS
## *With White Wine Mushroom Sauce*

¼ cup unsalted butter (1 stick)
2 tablespoons unsalted butter
½ pound mushrooms, trimmed and sliced
¼ cup flour
2 cups chicken stock

½ cup dry white wine
salt & ground pepper to taste
1 tbs. finely chopped fresh parsley
4 game hens (1 ¼ pound each)

Preheat oven to 350 degrees, lightly oil a rack of a roasting pan.

In a large skillet over medium-high heat, melt ¼ cup butter. Add the mushrooms and cook, stirring often, until well browned, about 10 minutes using a slotted spoon, transfer mushrooms to a paper towel. In the same skillet add ¼ cup more butter and melt. Add flour and stir until well blended and lemon colored, about 3 minutes; pour in the chicken stock, increase the heat to high, and bring to a boil, stirring often. Reduce heat to medium and simmer until thick and creamy, about 5 minutes. Stir in wine, add the mushrooms and simmer an additional 5 minutes. Season with salt and pepper. Stir in parsley.

Rub the game hens with the remaining 2 tablespoons softened butter. Season well with salt and pepper. Arrange, breast side up, on oiled rack and reduce the oven temperature to 350 degrees. Roast the game hens, basting often, until golden brown and the juices run clear when pierced at the thickest part of the thigh, about 45 minutes to 1 hour. Let the hens rest for about 10 minutes, covered in foil, before serving. While meat is resting re-heat the sauce over low heat. Place the hens on individual plates and spoon over a small amount of the sauce. Serve the remaining sauce on the side.

Makes 4 servings.

*If you wish you can substitute water or additional broth for the white wine. Although the wine gives it a really nice flavor.*

# SOUTHERN FRIED CHICKEN

1 cup buttermilk
2 cups self-rising flour
OR 2 cups flour with 4 tsp. baking powder &
1 teaspoon salt

3 whole chicken breasts, @ 12 oz.
each halved lengthwise
1 teaspoon lemon-pepper seasoning
1 quart vegetable oil

Pour buttermilk into a shallow plate. Measure flour onto wax paper.
Dip chicken into buttermilk; sprinkle with lemon-pepper seasoning; then roll in flour, coating well and shaking off excess. Pour enough vegetable oil into a large saucepan to make a 2" depth. Heat oil to 350 degrees on a deep-fat frying thermometer. (fry between 325 and 350 degrees otherwise it gets greasy!). Fry chicken, a few pieces at a time, for about 15 minutes, turning once, or until crisp and richly browned. Keep oil as near temperature as possible by raising and lowering heat. Keep browned pieces warm in oven.

Transfer cooked chicken to paper toweling to drain. Keep in warm oven until all chicken has been fried.

*Can use 1 broiler-fryer (3 ½ pounds) cut up instead of chicken breasts.*

Makes 4 servings.

# TURKEY GOODBYE
*Gwen B.*

1 1/3 cups long grain/wild rice, packaged  
½ cup grated cheese  
1 pint can of asparagus  
5 tablespoons flour  
1 teaspoon salt  
¼ teaspoon pepper  

4 cups chicken broth  
2 cups turkey, cut into pieces  
(or chicken)  
¼ cup cooking oil  
¼ teaspoon onion salt  
2 tablespoons slivered almonds, optional  

Sprinkle uncooked rice evenly into well-greased 13x9x2" pan. Pour on 1 ½ cup broth gently. Sprinkle with rice seasoning packet and ¼ cup cheese. Add layer of turkey and layer of asparagus. In separate saucepan, stir flour into oil, add seasonings and remaining broth gradually. Heat until thickened, stirring constantly. Pour over asparagus layer, sprinkle remaining cheese over top. Bake for 20 minutes at 375 degrees. Sprinkle almonds over top. Bake 5 minutes more.
2 ½ cups milk may be substituted for broth for a white sauce.
Makes 10 servings.


# WILD RICE AND TURKEY CASSEROLE

2 cups cut-up cooked turkey or chicken  
2 ¼ cups boiling water  
½ cups milk  
1 pkg. (6 oz) original flavor long-grain & wild rice mix  

4 med. green onions, sliced (1/4 cup)  
1 can (10 ¾ oz) condensed cream of mushroom soup  

Heat oven to 350 degrees F. In ungreased 2 quart casserole, mix all ingredients, including seasoning packed from rice mix. Cover casserole. Bake 45 to 50 minutes or until rice is tender. Uncover, bake 10 to 15 minutes longer or until liquid is absorbed. If desired, sprinkle with additional green onion.

*I love this served with asparagus as a side dish.*

Makes approximately 3-4 servings.

# YAKITORI
## For Grilling

2 chicken breasts about 1 ¾ pounds, skinless, boneless, and cut into 1" cubes
8 green onions, cut into pieces
8 green peppers, cut into strips
TERIYAKI SAUCE:
1 cup soy sauce

1 cup dry sherry
¼ cup canned beef broth
1 teaspoon sugar
1 clove garlic, crushed
1 tablespoon finely minced ginger

Combine Teriyaki Sauce ingredients. Marinate meats and vegetables in sauce for 1 hour. Thread about 4 pieces of meat with either a green onion or green pepper strip, close together, on a wooden cocktail skewer. Brush with sauce, grill, 3" about white hot charcoal, for 4-5 minutes on each side, brushing with extra sauce when turning.

Makes 2 servings.

# GIBLET GRAVY
*Eleanor Bohlen Hinsch*

Turkey giblets and neck
1 medium onion, chopped (1/2 cup)
celery tops (a few)
salt and pepper to taste

1 bay leaf
4 cups water
½ cup flour
gravy master or similar

Combine turkey giblets, except liver, and neck with onion, celery tops, salt, bay leaf and water in a medium-size saucepan. Heat to boiling; reduce heat to low, cover. Simmer 1 hour, or until onion and celery is tender. Add liver, simmer 20 minutes longer or until liver is done.

Strain broth, measure, add water, if needed, to make 4 cups. Chop giblets finely and stir into broth, discard neck. After turkey has been removed from roasting pan, pour all fat into a cup, leaving juices in pan. Measure 8 tablespoons fat and return to pan; blend in flour.

Cook; stirring constantly, just until bubbly, stirring in the broth with giblets, while stirring. Continue cooking and stirring, scraping baked-on juices from the bottom and sides of the pan, until the gravy thickens and bubbles 1 minute. Season to taste with salt and pepper, stir in a little bottled gravy coloring to darken, if desired.

*The trick to good gravy is to mix the flour with cold water in a small jar; cover and shake until well blended. Add a bit at a time, stirring constantly to prevent lumps to the gravy mixture.*

*A good substitute for water is potato water if available (water that potatoes have been boiled in). The starch in the water is a natural thickener and adds flavor also. You can also substitute chicken broth for the water.*

Makes enough for 6-8 servings. Can be doubled.

# APPLE STUFFING
## *For duck or goose*

| | |
|---|---|
| 1 slice onion | 2 tablespoons butter |
| ½ cup chopped celery | ½ cup bread crumbs |
| ½ cup peeled, chopped tart apples | salt and pepper |

Melt the butter in a skillet and brown the onion. Add the rest of the ingredients, seasoning to taste, and mix thoroughly. Heat through. Stuff the bird as directed.

This recipe is sufficient for one duck, double the recipe for goose.

# BREAD STUFFING
## *For turkey*

| | |
|---|---|
| 6 to 8 cups crumbled day old bread | ¼ teaspoon pepper |
| 2 teaspoons poultry seasoning | ¼ cup minced onions |
| ½ to ¾ cup butter, melted | ¾ cup giblet stock, or hot water |
| 1 egg | |

Combine the bread, seasonings, the onions (first cooked but not browned, for 5 minutes in 2 tablespoons butter), and the stock. Blend thoroughly; add the remaining butter with the beaten egg. The chopped cooked giblets may be added also, if desired. For chicken, reduce the amounts by ½.

*You can use packaged bread crumbs for stuffing instead of the bread if you don't have the bread available.*

# CORN BREAD FOR STUFFING

½ cup flour
1 cup white cornmeal
1 teaspoon baking powder
½ teaspoon baking soda

1 teaspoon salt
1 cup buttermilk
1 egg
2 tablespoons butter, melted

Preheat oven to 400 degrees.

Put the flour, cornmeal, baking powder, soda and salt into a sifter and sift together into a bowl. Add the buttermilk and stir well. Add the egg and butter and beat well. Pour the mixture into a hot, greased 9 inch iron skillet or a 9" square baking pan. Bake until brown, about 20 minutes. Check for doneness. Remove the corn bread from the skillet or pan and let cool. When completely cooled use in stuffing recipe.

Makes 12 servings.


# CORN BREAD DRESSING

3 cups chopped onion
1 cup unsalted butter (16 tablespoons)
½ cup fresh sage, chopped
freshly ground pepper to taste
1 loaf corn bread (see above)

3 cups chopped celery
1 tablespoon olive oil
3 cups turkey or chicken stock
salt to taste

Heat oven to 350 degrees. In large skillet, sauté onion and celery in 12 tablespoons butter and olive oil until vegetables are softened, about 6-7 minutes. In bowl, mix onion mixture, sage, salt, pepper and corn bread cut into 1" cubes. Spoon in 13x9x2 glass baking dish. Melt remaining butter; drizzle over top, with stock, cover with foil. Bake at 350 degrees for 20 minutes. Remove foil and bake 10 minutes, until browned.

# GIBLET STUFFING
## *For turkey*

2 quarts crumbled, day old bread
½ teaspoon pepper
¾ cup butter
3 tablespoons finely minced celery
giblet broth

2 teaspoons salt
1 teaspoon sage
1 onion, finely minced
minced cooked giblets

Combine the crumbs and seasonings with the onion and celery first, simmer until tender, but not brown, in 2 tablespoons of the butter. Add the remaining butter with the minced cooked giblets. If a more moist stuffing is desired, add giblet or chicken broth.

Enough stuffing for medium sized turkey.

# RICE STUFFING

2 cups uncooked rice
½ cup cooking oil
1 cup chopped celery
1 cup chopped onion
2 cups meat stock or tomato juice

2 teaspoons salt
½ teaspoon pepper
1 tablespoon catsup
1 tablespoon Worcestershire sauce
1 tablespoon chopped parsley

Wash and dry the rice, then cook in the oil with celery and onion, stirring frequently, until the rice is golden brown. Add stock, cover closely and cook gently for ½ hour. Stuff loosely into bird. Roast as usual. *This is my great-grandma's recipe. I substitute a box of wild rice, adding all ingredients except tomato juice and catsup. Follow directions on rice box using stock instead of water. Sauté onion, celery in oil and gradually add to rice. This is great for Rock Cornish Game Hens. Scallions can also be added, but keep to a minimum.*

Enough for 1 bird.

# HERB STUFFING

2 cups finely chopped celery
½ cup (1 stick) butter or margarine
1 teaspoon leaf sage, crumbled
¾ cup water

1 med. size onion chopped (1/2 cup)
1 pkg. herb seasoned cubed stuffing
1 can chicken broth

Cook celery and onion in the butter in a large skillet until tender but not browned, about 15 minutes. Combine stuffing mix and sage in a large bowl. Add celery mixture, chicken broth and water and toss until well mixed. Use to stuff turkey. *Reduce to half to stuff a large chicken (6 cups)*.

Makes about 12 cups.

# MUSHROOM STUFFING

1 ½-1 lb. loaves white bread, cut into cubes
1 ½ bunches celery with leaves, coarsely chopped
3 tablespoons poultry seasonings
3 sticks (12 ounces) unsalted butter
2 eggs, beaten with 2 tablespoons water

1-10 ounce package sliced white mushrooms
1 ½ onions, chopped
1 tablespoon salt

Preheat the oven to 250 degrees. Arrange the bread cubes on a baking sheet and bake, tossing occasionally, until dried but not browned, about 40 minutes, let cool. Increase the oven temperature to 350 degrees. Meanwhile using a food processor and working in batches, pulse the celery until finely chopped. In a large, deep skillet, melt the butter over medium-high heat. Add the onions and cook until softened, about 10 minutes. Mix in the celery and mushrooms and cook over high heat, stirring frequently, for 10 minutes. Stir in the poultry seasoning and salt. In a large bowl, toss the bread cubes with the beaten egg mixture. Add the vegetable mixture and toss until well combined. Spoon the stuffing into 2 buttered 2 quart casserole dishes and bake, uncovered, for 40 minutes.

Approximately 12 servings.

# TRADITIONAL STUFFING

½ cup finely chopped celery
½ cup finely chopped onion
½ cup butter
½ cup chicken broth

¼ teaspoon salt
¼ teaspoon pepper
¾ bag bread cubes
1 teaspoon poultry seasoning

Sauté celery and onion in butter until soft, not brown. Add broth, poultry seasonings, salt and pepper. Heat, stirring to mix well. Add bread crumbs and mix lightly. Add more broth if needed. Should be moist but not wet. Turn into buttered baking dish (or stuff into chicken or turkey for roasting). Bake at 350 degrees, uncovered, for 30 minutes, or until lightly toasted.

Makes 5 cups.

Double recipe to stuff 12-15 pound turkey.

# LAMB AND VEAL

# CROWN ROAST OF LAMB

1 crown roast of lamb (ask butcher to prepare ahead) approximately 14-16 chops
¾ pound ground lamb for stuffing
1 ½ cups soft fresh bread crumbs
1 egg
¼ cup milk
¾ teaspoon onion salt
½ teaspoon rosemary, crumbled
salt and pepper to taste
parsley sprigs for garnish

The meat should be at room temperature when it goes into the oven. Remove paper frills and save. In bowl, combine ground lamb, bread crumbs, egg, milk, onion salt, rosemary and 1/8 teaspoon pepper; mix well.

Sprinkle surface of roast with salt and pepper, place on rack of roasting pan. Fill center of crown loosely with the ground meat mixture. Wrap tips of bones tightly with foil to prevent burning. Roast at 450 degrees for 20 minutes, reduce temperature to 325 degrees, continue roasting for 1 hour 10-15 minutes. Remove lamb from oven, place on serving platter and allow to rest for 10-15 minutes. Remove foil from bones, cover with paper frills, surround crown with roasted potatoes, or Swedish potatoes, and parsley sprigs. To carve, insert fork at side of crown at an angle to steady it; using a sharp knife, slice between ribs.

Note: *reduce roasting time by 10 minutes for rare.*
*A bit of lemon juice rubbed into crown roast before roasting will add additional flavor.*

Makes 8-10 servings.

# ROAST LEG OF LAMB

6 pounds leg of lamb, boned and tied
2 tablespoons oil or olive oil
3 crushed cloves of garlic

salt and pepper to taste
½ teaspoon ground thyme
1 tablespoon rosemary leaves

Preheat oven to 400 degrees. Put lamb into large roasting pan and rub well with oil, garlic, salt and pepper, thyme and rosemary. Roast for 1 hour, turn the oven off and leave the leg of lamb in the warm oven for ½ to 1 hour longer, until you are ready to serve. Potatoes, carrots and onions may be roasted in the pan with the lamb, baste occasionally. Serve with gravy and/or mint jelly.

Makes 8 servings.

# LAMB SHISH KEBOB
## For Grilling

3 pounds of lamb, trimmed, cut into 2" chunks
¼ cup olive oil
¼ cup red wine
¼ fresh lemon juice
½ small onion, finely chopped
1 clove garlic, minced
½ ginger root slice, minced
½ teaspoon black pepper
¼ teaspoon cayenne pepper
1 teaspoon curry powder

1 teaspoon turmeric
1 teaspoon coriander leaf, ground
18 cherry tomatoes
1 green pepper, cut into 2" pieces
1 red or yellow pepper, cut into 2" pieces
3 medium potatoes, par-boiled
18 large mushrooms
18 pearl onions, par-boiled
3 bacon slices
lemons, cut in quarters (optional)

Place cubed lamb in deep glass or ceramic dish. Combine oil with wine and lemon juice. Stir in onion, ginger, garlic and spices. Pour over lamb to marinate, turning every 2-3 hours for 8-10 hours or overnight. Remove lamb from marinade; sprinkle with salt and pepper. Prepare skewers wiping with oil Cut bacon, potatoes and peppers into 2" sized pieces. Thread meat and vegetables onto skewers; placing a piece of bacon over each meat chunk. A quarter of lemon can be also put on each skewer.

Grill 4 inches above white-hot charcoal, turning frequently so lamb cooks on all sides, and allowing 10 minutes cooking time for pink lamb; lamb is juiciest and most flavorful if it is not overcooked. Slide off skewers onto hot cooked rice.

Makes approximately 6 to 8 servings.

# LAMB STEW
## FOR 4

1 ½ lbs. boneless lamb shoulder, diced into cubes
all-purpose flour, seasoned with salt & pepper
2 tablespoons cooking oil
2 cloves garlic, finely chopped

2 cups water
1 pkg. frozen mixed vegetables, 10 oz.
salt and pepper to taste
½ teaspoon dried rosemary

Coat lamb with the flour seasoned with salt and pepper. Heat oil, add lamb and brown on all sides. Add garlic and water. Cover and cook for 1 hour over low heat, stirring occasionally. Add remaining ingredients, cover and cook for 10 minutes, or until vegetables are tender, stirring occasionally.

Makes 4 servings.

# SCHWEIZER SCHNITZEL
### Veal Rolls with ham and cheese

4 slices boiled ham
4 slices Swiss cheese
1 pound veal round steak, cut into 4 pieces
2 tablespoons flour
½ teaspoon salt
¼ teaspoon pepper

1 egg, beaten
½ cup dry bread crumbs
2 tablespoons shortening
½ cup dry white wine
package egg noodles
¼ teaspoon allspice

Pound veal pieces very thin. Place 1 slice each of boiled ham and Swiss cheese on each piece of veal steak. Roll up carefully, beginning at narrow end; secure rolls with wooden picks. Mix flour and seasonings; dust veal with seasoned flour. Dip floured rolls into beaten egg; coat with bread crumbs. Brown in hot shortening. Pour wine over meat. Cover and simmer 55 minutes; uncover, simmer 5 minutes longer. Serve on hot egg noodles; pour liquid and melted cheese from skillet over meat and noodles.

Makes 4 servings.

*This is a variation of Veal Cordon Bleu, but German style.*

# VEAL CORDON BLEU

4 thin veal scaloppini, about ½ pound cut from leg
4 slices Swiss cheese at room temperature
4 thin slices baked or boiled ham
salt and pepper to taste
¼ cup flour

1/3 cup dry seasoned bread crumbs
2 tablespoons butter
1 egg
1 tablespoon oil

Put the veal between sheets of waxed paper and pound them with a mallet until they are about 1/8" thick. Salt and pepper the veal slices. On top of each veal slice place a slice of cheese trimmed to be a fraction smaller than the veal, next a trimmed slice on ham. Roll, tucking in ends as you roll. Spread out the flour and bread crumbs in separate plates or sheets of waxed paper. Beat the egg in a bowl, coat each veal roll lightly with flour, then dip in egg and then dust with crumbs. This can be done ½ hour ahead of cooking time.

In a large skillet, heat the butter and oil. Add more butter if the bottom of the skillet is not well covered. Sauté the rolls for 4 minutes on each side (4 sides) or until the meat is golden brown. The cheese should be melted inside. Regulate the heat so fat is hot but not burning.

Serve immediately.

Makes 4 servings.

# VEAL PARMIGIANO

1 pound veal cutlets, very thinly sliced or pounded
1 teaspoon salt
1/8 teaspoon pepper
1 egg
water
1 onion chopped
1 can tomato paste, 6 ounces

1 teaspoon salt
½ teaspoon basil
1/3 cup grated Parmesan cheese
1/3 cup fine dry bread crumbs
¼ cup vegetable oil
6 slices Mozzarella cheese

Cut veal into 6-8 pieces; sprinkle with salt and pepper. In a shallow bowl, lightly beat egg with 2 teaspoons water. On a sheet of waxed paper combine Parmesan and bread crumbs. Dip veal into egg then in Parmesan mixture.

In a skillet, brown veal on both sides, a few pieces at a time, in oil. Remove to a large baking dish. To skillet add onion and cook until tender. Stir in tomato paste, 2 cups water, salt and basil. Simmer 5 minutes; scrapping up any browned bits from bottom of skillet. Pour most of the sauce over veal. Top with cheese, pour remaining sauce over top.

Bake at 350 degrees for 20-25 minutes.

Makes 4 servings.


# VEAL SCALOPPINI
## FOR 2

2 slices veal cutlet
all-purpose flour, seasoned with salt and pepper
1 tablespoon oil
1 minced green pepper

1 small onion, sliced
1 can tomato sauce, small size
3 tablespoons grated cheese

Dust 2 slices of veal with seasoned flour, brown in the oil. Add pepper, onion and sauté until tender, about 5 minutes. Add tomato sauce, sprinkle with grated cheese. Cover and simmer until cheese melts, about 10 minutes. Can be served over noodles, spaghetti or flavored rice.

Makes 2 servings.

# WIENER SCHNITZEL
# GERMAN VEAL CUTLETS

All-purpose flour, seasoned with salt and pepper
2 eggs, lightly beaten
2 tablespoons milk
1 cup fine bread crumbs

4 veal cutlets, pounded thin, chilled
vegetable oil
lemon wedges, for garnish

In a small bowl whisk together milk and eggs, on waxed paper put approximately 1 cup all-purpose flour seasoned with salt and pepper. On separate piece of waxed paper put bread crumbs. Coat each cutlet with flour, then dip into egg mixture, and finally cover with bread crumbs, making sure they are completely coated. Place one layer of cutlets on a baking sheet, cover with plastic wrap and refrigerate for at least 30-45 minutes before cooking. Pour the oil to a depth of ¼" into a deep skillet. Heat over a medium-high heat. Gently add a few cutlets at a time, and cook until golden brown on both sides, approximately 2-3 minutes per side. Transfer to paper towels to drain. Keep warm until ready to serve.

Serve with red cabbage.

*Can be served with mushroom sauce or veal gravy, served with mashed potatoes or French fries.*

Makes 4 servings.

# PORK, HAM AND SAUSAGES

# APPLE GLAZED ROAST PORK

4 pounds loin of pork
¼ cup sherry
salt and pepper to taste
dash sage
dash thyme
½ cup white wine

½ cup apple juice
1 thinly sliced onion
1 bay leaf
½ cup drained apple sauce
2 tablespoons brown sugar

Rub loin of port with sherry, salt, pepper, sage and thyme. Place in roasting pan with ½ cup white wine, apple juice, onion and bay leaf. Roast 2 hours in 350 degree oven, basting frequently; then coat with ½ cup drained apple sauce. Sprinkle with 2 tablespoons brown sugar. Roast 45 minutes longer or until done.

Makes 6 servings.

*Apples are just delicious with pork, this recipe makes the pork extra special. I prefer bone in pork loin, as it has more moisture and more flavor. I use my homemade apple sauce with this recipe.*

# BAKED FRESH HAM

10 pounds fresh ham
2 whole garlic cloves minced
2 tablespoons olive oil

½ teaspoon dried rosemary
½ teaspoon ground thyme
1 cup beer

Trim excess fat from ham. Mix oil with herbs and rub all over ham. Bake at 350 degrees for 30-35 minutes per pound of meat, until meat thermometer registers 185 degrees. Baste occasionally with the beer.

Makes 12 servings.

*This recipe is good with ale or stout also.*

# BROCCOLI-HAM ROLLS

1 package frozen chopped broccoli (10 oz)
1 can condensed cream of mushroom soup
1 can (6 ¾ oz) chicken or ground ham
½ cup sour cream

4 eggs
¼ cup water
butter

In 2 quart saucepan; prepare broccoli as label directs, drain. To cooked broccoli, add undiluted cream of mushroom soup and ham with its juices. Cook; stirring often, until ham is heated through and broken into small chunks; keep warm. Meanwhile in small bowl, with fork, beat eggs and water until well mixed. In a 6 or 7" skillet, over medium heat, melt 1 teaspoon butter, tilting skillet to grease sides, pour 2 to 3 tablespoons egg mixture into skillet, tilting to make a thin pancake.

When top of pancake is set and underside is delicately browned, run spatula around side and bottom to loosen; slide pancake onto plate. Repeat to make 7 more. Fill each pancake with some broccoli mixture; roll and arrange them in one layer on warm platter. Top with sour cream.

Makes 4 servings.

# CHOP SUEY

3 pounds boneless ground pork
6 tablespoons vegetable oil
½ teaspoon salt
½ teaspoon pepper
3 medium onions
8 celery stalks

2 cans chicken broth 15.75 oz
¼ cup soy sauce
1 can bean sprouts, drained, 1 pound
4 tablespoons cornstarch
½ cup water
hot rice & Chinese noodles

Cut pork into ¼" cubes, heat oil in large saucepan, add pork cubes or ground pork, salt and pepper. Cook over medium heat for 5 minutes, stirring frequently. Cut each onion into 6 wedges, cut celery into 1" pieces. Heat chicken broth; add to meat with onion wedges, celery pieces, and soy sauce, mixing well. Cook over low heat, stirring occasionally, for 15 minutes. Add drained bean sprouts and cook 3 minutes longer. Mix cornstarch with water and add to the saucepan. Stir until thickened and cook 2 minutes longer. Serve hot over rice and noodles.

*Cooked chicken strips can be added to this dish, or pork strips, instead of ground pork. (use 3 pounds, leftovers can be used). My children love Chop Suey and it was really hard to find when we moved to North Carolina so this was my answer! The hardest part now is getting the Chinese noodles.*

Makes 8 servings.

# CROWN ROAST OF PORK

7 ½ to 8 lb. pork crown roast (about 20 ribs)
1 teaspoon fresh ground pepper

2 teaspoons salt
2 lbs. of Pork sausage (mild or spicy)
or your favorite stuffing mixture

Heat oven to 325 degrees F. Sprinkle roast with salt and pepper. Place bone ends up in roasting pan; wrap bone ends with aluminum foil to prevent excessive browning. Place a small mixing bowl in crown to hold shape of roast. Make sure the bowl is oven proof. Insert a meat thermometer so tip is in thick part of meat. Roast uncovered 3 to 4 hours, or until meat is done. Thermometer should read 185 degrees.

An hour before meat is done, remove bowl and fill with the stuffing and cover the stuffing only with foil. This can be the pork sausage, removed from casings or your favorite stuffing, my favorite one is the rice stuffing. Bake for 30 minutes and remove foil. Continue baking for 30 minutes more. When done, place roast on a large platter. Remove foil wrapping; place paper frills, if available, on bone ends. To carve, slice between ribs. Use pan drippings to make gravy.

Makes 12 servings.

*This is a family favorite for the Holidays. I serve it with red cabbage, apple sauce, and mashed potatoes. My butcher has a pork stuffing that is really great, the closest I found was the mild pork sausage mixed with some finely diced apples and approximately ½ cup of flavored bread stuffing, crumbled.*

# KOO LOO YUK
# SWEET & SOUR PORK

SAUCE:
1 cup white vinegar
¼ cup pineapple juice
¼ cup ketchup
1 tablespoon soy sauce
¼ cup sugar
1 clove garlic, minced
10 bamboo shoots diced
¼ teaspoon dried, ground red pepper
1 green pepper, cut julienne style
6 slices canned pineapple, cut into eighths

1 tablespoon cornstarch
1 tablespoon vegetable oil
PORK:
1 ½ pounds pork tenderloin
2 tablespoons soy sauce
1 egg, beaten
2 tablespoons dry sherry
dash salt and pepper
¼ cup cornstarch
1 quart vegetable oil

SAUCE:

In a saucepan, combine the vinegar, pineapple juice, ketchup, soy sauce, and sugar. Bring to a boil and add the garlic, bamboo shoots, red pepper, and green pepper. Cook over low heat 3 minutes. Add the pineapple; mix the cornstarch with a little water until smooth, then stir into the sauce until thickened. Mix in the oil.

PORK:

Pound the pork lightly and cut into 1" cubes. Toss the pork with a mixture of the egg, soy sauce, sherry, salt and pepper. Sprinkle with the cornstarch and mix until fingers are not sticky. Heat oil to 350 degrees, and fry the pork until lightly browned. Drain. Raise temperature of oil to 375 degrees and fry pork again until browned. Drain. Pour sauce over the meat.

Makes 4 to 6 servings.

# OMA'S KALE MIT PINKELWURST
## Kale with pinkelwurst
*Mathilde Bohlen*

3-4 lbs. kale, washed and stripped,*and chopped
4 cups water or more
1 3 pound smoked pork butt
6-7 boiled potatoes

1 pinkelwurst (about 1 lb.)**
1 medium onion, finely chopped
salt and pepper to taste

*break stalks apart, discarding leaves that are brown, yellow, faded or bruised. Strip leafy portion from stems and ribs. Discard stems and ribs. Do not use an unclad iron or an aluminum pot, as the kale will become bitter flavored. Chop or put through food processor, until coarsely chopped.

**Can be purchased at a German butcher(such as Karl Emhers butcher shops).

Place kale in a 2-3 quart Dutch oven. If pinkelwurst casing is closed with metal bands, cut them off and discard. Add water (enough to cover kale half way). Cover pot and bring to a boil. Reduce heat and simmer slowly but steadily for about 20 minutes. Nest pinkelwurst in the kale, add onion and continue to simmer. The sausage, if it doesn't burst after about 20 minutes, should be slit open and casing discarded. As the sausage cooks and softens, cook boiled potatoes to serve with this dish. This dish can be frozen (without potatoes) and tastes even better reheated.

Oma usually added a little bit of rolled oatmeal and a few pieces of the large smoked bacon that you can get at the German butcher to the kale while it is cooking.

A smoked pork tenderloin can be added to the pot for a total meal. Remove wrapper, but keep in netting while cooking in pot with kale. Remove netting before slicing. The longer this pot simmers the better it tastes. When reheated it tastes even better. Bacon, fried and crumbled, can be added for additional flavor. Serve with boiled potatoes.

# KRAUT AND KNACKWURST

1 large onion, sliced
¼ cup butter
1 large red apple, cored, quartered, diced
1 can sauerkraut, washed and drained (1 ½ lbs)

3 tablespoons brown sugar
1 teaspoon caraway seeds
1 pound knackwursts, sliced
½ cup beer; or dry white wine

Sauté onion in 3 tablespoons butter in a large skillet until just soft, add apple and sauté apple 2 minutes. Stir in sauerkraut, brown sugar, and caraway seeds; toss lightly with a fork to mix well; spoon into an 8 cup shallow casserole dish. Sauté knackwursts in remaining 1 tablespoon of butter, in same pan, for 5 minutes, or until browned; arrange on sauerkraut, drizzle beer or wine over; cover casserole with foil.

Bake in moderate (350 degree) oven for about 30 minutes or until bubbly hot. Serve with mustard, dill pickles and pumpernickel bread if desired.

Makes 4 servings.

*Bratwurst can be substituted for the knockwurst in this dish. Use beer for the bratwurst. Nice served with pickled beets. Adds color and flavor.*
*I love this made with bratwurst. Unfortunately I have to fight the children for this one.*

# OVEN BARBECUED SPARERIBS

4 pounds spareribs
2 tablespoons butter
½ cup chopped onions
2 tablespoons vinegar
2 tablespoons lemon juice

2 tablespoons Worcestershire sauce
2 tablespoons brown sugar
1 teaspoon dry mustard
1 teaspoon salt
¼ teaspoon black pepper

Remove skin from back of ribs. Place ribs in a foil-lined baking pan in a single layer. Cut into 2 pieces in necessary. In a skillet; melt butter and sauté onion until brown and limp. Add remaining ingredients along with 1 cup water. Stir to blend and simmer for about 20 minutes. Pour mixture over ribs, cover tightly with foil or place ribs in plastic bag with marinade. Allow to marinade in the sauce mixture for at least 20 minutes.

Bake in a 275 degree oven for 3 hours. Using a slow oven makes the spareribs tender and ready to fall off the bones.

Makes 6 servings.

# BAKED VIRGINIA HAM
*Richard Bohlen*

12 lbs. whole, smoked ham butt & shank
parsley, for garnish
½ cup brown sugar

1 can pineapple slices, 32 ounces
whole cloves
1 cup beer

Remove brown outer skin from ham. Trim entire surface fat evenly to leave a covering ½" deep. Stud with whole cloves after scoring top of ham (1" crisscross). Coat ham with brown sugar and put beer in bottom of roasting pan. Bake in shallow roasting pan in preheated 325 degree oven for 2 ½ hours, basting with the beer.

20 minutes before end of cooking time open and drain pineapple slices. Place slices on top of ham. Bake for an additional 20 minutes until pineapple is cooked but not brown. Place on large serving platter. Surround with remaining fruit.
Serves 12-16.

This ham is not only what we made for Easter Sunday but what we made for the Virginia Ham sold in the Deli.

# PIZZA RUSTICA

PASTRY:
1 stick unsalted butter, softened
2 cups unbleached flour
2 tablespoons sugar
2 egg yolks
3 tablespoons iced water
FILLING:
3 egg yolks

1 cup whole milk ricotta cheese
¼ pound Proscuitto cut in ½" pieces
¼ pound boiled ham cut in ½" pieces
¼ pound Mortadella cut in ½" pieces
½ lb. mozzarella cheese cut in ½" pieces
1 cup plum tomatoes, drained, chopped
¼ cup grated Parmesan cheese
salt and pepper to taste

## PASTRY:

Cut butter into dry ingredients; add egg yolks and water; knead lightly with hands until well mixed. Form two balls, 1 slightly larger than the other; chill 1 hour.

When ready to use, roll larger dough ball in circle to fit 9" pie plate, and smaller ball for top. Roll out scraps and cut out decorative designs if desired, such as leaves, etc.

## FILLING:

In a large bowl, with a fork, lightly beat egg yolks. Stir in ricotta; beat until creamy. Stir in remaining ingredients. Spoon into buttered pastry lined pie plate, cover with top pastry, trim and crimp edges. Moisten bottom of pastry cutouts and affix to top of pie.

Bake in preheated 375 degree oven 45-50 minutes, until crust is light golden brown. Serve warm or at room temperature.

Makes 6 servings.

*Makes a nice change from bringing home a pizza from the local store, and more filling.*

# PORK CHOPS WITH GRAVY

4 pork loin chops, ½" thick
¼ teaspoon seasoned salt
½ cup sour cream
1 can condensed cream of celery soup (10.75 oz)

3 cups green beans
1 ½ cups potatoes, peeled, quartered
1 medium onion, sliced
1 medium green pepper, julienne

Spray large non-stick skillet with non-stick cooking spray. Heat over medium high heat until hot. Sprinkle pork chops with seasoned salt, add to skillet. Cook 5-6 minutes or until browned on both sides. Remove chops from skillet, cover to keep warm.

In medium bowl, combine sour cream, soup and sage; mix well, add to skillet; stir in frozen vegetables. Arrange chops over vegetable mixture. Press gently into mixture. Bring to a boil. Reduce heat to medium-low; cover and cook 10-15 minutes or until pork chops are no longer pink in center and vegetables are tender; stirring occasionally.

Makes 4 servings.

# PORK DIANE

2 tablespoons butter
2 pork tenderloins, cut crosswise into ¼" slices
1 cup chicken broth
2 teaspoons Worcestershire sauce
¼ teaspoon salt

1/8 teaspoon pepper
8 small new red potatoes, quartered
1 cup sliced fresh mushrooms
½ cup slices green onions
2 tablespoons flour

Melt butter in 12" skillet or Dutch oven over medium-high heat. Add pork slices; cook 3-5 minutes or until browned on both sides. Remove pork from skillet; set aside.

Reserve ¼ cup of the chicken broth. Add remaining chicken broth, Worcestershire sauce, salt, pepper and potatoes to skillet. Bring to a boil. Reduce heat to low; cover and simmer 10 minutes or until potatoes are tender. Stir in mushrooms, onions and pork slices. Cover; simmer an additional 5 minutes or until vegetables are tender.

In a small bowl, combine flour and reserved ¼ cup chicken broth; blend until smooth. Gradually stir into pork mixture. Cook and stir over medium-high until mixture is bubbly and thickened.
Makes 4-5 servings.

# PORK JAGER SCHNITZEL
## fried pork cutlets with mushroom sauce
## and with Jagermeister liqueur

PORK:
24-3 ounce pork scaloppini cutlets (4 ½ pounds)
1 ½ cups all-purpose flour,
seasoned with salt & pepper

SAUCE:
1 cup chopped bacon, 5 ounces
3 tablespoons chopped shallots

1 cup sliced shitake mushrooms caps
1 cup sliced white button mushrooms
1 tablespoon all-purpose flour
¼ cup vegetable oil
3 tbs. Jagermeister liquor
2 cups pork or beef broth
salt and pepper to taste
½ cup minced chives
½ cup minced parsley

PORK:
Dredge the cutlets in the seasoned flour. Heat 1 tablespoon of the oil in a skillet and
sauté one cutlet for about 1 minute each side and remove from pan. Drain on absorbent
toweling. Place on baking sheet, do not stack, uncovered, and keep warm in very low
oven until ready to serve. Repeat the process, adding oil as necessary, until all the cutlets
are browned.

SAUCE:
Place the bacon into the skillet and sauté until almost browned. Drain off most of the
fat from the skillet. Stir the shallots into the bacon and cook for several minutes, stirring
often, until they become translucent. Add the mushrooms and continue sautéing for 2
minutes. Sprinkle the flour over the bacon mixture and cook for 1 minute, stirring often.
Stir in the Jagermeister to deglaze the pan. Add the broth, bring to a simmer, and cook
for 14 minutes. Adjust the seasonings.

Makes 8 servings.

*Jagermeister is a potent (7o%) liqueur intensely flavored. I usually do this recipe without
the Jagermeister except for special occasions.*

# PORK SCHNITZEL
## pork cutlets with sauce

6 pork loin cutlets cut ½" thick
¼ cup all-purpose flour
1 teaspoon seasoned salt
¼ teaspoon pepper
1 egg, beaten
2 tablespoons milk
¾ cup fine, dry bread crumbs

1 teaspoon paprika
SAUCE:
3 tablespoons shortening
¾ cup chicken broth
1 tablespoon all-purpose flour
¼ teaspoon dried dill weed
1/3 cup dairy sour cream

Pound pork to ¼-1/8" thickness. Cut small slits around edges to prevent curling. Coat meat with mixture with the ¼ cup flour, seasoned salt and pepper. Combine egg and milk. Dip cutlets in egg mixture, then in mixture of crumbs and paprika. In large skillet, coat 3 cutlets at a time in hot shortening 2-3 minutes on each side.

Remove from pan to platter. Keep warm. Pour broth into skillet, scrapping to loosen crusty drippings. Blend the 1 tablespoon flour and dill weed into sour cream. Stir sour cream mixture into broth. Cook and stir till mixture is thickened, Do Not Boil. Pass sauce with cutlets.

Makes 6 servings.

# RAHM SCHNITZEL
## Pork cutlets with mushroom sauce

PORK:
16-3 oz. pork medallions, from center of loin
1 cup all-purpose flour
2 teaspoons salt
1 teaspoon ground black pepper
3 large eggs
3 tablespoons water
1 teaspoon Tabasco sauce
3 ½ cups dry breadcrumbs
oil for frying
SAUCE:

1/3 cup white onions, diced finely
2 cups sliced white button mushrooms
1 cup white wine
3 cups chicken broth
1 cup tomato puree
1 small bay leaf
3 tablespoons cornstarch
3 tablespoons water
¾ cup sour cream
salt and pepper to taste
1 tablespoon canola oil

Place plastic wrap over each pork medallion and with a meat mallet, pound until ½" thick. In a small bowl, combine the flour, salt and pepper. In a shallow container whisk the eggs and milk together. In a medium size bowl, place the bread crumbs. Entirely coat each medallion with the flour, then the egg mixture and finally the bread crumbs. Lay flat, in one layer, on a baking sheet. Cover and refrigerate until ready to cook. This can be done up to 6 hours before being ready to cook.

SAUCE:
In a 2 quart saucepan, heat the canola oil until hot; add the onions and sauté for 1 to 2 minutes. Add the mushrooms and continue to sauté for 3 to 4 minutes. Add the white wine and bring to a boil. Stir in the broth, tomato puree, and bay leaf, bring to a simmer, and cook for 30 to 45 minutes, stirring occasionally. Create a sherry of the cornstarch and water; whisk into the sauce, and bring to a boil, whisking constantly. Whisk in sour cream, adjust the seasonings, if needed, and remove from the heat, keep warm.

PORK:
Pour the canola oil to a 1" depth in a 12 inch skillet. Heat until medium hot. Gently add two medallions at a time to the pan and cook until golden brown on both sides, 2-3 minutes per side. Remove from heat and place on a baking sheet lined with paper towels. Repeat with remaining medallions. Place in a warm oven until ready to serve. Serve liquid over medallions.

Makes 8 servings.

# TWICE BAKED POTATOES
# WITH PORK AND HAM

8 large baking potatoes
½ pound bulk pork sausage
¼ cup butter, softened
2 cups shredded cheddar cheese, 8 ounces
1 ½ cups diced fully cooked ham

6 bacon strips, cooked and crumbled
1 cup sour cream, 8 ounces
½ cup Italian salad dressing
salt and pepper to taste

Scrub and pierce potatoes. Bake at 400 degrees for 40 to 60 minutes until tender. Meanwhile, in a skillet, cook the sausage over medium heat until no longer pink; drain. When potatoes are cool enough to handle, cut in half lengthwise; scoop out pulp, leaving a ¼ inch shell. In a large mixing bowl, mash the pulp with butter. Stir in the sausage, cheese, ham, bacon, sour cream, salad dressing, salt and pepper. Spoon into potato shells. Place on two un-greased baking sheets.

Bake at 400 degrees for 30 minutes or until done.

Makes 8-16 servings.

# SEAFOOD

# ASPARAGUS-TUNA CASSEROLE

1 package fine noodles—5 ounces
1 can tuna in oil—6 ½ ounces
1 can asparagus, drained
1 can cream of mushroom soup

½ cup grated cheese
¼ cup bread crumbs
butter

Cook noodles according to package directions, drain. Line buttered 2 quart casserole with noodles. Arrange tuna, asparagus, soup, cheese, and crumbs in layers. Dot with butter. Bake at 375 degrees for 30 minutes.

*Note: 3 hard boiled eggs, sliced, may be substituted for tuna.*

Makes 2-3 servings.


# BEER BATTERED FRIED SHRIMP

Beer batter-see below
½ teaspoon salt
1 pound shrimp, shelled and de-veined

vegetable oil for frying
1 tablespoon Dijon mustard
½ cup mayonnaise

Prepare beer batter. Wash, shell, de-vein shrimp leaving tails on. Dry on paper toweling. Pour enough vegetable oil into a large saucepan to make a 2" depth. Heat to 375 degrees on deep-fat frying thermometer. Holding shrimp by their tails, dip them into the batter, then carefully drop them into hot oil, a few at a time.

Fry until golden-brown, about 3 minutes. Drain on paper toweling. Put in warm oven to keep hot. Serve with mustard mixed with the mayonnaise and bottled tarter sauce.

Makes 2 to 3 servings.

# BEER BATTER

2 ½ cups beer
2 ½ cups all-purpose flour

1 ½ teaspoons baking powder
1 teaspoon kosher salt

Make the batter by mixing together in a large bowl; beer, flour, baking powder and salt. Set aside for at least 10 minutes before using as directed. Can be used for seafood and vegetables.

*You can substitute light beer for the regular beer.*

Makes 12 servings.


# BEER BATTER VEGETABLES

Beer batter-see above
16 small white button mushrooms
1 medium Spanish onion, cut into 1" pieces
1 medium carrot, cut into ¼" thick slices
vegetable oil for frying

1 red bell pepper, cored, seeded, cut into 1" squared pieces
1 yellow bell pepper, cored, seeded, cut into 1" squared pieces
1 small eggplant, peeled and sliced 1/8" thick

In a heavy deep pot, preheat the vegetable oil to 365 degrees F. Making sure they are absolutely dry before dipping, so the batter will cling properly, dip the vegetables into the beer batter, coating well. Carefully place the vegetables into the hot oil, taking care not to crowd them. Fry in batches for 3 to 5 minutes, or until the battered vegetables are golden brown and crisp. Remove from the oil and drain well on paper towels before serving with the sauce for dipping.

Use 1 tablespoon Dijon mustard mixed with ½ cup mayonnaise for a dipping sauce, or a commercially prepared sauce.

Makes 12 servings.

# BEER SHRIMP

1 quart beer
¼ cup lemon juice
2 teaspoons salt
1 teaspoon whole peppercorns

1 teaspoon tarragon
2 pounds raw shrimp in shells
sprig fresh dill
1 small jar stuffed green olives

Pour beer into 2 quart saucepan, add lemon juice, salt, peppercorns, tarragon, and bring to a boil. Reduce heat and simmer 10 minutes. Add shrimp, bring to a boil again, then simmer 3-5 minutes. (depending on size of shrimp cook until shrimp are deep pink). Drain, cool, shell, de-vein shrimp.

Arrange in a bowl on cracked ice, garnish with dill and olives.
Chill until serving.

Makes 8 servings.


# BROILED BAY SCALLOPS

1 tablespoon Sherry
8 ounces scallops
¼ cup cracker crumbs

2 tablespoons butter
¼ teaspoon paprika

In a small bowl; pour sherry over scallops. Combine crumbs, butter and paprika. Roll top of scallops in crumb mixture. Place uncoated side down on a shallow baking pan. Broil 5-6 inches from heat for 7-8 minutes.

*Note: melt butter in a small pan and then drop cracker crumbs and paprika into pan and coat scallops from pan. Can be broiled on clam shells.*

Makes 2-3 servings.

# BROILED SCALLOPS

1-1/2 pound scallops
½ cup dry vermouth
½ cup olive oil

½ teaspoon finely chopped garlic
½ teaspoon salt
2 tablespoons minced parsley

Marinate the scallops in the vermouth mixed with the remaining ingredients several hours in the refrigerator. When ready to serve, place the scallops and the marinade in a shallow pan. Place under a pre-heated broiler, two inches from the source of heat, and broil five to 6 minutes turning once.

Makes 4 servings.

# CRAB CAKES

1 lb. lump crabmeat, checked for cartilage & shell
3 slices white bread, crust removed
½ cup mayonnaise
1 tablespoon Dijon mustard
3 tablespoons chopped parsley
2 scallions finely chopped

1 large egg, lightly beaten
1 tablespoon Worcestershire sauce
1 tablespoon lemon juice
salt and pepper to taste
2 tablespoons unsalted butter
2 tablespoons vegetable oil

Make sure the crabmeat has no cartilage or shell fragments. Place the bread in a food processor and process for about 30 seconds to make fine, soft bread crumbs. In a large bowl, combine mayonnaise, mustard, parsley, scallions, egg, Worcestershire sauce and lemon juice. Add the crab and breadcrumbs. Gently stir just to mix and season with salt and paper.

Divide into uniform balls. Use hands to form them into small round cakes. Transfer to a plate or platter, cover, chill for 30 minutes. In large skillet over medium-high heat, melt the butter with oil. Add the crab cakes and cook until golden brown, about 3 minutes on each side. Drain on paper towels and serve at once.

*Form the cakes gently. Too much handling will make them compact and tough.*

Makes 4 servings.

# CRAB CAKES
*Richard Bohlen*

4 pounds crabmeat
1 egg
1 tablespoon lemon zest
¼ teaspoon Old Bay Seasoning
1 tablespoon fresh basil, chopped
1 cup saltine crackers, crushed
1 cup mayonnaise

4 tablespoon vegetable oil
3 egg yolks
3 ounces fresh lime juice
3 tablespoons chopped fresh cilantro
salt and pepper to taste
1 ¾ cups vegetable oil

In a large bowl; combine crabmeat, 1 egg, lemon zest, 1/8 teaspoon Old Bay Seasoning, chopped basil, crushed crackers and mayonnaise. Mix thoroughly. Form 5 ounce patties out of the crab mixture (should make 16 patties), and chill until cold.

In a skillet, heat 4 tablespoons of oil over medium heat. Sauté the crab cakes for 4 minutes on each side or until golden brown. In a blender; place the egg yolks, remaining Old Bay Seasoning, lime juice, cilantro, salt and pepper. Blend for 10 seconds. Keeping the blender running, slowly drizzle the oil into the blender. Blend until sauce is creamy. Serve sauce along side crab cakes.

Makes 16 servings.


# CRABMEAT REMOULADE

17 ounce can crabmeat
1 cup mayonnaise
¼ cup olive oil
2 tablespoon lemon juice
2 cloves crushed garlic

1 teaspoon celery seed
3 stalks celery, finely chopped
¼ teaspoon salt
1/8 teaspoon pepper

Pick over crab meat, remove any cartilage and shell. Blend all ingredients together, by hand. Refrigerate. Serve with crackers, chips or raw vegetables.

Makes 3 cups.

# CRAB STUFFED MUSHROOMS

24 large mushrooms with stems
3 tablespoons butter
1 small onion, finely chopped
1 large celery stalk, finely chopped
8 ounces fresh lump crabmeat
1 tablespoon all-purpose flour
½ teaspoon salt

¼ tsp. coarsely ground black pepper
1 cup milk
2 tablespoons dry sherry
2 slices white bread, finely chopped
2 tablespoons parsley, chopped
non stick cooking spray

Remove stems from mushroom caps. Chop stems. Cut, then slice from top of cap so that mushroom sits firmly. Arrange mushroom caps, cavity side up, in a 15-1/2x10-1/2" jelly roll pan.

In a 10" skillet, melt butter over medium heat. Add onion, celery, and mushroom stems and cook 15-20 minutes or until vegetables are tender and golden, stirring occasionally. Meanwhile, pick over crabmeat to remove any cartilage and shell. Increase heat to medium-high. Sprinkle flour, salt, and pepper over vegetable mixture. Cook 1 minute, stirring constantly. Gradually add milk, then sherry; beat to boiling stirring constantly. Remove skillet from heat. Add bread crumbs, crabmeat, and 1 tablespoon chopped parsley. Stir to mix well and break up crabmeat slightly.

Preheat oven to 400 degrees. Fill mushroom cavities with crabmeat stuffing. Spray large sheet of foil with nonstick cooking spray. Place foil, greased side down, over mushrooms. Bake 10 minutes, remove foil and bake 10 minutes more. Serve hot. Sprinkle with remaining chopped parsley.

Makes 8 servings.

# CRACKED CRAB

crab—1 per servings                                    melted butter
mayonnaise or tarter sauce

Plunge crabs into boiling, salted water. Bring water back to boiling, reduce heat. Simmer 15-20 minutes for Dungeness (California) crabs; 5-8 minutes for blue crabs. Remove crabs from water. Remove apron-shaped shell from underside. Separate shells, discard stomach of crab. Remove claws; crack them with a mallet or hammer. Cut body into 4 pieces with heavy knife or utility shears. Chill. Arrange on cracked ice. Serve with melted butter, mayonnaise or tarter sauce.

Makes 1 serving.

# CURRIED SHRIMP
*Marge K.*

2 pounds medium shrimp shelled, de-veined        4 cups hot chicken broth
1 tablespoon butter                                1 cup heavy cream
2 large onions, finely chopped                     salt to taste
2 large apples, finely chopped                     ground pepper to taste
1-1/2 cup water                                    lemon juice to taste
½ cup flour                                         cooked rice
2 tablespoons curry powder

Melt butter in a large saucepan. Add onions, apples and water. Cook over moderate heat until onions and apples are soft and water has boiled away. Add water if necessary, stirring in curry. Cook about 2 minutes. If desired, more curry can be added. Stir in flour until smooth. Cook another 3-4 minutes. Stir in 4 cups of hot, strained chicken broth. Simmer 10-15 minutes. Stir occasionally. Add cream, salt, pepper and lemon juice to taste. Add 2 pounds medium shrimp, thawed, shelled and de-veined. Bring to a boil and serve over rice.

Makes 6 servings.

*My cousin developed this recipe and its delicious. Thanks a lot Margret!*

# FILLETS BAKED IN SOUR CREAM

4 teaspoons butter, divided
2 pounds fish fillets, sole, haddock or flounder
1 teaspoon salt
½ teaspoon Tabasco sauce

1 tablespoon paprika
¼ cup grated Parmesan cheese
1 cup sour cream, 8 ounce
¼ cup bread crumbs, finely chopped

Grease a 2 quart baking dish with 1 teaspoon of the butter. Arrange fish in baking dish. Blend salt, Tabasco sauce, paprika and Parmesan cheese into sour cream. Spread over fish. Top with bread crumbs and dot with remaining 3 teaspoons of butter. Bake, uncovered, in 350 degree oven for 30 minutes until fish is easily flaked with a fork. Can be served with lemon slices, if desired.

Makes 4 servings.

# FLOUNDER AU GRATIN

¼ cup fine dry bread crumbs
¼ cup grated Parmesan cheese

1 pound flounder or sole fillets
¼ cup mayonnaise

In a shallow dish or on sheet of waxed paper combine crumbs and cheese. Brush all sides of the fillets with mayonnaise, coat with crumb mixture. Arrange in single layer in shallow baking pan. Bake in 375 degrees oven for 20 to 25 minutes or until golden and fish flakes easily.

Makes 4 servings.

*Microwave: place in oblong glass baking dish. Cover with waxed paper. Microwave with full power 6 to 7 minutes or until fish flakes easily. This is a quick meal that tastes good and is good for you.*

# FRYING BEER BATTER FOR FISH

½ cup flour
pinch salt
1 tablespoon melted butter

1 egg, beaten
½ cup beer
1 egg white, stiffly beaten

Enough to cover 1 pound shrimp or scallops, or fillets. Sift the flour and salt into a mixing bowl. Stir in the butter and egg. Add the beer gradually, stirring only until the mixture is smooth. Let the batter stand in a warm place one hour, then fold in the beaten egg white. Coat chosen fish or shellfish for deep frying.

# LINGUINE WITH SHRIMP

1 pound linguine
½ cup olive oil
3 cloves garlic, smashed
1 28 ounce can crushed tomatoes
½ cup chopped fresh Italian parsley

salt and pepper to taste
½ teaspoon oregano
¼ teaspoon red pepper flakes
1 pound shrimp, shelled and cleaned

In medium saucepan; heat oil and sauté garlic 2 minutes. Add next 6 ingredients, cook 15 minutes. Add shrimp and cook 10 minutes. Meanwhile cook linguine according to package instructions. Pour sauce on top to serve.

Makes 3-4 servings.

# LOBSTER AFRICAINE

6 lg. lobster tails (6 ounce each) or 12 small tails
4 tablespoons butter
¼ cup chopped onion
¼ pound mushrooms, chopped
4 tablespoons flour
1 ½ cups whole milk

1 teaspoon salt
¼ teaspoon pepper
½ cup dry sherry
½ cup plain bread crumbs
2 tablespoons melted butter

Par boil lobster 5 minutes, in boiling salted water. Do not over cook. Drain, and with sharp knife or kitchen shears cut the under shell around edges. Remove meat, cut in chunks, set aside. Wrap and refrigerate empty shells. Melt 4 tablespoons butter in large saucepan, add onions and mushrooms, and sauté until soft; about 5 minutes. Stir in flour, milk, salt, pepper and sherry; in that order. Continue to stir until sauce is thick and smooth. Remove from heat, blend in reserved lobster meat, cover and refrigerate. Oone half hour before serving—reheat lobster mixture over very low heat, stirring constantly. Fill lobster shells with hot mixture. Combine bread crumbs with 2 tablespoons melted butter, sprinkle over filled shells. Brown lightly under broiler for about 3 minutes.

Makes 6 servings.

# MAINE BOILED LOBSTER

4 Maine live lobsters (1 ¼ pounds each)
1 gallon boiling water
1 tablespoon salt

1 ½ cups melted butter
1 lemon, cut into wedges

Place 4 live Maine lobsters in a large kettle of briskly boiling water. Boil rapidly for 20 minutes for 1-1/4 pound lobsters, longer for larger-sized ones. Remove from the water and wipe dry. Place each lobster on its back, split lengthwise with a heavy knife and crack the large claws. Serve whole lobster with a side dish of melted butter and lemon wedges.

Makes 4 servings.

*Love lobster and love this recipe, fast and easy. My sister-in-law adds some white wine to the boiling water so that the lobsters don't suffer, it also adds flavor.*

# SCALLOPS SAUTEED IN GARLIC BUTTER

¼ cup butter
1 small clove garlic, split
1 pound scallops, fresh or defrosted

salt and pepper to taste
tarter sauce
lemon wedges

In a saucepan; heat the butter and garlic slowly. Add the scallops and cook five minutes. Season with salt and pepper and serve immediately with tarter sauce and lemon wedges.

Makes 4 servings.

*This is not only quick and easy, but if you like scallops, like I do, its a great tasting recipe. You can use either bay or sea scallops, cut sea scallops in half if large.*


# SEAFORD AU GRATIN

½ pound mushrooms, sliced
1 whole shallot, chopped
6 tablespoons butter
3 tablespoons all-purpose flour
¾ cup heavy cream
2 tablespoons brandy
salt, to taste

black pepper, to taste
paprika
½ pound crab meat cooked
½ cup lobster meat, cooked
½ pound large shrimp cooked
¼ cup Parmesan cheese

In a medium skillet, sauté mushrooms and shallots in butter for five minutes. Sprinkle flour over all and cook, stirring, for one minute. Add cream and bring to a boil, stirring constantly. Remove from heat and stir in brandy. Season with salt, pepper, and paprika.

Place crab meat, lobster meat, and shrimp in a shallow, buttered casserole dish. Cover with the mushroom-cream sauce and sprinkle with cheese. Bake at 450 degrees for 10 minutes, then brown under broiler (2-3 minutes).

Makes 6 servings.

# SEAFOOD MEDLEY CASSEROLE

1 pound fish fillets, sole, haddock or flounder
1 pound sea scallops
½ pound cooked, cleaned shrimp
1 can crab or lobster meat—7 ½ ounces
1 diced green pepper
4 tablespoons butter
4 tablespoons flour

¼ teaspoon dry mustard
1 teaspoon salt
1 cup heavy cream
2 tablespoons finely chopped onion
½ teaspoon Tabasco sauce
4 tbs. grated Parmesan, divided
2 cups toasted bread crumbs

*Note: this casserole may be prepared in advance and kept in the refrigerator. Allow and extra 15 minutes for baking.*

Poach fillets in water seasoned with a little parsley, onion, carrot, celery leaves, salt and Tabasco. Drain; reserve 1 cup of the liquid for cream sauce. With a fork, gently break fillets into pieces and place in a 2 quart buttered casserole. Cut scallops into bite-size pieces and add to fillets in casserole with shrimp, crab meat and green pepper. Toss lightly.

To make cream sauce, melt butter in heavy saucepan; blend in flour, dry mustard and salt. Gradually add reserved 1 cup fish liquid and heavy cream, and cook, stirring constantly until mixture thickens and comes to a boil. Remove from heat and stir in onion, Tabasco and 2 tablespoons Parmesan cheese. Mix with fish in casserole. Top with bread cubes and sprinkle with remaining cheese.

Bake in 350 degree oven for 30 minutes.
Makes 8 servings.

# SEAFORD THERMIDOR

1 pound fillets, fresh or frozen
1 small onion, quartered
lemon slices
1 can cream of shrimp soup
3 tablespoons all-purpose flour
¼ cup milk
¼ cup dry white wine

¼ cup shredded mozzarella cheese
2 tablespoons snipped parsley
½ cup soft bread crumbs
2 tablespoons grated Parmesan cheese
2 teaspoons butter
½ teaspoon paprika

Thaw frozen fish, skin if necessary, cut into ½" cubes. Place fish, onion and lemon in greased skillet. Add water to cover. Bring up to boiling, reduce heat and simmer, covered, 5-6 minutes, or till fish flakes easily. Meanwhile, in a small saucepan, blend soup and flour, gradually stir in milk and wine. Cook and stir till thickened and bubbly. Stir in the mozzarella and parsley. Heat through.

Carefully drain fish well; fold liquid into sauce. Spoon into 4 coquille shells. Combine bread crumbs, Parmesan, butter, and paprika. Sprinkle over sauce; broil foe 1-2 minutes.

Makes 4 servings.

# SHRIMP SCAMPI

1 ½ pounds large shrimp, cleaned
½ cup flour
salt and pepper to taste
cayenne pepper to taste
½ cup olive oil

½ cup parsley minced
4 cloves garlic, minced
2 shallots, chopped
½ teaspoon oregano
2 tablespoons wine
2 tablespoons brandy

Season flour with salt, pepper and cayenne pepper. Dredge shrimp in flour. Sauté shrimp in olive oil for 5 minutes over high heat; shaking briskly until cooked. Remove shrimp with a slotted spoon to a shallow casserole dish.

Add garlic, shallots, parsley, and oregano to olive oil, sauté over medium heat for 3 minutes, shaking the pan briskly. Remove herbs with a slotted spoon to casserole. Add wine and brandy to skillet and ignite. When flames die down, pour sauce over shrimp. Broil for 2 minutes.

Makes 4 servings.

# SHRIMP TEMPURA

2 pounds fresh shrimp
1 cup flour
½ teaspoon salt

1 egg, beaten
1 cup milt
6 cups peanut oil

Peel and de-vein the shrimp, leaving the tails on. Split each shrimp neatly down the back and spread open to form a butterfly shape. Pat shrimp dry with paper towels. Do not cut all the way through. Stir together flour and salt. Beat egg and milk together and beat into flour mixture. Heat peanut oil to 375 degrees F. in wok or fryer. Dip shrimp into batter, shaking off excess, and fry in hot oil, turning once, until brown on both sides, about 3-5 minutes. Serve with grated fresh ginger and soy sauce or tarter sauce.

Makes 4 servings.

*One of my personal favorites. Quick and easy. If you are allergic to peanut oil, substitute cooking oil.*

# PUDDINGS

# BAVARIAN CREAM

1 tablespoon plain gelatin
1 ½ cups milk, scalded
1/3 cup sugar
½ cup whipping cream

¼ cup cold water
3 eggs, separated
1 teaspoon vanilla

Soften the gelatin in the water for 5 minutes. Add the milk and stir until the gelatin is dissolved. Beat the egg yolks until thick and the whites until stiff. Combine the egg yolks and sugar in the top of a double boiler.

Add the gelatin mixture and cook over hot water for 5 minutes, stirring constantly, until the sugar is dissolved. Cool and chill until slightly thickened. Add the vanilla. Whip the cream until stiff and fold it into the mixture. Then fold in the beaten whites. Rinse a mold with cold water and pour in the mixture. Chill in the refrigerator until firm.

Makes 6 servings.

# BREAD PUDDING

4 slices white bread crusts removed
2 tablespoons softened unsalted butter
1/3 cup raisins
3 large eggs

½ cup sugar
1 tablespoon lemon zest
¼ teaspoon cinnamon
3 cups milk

You can substitute day old Italian or French bread for the white bread.
Preheat the oven to 325 degrees and butter a 1 ½ quart baking dish.

Cut the bread into thick fingers and butter one side. On the bottom of the dish lay half the bread. Sprinkle the raisins over the bread. Lay the remaining bread on top. In a large bowl beat the eggs sugar lemon peel, and cinnamon. Stir in the milk. Pour over the bread slices and set aside to soak for approximately 15 minutes. Bake at 325 degrees until browned on top and set in the center. Allow to cool for 40-45 minutes before serving.

# BRANDIED APPLE STEAMED PUDDING

1 tablespoon butter
1 tablespoon granulated sugar
1 cup all-purpose flour sifted
1 teaspoon baking powder
¼ teaspoon baking soda
½ cup bread crumbs packaged
¼ cup butter softened
½ cup firmly packed brown sugar

¼ cup milk
¼ cup brandy or apple cider
¼ cup molasses
1 med. baking apple pared, cored
and chopped
hard sauce (see sauces)
1 egg
1/3 cup raisins

Butter a 1 pound coffee can or a pudding steamer with the tablespoon butter sprinkle in the granulated sugar. Cover with lid and shake until bottom and sides are well coated with the sugar. Sift flour baking powder and baking soda onto waxed paper stir in bread crumbs.

Beat remaining butter, brown sugar and the egg in a large bowl until mixture is smooth. Combine milk brandy and molasses in a cup. Add to the butter mixture alternately with flour mixture. Cover and steam for 2 hours, follow general directions (see below). Serve warm with cream or hard sauce.

Makes 6 servings.

*This is one of my favorites of my steamed pudding recipes. These recipes were given to me by my Dad's cousin Catherine M. She also gave me the steamer. I have no idea how old the steamer is, but I never saw one offered for sale. The coffee can method works just as well. See basic directions next.*

# STEAMED PUDDING BASIC DIRECTIONS

*Basic Equipment:*
*1 pound coffee can or pudding steamer*
*trivet for bottom*

*aluminum foil*
*large kettle with tight lid*
*rubber bands or string*

## GENERAL DIRECTIONS FOR STEAMING AND UNMOLDING:

1. *to steam: tear off a 12" square of foil. With your fist make a "pouch" in the center like a chef's hat. Center the foil over the filled can, fasten to side of can with a rubber band or string. The space formed between the rim of the can and the foil will allow the pudding to rise fully. You do not have to do this with a pudding steamer.*

2. *Place the can or steamer securely on the trivet or ring of foil in the large kettle. Pour about 1" of boiling water carefully into the kettle. Cover the kettle heat to boiling then lower heat to just below simmering. Steam following time in each recipe. Check water level occasionally adding additional boiling water as needed.*

3. *To unmold: remove pudding from the kettle, remove foil or top of steamer let pudding stand for about 5 minutes. Partly open other end of can with a can opener and pudding will slide right out. Turn pudding over top side up. With pudding steamer, invert onto platter.*

4. *To reheat: wrap in foil and reheat in a slow oven.*

# CARMEL-APPLE BREAD PUDDING

butter softened
5 slices bread
2 eggs
1 ½ cups half and half
1 ½ cups applesauce
¼ cup sugar
1 teaspoon vanilla

¼ teaspoon salt
¼ teaspoon cinnamon
CARAMEL SAUCE
¾ cups brown sugar packaged
½ cup light corn syrup
½ cup half and half
2 tablespoons butter

Heat oven to 350 degrees. Lightly butter bread. Fit 2 ½ slices buttered sides up in ungreased square baking dish 8x8x2". Beat eggs in medium bowl. Stir in remaining ingredients except Caramel Sauce. Pour half of egg mixture into baking dish. Top with remaining bread and egg mixture.

Bake uncovered 50 to 60 minutes or until a knife inserted 1" from edge comes out clean. Serve warm or cold with Caramel Sauce and ice cream if desired. Refrigerate any remaining pudding immediately.

*CARAMEL SAUCE:*
Heat all ingredients to boiling in 1 quart saucepan over medium-low heat stirring constantly. Serve hot or cold.

Makes 8 servings.

*Another way to use my homemade apple sauce. Tastes great and easy to make. My younger daughters favorite.*

# CHOCOLATE NUT STEAMED PUDDING

1 tablespoon butter
1 tablespoon sugar
¾ cup all-purpose flour sifted
¼ cup unsweetened cocoa powder
2 tablespoons breadcrumbs packaged
3 tablespoons butter softened
¾ cup sugar

2 eggs separated
1/3 cup milk
2 tablespoons brandy or apple cider
½ cup finely chopped walnuts
orange liqueur sauce (see sauces)

Butter a 1 pound coffee can or pudding steamer with the 1 tablespoon butter. Sprinkle in the 1 tablespoon sugar. Close lid and shake until sides and bottom are well coated with the sugar. Sift flour, baking powder and cocoa onto waxed paper, stir in breadcrumbs.

Beat the remaining butter with the remaining sugar and the egg yolks in a large bowl until smooth. Combine milk and brandy in a cup. Add to butter mixture alternately with flour mixture, beating well after each addition. Stir in walnuts. Beat egg whites in a small bowl until stiff peaks form. Fold gently into batter; pour into prepared can. Follow general directions for steaming pudding.

Cover and steam for ½ hour following general directions for steamed puddings. Garnish top with walnuts and serve warm with orange liqueur sauce.

Makes 6 servings.

# CHOCOLATE PUDDING
*Aunt Helen B.*

1 Package Chocolate Pudding
milk as per both package directions

1 Package Vanilla Pudding

Mix together package of chocolate and vanilla pudding with the milk and cook in a double boiler until done and put into individual dishes to serve. This makes a lighter chocolate pudding than just chocolate. I like to slightly set the puddings separately and then stir them for a marbled effect. Kids seem to enjoy it.

# CUSTARD, DELI STYLE

10 eggs
1 cup sugar
2 quarts milk, scalded not boiling

1 teaspoon salt
1 tablespoon vanilla

Preheat oven to 350 degrees.
Beat the eggs to until very light. Add salt, sugar and continue mixing. Add vanilla and milk and beat together. Pour into custard cups and put in pan. Fill pan with water to encourage even baking. Water should be 2" below top of custard cups. Bake for approximately 1 hour or until set and tops are lightly browned.

Makes approximately 16 to 20 servings.

This makes a lot of custard, usually I cut the recipe in half (5 eggs, ½ cup sugar, 1 quart milk, ½ teaspoon salt and 1 ½ teaspoons vanilla). Then follow directions for baking. Still makes 8 to 12 servings depending on size of custard cups.

# EGG CUSTARD

3 egg yolks
1 egg
¼ cup sugar
1 cup heavy cream

1 cup milk
½ teaspoon vanilla extract
¼ teaspoon ground nutmeg

Beat together egg yolks and whole egg until light. Beat in sugar. Combine cream and milk; scald and beat gradually into egg mixture. Stir in vanilla. Pour into six individual custard cups. Sprinkle with freshly grated nutmeg. Place in baking pan and add hot water to reach halfway up sides of cups. Bake at 325 degrees for 1 hour or until a knife inserted into custard comes clean. Serve hot warm or cold.

Makes 6 servings.

# MINCEMEAT STEAMED PUDDING

1 tablespoon butter
1 tablespoon sugar
1 ¼ cups all-purpose flour sifted
2 teaspoons baking powder
2 tablespoons breadcrumbs
2 tablespoons butter softened

½ cup firmly packed light brown sugar
1 egg
1 cup mincemeat
1/3 cup milk
½ cup chopped walnuts
orange liqueur sauce-see sauces

Butter a 1 lb coffee can or pudding steamer with 1 tablespoon butter. Sprinkle with 1 tablespoon sugar cover with lid and shake until sides and bottom are well coated with sugar. Sift flour and baking powder onto wax paper; stir in bread crumbs.

Beat in remaining butter brown sugar and egg in a large bowl until smooth. Combine mincemeat and milk in a 2 cup measure. Add flour mixture and milk mixture alternately to butter mixture; blending well after each addition. Stir in walnuts. Pour batter into prepared can. Following general directions for steaming pudding; cover and steam for 2 hours serve warm with orange liqueur sauce or hard sauce.

Makes 6 servings.

# OLD FASHIONED CREAMY RICE PUDDING

3 tablespoons raw long grain rice
3 tablespoons sugar
1 quart milk
¼ teaspoon salt

1 teaspoon vanilla
½ cup golden raisins
dash cinnamon

Combine rice sugar, milk and salt in a 6 cup baking dish. Bake in a 325 degree oven for 2 hours or until rice is very soft stirring every 20 minutes. Stir in vanilla and raisins sprinkle with cinnamon, bake without stirring until a light golden crust forms about 15 minutes longer.

Makes 4-5 servings.

# OLD FASHIONED RICE PUDDING

1 quart milk
¼ cup raw long-grain rice
½ cup sugar
½ teaspoon salt

1/3 cup seedless raisins optional
1 teaspoon vanilla extract
¼ teaspoon grated nutmeg

Preheat oven to 300 degrees.
Mix the milk, rice, sugar and salt in a 6 cup buttered casserole and bake uncovered for 2 hours stirring the mixture every 30 minutes. If the raisins are not soft, let them stand in water to cover while the pudding bakes. Drain and add the raisins to the pudding. Add the vanilla and nutmeg and mix carefully.

Bake the pudding without stirring about ½ hour longer, or until the rice is very tender. Serve warm or cold.

Makes 6 servings.

# OLD FASHIONED CUSTARD

3 eggs
2 cups milk
¼ cup sugar

½ teaspoon ground nutmeg
1/8 teaspoon salt
¼ teaspoon vanilla extract

Preheat oven to 350 degrees.
Into a blender combine all ingredients and process until well blended. Pour custard into 4 custard cups, place cups into a baking dish. Pour boiling water into bottom of baking dish to a depth of ½". Bake 1 hour, or until a knife inserted in center comes out clean.

Makes 4 servings.

# ORANGE-LEMON STEAMED PUDDING

1 tablespoon butter
1 tablespoon sugar
½ cup candied lemon peel, chopped
¼ cup orange liqueur or juice
¼ cup breadcrumbs
¼ cup butter, softened

½ cup sugar
2 eggs
1 cup all-purpose flour, sifted
2 teaspoons baking powder
¼ cup orange juice
mandarin orange sauce, see Sauces

Follow directions for steaming puddings.
Butter a 1 pound coffee can or pudding steamer with 1 tablespoon butter; sprinkle in the 1 tablespoon sugar. Cover with lid and shake until sides and bottom are well coated with sugar. Combine lemon peel with orange liqueur or juice in a small bowl. Let stand while preparing batter.

Sift flour with baking powder onto wax paper, stir in breadcrumbs.
Beat remaining butter, sugar and eggs in a large bowl until mixture is smooth. Add flour mixture alternately with orange juice to butter mixture, blending well after each addition. Stir in lemon peel and any unabsorbed liquid. Pour batter into prepared can. Cover and steam for 2 hours, following general directions. Garnish top with mandarin orange slices. Serve warm with mandarin orange sauce.

Makes 6 servings.

# RAISIN APPLE BREAD PUDDING

4 cups of white bread, cubed
1 cup chopped, cored, peeled apple (approx 1 med)
1 ½ cups seedless raisins
2 eggs
½ cup sugar

12 ounces evaporated milk
½ cup apple juice
1 ½ teaspoons ground cinnamon
vanilla or caramel ice cream
to garnish

Combine bread, apple and raisins to large bowl. Beat eggs in medium bowl; stir in sugar, evaporated milk, apple juice, and cinnamon, mix well. Pour egg mixture over bread mixture. Let stand, 10 minutes. Spray or lightly grease a 9" square pan, put in mixture. Bake in preheated 350 degree oven for 40 to 45 minutes or until set and apples are tender. Serve warm with ice cream topping.

Makes 8 servings.

# RICE PUDDING

¾ cup raw long grain rice
½ cup sugar
dash nutmeg
1 quart milk
4 eggs, separated

1 teaspoon vanilla
1 cup raisins, seedless
dash salt
sugar, to taste

Put in the top half of a double boiler ¾ cup rice, ½ cup sugar and nutmeg and milk. Bring water to boil in the bottom half. Place the top over the bottom and let cook for 1 hour, stirring occasionally and replacing the boiling water if necessary. At end of hour, stir in four beaten egg yolks, 1 teaspoon vanilla extract and raisins. Let cook another 5 minutes, pour into an oven-proof dish, make a meringue with egg whites, dash of salt and sugar to taste, pile in on top of pudding, stick in hot 450 degrees oven to brown peaks, then chill.

Makes 5-6 servings.

# RUM RAISIN STEAMED PUDDING

1 tablespoon butter
1 tablespoon granulated sugar
1 cup all-purpose flour, sifted
1 teaspoon baking powder
½ cup breadcrumbs
¼ cup butter, softened
¼ baking soda
½ cup firmly packed light brown sugar

1 egg
½ cup molasses
¼ cup milk
¼ cup light rum
¼ cup chopped pecans
1/3 cup raisins
Butterscotch sauce, see SAUCES

Butter a 1 pound coffee can or pudding steamer with the 1 tablespoon butter. Sprinkle in the 1 tablespoon sugar. Cover and shake until bottom and sides are well coated with sugar. Sift flour, baking powder and baking soda onto wax paper, stir in breadcrumbs. Beat remaining butter, brown sugar and egg in a large bowl until smooth. Combine molasses, milk and rum in a cup. Add to butter mixture, alternately with flour mixture, blending well after each addition. Stir in the chopped pecans and the raisins. Pour batter into the prepared can or pudding steamer. Cover and steam 2 hours, following general directions for steaming puddings.

Garnish top with pear halves and serve warm with butterscotch sauce.

Makes 6 servings.

# ALL FRUIT DISHES

Fruit Compotes: means a mixture of fruits, fresh or dried, cut or whole, sometimes poached in a syrup, usually perfumed with a light or an eau de vie. Often called a fruit salad. But compote has also come to mean the bowl, crystal or porcelain, usually on a stem, in which the fruit mixture is served.

## AMBER MARMALADE

1 orange
1 lemon
1 grapefruit

Shave in very thin slices, rejecting only seeds, core and measure the quantity of fruit and add to it 3 times the quantity of water. Let stand in an earthen dish overnight and next morning boil 10 minutes only. Allow to stand another night and the second morning add a cup of sugar for every cup of fruit mixture and boil steadily until it jells. Stir as little as possible during the cooking period which will be approximately 2 hours. Put into sterilized jars and seal.

## ORANGE PEACH MARMALADE

25 peaches (washed and stones removed)  2 oranges (wash, cut, remove seeds)
sugar

Grind together peaches and oranges. Measure and use as much sugar as there is pulp. Cook until thick. Fill sterile jars and seal.

# APPLE BROWN BETTY

1 can sliced apples
½ teaspoon cinnamon
1/3 cup sugar

butter
bread crumbs

Mix apples with 1/3 cup buttered bread crumbs, reserve liquid from can. (melt butter to cover bread crumbs). Add 1/3 cup sugar, and ½ teaspoon cinnamon. Pour on apple juice reserved from can. Bake in greased dish in oven at 375 degrees for 40 minutes. Serve with cream.

# APPLE CRUNCH

4 cups sliced, pared apples
¾ cup sugar
1 teaspoon cinnamon
1 cup sifted flour

½ teaspoon salt
½ cup corn flake crumbs
½ cup softened butter

Combine ½ cup sugar with cinnamon; sprinkle over apples. Sift together flour, salt and remaining sugar, stir in corn flake crumbs. Cut in butter until mixture resembles coarse corn meal. Sprinkle over apples. Bake at 400 degrees for about 30 minutes. Serve warm with cream.

Makes 6 servings.

## APPLE OATMEAL CRISP

3-4 cooking apples, pared and thinly sliced ¼ cup quick oats
½ cup butter ½ cup flour
¼ cup brown sugar 1 teaspoon cinnamon

Arrange apples in a well buttered shallow baking dish. Melt butter and add other ingredients until well mixed. Sprinkle over apples. Bake at 350 degrees for 45 minutes. Until golden brown. Serve with whipped cream.
Makes 6 servings.


## DREI-FRUCHET KOMPOTT
### 3-Fruit Compote

1 can pitted sour cherries in syrup 1 ½ tablespoons cornstarch
1 10 ½ ounce package frozen raspberries 1 tablespoon lemon juice
½ 16 oz. pkg. frozen whole strawberries, thawed 1 teaspoon vanilla extract
few drops red food color heavy cream

Day before: with strainer, drain cherries, raspberries, and strawberries, keep juice and fruit separate. In small saucepan, blend these three juices with cornstarch; till smooth; cook, stirring over medium heat until thickened and clear. Cool; add lemon juice, vanilla, and red food color.

Now, with a fork, carefully fold in fruit. Refrigerate until well chilled. Serve in sherbet glasses with cream.

Makes 5 servings.

# FRESH APRICOTS IN HONEY SAUCE

3-4 apricots per person
1 cup honey
juice of 1 lemon
1/4 cup of water

¼ cup apricot brandy
heavy cream

Drop the apricots in boiling water for a couple of minutes. Peel, cut in half and remove the stones. Combine 1 cup of liquid honey, the lemon juice and boil in water for about 1 minute, you'll get about ¼ cup which is the amount you need, and add 14 cup of water. Bring the mixture to a boil. Add the apricot halves, reduce heat to simmer and cook until the fruit is tender when pierced with a toothpick. Chill right in the syrup then stir in ¼ cup apricot brandy.

To serve, pour into a large crystal bowl and serve with a pitcher of heavy cream. Some crisp sugar cookies would be a nice accompaniment.

# BLUEBERRY MOUSSE

4 cups fresh blueberries (2 pints)
juice of ½ lemon

2 cups sugar
2 cups heavy cream-whipped

Combine the blueberries with 2 cups of water in a heavy saucepan. Bring to a boil, then simmer for 15 minutes. Push through a very fine sieve to extract all the juices. Return the juice to the saucepan, with the sugar and lemon juice. Bring to a boil, reduce heat and simmer for 5 minutes. Chill. When cold, combine with heavy cream and pour into 2 ice trays. Freeze until firm.

Makes 8-10 servings.

# PORT BAKED PEACHES

1 cup medium sweet port wine
1 cup sugar
finely grated rind of one large lemon
¼ cup lemon juice
2 tablespoons orange liqueur

1/8 teaspoon freshly ground nutmeg
6 lg. ripe peaches, peeled, halved and de pitted
½ cup heavy cream
1 teaspoon sugar
½ teaspoon vanilla

Measure the port wine into a saucepan and add the sugar, grated lemon rind, lemon juice, orange liqueur, and nutmeg. Heat, stirring, until sugar dissolves. Place peaches in baking dish and pour on the syrup. Bake at 400 degrees for approximately 25 minutes, basting occasionally until fruit is soft.

Remove from oven and chill thoroughly. At serving time whip the heavy cream with a teaspoon of sugar and the vanilla until it holds soft peaks. Spoon on a little of the cream over each peach as its served.

# PEACH FLIPS

1 jar junior peaches
1 envelope unflavored gelatin
2-tablespoons sugar
cinnamon and nutmeg to taste

Put peaches into a small saucepan. Sprinkle in gelatin and stir over medium heat until dissolved. Remove from heat and add sugar. Cool slightly then stir in milk. Add seasonings. Pour into small bowls. Chill until firm Unmold and serve directly from bowl. Yields 3 4 ounce servings. Approximately 1 ½ cups.

# PEACHES POACHED IN APRICOT SAUCE

8 tablespoons apricot jam
6 tablespoons sugar

grated rind of 2 oranges
8 large fresh freestone peaches or
nectarines

Combine apricot jam, orange rind, sugar, and ¾ cup water in a saucepan. Bring up to a boil over moderate heat, reduce to simmer, and cook over low heat until mixture is syrupy take off heat. Meanwhile, peel the peaches by dropping into boiling water for a few minutes. The skin will slip off easily. Cut in half and return the saucepan to the stove and cook, again over low heat, until the peaches are barely tender when pierced with the point of a paring knife. Chill.

Serve plain, with a sprinkling of slivered, toasted almonds, or with whipped cream.

Makes 8 servings.


# PEAR AMBROSIA

8 winter pears
1 cup fresh or frozen orange juice

½ cup shredded coconut
½ cup chopped nuts

Peel and core pears, cut into quarters. Place fruit in sherbet glasses or shallow glass bowl. Pour orange juice over pears. Sprinkle with coconut and chopped nuts. Chill for several hours before serving.

Makes 4 servings.

# FRESH PEARS COOKED IN CREAM

2 pounds very firm pears          ½ cup (1 stick) butter
1/3 cup vanilla sugar             ½ cup heavy cream

Peel the pears, slice into eights, and cut out cores. Heat the butter in a large, heavy skillet. It should be large enough so the pears can be as nearly flat as possible. It may be necessary to use 2 skillets. Add the pears to the hot butter and sprinkle with the vanilla sugar. Turn them over a few times so they are well coated with butter and sugar. Cook over low-to-moderate heat until the pears are soft enough to be pierced with the point of a paring knife, but still shapely. The length of time depends on the firmness of the raw fruit. Add the cream and cook another couple of minutes, shaking the pan until the cream thickens lightly. Serve hot or lukewarm.

Makes 4-6 servings.

# STUFFED PEARS

Halve fresh pears and remove cores and seeds fill cavities with cream cheese, blended with honey or maple syrup and a little nutmeg. Put pear halves back together and slice into wedges.

# FROSTED FRUIT CENTER

Can be made a day ahead of time
Assorted fresh fruits wax paper
2 egg whites tooth picks
granulated sugar

Beat 2 egg whites just until frothy. Brush fruits with whites (using pastry brush), then either dip into sugar or pour sugar over them. Let fruit stand on broiler rack over wax paper until dry (about 1 hour). Arrange in bowl, use toothpicks to anchor fruit in place. Shape is similar to inverted cone.


# BAKED MELON GLACE

3 small cantaloupes 1 ¼ cups sifted sugar
½ cup cognac 1 quart very firm vanilla ice cream
6 egg whites crushed ice

Cut melons in half and scoop out the seeds. Cut the meat of the melons into balls or squares, pour the cognac over them, Reserve the shells. Beat the egg whites until peaks begin to form, then very gradually beat in the sugar until stiff. Half fill the shells with the melon balls. Cover with the ice cream, then heap the meringue over it, being sure the edges are well covered. Spread the ice in a baking pan and arrange the melons over it. Bake on the upper level of the preheated 475 degree oven for 3 minutes or until the meringue is delicately browned. Serve immediately.

Makes 6 servings.

## PARFAIT BANANA

2 bananas
1 cup whipped cream
¼ cup chopped nuts

¼ cup milk
grated chocolate

Mash or puree in blender 2 bananas with milk. Fold in whipped cream and finely chopped nuts. Chill in tall sherbet glasses, topped with grated chocolate minutes.


## GOLDEN FRUIT COMPOTE

1 29 ounce can pear halves
1 29 ounce can peach halves
1 20 ounce can sliced pineapple
1 17 ounce jar or can kadola figs
1/8 teaspoon salt

½ cup light brown sugar, packed
1/3 cup butter
1 teaspoon ginger
¾ teaspoon curry powder

Preheat oven to 350 degrees. Thoroughly drain fruits.
In saucepan (small) combine sugar, butter, ginger, curry powder, and salt. Heat to boiling, stirring often. Remove from heat. Arrange fruits in 2 ½ quart baking dish. Drizzle syrup-spice mixture over fruits, coating top well.

Bake 40 minutes, basting occasionally, serve hot, and if desired, with warm squares of plain cake and whipped cream.

Makes 6-8 servings.

# ELEGANT BRUNCH MELON

Carve whole watermelon to resemble large basket with handle. Fill with melon balls, strawberries, grapes, orange sections, blueberries, grapefruit sections, etc.

## MELON MOLD

4 tbs. (4 envelopes) unflavored gelatin
8 cups boiling water
¼ cup sugar
1" balls of cantaloupe, watermelon,
and honeydew approx. 12 cups

1 ½ cups cold water
2 packages lemon flavored gelatin
1 ½ cups sherry

Soak unflavored gelatin in cold water. Dissolve in boiling water. Add lemon flavored gelatin and sugar. Stir until gelatin and sugar are dissolved. Stir in sherry. Cool mixture to room temperature. Meanwhile, place 3 trays of ice cubes in a large open kettle. Place a bundt pan or 12 cup mold in ice to chill. Spoon enough gelatin mixture into mold to make a layer about ½" deep. Let set until thick and syrupy. Arrange melon balls on gelatin, alternating the colors. Let set until gelatin is firm. Add enough gelatin to cover melon balls completely. Let set until firm. Repeat layering of melon balls and gelatin, twice more. Spoon remaining gelatin on top. Remove mold from kettle. Refrigerate 4 hours or overnight if possible. To unmold, dip mold in warm water for about 15 seconds. Invert onto serving platter. Arrange extra melon balls in center of mold or around edge, if desired. Serve with salad dressing for a salad, or plain as a desert. Makes about 20 servings. Recipe may be cut in half and poured into a 6 cup mold.

## NECTARINES IN WHITE WINE

1 nectarine per person                          superfine sugar
white wine

Drop freestone nectarines or peaches (1 per person) in boiling water for a minute or so, then peel. Cut in half. Lift out the seed, then slice straight into a big wine glass. Sprinkle lightly with superfine sugar and add a couple of tablespoons of white wine. Should be done shortly before serving, otherwise fruit might get mushy.


## STRAWBERRIES JUBILEE

1 box defrosted strawberries                    1/4 cup brandy
½ cup red wine                                  butter pecan ice cream

At the table heat the berries in chafing dish with wine. Pour over heated brandy. Ignite. Spoon over butter pecan ice cream.

# STRAWBERRIES MELBA

1-1 ½ quarts large strawberries
sugar
whipped cream

2-3 boxes fresh raspberries or
3 frozen packages thawed, drained
grand marnier

Wash and hull 1-1 ½ quarts large strawberries and arrange them in a pyramid in a serving dish. Puree 2-3 boxes fresh raspberries or 3 frozen packages thawed and drained. Flavor with a little sugar if you like. Carefully spoon over the strawberries. Serve with sweetened whipped cream flavored with kirsch or Grand Marnier.

# STRAWBERRY SNOW

2 cups fresh strawberries, washed and hulled
3 egg whites

½ cup sugar
1 cup heavy cream, whipped

Puree strawberries in blender. Stir in sugar. Beat egg whites until stiff peaks form. Fold strawberry puree into egg whites, fold in whipped cream. Pour into serving bowl or individual sherbet glasses. Serve immediately or chill until serving time.

For extra flavor add 2 tablespoons orange liqueur to cream before whipping.

Serves 6.

# VANILLA FRUIT COMPOTE

1 cup firmly packed light brown sugar
juice of 1 orange
raspberries, strawberries, blueberries, pears

½ cup water
juice of 1 lemon
1 tablespoon vanilla

Combine 1 cup firmly packed light brown sugar with ½ cup water and the juices of 1 orange and 1 lemon. Bring to a boil and simmer 5 minutes. Take off the heat and stir in 1 tablespoon of vanilla. Pour the hot syrup over 4 cups of mixed fresh fruits, either sliced pears, raspberries, blueberries and strawberries. Chill.

# JAMS AND JELLIES

*For all jellies and Jams: cook together fruit with other ingredients. Place into sterile jars and put on lids. Heat in canner per directions for canner.*

**Blueberry Jam:** 2 ½ pints blueberries, crushed Measure 5 cups crushed blueberries plus 1 cup water plus 2 ½ cups sugar.

**Cherry Jam:** 3 ½ pounds sour cherries finely chopped, to make 5 cups cherries plus 3 ¼ cup sugar.

**Blackberry Jam:** 2 ½ pints blackberries crushed, measure 5 cups crushed blackberries plus 4 ½ cups sugar.

**Strawberry Jam:** 2 ½ quarts strawberries. Crushed. Measure out 6 cups crushed strawberries plus 4 ½ cups sugar.

**Blackberry Jelly:** Crush 4 quarts blackberries. Strain and retain 5 cups juice add 3 ¼ cups sugar.

**Grape Jelly:** Crush 4 ½ pounds of grapes, strain and retain 6 cups of juice, add 4 ½ cups sugar.

**Red Raspberry Jelly:** crush 3 quarts of raspberries, strain and retain 5 cups juice and add 3 ½ cups sugar.

# TORTES, TARTS AND PIES

# BASIC SHELL FOR FRUIT TARTS

3 1/3 cups all-purpose flour
4 tablespoons sugar

1 cup cold unsalted butter, cut into pieces
2 egg yolks
½ cup water

*To make in an electric mixer:* combine flour, sugar, salt and butter in the bowl of the mixer. Start at medium speed and mix until the mixture clumps together into pieces about the size of peas (2-3 minutes). Stop the beater. Beat the yolks with the water and add to the flour mixture. Mix at medium speed for 10 seconds. Turn out onto a piece of wax paper and gather up into a ball. Refrigerate for at least 30 minutes before using.

*To make by hand:* Combine flour, sugar, salt and butter in a large bowl. Mix with a pastry blender, cutting the butter into the flour using a cutting motion until the mixture clumps together into pieces about the size of small peas. Beat the yolks with the water. Add to flour and form into a ball, refrigerate for 30 minutes. With a decorative edge, press the rim of the pastry all around, on a slant, with the dull edge of a table knife. Prick the bottom of the pastry all over with a fork. So the sides of the pastry shell don't collapse, line the shell with foil or can be inverted over a custard cup. Wrap in wax paper and refrigerate at least ½ hour.

**To make 2-10" tart shells:**
Take out about 1/3 of the pastry. Roll out on a lightly floured board with a rolling pin, also lightly floured. 1/8" thick in a circle 1" larger than a flan ring. Roll the pastry up on the rolling pin. Place the flan ring on a baking sheet. Center the rolling pin over the ring, unroll and allow pastry to drop loosely into the ring. Press the dough lightly onto the baking sheet. To make the sides of the flan sturdier, fold the surplus dough inside the ring with your fingers, pressing it firmly against the sides. Run the rolling pin over the top of the ring to cut off the excess dough. Then, using your thumbs, push the dough about 1/8" above the edge of the ring, making an even rim of dough all around the inside of the ring. To make with dry beans or rice. Refrigerate, if not baked at once.

Bake in the center of a preheated 400 degrees F. oven for 25 minutes. Lift the foil from the shell and bake another few minutes, if needed, or until the center of the shell is cooked and lightly browned. When cooked, cool, then slide onto serving plate. Since pastry shrinks slightly after baking, the ring will lift off easily.

Note: pastry, not used, can be refrigerated, if securely wrapped for several days, or frozen (thaw before using).
Makes 2 tart shells.

# TENDER TART TIPS

BE PRECISE: Accurately measure your ingredients. Too much flour will toughen your dough, and too much butter or shortening can make it greasy and crumbly.

GIVE IT A REST: Before rolling the dough out, let it rest at room temperature for 20 to 30 minutes to allow the gluten to relax. Dough can be refrigerated for up to 2 days.

AVOID STICY DOUGH: Roll dough onto a lightly floured surface. Don't fear that your crust will be dry from the extra flour; you take a greater risk with dough that sticks, which requires you to re-roll it, making it tough and chewy.

# PREPARING FRUIT PIE FOR FILLING

1. chill the pie crust well before rolling it out.
2. use about ¼ cup of cornstarch for 6 cups of berries.
3. before filling, brush pie crust with an egg white to keep it from becoming soggy.
4. prick bottom shell with fork a few times to prevent bubbling.
5. if making a double crust fruit pie, make sure to vent the top pastry to prevent cracking

# CUSTARD FILLING

3 tablespoons cornstarch
1/3 cup sugar
1/8 teaspoon salt
½ cup cold milk

1 ½ cups milk, scalded
1 teaspoon vanilla extract
2 egg yolks beaten with 2 tablespoons milk

Mix cornstarch, sugar, salt and cold milk. Gradually add the scalded milk. Cook in a double boiler until thick, stirring constantly. Cover and cook 10 to 12 minutes. Stir some of the hot mixture into the beaten yolks, then add to the custard. Stir well, add the vanilla and cool.

*Can be used for éclairs.*

Enough to fill one cake.

# PASTRY CREAM FOR PIES AND CAKES

1 cup milk
2 egg yolks
½ cup sugar

¼ cup all-purpose flour
1 tablespoon butter
1 tablespoon vanilla extract

In a small saucepan, heat milk to boiling point and remove from heat.

In a heatproof mixing bowl, beat egg yolks until smooth. Gradually add the sugar and continue beating until pale yellow in color. Beat in the flour. Pour in the hot milk in a steady stream, beating constantly. When all milk has been added, place the bowl over the pan of boiling water (not in), approximately 1 ½" up the sides; or pour the mixture into the top of a double boiler. Heat, stirring constantly until thickened. Cook 2 minutes more, then remove from the heat. Stir in the butter and vanilla. Cover with plastic wrap and allow to cool. Preparation time approximately 30 minutes.

A thick egg custard that is good for fruit pies. Spread in a baked pie shell and cover with fresh fruit or can be used as a creamed filling for cakes.

Makes enough for 1 cake or pie.

# PUFF PASTRY

Thaw frozen pastry sheets at room temperature for 20-30 minutes before gently unfolding. Wrap unused sheets in plastic wrap or foil and return to the freezer.

Always preheat the oven prior to baking, as directed in the recipe.

Roll and shape the dough on a lightly floured (or sometimes sugared) surface. If cracks develop along the fold lines, rub with a little water on your finger and press pastry together to seal.

Choose the right baking pan. Dark baking sheets may bake pastry faster. Best advice: keep an eye on the pastry. When golden and puffy, its done.

Don't even think about baking puff pastry in the microwave or toaster oven. It just doesn't work.

Baking temperatures vary. Most pastry chefs agree with instructions on the box and bake puff pastry at a high temperature for a short time, usually 400 degrees for about 20 minutes. When the pastry is high and golden brown, it is done. Other chefs bake the pastry at 350 degrees for almost an hour to ensure that every layer is dried and crisp. Height and color are also measures of doneness.

Puff pastry is available in packages of 2 individual sheets or six ready to bake pastry shells. They store well in the freezer.

Sheets are buttered and layered, the sheets puff when baked.

**Custard-filled puff pastry**: using ready to bake shells, bake according to package directions, cool to room temperature and fill with custard of your choice. Garnish with fresh berries and fruit in season, mint and a dollop of cream.

**Palmiers**: Sprinkle a sheet of puff pastry generously with sugar. Starting with the short side, roll it up tightly, jelly roll fashion, but only to the middle of the sheet. Repeat with the other short side so the 2 rolls are the same size and meet in the middle. Wrap tightly in plastic, press down slightly and chill for at least 30 minutes. Then cut the dough into ¼" slices and transfer cookies to a sugar sprinkled baking sheet. Bake at 350 degrees for 20 to 20 minutes.

Note: berry jelly can be spread on the sheet before rolling, cookies should be refrigerated after cooled.

# CORN FLAKE CRUMBS PIE SHELL

For 8" pie:
¾ cup corn flake crumbs
2 tablespoon sugar
¼ cup butter melted

For 9" pie
1 cup corn flake crumbs
2 tablespoons sugar
1/3 cup butter, melted

Combine crumbs, sugar and butter in pie pan; mix well. Press evenly and firmly around sides and bottom of pie pan; reserving 2 tablespoons crumbs mixture for topping if desired. Chill. If more crisp crust is desired, bake shell at 300 degrees F. for 5 minutes before chilling. Fill with suitable filling, sprinkle with reserved crumbs, chill again until firm.

# GRAHAM CRACKER CRUST
## For cheese cakes (springform)

1 ¾ cups graham cracker crumbs
½ teaspoon cinnamon

3 tablespoons brown sugar
1 stick butter, melted

Mix together ingredients; push into springform using a flat bottomed glass.

# PIECRUST

1 cup all-purpose flour
½ teaspoon salt

1/3 cup vegetable shortening
4 tablespoons cold water

*The secret to a tender, flaky pie crust is to handle the dough as little as possible when mixing and rolling it out.

*This recipe is for a 2 crust pie, you can easily double this recipe.*

Combine flour and salt in a mixing bowl. Cut in solid shortening with a pastry blender or 2 knives until mixture is the size of small peas.

Use cold water only. Sprinkle water, a little at a time, in mixture while constantly tossing with a fork. Add water to driest parts while pushing lumps to sides, only until dough is just moist enough to hold together. Form into a ball; then flatten to ½" thick on lightly floured surface. Roll with rolling pin to the size to fit your pie plat plus 1 ½ inches. Roll from center outwards each time. Smooth edges with hands to keep it round.

Fit crust loosely into pan; flute edges and prick crust in several spots with a fork. Pat out any air bubbles. Bake in a preheated 450 degree oven for 10-12 minutes until golden brown. Cool completely before filling, if recipe calls for pre-baked pie shell.

# SHORTBREAD CRUST

1 cup all-purpose flour          ½ cup butter
1 tablespoon confectioner's sugar

Sift flour and sugar together into mixing bowl. With a pastry blender, cut in butter until mixture resembles cornmeal. Chill 30 minutes, then turn into a 9" tart pan or pie pan and press firmly onto bottom and sides. Bake in preheated oven (425 degrees F.) for 10 to 12 minutes or until golden brown. Cool on a cake rack.

Makes 1 crust.

# OMA'S PIECRUST
*Mathilde Bohlen*

2 cups flour          ½ cup unsalted butter, chilled
1 teaspoon salt          1/3 cup vegetable shortening, solid
2 tablespoons sugar          1/3 cup ice water

In a large bowl sift together flour, salt, and sugar; cut in butter and shortening using a pastry blender or 2 knives. Make a well in the center and add ice water. Mix quickly with a fork to form soft dough. Add another 1-2 tablespoons of ice water if needed if dough is dry. Turn out onto a floured board and work gently into a ball. Wrap in plastic wrap and refrigerate for 30 minutes. Roll out to fit a 10" pie plate.

# PERFECT PIE CRUST
## (Aunt) Anna R.

2 cups flour
½ teaspoon salt
1 ½ sticks butter

3 tablespoons shortening
¼ cup iced water

1.  In a large bowl, sift flour and salt. With pastry blender cut in butter and shortening. Mixture should resemble coarse meal (Like cornmeal).
2.  Avoid making pastry on humid days, handle as little as possible. Sprinkle iced water over mixture, 1 tablespoon at a time, with a fork work in until moistened. You might not need all the water, only use as much as you need. Dough should not feel sticky.
3.  Gather pastry in a ball, wrap in plastic wrap, chill at least 1 hour (up to 2 days)—if chilled a long time, remove pastry from refrigerator about 15 minutes before rolling out for pie crust.
4.  Divide pastry in half. Lightly flour pastry board (or table), pat ball to slightly flattened ball on pastry board. Turn over to flour other side. DO NOT OVER FLOUR.
5.  Rub rolling pin with flour, starting at center roll out pastry in one direction only, giving pastry a quarter turn to form an even circle. Always work from the center to the edge. Flour pin and board lightly with additional flour if needed.
6.  Measure with pie plate—it should be about 1" wider all around.
7.  Pick up pastry by gently rolling half on pie, do not stretch, it will shrink while baking. Lay it on the pie plate evenly. Press lightly, prick bottom lightly, fill with desired filling.
8.  Repeat for top. Crimp rim, using fingers. Vent top with about 4 slits. Brush with milk and sprinkle with sugar if desired.

*My aunt made the best pie crust. (its the iced water, according to my cousin!).*

# APPLE CRANBERRY TART

1 can apple cranberry pie filling—21 ounces     cinnamon sugar
1 egg     prepared double crust pie crust

Make or purchase piecrust for a 9" pie. Pour can of pie filling onto center of crust leaving a 3" border. Gently fold crust over filling, brush with egg wash (beaten egg with 1 tablespoon water) sprinkle with cinnamon sugar. Bake at 375 degrees for 40 minutes or until crust is golden brown.

Makes 6 servings.


# APPLE NUT TORTE

1 egg     1 teaspoon cinnamon
¾ cup sugar     1 cup chopped, cored, peeled tart apples
½ cup all-purpose flour     ½ cup chopped walnuts
1 teaspoon baking powder     ½ teaspoon salt
1 teaspoon vanilla     cool whip or whipped cream

Preheat oven to 350 degrees F., beat egg until lemon colored, add sugar, sift together flour, baking powder, cinnamon, salt and fold into egg mixture. Stir in apples and walnuts and vanilla.

Butter an 8" square pan. Pour in batter and bake for 35-50 minutes at 350 degrees until golden brown.

Serve warm with whipped cream or cool whip.

Makes 6-8 servings.

# BAVARIAN CREAM

A type of soft custard which gelatin and whipped cream are folded in after the mixture is cooled. Can be flavored with flavored extracts. It is then chilled and un-molded for serving.

| | |
|---|---|
| 1 tablespoon plain gelatin | ¼ cup cold water |
| 1-1/2 cups milk, scalded | 3 eggs, separated |
| 1/3 cup sugar | 1 teaspoon vanilla |
| ½ cup whipping cream | |

Soften the gelatin in the water for 4 minutes. Add the milk and stir until the gelatin is dissolved. Beat the egg yolks until thick and the whites until stiff. Combine the egg yolks and sugar in the top of the double boiler. Add the gelatin mixture and cook over hot water for 5 minutes, stirring constantly, until the sugar is dissolved. Cook and chill until slightly thickened. Add the vanilla. Whip the cream until stiff and fold it into the mixture. Then fold in the beaten whites. Rinse a mold with cold water and pour in the mixture. Chill in the refrigerator until firm.

*Variations: instead of vanilla, use almond extract. I like to add a bit of cinnamon with the vanilla extract for a flavoring.*

*Some lemon extract instead of vanilla can also be used. Also nice is orange flavoring.*

# BLUEBERRY-WALNUT TART

2 cups blueberries
1 jar red currant jelly (10 ounces)
shortbread crust (see above)

2 tablespoons finely chopped, lightly
toasted, walnuts
1 cup dairy sour cream

Rinse, drain, and dry blueberries. Spread in crust. Put jelly over low heat, stirring until melted. Stir to cool slightly, then spoon evenly over berries. Chill until jelly sets well. Stir sour cream until smooth. Spread evenly over all berries, not allowing cream to touch crust. Sprinkle nuts around edge of cream for decorative border.

Makes 8 servings.


# CHERRY BREEZE

1 8 ounce package cream cheese, softened
½ cup lemon juice
1-1 pound 5 ounce can chilled cherry pie filling

1 can sweetened condensed milk
1 teaspoon vanilla

Beat cream cheese until light and fluffy. Add condensed milk and blend thoroughly. Stir in lemon juice and vanilla. Turn into prepared corn flake crumbs pie shell (9") Refrigerate 3-4 hours until firm. Top with chilled cherry pie filling before serving.

Makes 8 servings.

# CHOCOLATE TORTE

Layers:
1 ½ cups sifted flour
½ cup sifted unsweetened cocoa
pinch salt
½ pound butter
1/3 cup heavy cream

Filling:
1 pound semisweet chocolate
¼ cup milk
5 egg yolks
¼ pound sweet butter, softened
grated chocolate

LAYERS:
Sift the flour, cocoa and salt into a bowl. With a pastry blender or 2 knives, cut in the butter until small particles are formed. Wrap in foil or waxed paper and chill 2 hours. Divide the dough into 3 pieces and roll each piece into an 8" square.

Grease 2 baking sheets and dust lightly with flour. Carefully transfer the squares to the pans and prick the tops all over with a fork. Bake in preheated 400 degree F. oven about 12 minutes. Cool on a cake rack. (these layers are extremely fragile, so handle carefully).

FILLING:
Break the chocolate into small pieces and combine in the top of a double boiler with the milk. Place over hot water until chocolate melts, stirring frequently. Beat the egg yolks in a bowl; gradually add a little of the melted chocolate, stirring to prevent curdling. Beat in all the remaining chocolate for 1 minute. Remove from the heat and gradually beat in the butter. Cool, mixing frequently. When chocolate is cold, spread the filling between the layers, reserving a little for the top. Sprinkle the top with grated chocolate. Chill 1 hour. Cut into small squares.

Makes 8 servings.

# CHOCOLATE MOUSSE TORTE

1 package (1 layer size) devil's food cake mix
1/3 cup chocolate ice cream topping
4 squares (4 ounces) semisweet chocolate
2 tablespoons powdered sugar
2 tablespoons coffee liqueur

2 egg yolks
½ cup whipping cream
1 tbs. chocolate ice cream topping
½ cup whipping cream
fresh raspberries, optional

Prepare mix and bake according to package directions. Cool 10 minutes. Remove from pan; cool completely. Place on a serving platter. Spread cake with the 1/3 cup ice cream topping. Chill till needed. Set aside.

For mousse, in a small saucepan melt semisweet chocolate over low heat, remove from heat. Stir in powdered sugar, liqueur, and egg yolks. Cook and stir over medium heat for 2 minutes or till mixture just coats a metal spoon. Remove from heat, cool completely. Beat the first ½ cup whipping cream with an electric mixer to soft peaks. Stir half of the chocolate mixture into whipped cream. Fold in remaining chocolate. Cover, chill mixture just till it mounds. Spread onto cake to within 1" of edge. Chill, covered, several hours.

To serve, drizzle cake with the 1 tablespoon topping. Beat the remaining whipping cream to stiff peaks. Using a pastry bag fitted with a large star tip, pipe whipped cream around cake edge. Garnish with raspberries, if desired, on cream stars.
Makes 12 servings.

# DOBOS TORTE
*Grandma Anna Margaretha*

5 eggs, separated
2/3 cup sugar
1 teaspoon vanilla
4 squares unsweetened chocolate, 4 oz., softened
1 cup butter, 2 sticks softened

2 egg yolks
2 ½-3 cups confectioner's sugar
½ cup light cream
Lace Cookies (recipe follows)
Brandy Cream (recipe follows)

Line two 15x10x1 inch jelly roll pans with parchment paper. Beat egg whites in large bowl until foamy white with electric mixer at high speed. Sprinkle in 1/3 cup of the sugar, 1 tablespoon at a time, until meringue forms soft peaks.

With same beaters, beat the egg yolks with remaining sugar and vanilla until thick and fluffy; fold in flour. Stir in 1/3 of the egg white meringue, fold mixture into remaining meringue. Spread batter into prepared pans, dividing evenly, smooth tops.

Bake in moderate oven, 350 degrees F, for 12 minutes or until center springs back when lightly touched with fingertip. Invert onto wire racks or clean towels, peel off paper, cool completely. Cut each cake crosswise into 4 strips, each about 10x4 inches.

Melt chocolate in the top of a double boiler over hot, not boiling, water. Remove from heat; beat in butter and egg yolks until well blended. Beat in confectioners sugar alternately with cream until filling is smooth and spreadable. Stir in vanilla.

Chill briefly if too soft. Trim layers, if necessary, and stack (8 in all) on serving plate using a slightly rounded ¾ cup of filling between each layer. Smooth remaining filling on sides, top.

Prepare Lace Cookies. Arrange about 12 on top of torte. Pipe Brandy Cream into ends of cookies and in small rosettes around base of torte.

Chill several hours or overnight.

Makes 12 servings.

**LACE COOKIES:**

¼ cup ground blanched almonds

¼ cup butter—1/2 stick

1 tablespoon milk

¼ cup sugar

1 tablespoon flour

Combine almonds, sugar, butter, flour and milk in small saucepan. Heat, stirring constantly, just until butter is melted and mixture is smooth. Drop by teaspoonfuls, 4" apart, onto buttered and floured cookie sheets. Work with only 4 or 5 at a time.

Bake in a 375 degree oven for 5 minutes or until lacy and golden brown. Cool briefly on the cookie sheet, then working quickly, turn upside down with a spatula and quickly roll around the handle of a wooden spoon. If cookies cool to fast and are too brittle to work with, return to warm oven for a few minutes. Slide off handle onto wire rack.

**BRANDY CREAM:**

Beat ¼ cup (1/2 stick) softened butter with 2/3 cup sifted confectioners sugar and 2 teaspoons brandy in a small bowl until smooth.

# EASY DOBOS TORTE

1 package yellow cake mix
8 ounces semisweet chocolate
¼ cup heavy cream
1 cup butter
1 cups confectioner's sugar

TOPPING:
1 cup sugar
1 teaspoon lemon juice
walnut halves

Grease and flour an 11 ½ x 4 ½ x 2 ½" straight-sided loaf pan; or a classic dobos pan. Prepare yellow cake mix according to directions. Bake in preheated 350 degrees F. oven for 40-45 minutes or until a cake tester inserted in the center comes out clean. Cool cake in pan on wire rack for 5 minutes. Loosen sides with spatula. Un-mold and cool on rack. This cake is best made a day before so it becomes firm to cut in very thin slices. Wrap in foil to store.

With sharp, serrated knife, level top of cake. Cut into 7 crosswise slices. After slicing, lift off each layer with a wide spatula and stack with waxed paper between slices. In top of double boiler over simmering water, heat chocolate and heavy cream. Stir to melt chocolate. In bowl, beat butter until light and fluffy. Cool chocolate slightly; beat into butter, alternating with confectioners sugar added through a sifter. Frosting should be of good spreading consistency.

Place bottom, well-browned cake layer on a sheet of foil, crust-side up. Set aside. Stack cake layers on serving platter, spreading frosting between each layer. Frost sides smoothly. Reserve ¾ cup frosting for piping. Chill cake.

Make caramel topping in small skillet, using sugar and lemon juice. Use to coat reserve layer as described below.

Set layer in place on top of cake. Pipe rosettes around top and bottom edge of cake using a meringue tip or piping tip. Place walnut halves between each rosette along bottom edge. Chill 30 minutes only, otherwise caramel top becomes sticky. Cut with serrated knife.

Makes 12 servings.

To Glaze Dobos Torte

Place the bottom layer upside down on a sheet of foil, so that the dark brown crust is uppermost. In a small skillet slowly heat 1 cup sugar and 1 teaspoon lemon juice until sugar liquefies underneath top layer. Only now stir the sugar and keep heating until syrup becomes rich brown. Candy thermometer should read 270 degrees or a small caramel drop placed in cold water separates into threads.

Remove from heat, let bubbles subside. Quickly pour syrup over cake layer to coat evenly. Cool 1 minute. Heat a dull knife edge and mark top of cake into 12 slices. Trim excess caramel, set layer in place on top of cake.

# FILBERT TORTE
*Margret K.*

6 eggs separated, room temperature
sugar
1/3 cup dried breadcrumbs
¼ cup flour

1 ¼ cups filberts, finely ground (or walnuts)
2 cups heavy cream
1 teaspoon vanilla extract

About 3 hours before serving or early in the day:
Preheat oven to 325 degrees F. In a large bowl with mixer at high speed, beat egg whites until soft peaks form. Gradually sprinkle in ¼ cup sugar, 2 tablespoons at a time, beating well after each addition until dissolved. Whites should stand in stiff, glossy peaks.

In a small bowl with mixer at medium speed, beat egg yolks and ½ cup sugar until thick. Stir in bread crumbs, flour and 2/3 cup ground nuts. Fold egg yolk, mixture into egg whites, spoon into 10x2" springform pan. Bake 40 minutes or until cake springs back when touched with finger. Invert cake with pan onto wire rack; cool.

In a small bowl with mixer at medium speed, beat heavy or whipping cream, vanilla and 2 tablespoons sugar until stiff peaks form. Remove cake from pan; with a long serrated knife, slice cake horizontally into two layers. Place bottom layer on platter, spread with ¼ whipped-cream mixture, top with second layer. Frost sides with half of remaining whipped-cream mixture then put remaining mixture into a pastry bag and with a large rosette tip; us to decorate top of torte.

Makes 12 servings.

# HAZELNUT TORTE
*Magret K.*

7 eggs, separated
¼ teaspoon salt
¾ cup sugar
2 teaspoons grated lemon rind
1 teaspoon vanilla
1 cup ground hazelnuts (or pecans)
powder

1/3 cup plain breadcrumbs, dried
1 teaspoon baking powder
1 cup heavy cream
¼ cup confectioners' sugar
Mocha Butter Cream Icing Recipe
2 tablespoons unsweetened cocoa

Line 3 8x1 ½" round layer pans with parchment paper. Beat egg whites with salt in a large bowl with electric mixer on high speed until foamy white. Beat in ½ cup of the sugar, 1 tablespoon at a time, until meringue forms soft peaks.

With same beaters beat egg yolks with remaining sugar until very thick and fluffy. Beat in lemon rind and vanilla. Fold yolk mixture into meringue. Do not beat the two together, just fold. Combine nuts, bread crumbs and baking powder, gently fold into egg mixture. Do not beat. Pour into prepared pans, dividing evenly, smooth top with spatula. Bake in 375 degrees oven for 25 minutes or until center springs back when lightly touched with fingertip. Turn pans upside down on wire rack, cool layers completely.

Loosen cakes from edges with knife and turn out of pans, remove parchment paper.

Beat cream and sugar in medium sized bowl until stiff. Stack layers on serving plate with whipped cream between each layer. Refrigerate while making Mocha Butter Cream icing. Spread butter cream on side and top of torte, reserving about 1 cup. Add 2 tablespoons unsweetened cocoa powder to reserved butter cream and pipe through a decorating tube onto top and around base of cake. Decorate with whole hazelnuts, if desired. Refrigerate 3 hours before serving.

## Mocha Butter Cream

½ stick butter
1 egg yolk
2 ¾ cups confectioners' sugar

3 tbs. unsweetened cocoa powder
3 teaspoons instant coffee powder
1/3 cup cold water

Beat butter in medium sized bowl until soft, beat in egg yolk; 1 cup of the sugar and the cocoa. Dissolve coffee in the water. Beat in alternately with remaining sugar until smooth.

*This is an old fashioned German favorite.*

# SACHER TORTE
*Magret K.*

ALMOND PRALINE (recipe follows)
6 eggs separated
½ cup sugar
½ cup butter, softened, 1 stick
1 pkg. 6 oz. semisweet chocolate pieces, melted & cooled

¾ cup sifted cake flour
1 teaspoon baking powder
1 jar apricot preserves 12 ounces
CHOCOLATE GLAZE (recipe follows)

Make almond Praline. Grease a 8x3" round springform pan.
Beat egg whites in a large bowl with electric mixer at high speed until foamy white. Sprinkle in 1/3 cup of the sugar, 1 tablespoon at a time, beating all the time until meringue forms soft peaks.

With same beaters, beat butter until soft in a small bowl; add remaining sugar and egg yolks; beat until light and fluffy, about 3 minutes. Beat in chocolate and ½ cup Almond Praline at low speed, gently fold into egg whites. Sift flour and baking powder over bowl; fold in just until blended. Pour into prepared pan.

Bake in 325 degree oven 1 hour and 15 minutes or until cake tester inserted into center comes out clean. Let cool 10 minutes in pan on wire rack. Loosen around edge; remove ring from pan; cool completely.

Even off top, then split cake horizontally into 3 layers. Spread about ½ of the preserves on bottom layer, replace top. Brush or spread remaining preserves on top and sides of cake. Let stand at least 2 hours for preserves to soak in a partially dry cake.

Prepare Chocolate Glaze and pour over top of cake, letting it drip down side, smoothing with a warm spatula. Reserve about 2 tablespoons glaze to drizzle over top. Sprinkle top with reserved praline powder. Drizzle reserved glaze from a wax paper cone over praline.

Serve with whipped cream.

Makes 8 servings.

*ALMOND PRALINE*: Heat 1/3 cup sugar in a small skillet just until melted and starting to turn golden in color. Add 1/3 cup slivered almonds. Continue heating over medium heat until almonds start to "pop", and mixture is deep golden in color. Pour onto buttered cookie sheet. Cool completely. Break into smaller pieces and crush finely in blender or with rolling pin. Makes about ¾ cup.

*CHOCOLATE GLAZE*: Blend 2 tablespoons water, 2 tablespoons light corn syrup and 1 ½ cups confectioner's sugar in medium-size bowl; stir in 1 ½ squares unsweetened chocolate. Set bowl over hot water, until chocolate melts and glaze is thin enough to pour over the cake. Makes about 1 cup.

*This takes a bit of time but is definitely worth the time spent making it.*

# SCHICHT TORTE
# 8 LAYER TORTE
*Mathilde Bohlen*

1 cup butter
1 cup sugar
4 eggs, separated
2 cups sifted flour
½ pint dairy sour cream
1 cup finely ground almonds
1 teaspoon vanilla extract

1 ounce each marmalade, apricot jam, apple &
current jelly
2 squares unsweetened chocolate, melted
½ teaspoon vanilla extract
1 tablespoon butter
½ cup milk
2 cups confectioner's sugar

In a bowl cream the butter until light and fluffy. Add the sugar gradually, beating until well blended. Beat in the egg yolks. Mix in the flour, beat the egg whites until stiff but not dry, fold into the mixture. With a spatula spread a thin layer of batter over the bottom of two inverted greased and floured cake pans (9"). Bake in moderate oven until edge is a light brown. Remove from cake pan carefully to a rack.

Repeat until 8 layers are baked. Spread three tablespoons of jelly over bottom layer.

In a bowl combine the sour cream, almonds and vanilla. Top jellied layer with two tablespoons of the almond mixture Now place the next baked layer on top and continue spreading alternate colored jams and almond mixture between layers. Then place a piece of foil over the cake. Let stand overnight with a weight on top (heavy telephone directory). Using a sharp knife trim the edges of the cake. Cut a round small cake (3 inches in diameter), from the center. Remove carefully, insert an inverted glass custard cup in the hole Place the piece of cake on top of the glass.

*For the frosting:*
Put the chocolate, butter and milk in a saucepan. Cook until the chocolate melts. Let stand until lukewarm. Beat in sugar until mixture is thick enough to spread. Add vanilla extract. Frost entire cake. Garnish with frosted almonds. Refrigerate. Remove to cake platter. Serve cut in bars (1 inch). Bake cake at 350 degrees for approximately 12 minutes.

Makes 12 servings.

*My Mom made this often when I was growing up. It is a traditional German cake, and great tasting. It takes time to make but it is a joy to eat.*

# STRAWBERRY TART

3 cups strawberries                               shortbread crust (see above)
1 jar red raspberry jelly (10 ounce)

Rinse and dry berries, pinch out stems (do not slice off). Arrange berries, pointed side up in crust. Put jelly over low heat, stirring until melted. Stir to cool slightly, then carefully spoon over berries to cover each. Chill until jelly sets.

Makes 6 servings.

# FRESH STRAWBERRY TART

1-10" pastry shell
1-cup strawberries, washed, hulled
Crème Patissiere

| | |
|---|---|
| 2 cups milk | 1 teaspoon vanilla |
| 4 egg yolks | ¼ cup flour |
| ¾ cup sugar | |

*red current jelly glaze

red current jelly glaze; combine 1 cup of red current jelly with 2 tablespoons sugar in a small saucepan. Bring to a boil and cook until mixture reaches 228 degrees on a candy thermometer. Add 2 tablespoons Kirsch or Cognac; if you like, when cool.

While the tart is baking, make the crème. Bring the milk to a boil over a medium high heat but watch that it doesn't boil over.

Combine the yolks, sugar and vanilla in a bowl and beat with an electric mixer until the mixture makes ribbons, about 3 to 4 minutes. Beat in the flour. Add the milk slowly, beating constantly.

Pour the mixture back in the saucepan, place over a moderate heat and bring to a boil, stirring constantly with a wooden spatula. Boil over low head, still stirring constantly, for 5 to 6 minutes.

This makes a very thick crème that can also be used for filling éclairs, crème puffs, cakes or as a base for sweet soufflés. To finish the tart: coat the bottom of the cooled tart with current glaze and allow it to set for a few minutes. Spread a thick layer of crème (about half the depth of the pastry shell) over the bottom. Arrange the strawberries, stem end down, as close together as possible in a design on top of the crème. Spoon or brush a coating of the current glaze over the berries. DO NOT REFRIGERATE.

# TIRAMISU TOFFEE TORTE

1 package white cake mix
1 cup strong coffee, room temperature
4 egg whites
4 toffee candy bars, very finely chopped 14 oz. size
FROSTING:
2/3 cup sugar
1/3 cup chocolate syrup

4 ounces cream cheese, softened
2 cups whipping cream
2 teaspoons vanilla
1 cup strong coffee, room temp.
GARNISH:
chopped toffee bars or chocolate curls, if desired

Heat oven to 350 degrees.
Grease and flour two 9 or 8" round cake pans. In a large bowl, combine cake mix, 1 cup coffee and egg whites at low speed until moistened, beat 2 minutes at low speed until moistened; beat 2 minutes at high speed. Fold in chopped toffee bars. Spread batter in greased and floured pans.
Bake 9" for 20-30 minutes.
Bake 8" for 30-40 minutes
Until toothpick comes out clean. Cool 10 minutes; remove from pans. Cool completely.

In a medium bowl; combine sugar, chocolate syrup and cream cheese, beat until smooth. Add whipping cream and vanilla, beat until light and fluffy. Refrigerate until ready to use. To assemble cake: Slice each layer in half horizontally to make 4 layers. Drizzle each cut side with ¼ cup coffee. Place 1 layer, coffee side up, on serving plate, spread with ¾ cup frosting. Repeat with second and third cake layers. Top with remaining cake layer. Frost sides and top of cake with remaining frosting. Garnish with chopped toffee bars. Store in refrigerator.

Makes 12 servings.

# BEST APPLE PIE RECIPE
### Eleanor Hinsch

2 ½ lbs. cooking apples, pared, cored & peeled
sliced very thin (8 cups)
1/3 cup firmly packed light brown sugar
1/3 cup sugar (for tart apples use 2/3 cup)
1 tablespoon cornstarch
1 teaspoon ground cinnamon

¼ teaspoon ground nutmeg
¼ teaspoon salt
1 piecrust, top and bottom
2 tablespoons butter
milk and sugar for top

Place apples (already sliced) into a large bowl, mix sugars, cornstarch, cinnamon, nutmeg and salt in a small bowl, sprinkle over apples, toss gently to mix. Let stand until a little juice forms, about 10 minutes. Meanwhile prepare the piecrust. A 9" deep dish piecrust is desired.

Pile apple mixture into pastry, dot with butter. Moisten edge of bottom pastry with water, place top on, trim overhang to 1" wider than pie plate, turn edges under and press together to seal. Pinch to make fluted edges. Brush top of pastry with milk, and sprinkle lightly with sugar. Slit top decoratively for vents. (about 4).

Bake at 425 degrees F. for 40 minutes or until juices bubble through slits and apples are tender. If edge browns to fast cover with a narrow strip of foil.

*I have frozen these pies and reheated in a warm oven when needed. Can stay up to 2 months in the freezer without losing flavor.* Makes 8 servings.

*Variation:* **Caramel-Pecan Apple Pie**: *combine 18 caramels (light or dark) and 3 tablespoons water in a saucepan. Melt over low heat until smooth. Pour topping evenly over prepared apple pie and decorate with pecan halves.*

*This is the family favorite. I make it for all the holidays and whenever I'm in the mood.*

# APPLE CRUMB PIE

1 package piecrust
5-6 medium tart apples
2/3 cup sugar
3-4 tablespoons flour
2 tablespoons cinnamon candies
pinch salt
1-teaspoon butter

1 tablespoon lemon juice
CRUMB TOPPING;
¼ cup butter softened
¼ cup sugar
½ cup all-purpose flour, sifted
2 teaspoons cinnamon

Make piecrust as label directs. Line 8" pie plate with pastry. Pare, core and slice apples 1/8" thick. Lay apple slices carefully in pie plate. When half the apples are in, sprinkle with half the combined sugar, flour, and cinnamon candies. Add remainder of apples; sprinkle with the remaining sugar mixture. Dot with butter, add lemon juice. Top with crumb topping.

*TOPPING:*
Cream butter and sugar together. Blend flour and cinnamon and add to butter-sugar mixture. Sprinkle over apples in pie. Bake in hot oven of 450 degrees F. for 10 minutes. Reduce heat to 350 degrees F. and bake 20 to 25 minutes or until apples are tender. Makes 6 servings.

# BANANA PIE

1 9" piecrust
¾ cup sugar
¼ cup cornstarch
½ teaspoon salt
1 envelope unflavored gelatin
3 cups milk
1 egg yolk

2 tablespoons butter
1 tablespoon vanilla extract
1 cup heavy cream
4 medium bananas
1 medium lemon
½ cup apple jelly

Early in day:
Prepare and bake piecrust mix as label directs; cool. In 2 quart saucepan combine sugar, cornstarch, salt, and gelatin, with wire whisk, beat in milk and egg yolks. Cook mixture over low heat, stirring constantly until thickened, about 15 minutes. Stir in butter and vanilla, cover surface of custard with plastic wrap, chill.

Whip cream. Slice 3 bananas. Fold cream and bananas into custard. Spoon into piecrust. Chill until set. Grate peel of lemon. Halve lemon, squeeze juice into bowl. Slice remaining banana into lemon juice. In small saucepan over low heat, heat jelly until melted. Drain banana, pat dry and arrange on pie. Brush banana with jelly. Sprinkle edge with peel. Refrigerate.

Makes 8 servings.

# BLUEBERRY PIE

1 9" piecrust
6 cups fresh blueberries, rinsed and dried
1 cup sugar
1 tablespoon sugar

¼ teaspoon ground cinnamon
2 teaspoons finely grated lemon zest
1 teaspoon vanilla extract
1 large egg white, beaten with 1 tbs. water

Preheat the oven to 400 degrees F.

Toss the blueberries with 1 cup of sugar; the cornstarch, cinnamon, lemon zest and vanilla.

Remove the prepared pie shell from the refrigerator, brush the bottom and sides with the egg-white mixture to prevent sogginess. Spoon the blueberry mixture into the pie shell. Remove the top crust from the refrigerator and unfold it over the filling. Trim the overhang to 1". Moisten the edges where they meet, then press them together lightly and turn under. Crimp the edge decoratively. Cut several decorative slashes in the top crust, then brush lightly all over with water, sprinkle with the remaining tablespoon of sugar.

Bake the pie in lower third of the oven until the filling is bubbly and crust is golden brown, 1 to 1 ¼ hours. Cool on rack before serving warm or at room temperature.

Makes 8 servings.

# BOSTON CREAM PIE

3 large eggs, separated
1 teaspoon vanilla
½ cup granulated sugar
¾ cup cake flour

FILLING
½ cup granulated sugar
¼ cup all-purpose flour
1 ½ cups milk

6 large egg yolks
2 teaspoons vanilla
pinch salt
GLAZE
½ cup granulated sugar
3 tablespoons light corn syrup
2 tablespoons water
4 oz semisweet chocolate, coarsely chopped

Preheat oven to 350 degrees F. grease a 9" round cake pan. Line with waxed paper. Beat together egg yolks and vanilla at medium speed until blended beat in half of sugar until very thick and pale. Using clean, dry beaters beat together egg whites and salt at medium speed until very soft peaks form. Gradually beat in remaining sugar until stiff, but not dry, peaks form. Fold yolk mixture into egg whites. Sift flour over mixture; fold in gently. Do not over mix. Pour batter into prepared pan.

Bake cake until top springs back when lightly pressed, 25 minutes. Loosen cake by running a metal spatula around sides of pan. Invert cake onto a wire rack. Remove pan, leaving waxed paper on cake Turn cake right side up. Cool completely on rack.

Meanwhile, prepare filling. In a saucepan, mix together sugar and flour. Gradually whisk in milk, then egg yolks, vanilla and salt. Bring to a boil over medium heat; boil for 1 minute, whisking constantly. Strain through a fine sieve into a bowl. Press plastic wrap on surface. Chill for 30 minutes.

Using a serrated knife, cut cake horizontally in half. Carefully remove waxed paper. Place bottom layer on a serving plate. Spread evenly with filling. Top with remaining cake layer.

To prepare glaze, in a saucepan, bring sugar, corn syrup, and water to a boil over low heat, stirring constantly, until sugar has dissolved. Remove from heat. Add chocolate; let stand for 1 minute. Whisk until smooth. Gradually pour glaze over cake, allowing it to drip down sides. Let stand until glaze sets.

Must be stored in the refrigerator.

Makes 8 servings.

# CHOCOLATE CREAM PIE

1 9" pie shell, baked
1 cup sugar
1/3 cup cornstarch
½ teaspoon salt
4 egg yolks

3 cups milk
2 squares unsweetened baking chocolate, chopped
3 teaspoons vanilla
1 cup heavy cream

Prepare pastry shell with a high fluted edge to hold filling. A deep dish shell is best. Beat sugar, cornstarch, salt and egg yolks in a large saucepan until blended. Stir in milk gradually, then stir in chocolate pieces.

Cook over medium heat, stirring constantly, until mixture thickens and comes to boiling. Continue stirring, for an additional minute on the heat. Remove from heat, stir in vanilla. Pour into prepared shell. Put a piece of plastic wrap directly on the surface of the hot filling to keep it from forming a skin. Refrigerate pie at least 3 hours. Just before serving, remove plastic from pie. Whip cream in a small bowl until stiff. Spread over pie in a smooth layer. Decorate with shaved chocolate, if desired.

# COCONUT CREAM PIE

1 pie shell, baked
½ cup sugar
4 tablespoons cornstarch
¼ teaspoon salt
1 ½ cups milk, scalded
1 tablespoon butter

3 egg yolks
2 teaspoons vanilla
1 ½ cups flaked coconut, divided
1 cup heavy cream
2 tablespoons confectioners' sugar

In top of a double boiler, mix sugar, cornstarch and salt.
Stir in milk until smooth, add butter. Cook directly over medium heat until mixture thickens.

Beat egg yolks, stir in 4 tablespoons of the hot milk mixture, until well blended. Then stir egg mixture into remaining milk mixture, cook and stir over hot water until custard is smooth and thickened. Remove from the heat. Stir in vanilla and 1 cup coconut. Pour into pie shell, refrigerate until completely cold.

Whip cream with the confectioners' sugar, stir in remaining ½ cup coconut. Spread over the filling. Chill until serving.

# DEEP DISH MOLASSES APPLE PIE

10 cups apples, pared, quartered, and sliced thin
¾ cup sugar
4 tablespoons flour
1.2 teaspoon ground cinnamon
¼ teaspoon ground nutmeg
½ cup apple cider or apple juice

¼ teaspoon salt
½ cup light molasses
4 tablespoons butter
1 package piecrust mix
heavy or light cream

Mix flour, sugar, cinnamon, nutmeg and salt in a small bowl. Sprinkle over apples in large bowl, toss gently to mix, turn mixture into an 11 ¾" x 7 ½" x 1 ¾" baking dish or a shallow 10 cup baking dish. Heat molasses and apple cider or juice in small saucepan. Boil, uncovered, 5 minutes, stir in butter until melted. Pour over apples in baking dish.

Prepare piecrust mix, following label directions. Roll out on lightly floured surface to a rectangle 13"x9", cut a few slits near center to allow steam to escape. Fit over top of baking dish; press edges firmly against edges of dish.

Bake at 375 degrees for 50 to 60 minutes or until juices start to bubble through slits.

Serve warm with cream poured over or topped with whipped cream or ice cream.

Makes 8 servings.


# KEY LIME PIE

1 10" pie crust, baked
1 tablespoon grated lime zest
1 cup fresh lime juice (30 key limes)

1 can sweetened condensed milk
1 3/5 oz. pkg. instant vanilla pudding
1 8 oz. container frozen whipped topping, thawed

In a large bowl, mix together lime zest, lime juice, and condensed milk. Whisk in pudding mix and allow to set up to 5 minutes. Fold in 8 ounce tub of whipped topping. Pour mixture into pastry shell. Chill at least 2 hours before serving. Garnish with additional whipped topping if desired.

*This tastes best with key limes, but regular limes can be used instead, and they aren't as tart as the key limes.*

# LEMON MERINGUE PIE
*Traditional*

3 eggs separated
¼ cup fresh lemon juice
1 tablespoon lemon zest
3 tablespoons all-purpose flour
1 cup sugar

2 tablespoons butter
1 ¼ cups boiling water
1 9" pie crust, baked
3 tablespoons sugar

Beat egg yolks with lemon juice and zest. Pour into heavy saucepan and heat on low heat. Beat in flour, sugar and butter. Add boiling water, cook and stir until mixture thickens. Pour into prepared pie crust. Beat egg whites until stiff, but not dry. Gradually add sugar. Spread over filling. Make sure to cover the pie completely as it will shrink back when baking.

Bake at 450 degrees until brown.

*This is the pie my Mom made, its great and melts in your mouth, just tart enough and sweet enough.*


# LEMON MERINGUE PIE
*Quick and Easy*

1 9" pie shell, baked
2 tablespoons fresh lemon juice
4-5 tablespoons sugar
1 teaspoon lemon zest

1 package lemon pudding
2 eggs, separated (as package directs)
½ teaspoon cream of tarter

Prepare the pudding as per the package directions using the 2 egg yolks. Also add the 2 tablespoons of fresh lemon juice into the pudding mixture as it cooks. When done pour into pre-baked pie shell. Allow to cool completely, then prepare meringue by whipping the 2 egg whites, adding, a tablespoon at a time, either granulated or confectioners' sugar. Also add the cream of tarter and lemon zest. Whip until stiff peaks form and spread gently over the top of the filling being sure to cover the entire surface to the edges of the pie shell to prevent the meringue from shrinking back. Brown in the oven according to pudding package directions. Chill until serving. Decorate with thin slices of lemon, if desired.

# MINCEMEAT PIE

1 piecrust shell, top and bottom, baked
top cut into ½" strips for lattice top
10" size
FILLING:
1 pound apples, cored, peeled, chopped
½ pound walnuts or almonds, chopped
½ pound brown sugar, firmly packed
½ pound raisins
½ cup brandy

½ pound suet
½ pound currants
¼ cup chopped citron
1 cup apple cider
¼ teaspoon mace
¼ teaspoon cinnamon
¼ teaspoon ground cloves
¼ teaspoon ground nutmeg
EGG GLAZE: 1 beaten egg with 1
tablespoon water

In large saucepan combine apples, nuts, sugar, raisins, suet, currants, citron and cider. Cook over low heat for 1 ½ hours. Stir in spices, brandy and cool.

Fill pie shell with mixture. Then weave pastry strips in lattice pattern over filling (leaving spaces, not packed together). Secure ends of strips to rim of the pie with the glaze, then brush over strips. Bake in preheated 350 degrees oven for 40-50 minutes, or until golden brown. Remove and cool on rack.

Before serving, gently lift pie with removable pan bottom away from sides of pan to serving plate.

Makes 8 servings.

# LATTICED PEACH PIE
## *and deep dish peach pie variation*

½ cup sugar
1/8 cup all-purpose flour
½ teaspoon ground cinnamon
¼ teaspoon salt
6 ripe peaches (about 1 ½ pounds)

1 tablespoon lemon juice
¼ teaspoon almond extract
1 piecrust, top and bottom
milk and sugar to top

Mix sugar, flour, cinnamon and salt in a small bowl. Drop peaches, 3 or 4 at a time, into boiling water, leave in 15-20 seconds, lift out with slotted spoon. Peel off skins, cut in half, remove pits, then slice (should be about 5 cups).

Place peaches in large bowl and sprinkle with lemon juice and almond extract, toss lightly. Sprinkle with sugar mixture. Toss gently to mix together.

Prepare piecrust, roll out to fit 9" pie plate, bottom to ½" overhang; top 11" round and cut into 10 strips. Put in pie filling and dot with butter. Weave the 10 strips over the top of the pie, turn edge under, flush with rim and flute edge. Brush top with milk and sprinkle with sugar.

Bake at 425 degrees for 15 minutes then lower oven to 350 degrees and continue to bake 35-40 minutes longer, or until pastry is golden and juices bubble up near center. Cool 1 hour.

*For deep dish peach pie. Instead of a 9" piecrust. Put fruit mixture into a 1 ½ quart casserole dish. Dot with 2 tablespoons butter. Make and roll out pastry to cover top of casserole dish. Cover the casserole dish with the pastry. Trim the edge and flute the pastry to the side of the casserole, but not over the edge. To prevent over-browning, cover the edge of the pastry with foil.*

*Place the casserole on baking sheet in oven (mixture may bubble over slightly). Bake in 375 degrees oven for 25 minutes. Remove foil bake for 30-35 minutes longer or till crust is golden brown. Cool the pie on a wire rack. Serve pie warm or cool. Spoon into dessert dishes to serve.*

# PEACH TOFFEE PIE

1 9-10" piecrust, top and bottom
5 cups slices peaches, peeled pitted, sliced
¾ cup sugar

3 tablespoons flour
3 tablespoons quick-cooking tapioca
1 teaspoon butter
16 pieces toffee candies

Preheat oven to 350 degrees.

Prepare crust, chill shell while preparing filling. Combine peaches, sugar, flour, tapioca and butter. Grind candies in a food processor to make very small pieces and stir into peach mixture.

Put prepared filling into pie shell, layer remaining pastry on top, seal and flute the edges. Cut vents in top crust for steam to escape. Bake for 45 minutes at 350 degrees, or until crust is golden brown.

Makes 1 double-crust pie.


# PECAN PIE

1 cup white corn syrup
1 cup dark brown sugar, packed
1/3 cup melted butter
1 cup shelled pecans (heaping cup)

3 eggs, beaten
dash vanilla
pinch salt
1 unbaked 9" pastry pie shell

Mix the ingredients together in mixing bowl, retaining on the side a few whole pecans for decorating the top of the pie. Pour into the unbaked pastry shell and arrange the whole pecans on the top of the pie. Bake at 350 degrees for 45 to 50 minutes. Cool and top with whipped cream or ice cream.

*This is the recipe I used for cake sales, and for the family—it's a winner!*

# SOUTHERN PECAN PIE

Filling:

4 eggs
1 cup sugar
1 cup light corn syrup
½ tablespoon flour
¼ teaspoon salt
1 9" unbaked pie shell

1 teaspoon vanilla
¼ cup butter, melted
2 cups pecan halves
whipped cream

Prepare pie shell and refrigerate. Preheat oven to 350 degrees. In a medium bowl, with a rotary beater or whisk, beat eggs well. Add sugar, corn syrup, flour, salt and vanilla, beat well, until combined. Stir in butter and pecans, mixing well. Turn into pie shell. Bake 50 minutes or until filling is set in the center when the pie is shaken gently. Cool pie completely on a wire rack. Chill slightly before serving. Just before serving decorate with whipped cream.

Makes 8 servings.

# PUMPKIN PIE
*Quick and easy*

2 piecrusts deep dish
2 eggs, slightly beaten
1 can solid pack pumpkin (16 ounce)
¾ cup sugar
½ teaspoon salt

1 teaspoon cinnamon
½ teaspoon ginger
¼ teaspoon cloves
1 can evaporated milk (13 ounces)

Re-crimp edges of pie shell to stand ½" above the rim. Combine the ingredients and pour about half of filling into shell place on preheated cookie sheet near center of oven. Pour remaining filling into pie shell. Bake for 15 minutes at 425 degrees, then 40-50 minutes at 350 degrees or until knife inserted near center comes out clean. Cool pies on wire rack. Garnish with whipped cream.

*After years of making pumpkin pie with real pumpkins I switched to this recipe that is less watery. If you really want to use fresh pie-pumpkin, cut in half and bake in oven till soft and scoop out pumpkin and puree in food processor. Then continue with the recipe just substituting the fresh pumpkin for the canned.*

# SOUR CREAM AND CHERRY PIE

1 9" piecrust, baked
1 container sour cream 16 ounces
1 can cherry pie filling, 21 ounces
¼ cup sugar

1 envelope unflavored gelatin
¼ cup water
1 tablespoon cornstarch
½ teaspoon almond extract

Early in day: Prepare piecrust. In a small bowl stir 1 ¾ cups sour cream with ¼ cup syrup from cherry pie filling until well mixed. Set aside, do not refrigerate. In small saucepan stir together sugar and 1 envelope gelatin, stir in water, heat over low heat until gelatin is dissolved. Cool slightly, add to cherry-sour cream mixture. Spread in bottom of prepared crust. Refrigerate for 1 hour or until set.

In 1 quart saucepan, mix remaining cherry pie filling, cornstarch and almond extract over medium high heat, heat to boiling, stirring constantly, boil for 1 minute. Cool to room temperature about 45 minutes. Pour over sour-cream mixture. Refrigerate 1 hour or until set.

Makes 6 servings.


# SOUR CREAM AND RAISIN PIE

1 piecrust, top and bottom. With top cut into
½" strips
1 ½ cups Muscat raisins
½ cup water
2/3 cup sugar
EGG GLAZE:
1 egg, beaten with 1 tablespoon water

1 tablespoon flour
¼ teaspoon nutmeg
¼ teaspoon ground cloves
¼ teaspoon cinnamon
1 lemon, zest and juice
3 eggs beaten

Cook raisins in water over low flame until plump and tender, about 5 minutes. Stir in sugar, flour, spices lemon zest and juice. Cook until mixture thickens, cool. Beat eggs into sour cream. Stir in raisin mixture. Spoon into pie shell, cover with pastry strips woven into lattice pattern. Secure ends to rim of pie with glaze, then brush over strips. Bake in preheated 450 degrees oven for 10 minutes. Reduce heat to 350 degrees and bake an additional 20 to 25 minutes longer or until filling is set. Makes 6-8 servings.

Makes 6 servings.

# STRAWBERRY CHIFFON PIE

1 envelope unflavored gelatin
¼ cup sugar
¾ cup water

1 package frozen strawberries, cut into
pieces (10 ounces)
1 8" graham cracker pie shell
1 container non-dairy whipped cream (9 oz)

Combine gelatin and sugar in small saucepan. Stir in water, let stand for 2 minutes. Heat slowly, stirring constantly, 3 minutes, or until gelatin is dissolved. Pour into container of electric blender, cover, whirl at low speed 30 seconds, until mixture is foamy. Remove inner cap from cover, (whirl at high speed), gradually adding pieces of strawberries until mixture is smooth. Measure 1 ½ cups non-dairy whipped topping into large bowl. Gradually fold in strawberry mixture. Place in refrigerator 10 minutes, until mixture just begins to firm. Spoon into pie shell. Chill.

Garnish with additional cream and fresh strawberries.

# STRAWBERRY AND RHUBARB PIE

2 cups rhubarb, diced
1 pint strawberries
1 ¼ cups sugar
1 tablespoon quick cooking tapioca

¼ teaspoon salt
3 tablespoons butter
1 9" piecrust, top and bottom

Wash rhubarb, cut away any tough parts and chop into small pieces. Slice the strawberries and add to rhubarb. Mix the remaining ingredients and add to fruit. Blend well and allow to stand for up to 30 minutes to allow sugar to penetrate strawberries.

Pour mixture into a 9 inch piecrust, dot with butter and cover with second crust. Cut slits in top crust. Seal edges and crimp. Bake in preheated 375 degree oven for 50 to 55 minutes. Cover pie with aluminum foil tented over it during the first 30 minutes of baking time, removing it to allow crust to brown during last part of baking. About 10 minutes before done, brush on warm milk and sprinkle top crust lightly with sugar if desired.

# CAKES AND ICINGS

# QUICK BUTTER FROSTING

¼ cup butter, softened
1 pound (3 ½ cup) sifted confectioner's sugar
¼ teaspoon salt

1 tablespoon heavy cream
1 teaspoon vanilla extract

Cream the butter, add about one cup of the sugar and the salt and cream well. Add the remaining sugar alternately with the cream, using enough cream to give a slight gloss and a good spreading consistency. Add the vanilla.

Enough for a layer cake.

# UNCOOKED BUTTER FROSTING

½ cup butter
3 cups confectioners' sugar

4 tbs. evaporated milk, undiluted
1 teaspoon vanilla

Cream butter and add remaining ingredients. Continue creaming until the mixture is well blended and light and fluffy.

Enough for a layer cake.

# BANANA FROSTING

1 large ripe banana
1 ½ teaspoon lemon juice

3 cups confectioner's sugar
salt

Crush the banana and gradually beat into the banana the sugar, lemon juice and salt. Spread between and on top of layer cake or use on small cup cakes.

# CARAMEL ICING

2 cups brown sugar                          ½ cup sweet milk
3-4 tablespoons butter

Heat in double boiler for 15 minutes, and stir. Place in cold water and stir until cool.
Enough for double layer cake.


# CHOCOLATE BUTTER-CREAM FROSTING

4 squares unsweetened chocolate; 1 ounce squares          2 2/3 cups confectioners' sugar
½ cup butter                                              1/8 teaspoon salt
1 egg

Fill large bowl half full of ice cubes, add ½ cup cold water. In top of double boiler; combine
chocolate and butter. Place over hot, NOT BOILING, water, stirring occasionally, until
chocolate is melted. Remove from hot water. Quickly stir in egg. Add sugar, 1/3 cup
water, the vanilla, and salt, stir until well blended. Place pan in prepared ice water. With
portable electric mixer at high speed, beat until it is of spreading consistency—about 5
minutes.

Makes enough frosting for a 2 layer cake.

# CHOCOLATE LOVERS FROSTING

3 cups confectioner's sugar, divided          5-6 tablespoons milk, divided
½ cup cocoa                                   1 teaspoon vanilla extract
½ cup butter, softened, 1 stick

In a small mixer bowl, beat 1 cup confectioners' sugar, cocoa, butter, 2 tablespoons milk and vanilla extract until creamy. Gradually add remaining 2 cups of confectioners' sugar alternately with remaining 3 to 4 tablespoons milk. Beat until smooth.

Makes about 2 1/3 cups.

# CHOCOLATE FROSTING FOR ECLAIRS

1 egg                                         1 teaspoon vanilla
1/3 cup melted butter                         1 ½ cups confectioners' sugar
1 ½ squares (1 ½ oz) unsweetened chocolate, melted

Beat egg; add melted butter, chocolate, vanilla and confectioners' sugar. Beat until well blended.

Makes enough for 12 éclairs.

# CHOCOLATE FILLING

¾ cup milk
1 ½ squares unsweetened chocolate
¼ cup flour
1 tablespoon butter

½ cup sugar
1 egg
¼ teaspoon salt
½ teaspoon vanilla extract

Scald milk with chocolate and thicken with flour mixed with ¼ cup cold milk; add butter. Beat sugar, egg and salt together and mix together. Cook over hot water until smooth and thick. Add vanilla and spread on cake.

# COCOA FROSTING

¾ cup cocoa
4 cups confectioners' sugar
½ cup butter

1 tablespoon vanilla
¼ cup light cream

Sift together cocoa and confectioners' sugar. Cream part of cocoa-sugar mixture with butter. Blend in the vanilla and cream. Add remaining cocoa-sugar mixture and beat until desired consistency is reached.

Makes enough frosting for a layer cake.

# COFFEE BUTTERCREAM ICING

2 cups confectioners sugar                    2 tablespoons soft butter
3-tablespoons cold strong coffee (instant-heaping teaspoon)

Mix sugar and coffee together and beat until smooth. Beat in the soft butter (not melted). Add more coffee if necessary to make icing good consistency to spread.

*This makes a great icing and can also be dribbled over cinnamon buns and coffee cakes.*


# CREAM CHEESE FROSTING

2 tablespoons butter                          2-3 teaspoons milk
2 packages of cream cheese (3 ounces each)    1 teaspoon vanilla
1 cup sifted confectioners' sugar

Cream butter and cream cheese together. Add confectioners' sugar alternately with the milk. Beat until blended. Add vanilla. Use extra teaspoon of milk if frosting is dry.

Makes enough frosting for 2 layers.

This is a nice icing for spice or carrot cake or cupcakes.

# QUICK POUR FONDANT

1 pound fondant mix
¼ cup water
1-teaspoon vegetable oil

¼ teaspoon flavoring (your choice)
coloring as desired

Mix dry fondant mix and put in the top of a double boiler, place over boiling water. Heat to 150 degrees F. stirring constantly. Remove from the heat. Stir in vegetable oil, color and flavoring until well blended. Continue to stir until mixture thickens slightly. To cover cake, ice with thin coating of butter cream icing or apricot glaze and allow to set. Place cake on racks over a drip pan. Pour fondant starting at center of cake and work towards edges. Excess fondant can be reheated and poured again. Additional water may be added to obtain the proper pouring consistency.

Makes 1 ½ cups.

*Variation: Chocolate Quick Pour Fondant:*
   *Add 1 tablespoon water to Fondant recipe. After heating, stir in 1 to 2 ounces melted unsweetened chocolate then add vegetable oil and flavoring.*

Flavorings that can be used: vanilla, almond extract, etc.

# FLUFFY 7 MINUTE FROSTING

1 ½ cups sugar
¼ cup water
2 egg whites

2 tablespoons light corn syrup
¼ teaspoon salt
1 teaspoon vanilla

Combine sugar, water, egg whites, corn syrup and salt in top of double boiler; beat mixture until well blended. Place over simmering water, cook, beating constantly at high speed with electric hand mixer about 7 minutes, or until mixture triples in volume and holds firm peaks. Remove from heat, beat in the vanilla. Spread on cool cooked cake while still warm.

Makes enough for 1 sheet cake or a two layer cake.

# FLUFFY CHOCOLATE FROSTING

½ cup butter, softened
½ teaspoon vanilla
1 pound confectioners' sugar

½ cup cocoa
2 egg white unbeaten
¼ cup boiling water

Cream butter with vanilla and ½ cup of powdered sugar. Add cocoa and egg whites. Continue beating, adding the confectioners' sugar and boiling water alternately until desired consistency is reached.

Makes enough frosting for a two layer cake.

# FRENCH BUTTERCREAM ICING

2/3 cup confectioners' sugar
¼ cup flour
¼ teaspoon salt

¾ cup milk
1 cup cold butter
1 teaspoon vanilla extract

Place sugar, flour and salt in saucepan and mix thoroughly. Stir in milk. Cook over medium heat and stir constantly until very thick. Remove from heat and pour into a medium mixing bowl. Cool to room temperature. Add ½ cup butter a little at a time (cut butter into pieces) and beat at medium high speed until smooth. Add vanilla and beat well. Chill icing for a few minutes before decorating cake. Iced cake must be refrigerated until serving.

Makes 2 cups of icing.

# ROLLED FONDANT
## For 9" cake, 3" height

2 pounds confectioner's sugar, sifted
1 tablespoon unflavored gelatin
1 ½ tablespoons glycerine
cornstarch

¼ cup cold water
½ cup glucose or white corn syrup
1 teaspoon desired flavoring (vanilla will give fondant an off-white color)

In a large bowl (do not use metal) sift the sugar and make a well in the center. In a small saucepan, add the water and sprinkle the gelatin on top to soften for about 5 minutes. Begin to heat the gelatin and stir until the gelatin is dissolved and clear. Do not boil. Turn off the heat and add the glucose and glycerine stirring until well blended. Add the flavoring. Pour into the well of sugar, and mix until all of the sugar is blended. Use the hands to knead icing until it becomes stiff. Add small amounts of confectioner's sugar if the mixture is sticky.

Form the mixture into a ball and wrap tightly in plastic wrap. Place in a airtight container. This icing works best if allowed to rest at room temperature for about eight hours before using, particularly if the weather is humid. Do not refrigerate.

To cover a cake with fondant; dust a clean pastry cloth, or a smooth, clean surface, with cornstarch and roll the fondant with a rolling pin until it is approximately ¼ inch thick. Make sure that the fondant is large enough to fit over the top and sides of the cake. Slide both hands under the fondant and carefully center it on top of a cake that has been freshly iced with butter cream. (the icing makes the fondant adhere to the cake).

Dust your hands with cornstarch and smooth the fondant, starting at the top and working down the sides until the entire surface is even and flat. Cut off the excess icing around the bottom of the cake with a pizza outer or sharp knife. Decorate the cake with butter cream or royal icing. This fondant keeps a cake fresh for two days at room temperature. **Do not refrigerate a cake with fondant icing.**

# FUDGE ICING

1/3 cup butter
¼ cup water
1/3 cup unsweetened cocoa powder

3 cups confectioners' sugar
½ teaspoon pure vanilla extract

In a saucepan, melt butter in the water, do not boil. Add cocoa immediately. Add confectioners' sugar and beat until smooth. Add vanilla last.

Makes enough to frost 1 large cake.

# QUICK FUDGE FROSTING

2 squares unsweetened chocolate
¼ cup butter, softened
1 cup confectioners' sugar

1/8 teaspoon salt
¼ cup light cream or evaporated milk, undiluted hot
1 teaspoon vanilla or rum extract

Melt chocolate over hot water. Remove from heat, let cool. In medium bowl, combine butter, sugar, salt and 3 tablespoons hot cream. With a wooden spoon or portable mixer mix at medium speed, beat until smooth. Add chocolate; continue beating until frosting is thick enough to spread. Add vanilla, mix until blended. If frosting seems too thick, gradually beat in a little more hot cream.

Makes enough frosting for a 2 layer cake.

# MOCHA FROSTING

3 tablespoons butter, softened
1 ½ cups confectioners' sugar
2 tablespoons cocoa

½ teaspoon instant coffee
½ teaspoon vanilla
1 tablespoon milk

With wooden spoon mix butter, sugar, cocoa and coffee. Add vanilla and milk and beat until smooth.

Makes enough frosting for layer cake.

*This icing is good on booth vanilla and chocolate cakes. This can also be used in the Schicht Torte.*


# NUT AND FRUIT FILLING

2 cups granulated sugar
2/3 cup boiling water
whites of 2 eggs

¼ cup chopped nuts
1 cup mixed raisins, citron, cherries, pitted plums cut fine

Boil sugar and water without stirring until syrup spins a thread at 238 degrees. Beat whites until dry, add syrup, gradually beating constantly; when cool add nuts and fruit. Spread between layers of cake.


# STRAWBERRY FILLING

1 egg white (unbeaten)
½ cup drained strawberry pulp

½ cup granulated sugar
confectioners sugar to thicken

Place all in bowl and beat with wire egg beater until very stiff.

# VANILLA CREAM FILLING

½ cup sugar
2 tablespoons cornstarch
1/8 teaspoon salt
3-eggs

1 cup scalded milk
2 teaspoons butter
½ teaspoon vanilla extract

Mix sugar, cornstarch, salt and beaten eggs; gradually pour in scalded milk, add butter, cook in double boiler until thick and smooth, stirring constantly, add the vanilla.

# COFFEE CREAM FILLING

Follow directions for Vanilla Cream Filling, adding one tablespoon very finely ground coffee to scalded milk. Strain before adding to dry ingredients.

# LEMON FILLING

3 tablespoons cornstarch
1 cup sugar
¾ cup water
¼ cup lemon juice

2 egg yolks
2 tablespoons butter
grated rind of 1 lemon
½ teaspoon lemon extract

Mix cornstarch and sugar (holding back 2 tablespoons back) in top of double boiler. Add water slowly and cook over hot water until thick, stirring to prevent lumping. Add lemon juice. Add egg yolks mixed with the 2 tablespoons sugar, cook 3 minutes longer and beat until smooth. Add butter, grated lemon rind and lemon extract.

# REASONS FOR CAKE FAILURE

*There are many reasons for cakes to fail. It is important to start with fresh ingredients and that butter and eggs, if used, are at room temperature. There are other reasons for failures also. Too much baking powder or baking soda can cause a cake to be dry, crumbly, or the cake to fall. If you use too little baking powder or baking soda the cake can be undersized. Too much flour will cause the top of the cake to split or be crumbly. If too much sugar or shortening is used the cake will be dry or "heavy." If you fail to mix the ingredients well enough the bottom of the cake will be heavy or under-sized or coarse.*

*If you under bake the cake it will be sticky, if you over bake the cake it will be too dry.*

# ANGEL FOOD CAKE

1 ¼ cups confectioners' sugar
1 cup flour
1 ½ cups eggs whites, at room temp. (12-14 eggs)
1 ½ teaspoon cream of tartar
1 ½ teaspoon vanilla
¼ teaspoon salt

¼ teaspoon almond extract
1 cup sugar
SUGAR GLAZE:
1 ½ cups confectioners' sugar
¼ teaspoon almond extract
4-5 teaspoons water

Early in day:
Preheat oven to 375 degrees F. In a small bowl, stir confectioners' sugar and flour, set aside. In a large bowl (DO NOT USE PLASTIC), with mixer at high speed beat egg whites; cream of tartar; vanilla; salt and almond extract until well mixed. Beating at high speed gradually sprinkle in sugar 2 tablespoons at a time beat just until sugar is dissolved and whites stand in stiff peaks. Over-beating causes cake to fall later. Do not scrape sides of bowl during beating. Fold in flour mixture about ¼ at a time but cutting down with rubber spatula through center of whites across bottom and up side of bowl. Give bowl a quarter turn and repeat cutting motion just until flour disappears.

Pour mixture gently into ungreased 10" tube pan. With metal spatula cut through batter to break large air bubbles. Bake on lowest rack level 35 minutes or until cake springs back when lightly touched with finger. Invert cake in pan on funnel, cool completely. With metal spatula, gently loosen cake from pan and remove to plate. Spread top of inverted cake with sugar glaze. Serve with strawberries.
Makes 16 servings.

SUGAR GLAZE: *In a small bowl, stir in confectioner's sugar, almond extract and water until smooth.*

# OMA'S APPLE KUCHEN
*Mathilde B. apple cake*

1 ¼ sticks butter, softened
½ cup sugar + extra for topping
3 eggs
1 cup flour

pinch salt
2 teaspoons baking powder
brown sugar & cinnamon for topping

Cream butter and sugar together, then add eggs. Mix well, then add flour, salt and baking powder. Spread thinly on a greased baking pan. (about ½-3/4" thick). Put on sliced, peeled, cored and pitted apples and sprinkle with sugar, brown sugar and cinnamon (for apple topping), dot with butter and bake at 375 degrees or until golden, about 30 minutes.

Serve with whipped cream.

*You can use sliced and pitted plums, peaches, etc instead of apples on this cake, just omit the cinnamon as part of the topping. My favorite is still the apple, my Mom loved the black plum.*


# GRANDMA'S APPLE SAUCE CAKE
*Oma Anna Catherina*

2 ¼ cups flour
1 teaspoon salt
1 teaspoon baking soda
1 teaspoon cinnamon
½ cup butter, softened

1 cup molasses
1 egg
1 cup apple sauce
¾ cup raisins

Combine dry ingredients in mixing bowl. Cut in butter. Add molasses, egg and apple sauce. Beat well. Stir in raisins. Bake in a greased, floured 8" square pan at 350 degrees for 40-50 minutes. Turn out on cake rack. Sprinkle with confectioner's sugar or glaze. For glaze mix 1 ½ tablespoons lemon juice and ¾ cup confectioner's sugar.

Makes 8 servings.

# GERMAN APPLE SPONGE CAKE

CAKE:
1 stick butter
4 ½ ounces sugar (1/2 cup +2 tablespoons)
3 eggs
4 drops lemon extract
7 ounces flour (1 ¾ cups)

2 teaspoons baking powder
1-4 tablespoons milk
TOPPING:
1 ½ lbs. apples or 1 ¾ lbs cherries
dusting of confectioner's sugar

Cream butter and gradually add sugar, eggs and flavoring. Mix and sift together flour and baking powder, and adding a tablespoon at a time, mix flour mixture into creamed ingredients. As mix becomes firmer, add milk, but use only enough to give it a firm dropping consistency. Turn mix into a well-greased round cake time (10 ½" spring form). Peel apples and cut into quarters, make shallow slits on back of quarters, lengthwise, and lay on mixture (ring around outside, one in middle, and ring around middle ring, until covered). Bake at 325-350 degrees F. for 40-50 minutes, or until golden brown. Dust with confectioner's sugar when cooled. Makes 8 servings.

*My Mom made this cake as a special treat for my Dad, who loved it! I like it myself. It is a light cake, can be used as a dessert or as a breakfast treat, although I never tried the cherry sponge cake for breakfast. Either way it is a lovely cake. The slits in the backs of the apples make it really pretty and decorative for any occasion.*

# APPLE-STRAWBERRY CRISP

8-9 cooking apples, peeled cored
& cut into 1" slices
3 tablespoons sugar
¼ teaspoon ground cloves
½ teaspoon ground cinnamon
½ lemon, juice of
1 cup all-purpose flour
2 tablespoons all-purpose flour

1 pint strawberries, washed & halved
1 cup almonds, toasted and chopped
1/8 teaspoon salt
1 cup light brown sugar
8 tbs. unsalted butter, cut into pea
sized pieces
whipped cream or ice cream for garnish

Preheat oven to 350 degrees. Toss apples with sugar, cloves, cinnamon, lemon juice and 2 tablespoons flour. Place in a 9x13 ½ x 2" deep baking dish. Distribute strawberries evenly over apples. Toast almonds lightly, about 5 minutes, in 350 degrees oven. Cool completely. Using hands, rub together 1 cup flour, salt, brown sugar and butter until mixture clumps. Add toasted nuts and spread dough evenly over fruit.

Bake on bottom shelf of 350 degree oven for 1 hour, until fruit in bubbling and topping is crisp. Serve with vanilla whipped cream or vanilla ice cream.
Makes 8 servings.

# APPLE STREUSEL CAKE

STREUSEL:
1 cup light brown sugar
1 cup chopped apples
1 cup sliced almonds, pecans or walnuts (optional)
¼ cup all-purpose flour
1 teaspoon ground cinnamon
1 tablespoon butter, melted

CAKE:
2 cups all-purpose flour
1 teaspoon baking powder

1 teaspoon baking soda
½ cup butter, softened
½ cup granulated sugar
3 large eggs
½ teaspoon vanilla extract
1/3 cup orange juice

GLAZE:
½ cup confectioner's sugar
2 ½ teaspoons orange juice

STREUSEL: Preheat oven to 350 degrees F. Grease a 9 or 10" tube pan. To prepare streusel, in a medium bowl, combine brown sugar, apples, almonds, flour and cinnamon. Stir in melted butter.

CAKE: In a medium bowl, combine flour, baking powder and baking soda, mix well. In a large bowl, using an electric mixer on medium speed, beat butter and sugar until light and fluffy. Add eggs, one at a time, beat well after each addition, add vanilla.
Set mixer to low, alternately beat flour mixture and orange juice into egg mixture. Spoon half of batter into tube pan. Sprinkle with half of streusel. Spoon the remaining batter over the streusel, spreading to make an even layer. Swirl batter with a knife to create a marble pattern.

Bake for 15 minutes. Remove cake from oven, sprinkle top with remaining streusel. Return cake to the oven; bake until a toothpick inserted in center comes out clean, about 30-35 minutes. Transfer to a wire rack, cool completely.

GLAZE: Combine confectioners' sugar and orange juice, mix well. Turn cake out onto a serving plate, invert so streusel is on top. Drizzle glaze over cake, serve. This cake can also be cooked in a cast-iron skillet. Watch closely as iron absorbs and retains heat more efficiently. Can also be made into muffins, baking time should be cut back.

*Adding fruit to recipe: chopped pears, fresh or dried cranberries, dark or golden raisins, fresh raspberries or flaked coconut can be added to streusel mixture. Cinnamon can be sprinkled on glaze for added flavor.*

Makes 12 servings.

# TANTE MIMI'S BIENENSTICH
*Tante Mimi B.*

CAKE: (all German measures)
100 grams butter (2 cups)
100 grams sugar (2 cups)
½ pound flour (5 cups)
2 eggs
2 teaspoons baking powder
TOPPING:
Melted together:
100 grams butter (2 cups)
100 grams sugar (2 cups)
100 grams slivered almonds (1 cup)

1 teaspoon vanilla
1 tablespoon milk
BUTTER CREAM FILLING:
2 cups milk
½ cup sugar
3 tablespoon flour (level measure)
2 tablespoons corn starch (level)
2 eggs, beaten
1 stick butter

Mix ingredients for cake together, bake at 350 degrees in spring form until done. Cool, then split in half and fill with the butter cream filling.

For filling: beat first 4 ingredients together, then add 2 beaten eggs gradually, add some of the milk mixture first so the eggs don't scramble.

Cool, then cream 1 stick of butter and gradually add in the milk mixture.

The German weight is different than ours but 100 grams is about 3 ½ ounces or about 2 cups (there are 500 grams to a German pound and 454 grams to an American pound. So 100 grams would be a bit different than ours, but it should be close. I have made this recipe and it tastes great.

# BIENENSTICH

1 ¾ cups sifted all-purpose flour
3 teaspoons baking powder
¼ teaspoon salt
1 cup slivered blanched almonds
1/3 cup granulated sugar
¼ cup butter
1 tablespoon milk
2/3 cups granulated sugar

1 teaspoon vanilla extract
½ cup butter
2 eggs
5 tablespoons milk
1 tablespoon flour
½ cup butter
1 package vanilla pudding

Day before:

Heat oven to 375 degrees F.

Grease and lightly flour 9" spring form pan. Sift together 1 ¾ cups flour, baking powder, and salt. In small saucepan, place almonds 1/3 cup sugar, ¼ cup butter and 1 tablespoon milk, set aside. In large electric mixing bowl, with mixer at medium speed gradually add 2/3 cup sugar and vanilla to ½ cup butter, while beating until very light.

Now add eggs one at a time, beating well after each addition. Then at low speed, alternately beat in flour mixture and 5 tablespoons milk. Pour into pan. Heat almond mixture just till sugar dissolves. Sprinkle batter with 1 tablespoon flour, then lightly pat surface with hand to spread flour evenly. Now carefully spoon warm almond mixture over batter.

Bake cake 25 minutes or until cake tester inserted in center comes out clean. Cool thoroughly. Meanwhile, let ½ cup butter warm to room temperature. Prepare pudding as label directs; cool to room temperature, carefully stir in butter until smooth, to make custard filling. Cut cake crosswise into two layers. Set bottom layer, cut side up, on cake plate. Spread with custard filling. Top with second layer cut side down. Refrigerate at least 1 hour or until serving time.

# BLACK FOREST CHERRY CAKE
*Swartz Walde Kirche Torte*

Cake:
1 ¾ cups flour
1 ¾ cups sugar
1 ¼ teaspoon baking soda
1 teaspoon salt
¼ teaspoon baking powder
2/3 cup butter, softened
4 squares (1 ounce each) unsweetened chocolate, melted and cooled
1 ¼ cup water

3 eggs
Chocolate Filling:
1 ½-4 ounce bars sweet German chocolate
¾ cup butter, softened
½ cup toasted almonds
Cream Filling:
2 cups whipping cream
1 tablespoon sugar
1 teaspoon vanilla

Preheat oven to 350 degrees F. Brush sides and bottom of four 9" round layer cake pans with butter or solid shortening. Bake 2 layers at a time, if desired. Measure into large mixing bowl, mix first 8 ingredients together and beat at low speed until blended, beat at medium speed for two minutes scraping sides and bottom of bowl often. Add 3 eggs and beat an additional 2 minutes. Divide batter into quarters and pour 1 quarter into each prepared pan. Layers will be thin. Bake for 15 to 18 minutes or until cake is done. Cool slightly and remove from the pan. Cool thoroughly.

Chocolate Filling: Melt chocolate in top of double boiler. Cool, then blend in butter. Stir in almonds.

Cream Filling: Whip cream, sugar and vanilla together until stiff, but do not over-beat. To finish torte: Place bottom layer of cake on a serving plate. Spread with ½ of chocolate filling. Put on next layer and spread with cream filling. Repeat, ending with cream filling on top. Do not frost sides. Make chocolate curls with remaining chocolate and decorate the top of cake. Wrap carefully and refrigerate until ready to serve. This torte can be frozen.

# MOCK SWARTZ WALDE KIRCHE TORTE
*Easy Black Forest Cherry Cake*

1 package chocolate cake mix, prepared as directed
1 can baking cherries in syrup
1 pint heavy whipping cream, whipped with
1 tablespoon sugar and 1 teaspoon vanilla

1 chocolate bar, milk or dark
1 can chocolate frosting

Prepare cake as directed. Freeze. When frozen, using one layer, cut in half, lengthwise, making 2 thin layers. Leave second layer in freezer for another time or double recipe and make two or make a 4-layer cake. Put lower layer on a serving plate with cut side facing down. Spread a thin layer of icing on top. Do not cover the sides of this cake. Put ½ of the cherries over the chocolate icing, put on thin layer of whipped cream. Put on top ½ of layer with cut side down. Repeat with chocolate icing, cherries and ring whipped cream around edge of cake. Using a vegetable peeler, make chocolate curls on top of the cake using either the milk or dark chocolate.

Keep refrigerated until use. *This is very good, and very rich and very fast to make. The cakes layers can be made ahead and used when needed. I had a co-worker who constantly requested this cake, although she called it "death by chocolate."*

Makes 8 servings.

# BUCHE DE NOEL

1 package angel food cake mix
sifted confectioners' sugar

Filling:    1 can dark chocolate frosting
           1 cup coarse, crumbled, soft macaroons
           1 tablespoon freeze-dried coffee granules

Frosting: ¼ cup heavy cream
           ½ cup butter
           3-4 cups sifted confectioners sugar

Grease a 15"x10"x1" jelly roll pan. Line bottom and sides with foil. Grease foil on bottom only.

Prepare angel food cake mix, according to package directions. Pour into prepared pan, spreading evenly. Bake in preheated 350 degrees oven for 20 to 25 minutes, until top is golden. Do not over bake or cake will not roll.

Coat a tea towel heavily with sifted confectioners sugar. Invert cake onto sugared towel. Remove foil carefully. Trim crusts quickly and gently with serrated knife. While cake is hot roll up in tea towel, starting from 10" side. Set on wire rack to cool. Meanwhile make filling by blending canned frosting with macaroon crumbs. Crush coffee granules to a powder. Add to filling.

Make frosting by heating heavy cream and coffee granules, until dissolved. Cool. Beat butter until fluffy, adding cooled coffee mixture alternately with sifted confectioners sugar. Frosting should be of spreading consistency.

Unroll cake, spread thickly with chocolate filling. Re-roll. Cut 1" thick diagonal slice from roll. Set in place on top of roll with a little coffee frosting. It should be slightly off center.

Cover with remaining frosting as directed. Chill until serving time.

Makes 8 servings.

# OMA'S BUTTER CAKE
*Mathilde B.*

5 cups flour
½ pound butter, softened
1 ½ cups warm milk
2 eggs, beaten
cinnamon & sugar, mixed
(about ¾ cup sugar + 1 tsp. cinnamon)

2 active yeast cakes
10 tablespoons sugar
1 tablespoon salt
¼ pound butter, melted
slivered almonds (optional)

Dissolve yeast in ¼ cup lukewarm water with ½ teaspoon sugar, set aside. Sift flour, sugar, and salt together. Beat eggs and add to flour mixture (make a hole in the center and add the other ingredients as follows; add yeast, melt the ½ pound butter into the milk to lukewarm and add slowly to flour. If raisins are prepared, you can add them now (1/2-1 cup either golden or dark seedless or mix of the 2).

Allow to raise once and then spread thinly on lightly greased jelly roll pan or 2 round 8-9" cake pans. (about ½" thick). Brush the ¼ pound melted butter on top and then sprinkle the mixed sugar and cinnamon to lightly cover top. Sprinkle with almonds. Cover and let raise again Prick tops with fork. Bake 10-15 minutes at 400 degrees F.

Makes 16 servings.

*This was my Dad's ultra favorite. I like to cut it lengthwise and put a custard filling between the two resulting layers. Its a quick Bienenstich (filled cake).*

# BUTTER CAKE: TRADITIONAL STYLE

1 cup butter
1 teaspoon vanilla
2 cups sifted cake flour
½ teaspoon salt

1 cup sugar
2 eggs
2 teaspoons baking powder
2/3 cup milk

Cream butter until very light, then gradually add the sugar and continue beating until the mixture is light and fluffy. Add the vanilla, then the eggs, one at a time, beating each in thoroughly. Add the sifted dry ingredients alternately with the milk. Beat until smooth. Turn batter into greased cake pans and bake in a 350 degree F. oven for about 25 minutes. After baking, place the cake (still in pan) on a cooling rack for 3 to 4 minutes, then loosen the edges of the cake from the pan with a spatula and turn out onto the cooling rack. Make sure the cake is thoroughly cooled before filling or icing.

If desired 1 cup sugar combined with 1 cup butter (heated over moderate heat until blended) with ½ cup slivered almonds (optional) can be poured over top of cake.

# CARROT CAKE

1 ½ cups flour
1 ¼ cups sugar
1 ½ teaspoons baking soda
1 ½ teaspoons cinnamon
¼ teaspoon salt
2 jars strained carrots (4 ½ ounces each)
2/3 cup oil

2 eggs slightly beaten
½ teaspoon vanilla
1 8 oz. can crushed pineapple drained
2/3 cup coconut
½ cup chopped walnuts
Cream Cheese Frosting (see icings)

In a 9" square pan using a fork mix flour sugar baking soda cinnamon and salt, together. Add carrots, oil, eggs and vanilla. Mix briskly with fork until thoroughly blended. Stir in pineapple, coconut and nuts. Bake in preheated 350 degree oven for 40-45 minutes or until pick inserted in center comes out clean and cake pulls away from sides of pan. Place the pan on a rack to cool. Spread with frosting. Makes 9 servings.

# CHEESECAKE

CRUST:
1 ½ cups graham cracker crumbs
1 tablespoons sugar
½ teaspoon ground cinnamon
¼ cup sweet butter, melted
FILLINGS
3 packages cream cheese, 8 ounces each

1 ¼ cups sugar
6 eggs, separated
1 pint dairy sour cream
1/3 cup all-purpose flour
2 teaspoons vanilla
1 grated lemon rind
juice of ½ lemon

CRUST:
Generously grease a 9x3 inch spring form pan with butter. Place pan in center of a 12" square of aluminum foil and press foil up around side of pan. Combine graham cracker crumbs, sugar, cinnamon and melted butter in a small bowl until well blended. Press ¾ cup of crumb mixture into bottom and sides of pan. Chill prepared pan while making filling. Reserve remaining crumb mixture for topping.

FILLING:
With electric mixer on low speed or with a wooden spoon, beat cream cheese in a large bowl until soft. Gradually beat in sugar until light and fluffy. Beat in egg yolks, one at a time, until well blended. Stir in sour cream, flour, vanilla, lemon rind and juice until smooth.

Beat egg whites until they hold stiff peaks. Fold whites into the cheese mixture, soufflé fashion, until well blended. Pour into prepared pan. Bake at 350 degrees for 1 ¼ hours, or until top is golden, turn off oven heat and allow cake to cool in oven for 1 hour. Remove cake from oven and allow to cool on a wire rack at room temperature. Sprinkle remaining crumbs on top.

Chill overnight before serving. Dust with confectioners' powdered sugar just before serving.

# CHOCOLATE LAYER CAKE

1 ¾ cups all-purpose flour
1 cup unsweetened cocoa powder
less 1 tablespoon
1 ¼ teaspoons baking soda
¾ cup butter, softened
2/3 cup granulated sugar
2/3 cup firmly packed brown sugar
1/8 teaspoon salt
3 large eggs

2 teaspoons vanilla extract
1 1/3 cups buttermilk
FROSTING:
½ cup butter, softened
1 cup confectioners' sugar, sifted
3 ozs. unsweetened chocolate, melted
2 teaspoons vanilla extract
chocolate shavings for topping (optional)

Preheat oven to 350 degrees F. Line bottoms of two 9" round cake pans with parchment paper. Grease paper and sides of pans, dust with flour. Mix flour, cocoa, baking soda, and salt. In another bowl, beat butter, granulated sugar, and brown sugar at medium speed until light and fluffy. Add eggs, 1 at a time, beating well after each addition, add vanilla.

At low speed, alternately beat flour mixture and buttermilk into butter mixture just until blended. Divide batter equally between prepared pans. Bake cakes until a toothpick inserted in center comes out clean, 25 to 30 minutes. Transfer pans to wire racks, cool for 10 minutes. Turn out onto racks and remove paper. Turn layers top side up and cool completely.

To prepare frosting, beat butter and confectioners' sugar at medium speed until light and fluffy, add melted chocolate and vanilla, continue beating until shiny and smooth. Place 1 cake layer on a serving plate, spread with frosting. Top with remaining cake layer. Spread frosting on top and sides of cake. Let cake stand for at least 30 minutes before sprinkling with chocolate shavings and slicing.

Makes 12 servings.

# COFFEE CAKE

STREUSEL:
1 cup brown sugar, firmly packed
2 tablespoons flour
¾ cup chopped nuts
1 teaspoon cinnamon
1 tablespoon melted butter
CAKE:
½ cup butter

1 cup sugar
3 eggs
2 cups flour
1 teaspoon baking soda
1/8 teaspoon salt
1 cup sour cream
1 teaspoon vanilla

Streusel: mix all ingredients together until crumbly.
Cake: cream butter and sugar, add eggs and beat well. Sift dry ingredients together and add alternately with sour cream and vanilla to the butter mixture. Grease an angel food or bundt pan. Put half of streusel in pan, then half batter, repeat streusel and then batter. Bake at 350 degrees F. for 55-60 minutes. Cool in pan for 10 minutes, then invert onto cooling rack.

# FRANKFURTER KRANZ
*Great-Grandma Meta B.*

3 ½ cups sifted all-purpose flour
4 teaspoons baking powder
1 cup butter

1 ½ cups granulated sugar
6 eggs, separated
1 ½ teaspoons vanilla

Early in day:
Preheat oven to 275 degrees F. Sift flour with baking powder. Grease 8 ½ x 3 ¾" Turk's head mold.

In a large electric mixing bowl, with mixer at medium speed, mix butter with sugar until very light and fluffy. Add egg yolks, one at a time, mixing well after each addition. Mix in vanilla. With mixer at low speed, mix in flour mixture just until blended.

Beat egg whites until stiff but not dry, with rubber spatula, blend thoroughly with batter. Turn batter into Turk's head mold, and bake 1 hour 10 minutes or until cake tester, inserted in center, comes out clean.

Immediately remove from pan, cool on cake rack.

Now split cake into three layers. Fill and frost them with butter-cream frosting (see below), sprinkling with sugar-toasted almonds, see below. Or top whole un-split cake with Apricot Glaze, see below.

*Butter-cream frosting: In a small electric mixing bowl, with mixer at medium speed, mix 1/3 cup soft butter, 1/8 teaspoon salt, 1 cup sifted confectioners' sugar, 1 ½ teaspoon vanilla till light and fluffy. Now alternatively add 2 cups sifted confectioners' sugar and ¼ cup milk or light cream, beating till smooth.*

*Sugar-toasted almonds: cook 1 cup slivered blanched almonds with 1/3 cup granulated sugar, 1/3 cup butter, 1 tablespoon milk over low heat till nuts are coated and a light caramel color. Turn onto waxed paper; cool, separated into small pieces, each of one or two nuts, not slivers. Sprinkle half of nuts over fillings, press rest on frosting.*

*Apricot Glaze: press 1/3 cup apricot jam through strainer, stir in 1 tablespoon lemon juice. Just before serving, spread over coffeecake, letting excess drip down sides.*

# EASY FRANKFURTER KRANZ

1 package yellow cake mix
Filling
1 ½ cup crushed almonds

can vanilla frosting (16.5 ounce)
Topping
½ cup apricot preserves, sieved

Grease and flour a 9" bundt pan. Prepare yellow cake mix according to package directions. Pour batter into prepared pan. Bake in preheated 350 degree F. oven for 40-45 minutes, or until a cake tester inserted in center comes out clean. With handle of wooden spoon, tap sides of pan to loosen cake. Invert onto wire rack. Let cool 10 minutes. Shake gently and remove pan. Cool completely.

Crush almonds with a rolling pin and measure 1 ½ cups. Beat canned frosting until soft, adding 1 cup crushed nuts. Cut bundt cake into 3 even layers. Spread frosting between each layer, reassembling cake on serving platter. Heat apricot preserves. Use to brush entire cake. Sprinkle with remaining almonds.

Makes 12-16 servings.


# QUICK AND EASY FRUITCAKE

3 eggs, slightly beaten
1 can sweetened condensed milk
2 2/3 cups ready to use mincemeat filling
1 cup mixed candied fruit-1 pound jar

1 cup chopped nuts, coarse
2 cups cornflake crumbs
1 teaspoon baking soda

Butter a 9" tube pan. Line with parchment paper, butter again. In a large bowl, combine eggs, sweetened condensed milk, mincemeat, fruits and nuts, mix well. Add cornflake crumbs and baking soda, blend well, turn into prepared pan. Bake in a 300 degrees F. oven for 2 hours or until a cake tester comes out clean. Cool in pan for 5 minutes. Turn out of pan, remove paper. Cool. If desired, decorate with glazed cherries.

To store, wrap well in foil and refrigerate or freeze.

Make 8 servings.

# GOLDEN FRUITCAKE

16 ounces red candied cherries (2 cups)
8 ounces diced, candied lemon peel (1 cup)
8 ounces diced, candied orange peel (1 cup)
8 ounces candied pineapple wedges, diced (1 cup)
10 ounces pitted dates, diced
2 cups golden raisins
1 cup walnuts, chopped
3 ¾ cups all-purpose flour
1 cup sugar

1 cup butter, softened
6 eggs
1 cup cream sherry
2 tsps double acting baking powder
½ teaspoon salt
2 whole angelica for garnish
2 tablespoons lemon juice
2 cups confectioners' sugar

**Up to 2 months ahead:** Line a tube pan with foil, which will make the cake easy to remove. Make sure foil is smooth, so side of cake will be smooth. Mix the fruit and nuts with flour to help keep them evenly suspended in the batter, to prevent them from sinking to the bottom as the cake bakes.

Cream the cake batter until fluffy and light. This ensures that the cake will have a moist, velvety texture. When spooning batter into pan, pack it evenly to eliminate air pockets that could make the cake rise unevenly and leave unsightly holes. Move oven rack to lower position to be sure whole cake is in middle of oven while baking.

Preheat oven to 300 degrees. Line the pan as noted. Cut cherries in half. Reserve 15 halves for garnish. In large bowl, combine remaining cherries, next 6 ingredients and ¾ cup flour. In another large bowl, with mixer at medium speed, stir in fruit mixture.

Spoon batter into pan. Bake 3 hours until toothpick inserted in center comes out clean. Cool on rack, remove from pan and peel off foil carefully. Wrap tightly with plastic wrap. Refrigerate cake up to 2 months.

**To Serve:** Cut angelica into 15 leaves. In small bowl, stir lemon juice, a little at a time, into confectioners' sugar until spreading consistency, garnish cake with glaze, leaves and reserved cherry halves.

Makes one 7 pound fruit cake.

Makes 16 servings.

# GINGER CAKE
*Great-Grandma Anna Catharina P.*

2 ½ cups sifted flour
1 ¾ teaspoons baking soda
1 teaspoon ground ginger
1 teaspoon ground cinnamon
¼ teaspoon ground cloves
¼ teaspoon salt

1 cup sugar
½ cup solid shortening
1 cup molasses
1 cup boiling water
2 eggs, well beaten

Sift together flour, baking soda, spices and salt and set aside. Cream sugar with shortening and molasses until well blended. Add dry ingredients to creamed mixture alternately with boiling water, beginning and ending with dry ingredients. Stir in eggs quickly. Pour into a well greased 13x9x2" baking pan and bake in a 350 degree oven for 30 minutes. Cut into squares and serve.

Makes approximately 8 servings.

*This is a quick cake and has a distinct taste, which I like. It can be served as is or with some whipped cream or ice cream, or just sprinkle with a bit of confectioners' sugar over the top, just like my Grandma did.*


# YELLOW LAYER CAKE
*Aunt Helen B.*

½ cup butter, softened
4 eggs
3 cups flour
1 teaspoon salt

½ cup sugar
1 cup milk
2 teaspoons baking powder
1 teaspoon vanilla

Mix all ingredients together and pour into buttered and floured layer cake pans. Bake at 375 degrees until done, approximately 15 to 25 minutes. Test with a toothpick to check doneness.

Makes 2 layers.

# INDIVIDUAL CHOCOLATE LAVA CAKES

*Center:* ½ bar bittersweet choco. baking bar (2 oz)
Cake: nonstick cooking spray
8 tablespoons unsalted butter (1 stick)
2 egg yolks
½ teaspoon vanilla extract
Garnish: raspberries and whipped cream

¼ cup heavy cream
1 bar bittersweet chocolate baking bar
2 whole eggs
1/3 cup sugar
½ cup cake flour

To make center: melt chocolate and cream together in the top of a double boiler. Whisk gently to blend. Refrigerate for about 2 hours or until firm. Form into 6 balls and refrigerate until needed. A melon baller makes this easy.

To make cake: preheat oven to 400 degrees. Spray 6 ramekins, silicon cupcake tray with plain sides or custard cups with nonstick spray. Melt chocolate and butter together in top of double boiler. Whisk gently together until blended. With an electric mixer, whisk eggs, yolks, sugar and vanilla on high speed about 5 minutes or until thick and light. Fold melted chocolate mixture and flour into egg mixture just until combined. Spoon cake batter into ramekins, place chocolate ball in the middle of each ramekin.

Bake about 15 minutes, or until cake is firm to the touch. Let it sit out of the oven for about 5 minutes. Run a small, sharp knife around inside of each ramekin, place plate on top, invert and remove ramekin. Garnish with raspberries and a dollop of whipped cream. Strawberries or blackberries can be used instead.

Makes 6 servings.

*This is a quick recipe to make and totally decadent.*

# MOCHA CAKE

1 ¼ cups flour
¼ cup cornstarch
1 teaspoon baking soda
½ teaspoon salt
1 tablespoon vinegar
Mocha frosting:

1 cup packed brown sugar
3 tablespoons cocoa
1 teaspoon instant coffee powder
1/3 cup oil
1 cup water
½ teaspoon vanilla

In 8" or 9" square pan, with fork, mix well flour, sugar, cornstarch, cocoa, baking soda, coffee powder and salt. Add oil, vinegar, vanilla and water. Mix briskly with a fork until thoroughly blended. Bake in preheated 350 degree F. oven for 40 minutes or until a tooth pick inserted in the center comes out clean and cake pulls away from the sides of the pan. Cool in pan on rack. Spread with frosting.

Makes 9 servings.

# NUT CAKE
*Aunt Helen B.*

1 package yellow cake mix
whipped cream

1 container caramel icing
nut meats (your choice)

Prepare cake mix as per package directions. When cold put layers together with caramel icing or other favorite icing of your choice. Whip icing with electric mixer before using, it makes it fluffy. Decorate top with nuts.

# OMA'S PINEAPPLE UPSIDE DOWN CAKE

½ cup butter
1 cup brown sugar
1 can sliced pineapple
1 dozen maraschino cherries, pitted, de stemmed
1 cup flour

1 teaspoon baking powder
1/8 teaspoon salt
3 eggs, separated
1 cup sugar
5 tablespoons pineapple juice

Melt butter in a large round baking pan. Spread brown sugar evenly in pan and arrange pineapple slices evenly on sugar following contours of pan. Fill in spaces in center of slices and along side slices with the cherries. Sift flour, baking powder and salt together, beat egg yolks until light, adding sugar then gradually add pineapple juice and flour. Fold in stiffly beaten egg whites. Pour batter over pineapple/sugar in bottom of pan. Bake at 375 degrees for 30 to 35 minutes. Turn upside down on cake plate.

Use a 9-10" cake pan.

Makes 8 servings.

*Love this cake, so do my children and the rest of my family. If you like pineapple this is the one!*

*Serve with a dollop of whipped cream.*

# UBER OMA'S POUND CAKE
*Great Grandma Anna B.*

1 pound butter, softened
3 cups sugar
10 eggs, separated
5 ½ cups sifted flour

6 teaspoons baking powder
¾ cup milk
2 teaspoons vanilla
1 teaspoon grated lemon rind

Beat softened butter with 3 cups of sugar for 5 minutes at low speed. Add 10 egg yolks and beat 2 minutes at low speed. Beat 10 egg whites for 2 minutes at high speed with same beaters. Then beat creamed mixture 5 minutes longer at low speed. Sift the flour and baking powder together. Beat 1/3 of flour into bowl at low speed. Beat in milk until smooth. Reserving ¼ cup of the flour, beat in another 1/3 of the flour into bowl. Add egg whites and beat until smooth. Add remaining flour to bowl. Increase speed to medium and beat for an additional 5 minutes. Grease 2 9 or 10" tube pans generously. Coat evenly with reserved flour, tapping excess into bowl. Add vanilla and grated lemon rind, beat at medium speed for 2 minutes. Pour batter into prepared pans. Bake at 300 degrees for 1 ¼ hours or until centers spring back when lightly pressed with fingertip. Cool in pans on wire rack for 10 minutes. Loosen around sides of pan with a knife and invert cake onto a wire rack to cool completely.

PLEASE NOTE: sugar and butter should be well creamed before adding the egg yolks. The egg whites are beaten separately and set aside while you measure the flour. If only 1 pan is available, just use half the batter, refrigerate the remainder until first cake is baked.

Makes 16 servings.

# RAISIN SPICE CAKE

½ cup butter, softened
1 cup firmly packed brown sugar
1 egg
2 cups all-purpose flour, sifted
3 teaspoons baking powder
½ teaspoon ground cloves
¼ teaspoon salt

1 teaspoon ground cinnamon
1 teaspoon ground nutmeg
¾ cup cooled coffee
1 cup raisins, seedless
¼ cup confectioners' sugar
1 tablespoon lemon juice

Combine butter, brown sugar and egg in a large bowl. Beat with electric mixer at medium/high speed until well blended and fluffy. Sift flour, baking powder, salt, cloves, cinnamon, and nutmeg onto waxed paper. Lower mixer speed to lowest speed, add sifted dry ingredients alternately with coffee. Mix just until blended. Stir in raisins. Turn batter into a buttered 9x9x2" baking pan.

Bake at 350 degrees F. oven for 40 minutes, or until center of cake springs back when lightly pressed with finger. Cool in pan on wire rack. Combine confectioners' sugar and lemon juice in a small bowl; add a few drops of water, if necessary, to achieve a spreading consistency. Spread over the top of cake while still warm. Frosting will form a thin glaze. Cut cake into squares. The remainder of the cake may be covered and stored in the pan.

*Instead of raisins you can add a cup of minced apples or a mixture of raisins and apples.*

# OMA'S SPONGE CAKE

4 eggs, separated  
½ teaspoon salt  
2 tablespoons cold water  
½ cup hot water  

1 ½ cups sugar  
1 teaspoon vanilla  
1 ½ cups sifted flour  
½ teaspoon cream of tartar  

Beat egg yolks and ¼ teaspoon salt in a 3 ½ quart mixing bowl, until thick and light colored. Add cold water and beat 1 minute, then hot water next and beat 5 minutes or until mixture fills bowl ¾ full. Gradually beat in sugar and stir in vanilla. Beat until very fluffy. Blend in flour. Beat egg whites until frothy; add cream of tartar and remaining salt and beat till stiff not dry. Fold whites into yolk mixture; pour into an ungreased 10" tube pan and bake in 350 degree oven for about 1 hour.

Makes 8 servings.

*Basic sponge cake that can stand alone or be used as a platform for fruit, served with whipped cream or spread with a thinned jam, marmalade, or preserves.*

# DESSERTS AND COOKIES

# EASY BAKED ALASKA

3 egg whites
3 tablespoons sugar
1 teaspoon vanilla

dash salt
1 quart ice cream
1 purchased sponge layer

Beat 3 egg whites until stiff, folding in sugar, vanilla and salt. Set sponge layer on a cold plate or wooden board. Place semi-frozen ice cream on the center, leaving a 1" border. Completely cover with meringue. Bake in hot oven at 450 degrees for about 3 minutes until lightly browned.

Makes 4 servings.

*An old time favorite, but still very impressive.*


# APPLE CRUNCH

4 cups sliced, pared apples
¾ cup sugar
1 teaspoon cinnamon

½ teaspoon salt
½ cup cornflake crumbs
½ cup soft butter

Spread apples in buttered 10x6x2" baking pan. Combine ½ cup sugar with cinnamon, sprinkle over apples. Sift together flour, salt and remaining sugar; stir in corn flake crumbs. Cut in butter until mixture resembles coarse corn meal. Sprinkle over apples. Bake at 400 degrees F. about 30 minutes. Serve warm with cream.

Makes 6 servings.

# APPLE STRUDEL

4 sheets phyllo dough
2 tablespoons cornstarch
3 c granny smith apples, peeled, cored, sliced ¼"
1/3 cup seedless white raisins
1 teaspoon ground cinnamon
1 cup apple cider+ 3 tablespoons (or apple juice)

¼ cup slivered almonds (optional)
6 tablespoons melted butter
3 tablespoons dried bread crumbs
1/3 cup sugar
1 beaten egg
confectioners' sugar

In a saucepan, over medium heat, cook the apples, that have been peeled, cored, and sliced ¼" thick, with 1 cup apple cider (or apple juice). Add the raisins, sugar and cinnamon until the apples are tender, about 10 minutes. In small cup, mix 3 tablespoons cider (or juice) with 2 tablespoons cornstarch and slowly add to cooking apples. Stir constantly until smooth and simmer, still stirring, for 1 additional minute. Remove from heat and cool. Stir in almonds and cover, refrigerate while preparing phyllo dough. Preheat oven to 450 degrees F. Line a cookie sheet with parchment paper.

Lay out one phyllo sheet on a surface lightly sprinkled with confectioner's sugar. Brush with melted butter, sprinkle with ¼ of the bread crumbs and carefully place the second sheet on top of the first sheet. Brush the second sheet with melted butter and ¼ of the bread crumbs and repeat with next two sheets.

Spread the apple filling evenly onto the prepared phyllo dough, leaving a ½" edge without fruit. Have lengthwise side facing you and place the fruit closer to one long edge (lengthwise) and roll into a log. tucking in ends to seal. Brush the top with the beaten egg and on ends to seal. With the sealed side down, Carefully place strudel on prepared baking sheet. Try to move the strudel as little as possible, since Phyllo dough is very fragile. Bake the strudel for approximately 16-18 minutes, or until golden brown. Remove from oven and cool for 15 to 20 minutes before scoring top into 1 ½" slices with a sharp knife. Cool completely before cutting into slices. Garnish with sprinkled confectioners' sugar before serving.

Makes 8 servings.

*This is a traditional apple strudel and real easy to make, phyllo dough can be difficult to work with, the trick is to make sure its defrosted fully but still cool enough to work with without tearing. My family and friends really like this one and they think I slaved over it. It is basically the same recipe I use for the apple turnovers, which everyone also likes.*

*The apples, prepared per directions, also make a delicious filling for crepes!*

# BAKED APPLES
*Berta H. (my Mother-in-law)*

4 large baking apples
½ lemon
½ cup seedless raisins
2 tablespoons hazelnuts, finely chopped

2 tablespoon corn syrup
1 cup apple juice
cinnamon
1 tablespoon butter

Preheat oven to 375 degrees. Wash apples and remove core with an apple corer or small knife. Leave about ½" of the core on the bottom so that each apple has a closed bottom. Peel apples halfway down from the top and rub peeled surfaces with the cut side of the lemon so the peeled sections will not brown.

Place apples in a baking dish. Mix raisins, nuts, 1 tablespoon of the corn syrup and 3-4 tablespoons of the apple juice. Stuff mixture into the apple hollows. Combine remaining juice with remaining corn syrup and pour over apples.

Sprinkle apples with cinnamon. Dot tops of apples with butter. Bake for 45 minutes, basting occasionally with pan juices, or until apples are tender. Serve either warm or at room temperature. Serve with cream or half and half.
Makes 4 servings.

Maple syrup can be substituted for the corn syrup.

*If you wish to make this en croute: simply take puffed pastry dough, defrosted, and roll out thinly. Cut into squares large enough to cover the apples, just sit each apple in middle of square and form like a purse around the apple leaving the top open like a purse. Bake as directed until golden brown. Cover with foil if dough is brown but apples aren't fork tender. Continue baking until apples are fork tender.*

# APPLE DUMPLINGS

2 ½ cups flour
1 teaspoon salt
light brown sugar
butter-flavored shortening
½ cup diced dried mixed fruit

ground cinnamon
6 small baking apples
1 large egg, beaten
6 whole cloves
light cream

One hour before serving: In a large bowl, mix flour, salt and 2 tablespoons brown sugar, cut in 1 cup of butter-flavored solid shortening. Stir in 5 to 6 tablespoons cold water until dough holds together. In a small bowl, mix dried fruit, ¼ cup brown sugar, 2 tablespoons butter-flavored shortening and 1 teaspoon cinnamon. Peel apples; remove cores but do not go all the way through to the bottom. Press fruit mixture into cavities.

Preheat oven to 400 degrees F. Grease 15x10 jelly roll pan. Reserve 1/3 cup dough. On floured surface, with floured rolling pin, roll remaining dough into 21"x14" rectangle. Cut dough into six 7" squares. On waxed paper, mix 2 tablespoons brown sugar and ½ teaspoon cinnamon. Roll an apple in sugar mixture, center apple on a dough square, brush edges of dough with some egg. Bring dough up over top of apple, press to shape, seal edges. Place in pan, repeat with remaining apples. Roll reserved dough ¼" thick. Cut leaves from dough, make veins in cutouts to resemble leaves. Brush dumplings with egg, attach leaves, brush with egg again. Press in cloves for stems.

Bake 35-40 minutes until pastry is golden and apples are tender when pierced. Serve with cream, garnish with lemon leaves if desired.

Makes 6 servings.

## APPLE COBBLER WITH CREAM

Heat 1 can of sliced apples with a dash of nutmeg and 1 tablespoon butter until boiling. Pour into a baking dish. Stir 3 tablespoons cream into ½ cup biscuit mix. Spoon over hot apples. Bake 15 minutes at 350 to 375 degrees.

*If you wish you can add a ¼ cup of raisins to the apples. I like this with plumped golden raisins.*

## APPLE OATMEAL CRISP

3-4 baking apples, pared, cored, thinly sliced   ½ cup butter
¼ cup brown sugar   ¼ cup quick oats
½ cup flour   1 teaspoon cinnamon

Arrange apples in well buttered shallow baking dish. Melt butter and add other ingredients until well mixed. Sprinkle over apples. Bake at 350 degrees F. for 45 minutes until golden brown.

Serve with whipped cream.

Makes 6 serving.

# APPLE PAN DOWDY

Peel and slice 4 tart apples into a buttered shallow baking dish. Sprinkle with ½ cup sugar, ½ teaspoon cinnamon, and dot with 2 tablespoons butter. Cover with biscuit dough (1 cup biscuit mix, 1/3 cup milk) rolled then bake 20 minutes in a moderate oven (350 degrees). Break crust into apples. Bake 10 minutes more. Serve hot with cream sweetened and then dusted with nutmeg.

*This is a universal dish. I've seen pan dowdy recipes in colonial cookbooks, English cookbooks, etc. In different variations it has been around for a long time. Canned, refrigerated biscuit dough can be used, or a homemade biscuit dough. It depends on how much time you have.*

# CINNAMON APPLE SLICES

1 cup light corn syrup
½ cup red cinnamon candies
½ cup cider vinegar
6-10 whole cloves

1-2 cinnamon sticks
4 medium baking apples (tart), cored and cut into ½" slices

In heavy 10" skillet combine corn syrup, candies, vinegar, cloves and cinnamon stick. Bring to a boil over medium heat and cook and stir until candies melt. Add enough apple slices to make a single layer in skillet and simmer just until slices are tender and transparent but do not lose their shape, 10 to 12 minutes. Remove the slices with the slotted spoon to clean wide mouth jars. Cook remaining apple slices and place in jars. Pour remaining syrup over slices removing cloves and cinnamon. Cover tightly and chill at least 1 week before serving. Good as a relish with roast meat or as a topping for puddings.

Keeps about 3 weeks.

Makes about 3 cups.

*Good way to use up those cinnamon candies you have for cake decorating.*

# APPLE TURNOVERS

Filling:
3 med. sized baking apples, peeled, cored, thinly sliced (about 3 1/2 cups)
½ cup sugar
¼ cup baking raisins or plumped white raisins
¼ cup sugar
1 tablespoon cornstarch
1 teaspoon ground cinnamon
1 cup apple juice or apple cider

Pastry:
melted butter, approx. ¾ stick
15 sheets phyllo dough, defrosted
Topping:
2 tablespoons sugar
¼ teaspoon ground cinnamon
1 teaspoon butter, melted

Preheat oven to 375 degrees F. In medium pot, combine filling ingredients. Heat together until apples are tender stirring until thickened and there are no lumps from cornstarch. Set aside.

Place 1 sheet of phyllo on a flat, dry work surface. (keep remaining sheets covered with plastic wrap to prevent drying out). Brush phyllo sheet with butter. Lay second sheet of phyllo over the first. Brush with butter. Cut layered sheets in half, lengthwise. Lay one half of cut sheets on second half, forming 4 layers.

Place ½ cup of filling at one end of layered sheets. Fold right bottom corner over filling, forming a triangle. Continue folding, keeping triangle shape. Place triangle with the seam side down on a baking sheet. Repeat with remaining phyllo and filling. Brush tops of triangles with butter. Sprinkle evenly with ½ teaspoon sugar. Bake for 16-18 minutes or until turnovers are golden brown. Serve with ice cream or cream if desired.

Makes approximately 12-14 turnovers.

*This recipe is very easy to make and tastes great. I like to drizzle the cooled turnovers with vanilla icing. My son requested this for his college fraternity cake sale (among others). One guy kept coming back buying more and more until he purchased 2 dozen of the turnovers, and then he ordered more!*

# BLACK FOREST CHERRY CUPCAKES
*Eleanor H.*

1 package Devil's Food Cake mix
1 can vanilla icing
bar of milk chocolate

1 can cherry pie filling
1 can chocolate icing
decorating bag for icing

Prepare cake mix according to package directions, using paper liners fill cup cake tray with batter to 1/3 full. Into each cup place a small piece of the chocolate bar. Put tablespoon full of batter into each cup. Bake as per package directions. Cool cupcakes.

Ice with chocolate icing. Pipe a ring of vanilla icing around edge of cupcake. Fill center with a small spoonful of cherry pie filling to cover chocolate icing. Using a vegetable peeler shave a few curls of chocolate from the chocolate bar on top of cherries. Makes approximately 20.

*Its amazing that this recipe came to me while I was sleeping and trying to think of something different to make for the bake sale I mentioned above (apple turnovers). Now its becoming a favorite of the family.*

# BRAUN KLUTTEN
## Browned and Fried Dumplings
### Great Grandma Meta B.

5 cups flour, sifted
10 ounces seedless raisins
2 eggs, room temperature, beaten
2 cups milk, warmed (not hot)

10 teaspoons sugar
2 active yeast cakes
cinnamon and sugar
¼ cup lukewarm water

Dissolve yeast in ¼ cup lukewarm water with 1 teaspoon sugar in 14 ounce drinking glass. Set aside and let rise to top of glass. (keep in a draft free warm area). Takes about 15 minutes. Sift flour and add sugar. Beat eggs slightly and make well in flour mixture and add eggs, raisins, warm milk, then yeast. Mix using a wooden spoon.

Cover with a towel and let rise till doubled. (approximately ½ hour). When doubled heat specialty frying pan (indentations for dumplings) or deep fry pan with 2" of cooking oil. Put ½ teaspoon of cooking oil in each dumpling indentation. Drop batter by approximately 1 tablespoon per opening and fry in oil until a golden brown. Remove from pan and drain on a paper towel or in a brown paper bag. Roll in cinnamon and sugar mixture while hot. Cool completely before storing.

*Can use dark or golden raisins or mix of both.*

Makes 3 ½ dozen.

*These are called olibooen in Holland. Since my parents come from a section of Germany that is close to the Dutch border it is entirely possible that they are one and the same. The only recipe I could find for olibooen was similar. Whatever its called its a quick and easy donut.*

*This was a special treat my Mom would make for my friends and I after school, she also made them for Christmas Eve.*

# BROWNIES

2 unsweetened baking chocolate squares
½ cup butter
2 eggs
1 cup sugar

1 teaspoon vanilla
½ cup all-purpose flour sifted
1/8 teaspoon salt
¾ cup chopped walnuts

Melt chocolate and butter in a small saucepan over low heat cool slightly. Beat eggs in a small bowl with electric mixer gradually beat in sugar until mixture is fluffy and thick. Gradually stir in chocolate mixture and vanilla, fold in flour and salt until well-blended stir in walnuts. Spread evenly in an 8x8x2" greased baking pan.

Bake in a 350 degrees F. for 30 minutes or until shiny and firm on top. Cool in pan on wire rack.

Makes 9 servings.

# CREAM PUFFS

1 cup water
½ cup vegetable shortening
dash salt
1 cup flour
3 eggs

Filling:
1 cup chilled whipping cream
1 teaspoon vanilla
1/3 cup sugar
confectioners' sugar

Preheat oven to 400 degrees F.

In medium saucepan over medium heat, bring water, shortening and salt to a simmer. Remove from heat and add flour all at once, mixing well. Adding 1 egg at a time, mixing very well until each egg is incorporated. Drop by rounded tablespoons (or use pastry bag to pipe out dough) on ungreased double baking sheet. Bake 30 to 45 minutes. Cool. Prepare filling by whipping together the cream, vanilla and sugar until thick. To assemble cut top 1/4 off each puff. With a fork remove any sticky dough inside. Fill with cream. Replace tops and dust with confectioners' sugar.

Make about 15 cream puffs.

Note: *can be made into swans—using a pastry bag with a large star tip, pipe body by holding the bag at an angle and pulling when done, to form tail. For neck, use pastry bag with plain #5 tip, form a backward "S". Bake necks for 10 minutes. To assemble cut open cream puff on angle opposite tail. Remove and cut in half for the wings. Fill body with cream and insert neck and wings. Dust with confectioners' sugar.*

# CRUMPETS

2 eggs
1 ½ cups milk
4 tablespoons melted shortening
1 teaspoon salt

1 tablespoon sugar
4 teaspoons baking powder
2 ½ cups flour

Add beaten eggs and milk to melted shortening and beat well. Add salt, sugar and baking powder sifted with the flour. Put greased muffin rings (large size) on hot slightly greased griddle or frying pan; fill 2/3 full with batter, cook slowly until brown and puffed up, turn with a pancake turner and cook other side. Split while hot, butter and serve with cottage cheese.

Makes 12 crumpets.

# ECLAIRS

½ cup butter
1 cup boiling water
1 cup sifted all-purpose flour

¼ teaspoon salt
4 eggs

Melt butter in boiling water. Add flour and salt all at one time stir vigorously. Cook, stirring constantly until the mixture forms a ball that doesn't separate. Remove from the heat and cool slightly. Add eggs one at a time, beating hard after each addition until mixture is smooth. Insert number 32 tip in the pastry press. Fill press with the mixture and form éclairs 1" wide and ¾" long leaving an inch of space between each on a greased cookie sheet. Bake. Cut éclairs in half lengthwise and fill with custard. Frost with chocolate frosting. See custard filling and chocolate frosting.

Makes 1 dozen éclairs.

**Custard Filling:** 3 tablespoons cornstarch
½ cup sugar
1/8 teaspoon salt
½ cup cold milk

1 ½ cups milk, scalded
1 teaspoon vanilla extract
2 egg yolks, beaten with 2 tbls milk

Mix cornstarch, sugar, salt and cold milk. Gradually add hot milk. Cook in double boiler until thick, stirring constantly. Cover, cook 10 to 12 minutes. Stir some of the hot mixture over beaten yolks, then add to the custard. Stir well, add vanilla extract, cool.

See frostings for chocolate frosting for éclairs.

# FRIED APPLE TURNOVERS
*Aunt Helen B.*

CRUST:
1 ½ cup flour
½ teaspoon salt
½ cup shortening
4 to 5 tablespoons cold water

FILLING:
apples
¼ cup apple juice
OR: apple sauce

Mix together ingredients for crust and roll out on floured counter. Either cook sliced, pared and cored apples in ¼ cup apple juice OR use prepared apple sauce for filling. Cut the dough in squares approximately 3x3" and put a spoonful of filling in each square. Fold over and press to seal. Fry in 2" of oil until golden.

# BERLINER PFANNKUCHEN
## Filled Berlin Doughnuts

1 package active dry yeast
¼ cup warm or lukewarm, water
¼ cup butter
¾ cup milk, scalded
¼ cup granulated sugar
1 teaspoon salt

2 eggs, unbeaten
3 ¾ cups sifted all-purpose flour
1 teaspoon grated lemon rind
1 egg white, slightly beaten
strawberry jam or applesauce
fat or salad oil
granulated sugar

Day before:
In a small bowl, sprinkle or crumble yeast into warm water; stir until dissolved. Melt butter in milk in a saucepan; then cool to lukewarm.

In large electric-mixer bowl, with mixer at medium speed, blend dissolved yeast, lukewarm milk, ¾ cup sugar, salt, and eggs. Add flour, a little at a time, and lemon rind; beat well. Cover with waxed paper, then clean towel; let rise in warm place (about 85 degrees F.) until doubled.

On lightly floured surface, knead dough a few times; then roll it 3/8" thick. Cut into rounds with floured 2 ¾" cookie cutter. Brush edges of half of rounds with egg white; then place 1 teaspoon strawberry jam or applesauce in center of each. Top with rest of rounds, firmly pinch edges together. Arrange on floured cookie sheets; cover with clean tea towel; let rise in warm place till almost doubled and light to the touch. In deep saucepan, place just enough fat or salad oil to come halfway up the side. Heat to 370 degrees F. on deep-fat frying thermometer.

Now fry doughnuts, two or three at a time, turning once, until golden brown and done—2 to 3 minutes each.

Lift out with a slotted spoon and drain on paper towels. Then roll each in granulated sugar.

Serve at once, with more strawberry jam or applesauce. If desired, store doughnuts in a covered container and serve next day for breakfast.

Makes about 20 donuts.

*Can use raspberry jelly instead of strawberry.*

# CHOCOLATE FUDGE

3 cups sugar
2/3 cup cream, milk or water
¼ teaspoon salt
2 tablespoons butter

2 squares chocolate
2 tablespoons light corn syrup
1 teaspoon vanilla

Combine the sugar, chocolate, cream syrup and salt in a large saucepan and bring slowly to boiling point, stirring constantly until the sugar in entirely dissolved and the ingredients blended. Continue cooking, without stirring, to the soft ball stage (238-240 degrees).

Add the vanilla and cool, without stirring, to lukewarm (110 degrees F) then add the butter and beat briskly until the mixture is creamy and loses its gloss. Turn into a buttered square pan and when partly cooled, mark into squares, cutting apart when cold.

Should the mixture become too stiff and is difficult to spread in the pan the candy may be kneaded or a very little water or cream added to bring it back to spreading consistency.

# FUDGE FILLING AND FROSTING

2 cups brown sugar
2 squares chocolate, grated
½ teaspoon butter

½ cup rich milk
1 tablespoon butter

Place the sugar and milk in a saucepan, stir over a very low heat until the sugar is dissolved. Then stir in the chocolate and continue stirring until mixture is melted. Beat a few seconds with egg beater to insure smoothness. Increase heat to medium and cook until the mixture forms a soft ball (238 degrees), when dropped into cold water. Remove from the heat and add the butter, cool to lukewarm then add the vanilla and beat until spreading consistency. Use 1/3 of the mixture as a filling and the remainder as frosting for the top and sides of the fudge.

Should the frosting become too firm to handle easily, it may be stirred over hot water for a few minutes until it again becomes creamy.

# DOUBLE FUDGE

Filling:
8 ounce package cream cheese, softened
2 tablespoons butter
¼ cup sugar
1 tablespoon milk
1 egg
½ teaspoon vanilla

Base:
1 package Devil's food cake mix
3 eggs
1/3 cup oil
1 cup water

Heat oven to 350 degrees F. Grease and flour 12x9" pan. In small bowl, blend all filling ingredients, beat at highest speed until smooth and creamy. Set aside. In large bowl, blend cake mix, eggs, oil and water until moistened. Beat 2 minutes at highest speed. Pour half of batter into pan. Pour cream cheese mixture over batter, spreading to cover. Pour remaining batter over cream cheese mixture.

Bake at 350 degrees F. for 45 to 55 minutes or until toothpick inserted in center comes out clean, cool completely. Frost with your favorite fudge frosting. Keep refrigerated.


# NO COOK CHOCOLATE FUDGE

½ pound sweet chocolate
1 pound confectioner's sugar
1 teaspoon vanilla
1 cup chopped nut meats

2 tablespoons butter
1/8 teaspoon salt
2 beaten eggs

Place the chocolate and butter in upper part of the double boiler, over hot water, and heat until the chocolate melts, stirring occasionally. Meanwhile, add the sugar, salt and vanilla to the eggs and blend thoroughly. Combine the two mixtures, stir in the nut meats, spread in a buttered pan and chill. Cut into squares and wrap in waxed paper. Can be frosted.

# VANILLA FUDGE

2 cups sugar
1 cup evaporated milk
1 teaspoon light corn syrup

¼ cup butter
1 teaspoon vanilla
chopped nuts, optional

Line an 8x4x2" loaf pan with foil, extending foil over edges of pan. Butter foil, set aside. Butter the sides of a heavy 2 quart saucepan. In the saucepan, combine the sugar, evaporated milk and corn syrup. Cook and stir over medium-high heat to boiling. Carefully clip a candy thermometer to side of pan. Cook over medium low heat to 238 degrees F. soft-ball stage, stirring frequently. This should take about 20 to 25 minutes.

Remove saucepan from heat. Add butter and vanilla, but do not stir. Cool without stirring to 110 degrees (about 45 minutes). Remove candy thermometer from saucepan. Carefully stir butter into cooked mixture to incorporate. Beat mixture vigorously with a wooden spoon till fudge becomes very thick (about minutes total), immediately spread fudge into prepared pan. Score into squares while warm. If desired, top each square with a nut piece, when candy is firm, use foil to lift it out of pan. Cut into squares. Makes about 1 pound.

Make up to 3 days ahead, make and cut fudge. Place in an airtight container and store in the refrigerator.

# GINGERBREAD

Solid shortening
1 cup molasses
½ cup butter
2 1/3 cups all-purpose flour, sifted
dash salt

¾ teaspoon baking soda
1 teaspoon ground ginger
1 teaspoon ground cinnamon
¼ teaspoon ground cloves
1 cup dairy sour cream

Grease a 9" square baking pan generously and set aside. Combine molasses and butter in a saucepan and bring to a boil. Take off the heat and pour into a large mixing bowl. Allow to cool slightly. Meanwhile, sift the flour with the salt, baking soda, and spices. Stir the sour cream into the cooled molasses and butter, then stir in the flour mixture thoroughly. Pour into the prepared pan and bake in a preheated 350 degrees oven for 35 to 40 minutes or until a toothpick inserted in the center comes out dry.

Turn out of the pan onto a cake rack to cool. Cut into squares.

Makes 8 servings.

# PEANUT BRITTLE

2 cups sugar
1 cup light corn syrup
¼ cup water
2 cups salted peanuts

3 tablespoons butter
1 teaspoon vanilla
1 teaspoon baking soda
1 tablespoon water

In a 3 quart saucepan combine sugar, corn syrup and water. Put over medium heat, stirring until sugar is dissolved. Simmer over medium heat until syrup reaches 270 degrees or soft crack stage on candy thermometer. Remove from heat. Stir in butter until melted, then stir in peanuts. Put back over heat and cook until syrup reaches 300 degrees or hard crack stage on candy thermometer. Combine vanilla, baking soda and water and stir into mixture until candy foams. Pour into buttered 15x10x1" baking sheet. Cool completely, then break into pieces.

Makes about 2 ¼ pounds.

# GERMAN FRUITED STOLLEN
### Great Grandma Sophie B.

1 package active dry yeast
¼ cup water
½ cup butter
1 cup milk, scalded
¼ cup sugar
¼ teaspoon ground cardamom
1 teaspoon salt
4 ¾-5 cups sifted enriched flour
1 egg
1 cup seedless raisins
½ cup currants

2 tablespoon grated lemon peel
¼ c coarsely ground blanched almond
¼ cup finely cut candied citron
¼ cup finely cut candied cherries
¼ cup chopped mixed candied fruit
2 tablespoons grated orange peel
Frosting:
¾ cup sifted confectioners' sugar
1 tablespoon milk or cream
1/8 teaspoon vanilla
sliced candied cherries
2 tbs chopped or slivered almonds

Soften active dry yeast in ¼ cup warm water or compressed yeast in ¼ cup lukewarm water. Melt butter in hot milk; add sugar, salt, and cardamom, cool to lukewarm. Stir in 2 cups of the flour. Add egg and beat well. Stir in softened yeast, fruits, peels and nuts. Add remaining flour to make soft dough. Turn out on lightly floured surface. Cover and let rest 10 minutes. Knead 5 to 8 minutes or till smooth and satiny. Place in lightly greased bowl, turning once to grease surface. Cover with a tea towel, let rise in warm place till double, about 1 ½ hours. Punch down, turn out on lightly floured surface and divide in 3 equal parts. Cover, let rest 10 minutes.

Roll each part into a 12x7 inch rectangle, without stretching dough. Fold long side over to within 1" of opposite side to make typical stolen shape (slightly curved or straight is fine); seal edges together. Place on greased baking sheets. Cover with tea towel, and let rise till almost double about 30 to 45 minutes. Bake in moderate oven (375 degrees) 20 to 25 minutes, or till golden brown.

Frosting: Mix sugar and milk (or cream) to make a smooth, thick frosting that will just pour. Add the vanilla. Pour over the top of the loaf, letting the frosting drip down the sides. Decorate with the sliced cherries and sprinkle with almonds. Form the cherries and almonds into flower type shapes, with the almond slivers for petals.
Makes 3 loaves.

*This is a German tradition for Christmas. It brings back all the memories of Christmas, the pine tree covered with tinsel and candles, the plates and plates of cookies and other special foods. And especially the family gathered all together.*

# TOFFEE AND CHOCOLATE DROP COOKIES

1 cup (2 sticks) butter softened
1 cup granulated sugar
1 cup packed light brown sugar
1 teaspoon vanilla extract
½ teaspoon salt
3 eggs

3 ½ cups all-purpose flour
2 teaspoons baking soda
2 teaspoons cream of tarter
1 1/3 cups Toffee Bits or Toffee
Bars broken into small pieces
1/3 cup mini chocolate chips

Heat oven to 350 degrees. Lightly grease cookie sheets.

Beat butter, granulated sugar, brown sugar, vanilla and salt in large bowl until blended. Add eggs; beat well. Stir together flour, baking soda and cream of tarter; gradually add to butter mixture, beating until blended. Stir in toffee bits and chocolate chips. (if using the bar candies, put in plastic bag and crush with a rolling pin or a heavy wooden spoon).

Drop by heaping teaspoons onto prepared cookie sheets. Bake 8 to 10 minutes or until lightly browned. Cool slightly; remove to wire rack. Cool completely.

Makes about 6 dozen cookies.

# HOW TO MAKE PERFECT ROLLED COOKIES

Mix dough as directed. Using part of the dough and keeping the rest of dough chilled, lightly roll dough to desired thickness, the thinner you roll the crisper the cookie. Rub flour into rolling pin cover with cloth to prevent sticking. To cut: dip cookie cutter in flour, shake off excess, cut with steady pressure. Cut as many cookies from each rolling as possible. Cut diamonds or squares with knife with remainder rolled dough. Carefully lift cut-out cookies to baking sheet with a spatula. Bake.

## OMA'S BROWN COOKIES
*Mathilde B.*

10-12 cups flour, sifted
½ pound butter (2 sticks), softened
1/8 pound shortening (1/4 cup)
2 cups sugar
1 ½ bottles corn syrup
1 lemon, juice of

1 ½ teaspoons cinnamon
1 teaspoon ground cloves
1 teaspoon vanilla
1 egg
1 ½ teaspoons baking soda

Mix butter, sugar, shortening, and syrup (slightly warmed). Add other ingredients except for flour. Slowly mix in flour, ½ cup at a time. Hold out enough flour to roll out dough. Batter should be dry but enough to form ball. Allow dough to rest 24 hours (leave covered with tea towel) and then knead thoroughly. Roll out on a lightly floured board. The thinner the dough is rolled the better the cookie will be. When dough is rolled out cut in shapes with cookie cutters. Bake at 350 degrees for 7 to 10 minutes. Watch closely.

Makes approximately 8 dozen cookies depending on size.

*This cookie is great for dunking into coffee or milk!*


## BROWN SUGAR PECAN COOKIES
*Aunt Helen B.*

½ cup butter or margarine, softened
1 ¼ cups brown sugar, packed firmly
1 egg
1 ¼ cup all-purpose flour

¼ teaspoon salt
¼ teaspoon baking soda
½ cup coarsely chopped pecans

Preheat oven to 350 degrees F. Mix butter, brown sugar and egg together. Stir in remaining ingredients and blend until mixed. Drop dough by teaspoonfuls onto ungreased baking sheet, about 2" apart. Flatten each cookie. Bake for approximately 10-12 minutes or until set.

Makes about 3 dozen cookies.

# OMA'S BUTTER COOKIES
*Mathilde B.*

2 cups butter, softened (1 pound)
1 cup sugar
4 cups flour
sugar or colored sugars

2 egg yolks
2 tsp. almond extract or vanilla extract
2 egg whites, slightly beaten
confectioner's sugar

Cream butter, add sugar, almond extract and egg yolks, mix well. Slowly beat in flour. Refrigerate for about 1 to 2 hours. Roll out on a board lightly dusted with confectioner's sugar and cut out shapes with cookie cutters. The thinner the dough the better the cookie.

Move the cookies to a lightly greased or sprayed with non-stick spray, cookie sheets. Brush egg whites on top of each cookie. Lightly sprinkle with sugar or colored sugar if desired. Bake 8 to 10 minutes at 325 to 350 degrees oven.

Makes approximately 4 dozen cookies.

*This cookie should be called butter/sugar cookies. These are my favorite!*

# CARAMEL THUMBPRINT COOKIES

large bag of caramels (approximately 42)
¼ cup cocoa
1 tablespoon vegetable oil
1 cup ground pecans

1 family sized brownie mix with syrup
2 eggs
1 tablespoon water
2 ½ teaspoons milk

Remove wrappers from the caramels, cut 24 in half, retain 18 whole caramels. Lightly grease cookie sheets. Beat brownie mix, pouch of syrup, cocoa, eggs, oil and water in medium bowl until well blended. Cover, refrigerate about 1 hour or until thoroughly chilled through (dough will still be sticky).

Heat oven to 350 degrees. Shape dough into 48 1-inch balls. Put balls onto wax paper-lined trays, leaving space between each and refrigerate about 10 minutes. Remove from refrigerator and then roll balls in pecans. Place on prepared cookie sheets, press thumb gently in center of each cookie. Bake 9 to 11 minutes or until set.

Cool slightly; remove from cookie sheet to wire racks and cool completely.

Place 18 whole caramels and milk in small microwave-safe bowl. Microwave at medium for 30 seconds and stir. If necessary microwave an additional 10 seconds on Medium until caramels are melted and smooth when stirred. Spoon slightly rounded ¼ teaspoons of melted caramel on each cookie indentation, then lightly press a caramel in center of each cookie.

Makes 48 cookies.

# TOBY'S CHOCOLATE CHIP COOKIES
*Toby R.*

½ cup unsalted butter, softened
½ cup butter flavored solid shortening
¾ cup brown sugar
¾ cup sugar
1 teaspoon vanilla
½ teaspoon salt

2 large eggs
2 ¼ cups flour
1 ¼ teaspoons baking soda
½ teaspoon baking powder
2 c. dark semi-sweet chocolate chips
1 ½ cups miniature white chocolate chips

Cream butter and shortening, vanilla, brown sugar and sugar together, add eggs and beat well. Combine flour, baking soda and salt, add to creamed mixture. Stir in chocolate chips. Drop by teaspoonfuls onto ungreased cookie sheet.
Bake at 350 degrees for about 10 minutes. Watch carefully the last minutes of baking. Edges should be slightly darker and centers puffed and just cooked through. Cool on sheets before removing.

Makes about 7 dozen.

*This recipe is delicious and was given to me by my niece's mother-in-law.*


# CHOCOLATE CHIP OATMEAL COOKIES

2 cups butter
4 cups flour
2 teaspoons baking soda
5 cups oatmeal, ground in blender
24 ounces chocolate chips
2 cups brown sugar

1 teaspoon salt
1 bar, 8 ounces, chocolate, grated
4 eggs
2 teaspoons baking powder
2 teaspoons vanilla
2 cups chopped nuts

Cream butter and both sugars together, add eggs and vanilla, mix together with flour, oatmeal, salt, baking powder and baking soda. Add chocolate chips, the grated chocolate bar and nuts. Roll into balls and place two inches apart on a cookie sheet. Bake for 10 minutes at 375 degrees.

Makes approximately 9 dozen cookies.

# CINNAMON COOKIES

½ cup shortening
1 cup sugar
1 teaspoon vanilla
2 eggs (or 4 yolks)

2 cups flour
½ teaspoon salt
2 teaspoons baking powder
2 teaspoons cinnamon

Cream shortening and sugar together, add vanilla. Beat eggs well. Sift dry ingredients together and add to the creamed ingredients alternately with beaten eggs. Chill for one hour. Mold with a cookie press or drop from a teaspoon and flatten with damp-towel covered glass. Bake at 425 degrees F. for 7 minutes.

Makes about 60 cookies.

*This is a delicious cookie and tastes great.*

# DOUBLE CHOCOLATE CHIP COOKIES

1 cup butter, softened (2 sticks)
1 ½ cups sugar
2 eggs
2 teaspoons vanilla
2 cups flour

2/3 cup cocoa
¾ teaspoon baking soda
¼ teaspoon salt
2 cups semisweet chocolate chips
½ cup coarsely chopped nuts (optional)

Preheat oven to 350 degrees F.

In a large bowl, cream butter, sugar, eggs, and vanilla until light and fluffy. Stir together flour, cocoa, baking soda and salt, add to butter mixture. Stir in chocolate chips and nuts. Drop by rounded teaspoons onto ungreased cookie sheet. Bake 8 to 10 minutes or just until set. Cool slightly and then remove from cookie sheet. Cool completely.

Makes 4 ½ dozen.

# GERMAN CHOCOLATE THUMBPRINTS

1 pkg. (7 ounce) almond paste
2 cups confectioners sugar
1 pkg. (14 ounce) flaked coconut
3 egg whites
1 tsp. Vanilla extract

1 carton (8 ounce) Mascarpone cheese
2 pounds white candy coating, chopped
2/3 cup sliced almonds
gold pearl dust (available Wilton Indust.)

Place almond paste in a food processor, cover and process until finely chopped. Transfer to a large bowl, add confectioners' sugar and coconut. Beat until mixture resembles coarse crumbs. In a small bowl, beat egg whites and vanilla until stiff peaks form, fold into coconut mixture. Drop by tablespoonfuls 2 inches apart onto parchment paper-lined baking sheets. Bake at 325 degree F for 14-18 minutes or until lightly browned. Remove to wire racks to cool. Spread about 1 tsp. Cheese over each cookie, refrigerate for 20 minutes, or until cheese is firm.

In a microwave, melt candy coating, stir until smooth. Dip cookies in coating, allow excess to drip off. Place on waxed paper, sprinkle with almonds. Let stand until set. Brush pearl dust over almonds. Store in an airtight container in the refrigerator.

# GINGER COOKIES

¾ cup shortening
1 ½ cups molasses
5 tablespoons boiling water

2 teaspoons baking soda
¼ teaspoon salt
1 ½ teaspoons ginger

Cream shortening, add molasses and water and blend. Sift the dry ingredients together and add to mixture. The resulting dough is very soft and must be chilled overnight. Roll out 1/8" thick on a well floured pastry cloth. Use shaped cutters. Bake at 375 degrees F. for 12 minutes.

Makes 144 2" cookies.

# KRUMKAKE
### Requires specialty iron

4 eggs
1 cup sugar
½ cup butter
5 tablespoons cream

1 teaspoon vanilla
1 to 1 1/4 cups all-purpose flour
2 teaspoons cornstarch

Heat krumkake iron over small burner on medium high heat. Beat eggs and sugar together thoroughly; add butter, cream and vanilla. Measure flour by dipping method or by sifting. Blend flour and cornstarch; stir into egg mixture. Beat until smooth. Form into small balls about 1 inch round, larger if larger cookie maker is used. Test iron with a few drops of water, if they jump, iron is at correct temperature. Drop batter (about ½ tablespoon for 6" diameter, more batter for larger iron) on ungreased iron. Close gently and bake on each side for about 15 seconds, or until light, golden brown. Keep iron over heat at all times. Remove cookie with a knife and immediately roll on wooden roller or by hand. This cookie resembles a canolli when rolled.

Makes approximately 5-6 dozen.

*Variations: Chocolate Krumkake: add 3 tablespoons cocoa and 3 tablespoons sugar to basic recipe. Can also substitute chocolate flavoring instead of the vanilla and cardamon flavoring.*

# OMA'S NEW YEAR'S COOKIES
## *Mathilde B.*

4 cups flour
2 cups sugar*
7 whole eggs, beaten

14 drops anise oil or 2 tsp. cardamom
1 cup milk
½ pound butter

Cream butter, add sugar and beaten eggs, beat and slowly add the flour a little at a time. Heat cookie iron and very lightly coat with solid shortening or cooking spray. (this cookie uses a cookie press) Add milk to batter slowly—adding just enough to make it the consistency of a thin crepe batter. It should spoon onto the press without running. Only use enough milk to reach this consistency.

Drop one spoon full of batter onto press and heat until both sides are golden brown, remove and roll cookie immediately into tube shape or cone shape as desired. Fill with whipped cream or ice cream, if desired, when cool. Or serve plain.

Makes 100-120 cookies.
*for a less sweet cookie you can use ½ cup less sugar.

**This cookies uses a specialty cookie maker.**

*This cookie is my family's favorite!*
*This cookie is similar to Krumkake which is Scandinavian in origin. See Krumkake recipe.*

# PFEFFERNUSSE
*Oma Meta B.*

3 cups flour (self-rising)
1 teaspoon ground cinnamon
1/8 teaspoon ground cloves
¼ teaspoon white pepper
3 eggs

1 cup sugar
1/3 cup finely chopped blanched almonds
½ cup finely chopped mixed candied orange peel and citron
confectioners' sugar

In a medium sized bowl, sift the flour with the spices and set aside. In a large bowl of an electric mixer, beat the eggs until frothy, slowly add sugar and continue beating until the mixture becomes thick and lemon colored. At low speed, gradually add the flour mixture, then the almonds and candied fruit and mix until well blended. Wrap dough in foil and refrigerate for 2 to 3 days so the flavors can meld.

Preheat oven to 350 degrees F.

Roll about 1/3 of the dough at a time to a ¼ to ½ inch thickness and cut with a 1 ¾ inch round cutter. Place the cookies 1 inch apart on greased baking sheets, and bake until lightly browned, 15 to 18 minutes.

Remove from baking sheets and let cool on wire racks. Store in an airtight container. If desired, dust with confectioners' sugar before serving.

*The secret of good pfeffernusse (pepper nuts) is to let the dough ripen for 2 to 3 days before baking and to store the cookies with a piece of apple to keep them moist before eating. Best if allowed to mature with apple slice for about 2-3 weeks.*

*Note: if you use all-purpose flour add ¼ teaspoon salt and ¼ teaspoon baking powder.*

# SHORTBREAD PUFFS
### *Gwen B.*

1 cup shortening
1 cup flour +
2 tablespoons flour

½ cup cornstarch
½ cup powdered sugar for rolling
¼ teaspoon almond extract

Cream shortening and sugar, add rest of ingredients, except powdered sugar. Drop by teaspoon full on cookie sheet. Bake for 30 minutes at 275 degrees then 3 minutes at 300 degrees F. Roll in powdered sugar while warm.

Makes between 24-30 cookies.

# SPICE COOKIES

2 ½ cups flour
2-teaspoons baking soda
½ teaspoon cloves
½ teaspoon allspice
½ teaspoon cinnamon
¼ teaspoon ginger

¾ cup butter, softened
1 cup sugar
1 egg
¼ cup light molasses
confectioner's sugar

Sift flour with baking soda, cloves, allspice, cinnamon and ginger onto sheet of waxed paper.

In a medium bowl, with an electric mixer, beat butter, sugar, and egg until light and fluffy. With a wooden spoon, beat in flour mixture alternately with molasses, beat well after each addition. Refrigerate dough, covered, 1 hour.

Preheat oven to 375 degrees F. Lightly grease cookie sheets.

Shape dough into ½ inch balls. Roll in confectioners' sugar, place on cookie in sheets, 1" apart. Bake 8 to 10 minutes. Remove to rack. Sprinkle with confectioners' sugar while still warm.

Makes 5 to 6 dozen cookies.

# SUGAR COOKIES

| | |
|---|---|
| Sugar | 2 ½ teaspoons baking powder |
| 3 ¼ cups all-purpose flour | 2 tablespoons milk |
| 2/3 cup shortening | 1 teaspoon vanilla |
| 2 eggs | ½ teaspoon salt |

About 4 hours before serving or up to 1 month ahead (keeping tightly covered).

Into a large bowl, measure 1 ½ cups sugar and remaining ingredients. With mixer at low speed, beat ingredients until well mixed, occasionally scraping bowl with rubber spatula. Shape dough into ball, wrap, refrigerate dough 2 to 3 hours until easy to handle.

Preheat oven to 400 degrees F. Lightly grease cookie sheets. Roll 1/3 of dough at a time, keeping rest of dough refrigerated. For crisp cookies, roll dough paper thin. For softer cookies, roll 1/8" to ¼" thick. With floured 2 1/2" round cookie cutter, cut into circles. Re-roll trimmings and cut again. Place cookies 1" apart on a cookie sheet. Sprinkle with ¼ teaspoon of sugar per cookie. Bake 8 minutes or until light brown. With spatula, remove cookies to wire racks, cool completely.

Makes approximately 6 dozen.

# HOW TO MAKE PERFECT PRESSED COOKIES

Mix dough as directed—dough for pressed cookies are high in shortening. Dough must be pliable. If very warm, chill a short time (if too cold, the dough will crumble). Using ¼ at a time, place dough in cookie press, force dough through cookie press, following manufacturers' directions, on ungreased baking sheet If baking sheet is too warm, fat in the dough will melt and cookies will pull away from the sheet when press is lifted. Bake until set. *See Oma's Spritz Cookies.*

# OMA'S SPRITZ COOKIES
## Mathilde B.

½ pound butter, softened
2 eggs
1 cup sugar

4 cups flour, sifted
1 teaspoon vanilla
1 teaspoon baking powder

Cream together butter, sugar and vanilla, add eggs and blend well. Sift together baking powder and flour. Slowly beat flour mixture into butter mixture. Force through a cookie press onto cookie sheet. Sprinkle with decorative sugars or cinnamon drops. Dough may be tinted.

Bake 10 to 15 minutes at 325-350 degrees F.

Makes approximately 60 cookies.


# ELEANOR'S SPRITZ COOKIES
## Eleanor H.

1 cup butter, softened
2/3 cup sugar
1 egg

½ teaspoon salt
2 teaspoons vanilla or almond extract
3 1/2 cups all-purpose flour

Preheat oven to 375 degrees F. In a 3 quart mixing bowl, combine butter, sugar, egg and flavoring, beat at medium speed, scraping sides of bowl often until smooth and fluffy. Add flour and salt, stirring until well combined. Dough can be divided and tinted (add 3-4 drops of green or red food coloring for Christmas, yellow or purple for Easter, etc) if desired. If dough is too soft, chill until workable.

Force dough through a cookie press onto un-greased baking sheets. Decorate with colored sugar or cinnamon candies, etc. Bake near center of 400 degree F. oven for 8 to 14 minutes, or until cookies are a light gold around edges.

Makes about 6 dozen cookies.

*Dough may be lightly tinted with food coloring.*

# THUMBPRINT COOKIES

½ cup shortening mixed with butter
¼ cup brown sugar, packed
1 egg, separated
½ teaspoon vanilla

1 cup all-purpose flour
¼ teaspoon salt
¾ cup finely chopped nuts
jelly or tinted confectioners sugar icing

Heat oven to 350 degrees. Mix shortening, sugar, egg yolk, and vanilla thoroughly. Measure flour by dipping or sifting. Blend together flour and salt, stir in. Roll dough into balls (1 teaspoon per ball). Beat egg white slightly with fork. Dip balls in egg white, roll in nuts. Place about 1" apart on ungreased baking sheet; press thumb gently in center of each. Bake 10 to 12 minutes or until set. Cool, fill thumbprints with jelly or tinted icing.

Makes about 3 dozen cookies.

*Chocolate thumbprint cookies: make thumbprint cookies except substitute ½ cup granulated sugar for the brown sugar, add 1 square unsweetened chocolate (1 ounce) melted, with the shortening.*

# CHOCOLATE CHIP COOKIES

2 ¼ cups all-purpose flour
1 teaspoon baking soda
1 teaspoon salt
¾ cup granulated sugar
¾ cup packed light or dark brown sugar

1 teaspoon vanilla extract
2 large eggs, beaten
2 cups semi-sweet chocolate morsels
1 cup chopped pecans
2 sticks (1/2 pound) butter, softened

Preheat oven to 375 degrees.
Combine flour, baking soda and salt in a small bowl. Beat butter, granulated sugar, brown sugar and vanilla extract in large mixer bowl until creamy, add eggs one at a time, beating well after each addition. Gradually beat in flour mixture. Stir in morsels and nuts. Drop by rounded tablespoon onto ungreased baking sheets.
Bake for 9 to 10 minutes or until golden brown. Cool on baking sheets for 2 minutes remove to wire racks to cool completely.

Makes 5 dozen cookies.

*Dark brown sugar makes a richer cookie.*

# FUDGE

1 ½ cups granulated sugar
2/3 cup evaporated milk
2 tablespoons butter
¼ teaspoon salt
2-cups miniature marshmallows

1 ½ c. semi-sweet chocolate, chopped
½ cup chopped pecans
1 teaspoon vanilla extract

Line 8" square baking pan with foil or parchment paper.

Combine sugar, evaporated milk, butter and salt in medium, heavy duty saucepan. Bring to a full rolling boil over medium heat, stirring constantly. Boil, stirring constantly for 4 to 5 minutes. Remove from heat. Stir in marshmallows, morsels, nuts and vanilla. Stir vigorously for 1 minute or until marshmallows are melted. Pour into prepared baking pan, refrigerate for 2 hours or until firm. Lift from pan, remove foil. Cut into pieces.

Makes 40 pieces.


# VANILLA WAFERS

1/3 cup shortening
1 cup sugar
1 beaten egg
¼ cup milk

2 cups flour
2 teaspoons baking powder
½ teaspoon salt
3 teaspoons vanilla

Cream shortening and sugar thoroughly. Beat the egg and add milk and vanilla. Sift all dry ingredients together. Add wet and dry ingredients alternately to the creamed mixture. Drop from a teaspoon onto a greased cookie sheet and bake at 300 degrees for 20 minutes.

Makes approximately 80—2" cookies.

# ZIMTSTERNE

A crisp cookie with a shiny glazed top.

3 tablespoons butter

1 ½ cups sugar

2 whole eggs

1 egg, separated

1 teaspoon lemon juice

2-1/3 cups all-purpose flour

2 ½ teaspoon baking powder

1 ¼ teaspoon cinnamon

¼ teaspoon salt

¼ teaspoon nutmeg

½ cup finely chopped walnuts

Heat oven to 375 degrees. Mix butter, sugar, 2 whole eggs, 1 egg yolk and lemon juice until fluffy. Measure flour by dipping or by sifting. Stir dry ingredients together; blend into sugar mixture. Stir in nuts, roll dough, 1/3 at a time, to 1/16" thick on lightly floured board. Cut with star cutter. Brush tops of cookies with remaining egg white, beaten until frothy. Bake on lightly greased baking sheet 6 to 8 minutes.

Makes 6 to 9 dozen cookies, depending on size of cutter.

Note: if using self-rising flour omit baking powder and salt.

*This is a very traditional German cookie I discovered while on a trip to Germany. I pestered my cousin until she gave up to recipe. It is traditional to make them in star shapes, approximately 1 ½" in width. They make a beautiful addition to the cookie plate.*

# GLAZES FOR COOKIES

Cookies can be glazed before or after baking. Simply brush the cookies with a thin layer of one of the following.

Before baking:
1. one egg white diluted with 1 tablespoon water.
2. one egg yolk mixed with 1 tablespoon water
3. milk or cream

*After baking:*
1. ¾ cup confectioners' sugar
2. 1 tablespoon hot liquid (more if necessary) like honey, etc.
3. 1 square chocolate melted for chocolate glaze

Mix and spread on cookie. Vary by changing the liquid or flavoring, or by tinting with food colorings.


# STABILIZED WHIPPED CREAM

1 teaspoon unflavored gelatin
4 tablespoons water

¼ cup confectioners' sugar
½ teaspoon vanilla

1 cup heavy whipping cream, very cold and at least a day old. Combine gelatin and cold water in small saucepan. Let stand until thick. Place over low heat stirring constantly until gelatin dissolves (about 3 minutes). Remove from heat and cool slightly. Whip cream, sugar and vanilla until slightly thickened. While beating slowly add gelatin to whipped cream mixture. Whip at high speed until stiff.

Makes about 2 cups.

Cakes iced with whipped cream must be stored in the refrigerator.

# DANISH—BASIC TIPS

1. It is important to keep butter enclosed in the dough. If it oozes out, immediately sprinkle with flour and, if dough becomes to sticky to handle its probably because butter has softened. Just chill 20 minutes before continuing rolling and folding.

2. Use more flour than you normally would for rolling out pastries, then brush off excess flour with a soft brush before folding or filling; this way flour will not build up in pastry.

3. Since dough is very rich, it is best to let pastries rise at room temperature. Do not try to hasten the rising by using heat; doing so would melt the butter. This would tend to ruin the texture of the pastry.

4. If using margarine, which is of softer consistency than butter, refrigerate 20 minutes between each rolling.

5. Have a rolling pin ready, and a soft pastry brush, ruler and working surface large enough to roll dough to 30".

6. For freezing: place shaped Danish on cookie sheets. Don't brush with egg or sprinkle with toppings until ready to bake. Cover with foil or plastic wrap; freeze.

7. To bake: remove Danish from freezer the night before and place in refrigerator. Next morning arrange on cookie sheets, 2" apart. Let rise at room temperature, away from draft, until double in volume, about 1 ½ hours. Brush with egg; sprinkle with topping, bake as per recipe.

8. for refrigerating: place shaped Danish on cookie sheet, cover; refrigerate.

9.To bake: remove Danish from refrigerator; let rise and bake as above.

# DANISH PASTRY DOUGH
*Basic recipe*
Makes 2 large or about 24 individual pastries

½ cup very warm water
2 envelopes active dry yeast
1/3 cup sugar
¾ cup cold milk
2-eggs

4 ¼ cups sifted all-purpose flour
1 teaspoon salt
1 pound butter
flour

Sprinkle yeast into very warm water in a 1 cup measure. (very warm water can be tested on wrist, should feel comfortably warm). Stir in ½ teaspoon sugar. Stir until yeast dissolves. Let stand undisturbed until bubbling and double in volume, about 10 minutes.

Combine remaining sugar, milk, eggs, 3 cups of the flour, salt and the yeast mixture in a large bowl. Beat with an electric mixer at medium speed for 3 minutes. Beat in remaining flour with a wooden spoon until dough is shiny and elastic. Dough will be soft. Scrape down sides of bowl. Cover with plastic wrap and refrigerate for 30 minutes.

Place the sticks of butter 1" apart, between 2 sheets of wax paper; roll out to a 12" square. Chill on a cookie sheet until ready to use.

Sprinkle working surface heavily with flour, about 1/3 cup, turn dough out onto flour, sprinkle flour on top of dough. Roll out to an 18"x 12" rectangle. Brush off excess flour with a soft pastry brush.

Peel off top sheet of wax paper from butter, place butter, paper side up, on one end of dough to cover 2/3 of the dough, peel off remaining sheet of wax paper. For easy folding, carefully score butter lengthwise down center, without cutting into dough. Fold uncovered third of dough over middle third. Brush off excess flour; then fold remaining third of dough over middle third to enclose butter completely. Turn dough clockwise so open side is away from you.

*roll out to a 24x12 inch rectangle using enough flour to keep dough from sticking. Fold ends in to meet on center, then fold in half to make 4 layers. Turn again so open side is away from you.

*repeat rolling and folding this way 2 more times. Keep the dough to a perfect rectangle by rolling straight up and down and from side to side. When it is necessary, chill the dough between rolling. Clean off the working surface each time and dust lightly with flour.

Refrigerate dough 1 hour or more—even overnight, if you wish, to relax dough and firm up butter layers. Cut dough in half—you can see the buttery layers, which when baked, become flaky and crisp. Work with only half the dough at a time keep the other half refrigerated until ready to use.

## PASTRY FILLING FOR DANISH

**Cheese Filling:** *makes 1 cup*
Combine 1 cup pot cheese, 1 egg yolk, ¼ cup sugar and 1 teaspoon grated lemon rind in container of electric blender, whirl until smooth.

**Almond Filling:** *makes 1 cup*
Beat ½ an 8 ounce package or can of almond paste, 4 tablespoons softened butter and ¼ cup sugar in a small bowl until smooth and well blended.

**Cinnamon-Pecan Filling:** *makes 1 cup*
Beat 4 tablespoons softened butter, ½ cup sugar, ½ teaspoon ground cinnamon and ½ teaspoon ground cardamom in a small bowl until smooth. Stir in ½ cup coarsely chopped pecans and ¼ cup currants.

# DANISH RECIPES

**Almond Crescent: makes 12**

½ Danish pastry dough                          sugar
almond filling                                 sliced almonds
slightly beaten egg

Roll pastry on floured surface to 2 20"x15" rectangle; trim edges even; with a sharp knife, cut into 12 5" squares. Spoon filling onto one corner of each square, dividing evenly. Roll each square around filling to opposite corner. Place point down 2" apart on cookie sheet. Curve into crescent shape. Let rise in warm place until double in volume, about 30 minutes. Brush with egg; sprinkle with sugar and almonds. Place in preheated 400 degree oven; lower heat to 350 degrees then bake 20 to 25 minutes, or until puffed and golden. Remove to wire rack, cool.

**Cheese Danish: makes 12**

1/2 Danish pastry dough                        slightly beaten egg
cheese filling                                 ½ cup corn syrup
cherry preserves

Roll and cut dough as in recipe for Almond Crescent. Spoon cheese filling onto center of each square, dividing evenly; fold in all 4 corners to meet and overlap slightly in center to enclose filling completely; press points down with finger tips. Place 2" apart on cookie sheet; let rise until double in bulk, about 30 minutes. Press down points again and fill center with a teaspoon of cherry preserves. Brush pastry with egg. Place in preheated 400 degree oven; lower heat immediately to 350 degrees and bake 20 to 25 minutes, or until puffed and golden brown. Heat corn syrup just until warm, brush over pastries. Remove to wire rack; cool. Add more preserves after pastries are baked, if you wish. Pastries will open up as they bake.

**Apricot Bow Ties: makes 12**

½ Danish pastry dough                          apricot preserves
slightly beaten egg                            2 tablespoons chopped walnuts
                                               mixed with 2 tablespoons sugar

Roll and cut dough as in almond crescent recipe. Place 1 teaspoon of apricot preserve along one of the edges of the pastry 1/2" in from the edge. Fold over opposite edge; press edges together to seal. With a sharp knife, make a lengthwise slit in folded pastry to within 1" of each end. Slip one end under and pull it through the slit. Place 2" apart, on cookie sheets. Let rise in a warm place until doubled in bulk, 30 to 45 minutes. Brush with egg; sprinkle with walnut mixture. Place in preheated 400 degree oven, lower heat immediately to 350 degrees. Bake 20 minutes or until golden brown. Remove to wire rack, cool.

## Cockscombs: makes 12

½ Danish pastry dough                    almond filling
slightly beaten egg                      sugar

Roll and cut dough as in Almond Crescent recipe. Spoon filing onto center of each square, dividing evenly. Spread slightly to parallel to one edge; brush edges lightly with egg, then fold opposite edge over; press edges together to seal. Make 4 to 5 slits in sealed edge; place on cookie sheet, curving pastries slightly to resemble a cockscomb. Let rise in a warm place until double in bulk, about 30 minutes. Brush with egg; sprinkle generously with sugar. Place in hot, 400 degree oven, lower heat immediately to 350 degrees. Bake 20 minutes, or until puffed and golden brown. Remove to wire rack, cool.

## Prune Danish: makes 12

½ Danish pastry dough                    1 12ounce can prune filling
½ cup corn syrup                         or 1-8 ounce jar Lekvar

Roll dough and cut as in Almond Crescent recipe. Spoon a rounded tablespoon prune filling or you may use canned cherry or apple pie filling, or apricot preserves, onto center of each square; bring 2 opposite corners over filling to overlap about 1". Place on cookie sheet 2" apart; let rise in a warm place, until double in bulk, about 30 minutes. Brush with beaten egg. Place in preheated 400 degree oven, immediately lower heat to 350 degrees, then bake 20 minutes. Warm corn syrup slightly in a small saucepan, brush over pastries; bake 5 minutes longer. Remove to wire rack; cool.

## Elephant Ears: makes 12

½ Danish pastry dough                    Cinnamon Pecan filling
slightly beaten egg                      sugar
coarsely chopped pecans

Roll pastry to a 12"x12" square; spread filling evenly over pastry; roll up jelly roll fashion with a sharp knife, cut into 1" pieces, then carefully cut each piece in half but not all the way through. Spread out the 2 halves, leaving them attached in center; place 2" apart on cookie sheet. Let rise in a warm place until double in bulk about 30 to 45 minutes. Brush with egg; sprinkle with sugar and pecans. Place in preheated 400 degree oven, lower heat immediately to 350 degrees. Bake 20 to 25 minutes or until puffed and golden brown. Remove to wire rack; cool.

## Mayor's Braid (Borgmester Krans): makes 1-10" round cake

½ Danish pastry dough
almond filling
slightly beaten egg

sugar
sliced almonds

Roll dough on a floured surface to a 30x9 inch rectangle; cut lengthwise into 3 strips. Spread the filling down the center of each strip; dividing evenly. Fold edges of strips over filling to enclose filling completely. Press ends of the 3 filled strips together; braid; press other ends together. Ease braid onto an ungreased cookie sheet, join ends together to form a ring, about 9" in diameter. Let rise in a warm place, 45 minutes, or until double in bulk. Brush with egg, sprinkle generously with sugar and almonds. Place in preheated 400 degree oven, lower heat immediately to 350 degrees. Bake 40 minutes or until puffed and golden; remove to wire rack, cool. Cut into wedges to serve. This cake is rich and will spread when baked. You may wish to place a collar of foil around the cake just before baking to keep it more compact.

# MINCEMEAT TARTS

1 ½ cups golden raisins
2 cups pared, cored and chopped tart apples
grated rind of 1 orange
1 tablespoon lemon juice
1 teaspoon ground ginger

Pastry:
2 cups flour
¼ teaspoon salt

¾ cup sugar
½ teaspoon cinnamon
½ teaspoon allspice
2 tablespoons quick cooking tapioca
2 tablespoons rum
½ cup orange juice

2/3 cup shortening
1/3 cup ice water

**Pastry:**
Sift together flour and salt. Cut in shortening with a knife or pastry blender until dough is texture of cornmeal. Sprinkle water over mixture and blend gently with a fork until it is well mixed. Roll out dough on pastry board.

**Filling:**
In a saucepan combine raisins, apples, orange rind and orange and lemon juices, bring to a boil. Simmer until apples are quite soft. Add spices and tapioca, simmer an additional 10 minutes. Stir in rum. Set aside. Roll out pastry and cut out tarts with cookie cutter in either circle or fluted circle. Cut 48 circles. Place 1 teaspoon mincemeat on top of each tart, cover with second cut out, then pinch together. Arrange tarts on cookie sheet and bake in 375 degree oven about 25 minutes.

Makes about 24 tarts.

*Note: Can use jar mincemeat instead of making you own mincemeat.*

**NOTE:** Leavenings for cookies. Most cookies contain no or very little leavenings. Baking soda makes a thin, crisp cookie; Baking powder makes a puffy, cake like cookie.

# BEVERAGES

# BLACK CHERRY PUNCH

2 bottles Extra Dry Champagne
1 cup brandy or cognac
1 12 ounce bottle of club soda

2 cups Kahlua
1 20 ounce jar glazed cherries

Chill all ingredients. Mix Kahlua, cognac, cherries and half the cherry liquid. Pour over ice. Add champagne, stir gently. Add club soda to taste. With a lighter cognac you will need less soda, a stronger brandy or cognac will need more soda.

Makes about 20 servings.

# CAPPUCCINO FROST

1 cup brewed coffee
Kahlua

scoop of ice cream
dash of cinnamon

In a blender combine all ingredients and mix until frothy.
Makes 1 serving.

# DAIQUIRI

Frost glass rim with sugar by rubbing the glass edge with lime or lemon juice and standing rim down in a bed of superfine sugar. Chill glass. Mix daiquiri ingredients (see below) in a cocktail shaker, omitting sugar. Add ice, shake, then pour into prepared glass, straining ice from the drink.

# FROZEN DAIQUIRI

2 ounces white rum
2 teaspoons superfine sugar
dash triple sec

2 tablespoons lime or lemon juice
(approximately 1 fruit)
½ cup cracked ice

Place white rum, lime or lemon juice, superfine sugar and Triple Sec in blender. Add ice, cover and blend 15-20 seconds at medium speed. Pour into a chilled stemmed glass.

Makes 1 serving.


# FROZEN STRAWBERRY DAIQUIRI

Same as frozen daiquiri but add 3 fresh or frozen strawberries to blender before adding ice. Blend 20 seconds, serve garnished with a whole strawberry.


# EGGNOG

Blend in blender, 5 ounces of rum and a pint of vanilla or eggnog ice cream. Sprinkle with nutmeg and serve immediately OR ½ bottle (12 ounce) of rum into a quart of dairy eggnog mix, fold in cup of whipped heavy cream. Chill. Stir. Sprinkle with nutmeg.

Makes 12 servings.

# CLASSIC EGGNOG

12 eggs, separated
1 cup sugar
1 ½ cups bourbon
½ cup brandy

6 cups milk
ground nutmeg
1 cup heavy or whipping cream

About 2 hours before serving or early in the day: In a large bowl with mixer at low speed, beat egg yolks and sugar until well blended. At high speed, beat until thick and lemon-colored, about 15 minutes, frequently scraping bowl with rubber spatula. One tablespoon at a time beat in bourbon and brandy (egg yolk mixture may curdle if bourbon and brandy are beaten in too quickly. Cover bowl and chill.

About 20 minutes before serving: In chilled 5 to 6 quart punch bowl, stir egg yolk mixture milk and 1 ¼ teaspoon nutmeg until blended. In large bowl with mixer at high speed, beat egg whites until soft peaks form. In small bowl, using same beaters, with mixer at medium speed, beat heavy or whipping cream until stiff peaks form. With rubber spatula or wire whisk, gently fold egg whites and whipped cream into egg-yolk mixture until just blended.

To serve, sprinkle some nutmeg over top of eggnog, ladle into 6 ounce punch cups or glasses.

Makes 19 cups or 38 ½ cup servings.


# HOT APPLE TODDY

1 quart sweet apple cider
2/3 cup brown sugar

½ lemon
¼ teaspoon aromatic bitters

In saucepan combine apple cider and brown sugar. Slice lemon, add to cider mixture. Bring to full rolling boil; simmer 5 minutes, add bitters. Serve warm, in mugs. Add a cinnamon stick, stir.

Makes 6 to 8 servings.

# HOT BUTTERED RUM

2 ounces dark rum
2 whole cloves
boiling water
cinnamon sticks

2 teaspoons sugar
1/8 teaspoon nutmeg
pat sweet butter

Blend dark rum, sugar, cloves and nutmeg in 1-8 ounce heat proof mug. Add ½ cup boiling water. Top with pat of sweet butter. Stir well with a cinnamon stick to dissolve sugar and flavor the rum.

Makes 1 serving.


# IRISH COFFEE

1 cup Irish whiskey
¼ cup sugar
8 cups strong hot coffee
1 cup whipped cream

For each serving: pour two tablespoons whiskey and one to two teaspoons sugar into warmed (with hot water) Irish coffee goblet, or coffee cup. Add hot coffee to within a ½" of glass or cup rim. Stir. Top with whipped cream.

# OPEN HOUSE PUNCH

1 46 ounce can chilled Hawaiian Punch
¼ cup lemon juice
2 cans (12 ounces each) lemon-lime soda, chilled

1 ½ cups orange juice
1 package (10 ounces) frozen sliced strawberries

Combine punch, citrus juices and strawberries. Mix well, stir in soda. Add punch cubes, garnish with orange slices and serve. Makes 22—4 ounce servings. Add punch cubes (pour additional can Hawaiian Punch into ice cube trays) it prevents punch from diluting.

For added zing, add liquor of your choice.

# RED RUM PUNCH

1 pint lime juice
1 quart pineapple juice
6 ounces Grenadine
fruits for garnish

1 quart orange juice
2 fifths white rum
2 quarts club soda

Mix together first 5 ingredients, stirring vigorously. Chill, or add a large block of ice to punch bowl. Just before serving add chilled club soda. Stir gently. Decorate with fruit slices.

Makes about 50 servings.

# RUBY PUNCH

6 ounces fresh lime juice
1 fifth vodka, chilled
mint for garnish

10 ounces cranberry juice, chilled
2 quarts club soda, chilled

Combine all but club soda. Stir well, pour over large block of ice in a punch bowl. Add club soda and stir gently. This can be served in punch bowls, but is best in tall glasses over ice, garnish with mint springs and lime shells.

Makes 12 servings.

# RUM SOUR

Crushed ice
1 tablespoon lemon or lime juice

1 ½ ounce gold rum
1-1 ½ teaspoon superfine sugar

Over crushed ice in a cocktail shaker pour gold rum, lemon or lime juice and superfine sugar. Shake well. Strain into chilled stemmed glass or old fashioned glass. Garnish with orange slice.

Makes 1 serving.

# WINE PUNCH

1 bottle dry red wine (3 ¼ cups)
¾ cup granulated sugar
3 whole cloves
½ cup orange juice
¼ cup lemon juice

3-1/2" strip orange peel
2-1/2" strip lemon peel
½ cup sugar cubes
¼ cup rum, heated

Heat wine with granulated sugar, cloves, fruit juices, and peels. Do not boil. Pour into flame-proof punch bowl. Soak sugar cubes in rum; place cubes in a strainer over punch. Ignite sugar cubes, as they flame, gradually spoon more heated rum from a long-handled ladle over the cubes when sugar has all melted into punch, add a few orange slices. Serve hot in cups.

Makes 8 servings.

# INDEX

## Meat and Dessert Sauces and Salad Dressings

## Soups

## Salads

## Breakfast and Brunch

## Breads and Muffins

## Hors D'Oeuvres

## *Vegetables and Vegetarian Dishes*

## Beef Dishes

## Chicken, Poultry and Stuffing

## Lamb and Veal

## Pork, Ham and Sausages

## Seafood

## Puddings

## All Fruit Dishes

## Tortes, Tarts and Pies

## Cakes and Icings

## Beverages